The Cuba-U.S. Bilateral Relationship

The Cuba-U.S. Bilateral Relationship

New Pathways and Policy Choices

Edited by

MICHAEL J. KELLY
ERIKA MORENO
RICHARD C. WITMER, II

OXFORD
UNIVERSITY PRESS

OXFORD
UNIVERSITY PRESS

Oxford University Press is a department of the University of Oxford. It furthers the University's objective of excellence in research, scholarship, and education by publishing worldwide. Oxford is a registered trademark of Oxford University Press in the UK and certain other countries.

Published in the United States of America by Oxford University Press
198 Madison Avenue, New York, NY 10016, United States of America.

Library of Congress Cataloging-in-Publication Data

Names: Kelly, Michael J., 1968– editor.
Title: The Cuba-U.S. bilateral relationship : new pathways and policy choices / edited by Michael J. Kelly, Erika Moreno, Richard C. Witmer, II.
Description: New York : Oxford University Press, 2019. | Includes bibliographical references and index.
Identifiers: LCCN 2019022946 (print) | LCCN 2019022947 (ebook) | ISBN 9780190687366 (hardback) | ISBN 9780190687373 (pdf) | ISBN 9780190687380 (epub)
Subjects: LCSH: United States—Foreign relations—Cuba. | Cuba—Foreign relations—United States. | United States—Foreign relations—21st century. | Cuba—Foreign relations—21st century.
Classification: LCC E183.8.C9 C82955 2019 (print) | LCC E183.8.C9 (ebook) | DDC 327.7307291—dc23
LC record available at https://lccn.loc.gov/2019022946
LC ebook record available at https://lccn.loc.gov/2019022947

1 3 5 7 9 8 6 4 2

Printed by Sheridan Books, Inc., United States of America

Note to Readers

This publication is designed to provide accurate and authoritative information in regard to the subject matter covered. It is based upon sources believed to be accurate and reliable and is intended to be current as of the time it was written. It is sold with the understanding that the publisher is not engaged in rendering legal, accounting, or other professional services. If legal advice or other expert assistance is required, the services of a competent professional person should be sought. Also, to confirm that the information has not been affected or changed by recent developments, traditional legal research techniques should be used, including checking primary sources where appropriate.

(Based on the Declaration of Principles jointly adopted by a Committee of the American Bar Association and a Committee of Publishers and Associations.)

Contents

List of Tables

Foreword

For me, Cuba is about unfinished business. About an opportunity I hope will not be squandered, to resolve long-standing, painful disputes between two neighbors, with overpowering historical, familial, and cultural affinities. I still remember my arrival on the island for the first time in October 1991. While I knew I was entering a parallel universe with a system wholly different from the one I cherished, I was immediately surrounded by the similarities between the two countries, right down to the street markers in Havana, identical to those in Coral Gables, Florida. It became clear to me straight away that Cubans and Americans had a lot more in common than each other knew or wanted to admit. I would go a step further and say that Cubans have more in common with Americans than they do with other Latin Americans. I have read many articles about the blending of American and Cuban culture and can attest to it after living in Cuba during 1991–1993, 1999–2002, and 2014–2017—a total of eight years as an American diplomat. Some Cubans and Americans would certainly disagree, but I saw it with my own eyes, from baseball, to music, to that stubborn sense of pride, to a talent for ingenuity and innovation, to that strongly held view their nation was the indispensable one. More profoundly, I discovered a yearning, often voiced in a whisper back then, among Cubans in Cuba and South Florida, for some way, some invisible bridge, to reconnect with family and friends on the other side of the Florida Straits.

Trying to make sense of what I was seeing during those first days in Havana, I made a note to myself about wanting to reread President John F. Kennedy's speech at American University on June 10, 1963 (my eighth birthday), a few months after the Cuban Missile Crisis. Kennedy was determined to construct a better relationship with the Soviet Union, despite our profound differences, to discourage another threat of nuclear war. The excerpt of the speech that resonated most was: "no government or social system is so evil that its people must be considered as lacking in virtue. As Americans, we find communism profoundly repugnant as a negation of personal freedom and dignity. But we can still hail the Russian people for their many achievements—in science and space, in economic and industrial growth, in culture and in acts of courage." Surely, we could find a better way to engage with a communist country ninety miles off our shore beyond trying to drive it to collapse. We managed to engage with China and Vietnam and, recently, have begun the process with North Korea, the only other remaining vestige of the Cold War.

I can't explain why necessarily, but after that first experience in Cuba, this issue, this bilateral relationship—the contradictions and inconsistencies—grabbed hold of me and never let go. In part, it was because I had come to that conclusion that our isolation policy was not working, and was wrong. Even though you could strongly disagree with someone about many things, you should still be able to have a civil conversation, learn something, find common ground, and influence your interlocutor along the way. Diplomacy should have been the vehicle then to develop a dialogue and some form of engagement with our longtime adversary.

Some twenty-one years and three months after I finished my first posting in Cuba, on December 17, 2014, to be exact, President Barack Obama announced to the world that the United States would change its relationship with Cuba. He said, "[W]e intend to create more opportunities for the American and Cuban people and begin a new chapter among the nations of the America." The "seemingly endless confrontation" he referenced was, I thought, finally coming to an end.

I was so fortunate to be in Cuba on that extraordinary day.

Well before 7:00 a.m. on December 17, 2014, American aid worker Alan Gross, wrongfully imprisoned for five years, was reunited with his wife, lawyer, and members of Congress who had worked hard for his release, at an airfield outside of Havana. There was something extraordinary about seeing a plane marked "The United States of America" sitting on the tarmac. After the plane took off, I rushed back to the U.S. Interests Section (not yet an embassy) to inform my American colleagues of what was about to happen. With more than fifty crammed into a small, secure conference room, I told them that Alan was on his way home, and that Presidents Obama and Raúl Castro would be speaking to their respective nations at noon to announce, among other things, their authorization of discussions to negotiate the re-establishment of diplomatic relations. The applause was deafening. Everyone knew we would henceforth be living history.

Later in the day, as the two presidents concluded their simultaneous speeches, I heard church bells ring in Old Havana. Thousands of Cubans gathered around television sets at their workplaces to watch President Castro and cheered with delight. I saw flags draped over balconies—Cuban and American—and wondered where they got the American flags. I felt joy in the streets. I saw tears, heard cries—and a little trepidation too.

Among the changes announced were steps to increase travel, commerce, and the flow of information to and from Cuba. Ultimately, this became a story about diplomacy—its transformative potential, high impact, and power. And how it affected people's lives on both sides of the Florida Straits. Conversations were begun between governments long estranged. Reconciliation between people was no longer unthinkable.

We began negotiating the re-establishment of diplomatic relations on January 22, 2015. Between that and the accompanying regulatory changes, within weeks, people-to-people travel skyrocketed, hundreds of thousands of Americans would visit, business delegations poured in. Cultural and educational leaders also came and organized exchanges. Noting that our sanctions on Cuba had denied access to technology, President Obama also authorized increased telecommunication connections between the two countries. Cell phones began to work. Wi-Fi hot spots sprouted up. People were starting to use some of the social media I still can't figure out. And Cubans coming online were seeing the same similarities, the same affinities I first saw twenty-three years prior. Cuba's nascent private sector, mostly in the service industry, thrived.

After decades of distrust and animosity, the process was never going to be linear or successful overnight. But, by the end of the Obama administration, we re-established relations, opened embassies, signed twenty-two agreements, and began seventeen dialogues on issues two countries ninety miles apart ought to have as a matter of course. We also began to talk directly about human rights, including civil and political rights. We began discussions about unresolved property claims for the first time. For those who have an interest in progress on these issues, you should want these conversations to continue.

While the Donald Trump administration appears to be returning to a policy approach that has failed for over fifty years, I remain convinced that, despite the ups and downs, the fits and starts, continuing the engagement begun during the Obama administration is the best way to advance American interests, to have an impact on the ground, and to promote the universal values we Americans hold dear. Reverting to rhetoric reminiscent of the axis of evil or—excuse me—triangle of tyranny, will solve nothing. It is a playbook those on the island resisting any change know well.

Given the current challenges and efforts to reverse what should be irreversible between the United States and Cuba, I especially welcome *The Cuba-U.S. Bilateral Relationship: New Pathways and Policy Choices* for its thoughtful approach to understanding the development of the relationship between the two countries and how they can move forward on a path that leads to the normalization of relations. This latest and comprehensive addition to the ongoing debate will contribute to our understanding of a seemingly intractable dilemma. It offers policy prescriptions on how we should think about and approach the toughest issues in the political, economic, and legal sectors, when both sides are ready to return to the negotiating table in a serious way.

Ambassador Jeffrey F. DeLaurentis (ret.)
Former Charge d 'Affaires
U.S. Embassy Havana, Cuba

Preface

Michael J. Kelly, Erika Moreno, and Richard C. Witmer, II

By December 2014, America's last two battle lines of the Cold War that remained intact were along the 38th parallel with North Korea and across the Florida Straits with Cuba. The Korean stalemate remains intractable so long as Kim Jong-un holds power in Pyongyang. However, with respect to the regime of Raúl Castro in Havana, successor to the dictatorship of Fidel Castro, an opening emerged that presented Washington, D.C. an opportunity to begin resolving the stalemate with Cuba.

President Barack Obama, working with Pope Francis and Vatican envoys, negotiated a breakthrough and then used his executive foreign relations power to re-establish diplomatic relations between Cuba and the United States in 2015. While Congress has been slow to follow with legislative adjustments that still must be made in order to fully normalize relations, the path toward normalization was underway until the election of Donald J. Trump.

As the Trump administration took shape, many questions emerged regarding the likelihood of normalization, especially considering that the island was on a path to witness its first peaceful transition of power to someone outside the Castro family. Today, most would suggest that the rhetorical reversals witnessed during the first few years of the Trump administration have not yet amounted to a substantial change in policy toward the island nation.

This book examines a number of issues that will continue to be encountered along the path of normalization. Drawing insight from the political, economic, and legal spheres, we suggest that much work remains to be done for the new Cuba-U.S. relationship to flourish. This includes the resolution of outstanding property claims that date back to the 1959 revolution, establishing U.S.-Cuban economic relationships in multiple sectors of the economy, and working through contentious political issues in both Cuba and the United States. Although the potential for a renewed freeze between the United States and Cuba is still likely, especially given some of the tensions experienced between the two states in 2017, this contribution seeks to identify avenues of potential cooperation and the potential for a permanent thawing of relations between the two countries.

Preface

[illegible] and Richard E. Feinberg

By December 2014, [illegible] one of the last [illegible] of the Cold War that remained largely [illegible] along the 90th parallel with North Korea and across the Florida Straits [illegible] [illegible] as long as [illegible] power in Havana. [illegible] the regime of Raúl Castro in Havana [illegible] to the [illegible] Washington, D.C. [illegible] to begin normalizing relations with Cuba.

President Barack Obama [illegible] was [illegible] behind the scenes [illegible] negotiations [illegible] to re-establish diplomatic relations between Cuba and the United States in 2015. While Congress has been unwilling to follow with a legislative [illegible] toward normalization [illegible] the election of Donald Trump.

[illegible] many questions remain regarding the future of [illegible] the first peaceful transition of power [illegible] during [illegible] the Trump administration has [illegible] to change [illegible] policy toward the island nation.

This book [illegible] along the path [illegible] the legal, economic, and [illegible] sphere [illegible] that much work remains to be done [illegible]. This includes the resolution of outstanding property claims [illegible] Cuban economic [illegible] both Cuba and the United States [illegible] trade between the United States and Cuba [illegible] in 2012 [illegible] this contribution [illegible] to identify [illegible] of cooperation and the potential for a [illegible] between the two countries.

Acknowledgments

This research stems from a USAID grant awarded to the Cuba research team at Creighton University in 2005. The original research team members included the three editors of this volume, as well as our colleagues at Creighton University: James Wunsch, Patrick Borchers, and Arthur Pearlstein. While the reports, publications, and presentations that resulted from that effort were important to understanding the complexity and possibilities of addressing unresolved property rights issues in Cuba, this strain of research subsequently launched a variety of new questions and research programs.

The Barack Obama administration's rapprochement with Havana spurred us to revisit the questions that we encountered almost ten years earlier. We are indebted to the many people and organizations that helped us in this effort, including the talented contributors, Creighton University School of Law, and College of Arts and Sciences, for their continuing support. Many thanks as well to the Southern Political Science Association for hosting a panel session with several of our contributors on the future of the bilateral relationship. The feedback received from that conference was essential to the completion of this book.

We are also grateful to Ashley Ritter and Hans de Sales-del Valle whose comments and suggestions on several chapters were invaluable. We also wish to thank the editors at Oxford University Press for their support and recommendations throughout the process. Finally, we thank our families—Gus and Lilia, Rick and Dorie, Richard, Sofia, and Gabriela, and Konni, Durham, Anderson, Kruz, and Kaylin—who patiently endured countless conversations about this volume or awaited our return from research trips to Cuba.

Notes on Contributors

Larry Catá Backer, W. Richard and Mary Eshelman Faculty Scholar & Professor of Law, Professor of International Affairs, Pennsylvania State University

Professor Backer researches globalization, especially as it relates to the emergence of ways of understanding constitutional and enterprise law. His most recent work touches on the regulation of multinational corporations, sovereign wealth funds, transnational constitutionalism, and the convergence of public and private law. He researches issues of governments as private actors in global markets, the development of law, and social norm systems to regulate business and human rights. He is author of "Ideologies of Sovereign Debt: Cuba and the IMF" in *Penn State International Law Review* and "Cuban Corporate Governance at a Crossroads" in *Transnational Law & Contemporary Problems*, among many other publications. Professor Backer is a member of the American Law Institute and the European Corporate Governance Institute. He received his JD from Columbia University and MPP from Harvard University.

Jonathan C. Benjamin-Alvarado, Professor of Political Science and Assistant Vice Chancellor for Student Affairs, University of Nebraska–Omaha

Dr. Benjamin-Alvarado joined the faculty at the University of Nebraska at Omaha in 2000 from a previous teaching and research position at the University of Georgia. Dr. Benjamin-Alvarado is the Director of the Intelligence Community Centers of Academic Excellence Program. Dr. Benjamin-Alvarado's research has been published in the *Journal of Political Science Education*, the *Nonproliferation Review, Political Science Quarterly*, and *Urban Affairs Review*. He is the author of *Power to the People: Energy and the Cuban Nuclear Program*, published by Routledge Press, and the editor of *Cuba's Energy Future: Strategic Approaches to Cooperation*, published by the Brookings Institution Press. He received his PhD from the University of Georgia.

Roger R. Betancourt, Emeritus, University of Maryland

Professor Roger R. Betancourt received his BA (cum laude) from Georgetown University (1962–1965) and his PhD from the University of Wisconsin–Madison (1965 to January 1970). He joined the Faculty at Maryland in September 1969 and became Emeritus in July 2007. With respect to the profession, he was one of the founders of the Association for the Study of the Cuban Economy (ASCE) in 1990 and led it (First President, 1990–1992) to become one of the Allied Social

Sciences associated with the American Economic Association, which is still the case. He has continued participating in its committees and intellectual activities to the present. (The latter are available in ASCE's Papers and Proceedings [Cuba in Transition, Volumes 1-2, 7- 9, 11,15, 17-20, 22-24, 26-27]), https://www.ascecuba.org/publications/annual-proceedings/. His research contributions in economics lie in three broad topic areas. With respect to production, a summary of his long-term contributions is available in "Capital Utilization" [entry in S. Durlauf and L. Blume (eds.) *The New Palgrave Dictionary of Economics*, 2nd edition, The Macmillan Press, 2008, or in the third edition, 2018].

Jeffrey F. DeLaurentis, Centennial Fellow, Georgetown University Walsh School of Foreign Service

Ambassador Jeffrey DeLaurentis currently serves as a Centennial Fellow for the Georgetown University after a year at the Harvard Kennedy School as a Senior Diplomatic Fellow with the Future of Diplomacy Project. DeLaurentis is a twenty-seven-year veteran of the Foreign Service; he served as the first Charge d'Affaires at the U.S. Embassy in Havana Cuba following the re-establishment of diplomatic relations between the United States and Cuba. Prior to taking up his Cuba post in August 2014, he was the Alternate Representative for Special Political Affairs at the U.S. Mission to the United Nations. Previously, he served as Deputy Assistant Secretary of State for the Bureau of Western Hemisphere Affairs, and as Minister Counselor for Political Affairs and Security Council Coordinator at the U.S. Mission to the United Nations.

Ambassador DeLaurentis began his State Department career in 1991 as a consular officer in Havana, and returned to Cuba as Political-Economic Section Chief in 1999–2002. In Washington, D.C., he served as Executive Assistant to the Under Secretary of State for Democracy and Global Affairs, Special Assistant to the Assistant Secretary of State for Western Hemisphere Affairs, and Director of Inter-American Affairs at the National Security Council. Ambassador DeLaurentis retired from the State Department in August 2018. He is a graduate of the Georgetown University School of Foreign Service and Columbia University Graduate School of International and Public Affairs.

Armando Nova-González, Senior Researcher and Professor at the Center for the Study of the Cuban Economy, University of Havana

Dr. Armando Nova-González, an eminent Cuban economist, has conducted more than eighty-four research studies on the Cuban economy and has published more than sixty-five articles in different Cuban and international journals. He is the author of *La agricultura en Cuba: Evolución y Trayectoria, 1959–2005* (Editorial de Ciencias Sociales, 2006), *Aspectos Económicos de los Cítricos en Cuba* (Editorial Científico-Técnica, 1988), and a third book, and has coauthored two other volumes. He received his Ph.D. from the University of Havana.

Mario A. González-Corzo, Associate Professor of Business and Economics, Lehman College, The City University of New York

Dr. González-Corzo's research interest and specialization covers various aspects of the Cuban economy, specifically on Cuba's post-Soviet economic transformations, the role of remittances, Cuba's banking and monetary reforms, and more recent economic development issues in Cuba. Prior to joining Lehman, Dr. González-Corzo provided consulting, strategic, and investment advice to global banks and financial institutions in the United States, Europe, and Latin America. His career in the financial services industry included senior positions at Price Waterhouse Coopers, LLP, JP Morgan Chase, and MetLife, Inc. Dr. González-Corzo received his PhD from Rutgers University.

Ted A. Henken, Associate Professor of Latino Studies, Baruch College, The City University of New York

Dr. Henken is president of the Association for the Study of the Cuban Economy (ASCE). His newest scholarly work, *Entrepreneurial Cuba: The Changing Policy Landscape*, is coauthored with the Canadian economist Archibald R. M. Ritter. One of Dr. Henken's current research foci is on the internet in Cuba, assessing the depth, breadth, representativeness, and social impact of the Cuban blogging phenomenon. His project, "In Search of Generacion Y: Citizen Journalism, The Cuban Blogosphere, and the Future of Cuban Civil Society," is particularly interested in how Cuban bloggers are connected to other new autonomous cultural and social projects and movements in today's Cuba and how they might together contribute to the strengthening of Cuban civil society. Dr. Henken received his PhD from Tulane University.

Gregg B. Johnson, Associate Professor of Political Science and International Relations, Valparaiso University

Dr. Johnson is chair of the Political Science Department. His research examines how political institutions (the rules of the game) affect elite and mass behaviors in Latin America and the United States. His work has appeared in the *American Journal of Political Science, Latin American Politics and Society, American Politics Research*, the *Journal of Legislative Studies*, and the *Journal of Politics in Latin America*. He teaches courses in Comparative Politics, Political Economy, and Research Methods. He received his PhD from the University of Arizona.

Michael J. Kelly, Professor of Law, Creighton University School of Law

Professor Kelly holds the Senator Allen A. Sekt Endowed Chair in Law. He coauthored the 2007 USAID *Report on Outstanding Property Claims between Cuba and the United States* and has offered testimony in Congress on this issue as well as expertise to media outlets such as the *Wall Street Journal* and *New York Times*. His current research focuses on cyberspace governance issues in his role as co-chair of the American Bar Association's Task Force on Internet Governance and international criminal law in his role as president of the U.S. National Section of the International

Association of Penal Law. He is author most recently of *Prosecuting Corporations for Genocide* (Oxford University Press, 2016); his articles have appeared in many articles including the *Harvard Law & Policy Review, Berkeley Journal of International Law, Cornell International Law Journal*, Illinois Law Review, and *Oregon Law Review*. He was the recipient of Creighton's 2017 University Research Award for his body of work in international law. Professor Kelly received his JD from Indiana University and LLM from Georgetown University.

Peter Kornbluh, Director, Cuba and Chile Documentation Projects at the National Security Archive in Washington, DC.

Peter Kornbluh is also co-author, with William M. LeoGrande, of *Back Channel to Cuba: The Hidden History of Negotiations Between Washington and Havana*. He is also the author of *The Pinochet File: A Declassified Dossier on Atrocity and Accountability*. His articles have been published in *Foreign Policy*, The *New York Review of Books, Cigar Aficionado, The Nation*, the *New Yorker*, The *New York Times*, The *Washington Post, Los Angeles Times*, and many other journals and newspapers.

William M. LeoGrande, Professor of Government, American University School of Public Affairs

Dr. LeoGrande is a specialist in Latin American politics and U.S. foreign policy toward Latin America and has been a frequent adviser to government and private sector agencies. He has written five books, including *Our Own Backyard: The United States in Central America, 1977–1992*. Most recently, he is coauthor of *Back Channel to Cuba: The Hidden History of Negotiations between Washington and Havana*. Previously, he served on the staffs of the Democratic Policy Committee of the U.S. Senate, and the Democratic Caucus Task Force on Central America of the U.S. House of Representatives. Professor LeoGrande has been a Council on Foreign Relations International Affairs Fellow, and a Pew Faculty Fellow in International Affairs. His articles have appeared in various international and national journals, magazines, and newspapers. He received his PhD from Syracuse University. He served as Dean of the School of Public Affairs from 1999 to 2011.

Zhimin Lin, Associate Professor of Government and Public Administration, University of Macau

Dr. Lin taught at Valparaiso University (Indiana, USA) from 1991 to 2014, where he chaired the Chinese and Japanese Studies Program and served as director for both the Master of Arts in Chinese Studies Program and the Valparaiso University China Center. Dr. Lin's research is focused on two areas: Chinese politics, especially budgetary politics and public policy, and international relations in East Asia. He is the author of *China under Reform* (Mason Crest, 2005 and 2013) and has coauthored or edited three books and published numerous journal articles in both English and Chinese. Presently, Dr. Lin is working on four book projects: (1) *Budgetary Politics in China, 1985–2015*, which examines the budgetary politics between central versus local governments and budgetary versus extra-budgetary income and expenditures; (2) *New Challenges to China's Growing Global Reach*, which studies how China is seeking to expand its global influence in Africa and Latin America; (3) *Measuring China's Diplomatic Capacity*; and (4) *Public Participation and Public Policy, International Comparisons and Lessons*, an edited volume that cross-nationally compares public involvement at various stages of policymaking. Dr. Lin received his PhD from the University of Washington and MPA from Princeton University.

Gary H. Maybarduk, Acting Secretary of ASCE

Dr. Maybarduk is a retired thirty-two-year veteran of the U.S. Foreign Service. He served as Counselor for Economic/Political affairs in the U.S. Interests Section in Havana, 1997–1999. He was chief of the economic section in Nicaragua for the first two years following the Sandinista revolution, Deputy Chief of Mission in Freetown, Sierra Leone during the beginning of the civil wars in Sierra Leone and Liberia, and Economic Counselor in Caracas during the first three years of the Chavez regime, 1999–2002. Other posts included Papua New Guinea and Mexico. He was Director of Central America Affairs in the Department of State, 1996–1997. In 2006 he directed the economic working group for the Commission on Assistance to a Free Cuba, CAFC II, and wrote most of the economic section of that report.

Dr. Maybarduk received his BS in economics from MIT, an MA in international relations from the Fletcher School of Law and Diplomacy, and a PhD in economics from the University of Minnesota. He later received an MS in International Security Policy from the National War College, 1994. In 2002–2004, he was a Professor of International Security Strategy at the Army War College.

Dr. Maybarduk has written more than twenty papers on the Cuban economy and U.S.-Cuban relations, mostly for the Association for the Study of the Cuban Economy (ASCE), where he is currently the Association's Secretary. His latest article, "Cuba's Political and Economic Arteriosclerosis—It Is Not Just the Castros," was published by ASCE in 2019.

Erika Moreno, Associate Professor of Political Science, Creighton University

Dr. Moreno specializes in comparative politics, with a focus on Latin American politics. Her scholarly interests focus on democratic institutions and interbranch relations and their implications for democratic accountability and representation. Her work has appeared in *Latin American Politics and Society*, *Comparative Political Studies*, *Electoral Studies*, the *Bulletin of Latin American Research*, and *Legislative Studies Quarterly*. She has also contributed to chapters in edited book manuscripts published by Notre Dame press, Oxford University Press, and Pennsylvania State Press on topics that include the Colombian peace process, government institutions and accountability, and the Colombian political system. Dr. Moreno was also part of the Creighton University team that wrote the *Report on the Resolution of Outstanding Property Claims between Cuba and the United States* (Creighton University Press 2007). She received her PhD from the University of Arizona.

Karen C. Sokol, Associate Professor of Law, Loyola University New Orleans

Professor Sokol joined the Loyola University New Orleans College of Law faculty in 2009. Her teaching and research interests include environmental law, torts, products liability, and law and philosophy. Her current scholarship focuses on legal controls on marketing of dangerous products, climate change resilience, particularly for vulnerable countries such as Cuba and India, and, most recently, on the potential for forging more robust environmental and public health protections by incorporating Indian philosophy into Western jurisprudence, law, and policy.

Professor Sokol graduated from Yale Law School, where she served as Articles Editor for the *Yale Human Rights and Development Law Journal* and was a member of the Allard K. Lowenstein International Human Rights Clinic. After law school, she clerked for Judge Carolyn Dineen King of the U.S. Court of Appeals for the Fifth Circuit and worked as an associate in the appellate section of Vinson & Elkins, LLP. She then worked as a policy analyst for the Center for Progressive Reform, writing a number of papers and articles on environmental and public health issues, with a focus on government transparency and corporate accountability. The year before coming to Loyola, she was a fellow at Georgetown University Law Center's O'Neill Institute for National and Global Health Law. She is admitted to practice in the state of Texas and the U.S. Court of Appeals for the Fifth Circuit.

Robert R. M. Verchick, Gauthier-St. Martin Chair of Environmental Law, Loyola University New Orleans

Professor Verchick holds the Gauthier-St. Martin Chair in Environmental Law at Loyola University New Orleans. He is also a Senior Fellow at Tulane University's Disaster Resilience Leadership Academy, in the School of Social Work, and President of the Center for Progressive Reform, a national policy institute focused on public health, public welfare, and environmental protection. Professor Verchick served in the Barack Obama administration as Deputy Associate Administrator for Policy at the U.S. Environmental Protection Agency in 2009 and 2010. In that role he helped develop climate adaptation policy for the EPA and served on President Obama's Interagency Climate Change Adaptation Task Force. In the fall of 2012, he researched climate adaptation policies in India as a Visiting Scholar at the Centre for Policy Research in New Delhi, supported by a Fulbright-Nehru Environmental Leadership Award. He holds an AB degree, with honors and distinction, from Stanford University and a JD degree, cum laude, from Harvard University.

Professor Verchick's writing focuses on environmental regulation, climate change adaptation, and the developing field of disaster law. His work has appeared in many venues, including the *California Law Review*, the *Southern California Law Review*, and the environmental law journals at Harvard, Stanford, and Berkeley. He is the author of three books, including *Facing Catastrophe: Environmental Action for a Post-Katrina World* (Harvard University Press 2010), which was selected as a CHOICE Outstanding Academic Title by the American Library Association.

Janet L. Walsh, Birchtree Global, LLC

Dr. Walsh is the CEO and President of Birchtree Global, LLC. Birchtree Global provides the legal, financial, tax, and human capital infrastructure for globalizing businesses. Her area of expertise lies in global startups, finance, infrastructure, and human capital performance. She has worked on the ground in seventy-nine countries directing multifunctional teams of legal, financial, tax, and human resource professionals in a wide variety of industries. Prior to working as CEO and President of Birchtree Global, Dr. Walsh worked in vice president and senior executive positions in Fortune 500, global multinationals. She is an adjunct professor of global business in MBA programs at the New York Institute of Technology, and Manhattanville College in New York.

Dr. Walsh holds a BA degree in Economics from Bucknell University, an MBA from Loyola University, and a DBA from the University of Phoenix. She speaks Spanish, French, and Japanese. She is a dual citizen of Ireland and the United States. Dr. Walsh can be contacted by email at walsh@birchtreeglobal.com.

Richard C. Witmer, II, Professor of Political Science, Creighton University

Dr. Witmer specializes in American Politics and Public Policy. Among his teaching and research interests are U.S.-Cuban relations, Congress, elections, and American Indian politics and policy. His work has appeared in a number of professional journals, including the *Journal of Politics, Political Research Quarterly, Social Science Quarterly, Politics and Policy, Social Science Journal, Creighton Law Review*, and *Cuban Affairs Journal*, among others. Dr. Witmer was also part of the Creighton University team (with Michael J. Kelly and Erika Moreno) that wrote the *Report on the Resolution of Outstanding Property Claims between Cuba and the United States* (Creighton University Press 2007).

Note on the Publication

As this book goes to press, the Trump Administration has decided to make one of the legal/choices available to it with respect to America's bilateral relationship with Cuba—but it is one that potentially affects the relationships of both countries with many others. The Administration announced that the United States will no longer fully block implementation of Title III of Public Law 104-114, or the Cuban Liberty and Democratic Solidarity (Libertad) Act of 1996 (110 Stat. 785), also commonly known as the Helms-Burton Act. This provision, held in abeyance for 23 years by every president since Clinton, authorizes U.S. nationals who have property claims in Cuba to bring suit in U.S. courts against persons or corporations who "traffic" in the property of those claims. The act broadly defines this as basically any use someone or some company makes of a property in Cuba that has a claim attached to it. Thus, a U.S. claimant can sue, for example, a Spanish or Swiss company doing business in Cuba that touches on the subject of that claim—whether it's a building, acreage, or perhaps even a trademark. As announced, the policy change also includes a provision for the U.S. to withdraw or deny visas from individuals that are tied to the trafficking of property formerly belonging to U.S. citizens.

This announcement has the potential to directly impact the findings in two chapters of this volume. First, Chapter 9, which focus specifically on Helms-Burton, and Chapter 10, which covers property claims of U.S. nationals against Cuba. However at this time it is difficult to forecast the actual impact that this will have on property claimants and/or Cuba-U.S. relations. For example, U.S. corporations may have foreign subsidiaries doing business in Cuba that could be liable or, alternatively, corporate claimholders may be reluctant to sour relations with Canadian firms or endanger trans-Atlantic business relationships by suing Canadian or European interests doing business in Cuba. Canada (https://www.canada.ca/en/global-affairs/news/2019/04/government-of-canada-will-defend-interests-of-canadians-doing-business-in-cuba.html [accessed May 17, 2019]) and the European Union (http://europa.eu/rapid/press-release_STATEMENT-19-2171_en.htm [accessed May 17, 2019]) were quick to issue statements opposing the Administration's activation of Title III provisions calling them a violation of international law. This pushback may help blunt any actual effect of the policy change.

Moreover, it is incredibly unlikely given jurisdictional issues, award enforcement issues, and location of assets (mostly outside the U.S.), that any claimholder in the U.S. would realize a meaningful return on that claim by taking advantage of Title III's pathway to litigation. An additional impediment is the number of possible suits seeking resolution. As noted in Chapter 10, most certified claims are for $10,000 or less. Of those over the Title III threshold for suit of $50,000, a filing fee of $6,548 for per case and an additional $350.20 filing fee (as of May 2019), prescribed for initiating any civil action (https://www.uscourts.gov/services-forms/fees/district-court-miscellaneous-fee-schedule [accessed May 17, 2019]) will likely reduce the number of corporations and individuals willing to engage in litigation.

Furthermore, as we detail in the following chapters, the Trump Administration's rhetoric has been far stronger than the actual implementation of the espoused policies. Whether this latest policy change is intended to be a symbolic nod to Cuban constituencies in South Florida as the incumbent Administration gears up for a reelection run in 2020, or is actually intended to provide real and significant opportunities for property claimants in the U.S. to engage in litigation in the US Court system, we are unable to discern at this time. Indeed, given the proclivity of this Administration to mete out rewards and punishments to those who act, or do not act, in accordance with its policy preferences, this move could be entirely about punishing Cuba for supporting the regime of Venezuelan President Nicolás Maduro, a move that Havana took expressly to counter Washington's support for his rival (Juan Guaidó).

Whatever the rationale, most experts would agree that the decision to allow for the implementation of Title III of the Libertad Act is not a beneficial move toward normalizing cross-strait relations with Cuba. It is, however, in line with other recent policy moves of the Trump Administration, however symbolic, that seek to move the U.S. and Cuba farther away from normalizing relations during this president's tenure in office.

1

Introduction

*Michael J. Kelly, Erika Moreno, and Richard C. Witmer, II**

It has been over five years since President Barack Obama traveled to Cuba for a memorable and, to many on the island, inspiring effort to bridge the divide between the United States and Cuba. Since then, many Cubans admit that the public mood rose rapidly on the hopes of a diplomatic normalization between the two political foes, only to be dashed by the election and rhetoric of Donald J. Trump. Today, the apprehension that characterized the months immediately after the 2016 election has eased somewhat. Although the Trump administration has repeated its desire to undo Obama-era policies vis-à-vis Cuba, few steps have been taken. Actions undertaken by the Trump administration were limited to the removal of diplomatic officers from Havana after a spate of mysterious illnesses afflicted members of the U.S. diplomatic corps in 2017 (Robles and Semple 2017), and small changes to rules guiding travel to the island. These events suggest that a normalization of relations between the two states are less likely as the United States shrinks its diplomatic efforts, literally and figuratively, on the island. Yet, at the same time, many of the changes ushered in under the last two years of the Obama administration remain in place, suggesting that the new status quo has largely remained untouched by the rhetorical flourishes of the current Republican administration.

Meanwhile, the Cuban government has continued to push forward on a range of policies that aim to bring the old regime up to date, including allowing for new leadership at the top with the appointment of President Miguel Díaz-Canel in 2018. As the first leader of the revolutionary government to bear a surname other than Castro, Díaz-Canel's appointment suggests that the regime is ready to move the revolution into a new era. Yet,

* Michael J. Kelly, Creighton University School of Law, michaelkelly@creighton.edu; Erika Moreno, Creighton University, erikamoreno@creighton.edu; Richard C. Witmer, II, Creighton University, witmer@creighton.edu.

The Cuba-U.S. Bilateral Relationship. Michael J. Kelly, Erika Moreno, and Richard C. Witmer, II.

it is important to remember that these efforts to launch the revolution into the twenty-first century are not without their own guardrails. As a relatively little-known party apparatchik, President Díaz-Canel's policy positions are relatively unknown, while his commitment to revolutionary institutions, like the Cuban Communist party, are clear. So far, the direction of the new administration bears many of the same guiding principles that kept the revolution alive over the last sixty years.

It is also worth noting that the regime has forged ahead with reforms that opened up several sectors of the economy and society. These reforms, as addressed in several of the chapters in this volume, have proven vital to the regime's longevity and will continue to play a role in the islands' development. Among the many changes that have altered the landscape of the nation are efforts to bring in market-oriented economic reforms, new rules guiding property rights, and the emergence of a new class of citizens, the *cuentapropistas*, or self-employed. As these changes filter through the bloodstream of the Cuban regime they will likely continue to help shape the manner in which these two countries relate to each other. Furthermore, as U.S. citizens and Cubans interact in greater numbers, a result of the expansion of Obama-era rules on visiting the island and noted in the second section of this volume, the chances will increase that people on both sides of the Florida Straits will continue to conduct small-scale, or person-to-person, diplomacy.

So while U.S.-Cuban relations appear to have experienced a recent brief thaw that helped to move a few policies toward normalization, the current political climate between the leadership of these two countries has been placed under a new freeze warning. In other words, the thaw cycle preceded a new freeze. Yet the ground shifted somewhat between those two cycles and has produced a new *status quo*—furnished by Obama's efforts at greater interaction—that will continue to shape how these nations deal with each other. The brief opening that took place in 2014 and that continues in many ways unabated today has the potential to have profound effects at the grassroots level. The Cuban government's efforts to modernize, as well as citizens from both countries continuing to engage in small-scale diplomatic and humanitarian interactions, facilitate the growing connection between the two nations.

This book examines a number of issues that will continue to be encountered along the path of normalization. Drawing insight from the political, economic, and legal spheres, we suggest that while much work is still needed for the new Cuban-U.S. relationship to flourish, the two states have seen important changes occur in a relatively short period of time. Among the greatest challenges facing the two states are the resolution of outstanding property claims that date back to the 1959 revolution, establishing U.S.-Cuban economic relationships in multiple sectors of the economy, and working through contentious political issues in both Cuba and the United States. Although the potential for a renewed freeze between the United States and Cuba is still possible, especially given some of the tensions experienced between the two states in 2017, the chapters in this volume seek to identify avenues of cooperation and the potential for a permanent thawing of relations between the two countries. The result is a collection of thought-provoking observations and commentary that posit viable policy choice across a range of contemporary issues.

While there are a variety of ways in which to categorize the kinds of challenges and opportunities faced by these two states, we focus on three key dimensions: political, economic, and legal. Although these are clearly intertwined in a variety of ways, often blurring the lines between one dimension and another, we see this tripartite division as essential for beginning a constructive dialogue on the most pressing roadblocks to normalization. As a result, each section and chapter approaches the challenges and opportunities that face these two nations in accordance with the disciplinary and theoretical lenses necessary to speak to experts and policymakers in those fields.

Three Dimensions and a Multilevel Game of Diplomacy

Among the myriad challenges and opportunities presented to both the United States and Cuba, our focus on politics, economics, and legal considerations highlight several key points. First, by disaggregating these three dimensions, we implicitly suggest that progress toward one does not necessarily constitute progress toward all. As we have seen in the recent past, movements toward easier access to the island—following a relaxation of the rules guiding travel to Cuba—did not incentivize elected politicians in the United States to encourage normalized diplomatic relations. Likewise, efforts to reform the agricultural sector have not translated into a clear and consistent approach to outstanding property rights issues. As should be clear across the various chapters, there are issues that cut across multiple dimensions and continue to pose intractable challenges to the restoration of diplomatic relations between the two states.

This is the case for a variety of thorny issues related to Cuba. After all, the lengthy history that has bound the two countries together, even before Cuba gained its independence, generated weighty, and emotional, baggage for the two neighbors. A history of intervention has made national sovereignty a critical component of the Cuban response to political, economic, or legal initiatives coming from the United States. Furthermore, the sheer number of issues related to politics, economics, and legal concerns means that the relationship is likely to remain multidimensional into the future. This despite the fact that changes in one country would likely be welcomed in the other. As an example, efforts like domestic reforms in Cuba to introduce market mechanisms in agriculture did not automatically result in a change in diplomatic relations between the two states. And while we have seen years of economic reforms on the island in the direction of a mixed market model, this has not brought about dramatic changes in diplomatic relations for a variety of reasons, many tied to the nature of the regime, evident in domestic legislation (see chapter 11, this volume), or domestic politics in each country that supersede these on-the-ground changes. For instance, the political stability of the Cuban government belies an ever-shifting set of policy goals and outcomes that produced an array of disparate, often competing economic policies (see Azicir 2004). The regime lurched from highly idealistic *Fidelista* models in the late 1960s to centralized state planning models, borrowed from the U.S.S.R. in the 1970s. The early 1980s then ushered in yet another approach through a series of pragmatic market-oriented reforms (Mesa-Lago 2015). Each shift in policy coincided with a concomitant shift in alliances among ministers and key figures close to Fidel Castro. As a result, the island saw broad policy changes in the economic realm over time even though the political realm has appeared to remain largely unchanged since 1959. Furthermore, the U.S. government has maintained a laser-like focus on political reform on the island while it has largely missed the fluctuations of policy in legal and economic affairs. The United States' insistence on dramatic political change on the island has thus frozen the dialogue between the two states in a Cold War–era stasis, even while important changes have taken place in other dimensions. Moving forward, for profound change to occur, all three of the respective dimensions covered in this volume—political, economic, and legal—require attention.

In order for progress to occur in these three policy areas, we suggest that another important facet of the U.S.-Cuban relationship includes the kinds of signals sent by both states. Diplomatic history between the United States and Cuba has given the incorrect impression that the two states ceased to communicate with each other after the 1959 revolution. The truth is that the two states have continually signaled their intentions over time. The broader literature on foreign policy suggests that there are several types of signals that states issue, including costly signals and cheap signals. Costly signals are the most credible because they require some action or a change in the status quo on the part of the signal-giver. Costly signals could take the form of troop movements or formulated policy changes. Cheap signals are sometimes referred to as "cheap talk" and suggest that the signal-giver is providing some information, positive or negative, but has not taken any actions to solidify that sentiment. Press statements or tweets to broad audiences with no substantive change in the status quo are examples of cheap signals. While both types of signals convey information, costly signals are generally more credible and indicative of a new policy direction for the signal-giver. What is more, costly signals are more likely to trigger actions by the receiver of the signal.

Although diplomatic relations were frozen in a Cold War–era dialogue, the two partners have found myriad ways to signal either a desire to reestablish a dialogue or to push each other away. At times those signals have been antagonistic in nature, as is the case for the embargo placed on the island decades ago. Yet, efforts to reopen channels of communication between Cuban families and their U.S.-based relatives during the 1970s and 1980s signaled renewed efforts at engagement. Here, the adoption of rules in 1977 that facilitated travel and communications for U.S. citizens and their relatives on the island served as a salve for years of verbal hostility.

Changes in U.S. presidential administrations have resulted in very different approaches to the island nation and, as a result, have sent an array of signals to the ruling elite. This is clear today, given the most recent swings in presidential administrations. President Obama's willingness to engage the island represented a credible signal that involved both rhetorical change, by calling on the Cuban people to see the United States as a potential partner, and policy changes that facilitated travel and exchanges with the island. Although President Obama was limited in his ability to alter the status quo and facilitate a normalization of relations, given the restrictions placed on U.S. presidents by congressional actions (for more details, see chapter 3 and chapter 9, this volume), he signaled an intention to move forward with diplomatic efforts.

The signal telegraphed by the Obama administration was thrown into doubt after the election of Donald J. Trump, who indicated a return to a hardline approach to the Castro regime. In the end, though, the Trump administration's posture toward Cuba has largely been rhetorical, with some statements indicating a desire to undo the progress made by Obama. However, two years into the new administration, the only tangible change has been the drawing down of a diplomatic presence on the island, owing ostensibly to health issues, and revocation of one of the original twelve rationales for U.S. citizens to travel to Cuba. Flights continue to depart from the United States to Havana, cruise ships continue to dock in Havana, and, as several of the chapters in this book indicate, there are a significant number of tourists traveling to Cuba every year. These signals are important precursors to a restoration of U.S.-Cuban relations. So although the cheap signals under the Trump administration have been hostile, little has been done, which is itself a signal to the Cuban government. Moving forward, as the United States approaches the 2020 election cycle, the outlook will become clearer as a new set of candidates for office articulate their own vision of U.S.-Cuban relations. And since the current administration has not moved to undo Obama's policy changes in any meaningful way, it is possible that a new president in 2020 will be able to pick up where Obama left off. Alternatively, a move to the far right of the political spectrum (as discussed by Johnson and Lin, chapter 4, this volume), will provide a new administration with an array of costly policy options to further isolate the island. In the end, the policy signals identified in a number of the chapters in this book could create opportunities, or provide additional challenges, for diplomatic normalization as we move forward.

A third consideration, identified in a number of chapters in this volume, is the fact that U.S.-Cuban relations have developed along two tracks over time. Since formal diplomatic relations were put on hold in the 1960s, much of the dialogue that has taken place has either occurred at the grassroots (or person-to-person) level or, sporadically, at the highest levels of state governance. Studies of diplomacy have identified several different tracks, including state-to-state interactions (or track one), unofficial interactions between nonstate officials (or track two), and business interactions (track three). Recent additions to this literature present a wider array of potential forms of diplomacy, including exchange programs, private voluntary organizations, nongovernmental organizations, and special interest groups, also known as person-to-person (or track four) diplomacy.

The U.S.-Cuban relationship after 1959 has developed primarily through a combination of track one and track four exchanges. The use of track one diplomacy has been sporadic after 1959, primarily because the context of the Cold War did not facilitate a means for the two countries to engage each other. In contrast to the Soviet Union and its satellite countries, which were connected by political and economic organizations (e.g., COMECOM and the Warsaw Pact), Cuba lacked membership in similar organizations that could advance its interests. Therefore, Cuba's geographic location kept the island at arm's length from its communist allies and ideologically isolated from its neighbors in the Americas. As a result, efforts at rapprochement have been halting. The wounds created by a sixty-year history of seemingly irreconcilable differences limited the kinds of statecraft that might be available to most other bilateral relationships. Yet, it bears noting that in spite of those differences, Cuba is not North Korea. While it faced suspicion and isolation, over time the Cuban regime has found ways to reintegrate itself into its neighborhood. So, the opportunities for additional state-to-state interactions are possible, although there remain myriad challenges as well. A number of chapters identify where these political, economic, and legal obstacles remain in place.

Person-to-person diplomacy, on the other hand, requires little more than rules that encourage citizen interaction. Citizen interactions are a means of de-escalating tensions across groups. What is more, this type of diplomacy requires citizen engagement in a variety of activities. Whether it is as a result of educational exchange, tourism, private volunteer organizations, or nongovernmental organizations, these activities break down stereotypes and build up a level of cultural competency needed to build partnerships. Track four diplomacy is often considered a small-scale approach to diplomacy, and although citizen interactions do not necessarily impact policymaking structures in the short term, they are potentially transformative over the longer term. Two chapters in the economic section specifically address citizen exchanges with Walsh (chapter 7) noting the characteristics of businesses that have been successful in tapping into the Cuban tourism market, and Betancourt (chapter 8) providing an overview of the flow of persons between Cuba and the United States. What is more, these person-to-person exchanges may also facilitate business exchanges (track three diplomacy), which are the subject of several of the contributions in the economics section of this volume.

Reliance on two track diplomacy presents an interesting set of opportunities and challenges. For instance, when state-to-state dialogue ceases, as it appears to have done during the Trump administration, pursuit of person-to-person diplomacy continues apace as long as U.S. citizens are allowed to continue traveling to the island. The Obama-era travel rules remain largely intact, allowing for an increasing stream of U.S. travelers to the island to conduct their own forms of person-to-person diplomacy, often sharing their ideals and or engaging communities in service activities that could exact change for both sets of participants. So while one channel is blocked, the other may continue to produce some grassroots change. After all, grassroots diplomacy continues the potential for long-term and substantive changes between the two nations increases. Moving forward, such interactions could produce the groundswell needed to ultimately pressure politicians to enact policy change, but of course, such change will be slow.

The multi-issue complexity of the relationship between the United States and Cuba is represented in the three sections of this edited volume that address political, economic, and legal dimensions. In addition, each of the chapters highlight one or more of the opportunities and challenges the two countries face. Throughout these chapters the authors also strive to elucidate the kinds of signals sent by the two states over time. While some of those signals speak loudly, as is the case for legislation like the Helms-Burton Act; others offer only minor glimpses into policy priorities. Lastly, as the two states move forward, the multi-track model of diplomacy that has developed over time will continue to foster additional opportunities while also make apparent numerous challenges in the near and distant future.

Organization of the Volume

This edited volume is organized around three key dimensions: political, economic, and legal. Contributions from experts in each of these fields are important to understanding what binds Cuba and the United States together and whether we might expect continued progress toward normalization, or continued discord. In each chapter, the authors, whether explicitly or implicitly, share important insight within an environment of political, economic, and legal flux in both nations. Within the United States, the election of Donald Trump signaled a change in foreign policy that continues to shape the interaction between the two countries. Similarly, the recent ascension of Miguel Díaz-Canel to the Cuban presidency marks the beginning of the post-Castro era in Cuba. Yet there are several key features that continue to shape the relationship between the United States and Cuba that remain relevant. For instance, as the first section of this volume suggests, the political challenges and opportunities that these two states are faced with are rooted in a full understanding of the history between the United States and Cuba. William LeoGrande's discussion in chapter 2 is especially important as he provides an in-depth analysis of the manner in which the Obama administration was able to negotiate a rapprochement with Havana. The negotiations occurred in the context of decades of animosity but were marked by repeated efforts to open up lines of communication. While the recent rhetoric coming out of Washington, D.C., is reminiscent of positions taken by prior administrations, LeoGrande's discussion provides a potential road map for the normalization of ties between the two countries, even under less-than-hospitable conditions.

Chapter 3 focuses on some of the challenges posed by a history of U.S.-Cuban relations that have been codified into laws (e.g., the Cuba Democracy Act and the Helms-Burton Act) that require the island to adopt democracy as a form of government before diplomacy can take place. These vestiges of Cold War–era policies have narrowed the scope of U.S.-Cuban relations by placing a significant precondition for formal discussions between the two neighbors. It is also worth noting that those legislative efforts reflected a concern that Democratic presidents might be tempted to restore diplomatic ties with the island too soon and without regard for a powerful voting constituency in South Florida that opposes the regime's existence. As the editors (chapter 3, this volume) note, the likelihood of a democratic transition in the near or medium term is low, relative to the chances of a continuation of the regime (or succession) through the appointment of new leaders, as approved by the existing regime. The challenges posed by these legal impediments and the demand for a regime change on the island did not preclude President Obama from reaching an informal rapprochement with Cuba. However, these limitations prevented the Obama administration from achieving a fundamental change in the status quo between the two nations.

Chapter 4 addresses the challenges and opportunities presented by the island's adoption of a new partner, China. The postrevolutionary regime's search for a foil to balance U.S. hegemony in the region has forced the island nation to seek out an array of allies. Given the steady disappearance of Cuba's key benefactors, including the U.S.S.R and, most recently, Venezuela, the regime has been forced to look elsewhere for economic partnerships. Johnson and Lim's discussion of the developing ties between China and Cuba place this burgeoning relationship within the context of Chinese expansion and Cuban needs. While Cuba might represent a rather small economic partnership for the Chinese, it is clear that the island—as one of the last Communist holdouts—holds a special place in China's foreign policy agenda. What is more, Cuba stands to benefit by fostering close ties with a nation that professes a continued devotion to communism and authoritarian systems that encourage central planning in the economy, while testing out the waters of market economies. Here, the Chinese are valuable partners to an island nation that has lost its top benefactors and is still seeking a viable political and economic model to guide its efforts to modernize.

So, the political dimension of U.S.-Cuban relations and the potential for normalization are contingent on understanding the deep, and often contentious, history between the two states, as well as the developing relationship with China. The manner in which these two states were able to produce an opening under the Obama administration (see chapter 2, this volume), in spite of the roadblocks placed by legal precedent and requirements for regime change (see chapter 3, this volume) provide an important backdrop for future efforts, which includes the presence of a new partner for the island. This new partner, China, aspires to serve as a global economic and political leader on the world stage, and may also condition the way in which future U.S.-Cuban relations are framed (see chapter 4, this volume). So, while the past is prologue, substantive changes on the world scene and a successful rapprochement suggest that U.S.-Cuban relations may yet see thawing in the future, but only under the right conditions.

Part two of this volume focuses on economic opportunities and challenges to normalization. Here, four chapters take turns addressing several key elements of the economic picture that have shaped the U.S.-Cuban relationship. Chapter 5, for instance focuses on changes in the non-sugar agricultural sector in Cuba. Gonzalez-Corso and Nova-Gonzalez's detailed discussion of changes to the agricultural sector on the island sheds a bright light on the myriad reforms that have been implemented domestically and their impact on U.S.-Cuban trade. What is more, their chapter makes a case for the potential benefits to both countries under normalized trade relations as well as some of the key challenges that have faced the agricultural sector on the island as the state has allowed for freer markets.

In contrast, Henken's contribution in chapter 6, focuses on entrepreneurial arrangements that have sprung up across the island in the form of *cuentapropistas*, like those featured in his discussion of Havana's *Artecorte*. Here, the kinds of reforms promulgated since the 2000s that have increased the number of private entrepreneurs in Cuba have helped to create a new ethos—one that values the basics of market transactions but without the zero-sum nature of most start-ups in the Western world. This form of self-employment has the hallmarks of a profoundly different market ethos that has gained attention in Cuba and beyond.

The last two chapters in this section focus on specific elements of the business relationship between Cuba and the United States. In chapter 7, Walsh discusses her research on the five characteristics of businesses that have found success in the tourism industry in Cuba, while Betancourt, in chapter 8 provides an overview of the ebb and flow of persons, goods, and services, and capital between Cuba and the United States. For Walsh, changes in the regulation of tourism, with Cuba opening up to more visitors, and citizens as well as businesses from the United States seeking to take advantage of recent changes, provide opportunities in the growing tourism industry. Importantly, Walsh's treatment of this new environment offers important lessons to actors seeking to make the most of the new landscape as she identifies five key characteristics of successful market entry.

Rounding out the discussion of economic concerns is chapter 8, which focuses on understanding the U.S.-Cuban relationship using the lens of a political economy approach. Here Betancourt's analysis suggests that the multilevel diplomatic game that has unfolded between the two states is inextricably linked to the flow of goods, services, and people over time. While he notes the wide variation in these three areas, he also identifies the trends that have developed as policies have recently changed. For example, changes to the wet-foot dry-foot policy have impacted the number of Cubans seeking entry into the United States. Similarly, the warming of relations between Cuba and the United States has resulted in increased U.S. tourism to the island as limitations were relaxed. Ultimately, these flows have, undoubtedly, impacted the calculus for both Presidents Obama and Trump to help fashion their approach to Cuba.

Overall, chapters 5 through 8 are important to illustrate the kinds of changes that have taken place in Cuba while providing some indication of how those changes have produced both unexpected and expected outcomes. Importantly, these changes are likely to continue the person-to-person diplomacy currently underway regardless of alterations to formal government-to-government relations between Cuba and the United States.

The final section of the book focuses on several legal challenges and opportunities facing the two states. In chapter 9, Benjamin-Alvarado addresses the tangled legal web that has bound U.S. policy for decades. Legal impediments, including the Helms-Burton Act of 1996, require action by members of the U.S. Congress before a full-scale normalization can occur. Importantly, chapter 9 addresses the likelihood of such changes taking place in the current political context with a focus on the structural barriers placed between the United States and Cuba that, barring action by members of the U.S. Congress, are likely to continue to serve as an impediment for years to come. In the current U.S. political context, the Trump administration's fecklessness on foreign policy has resulted in an inability to take advantage of a small window of Republican Party control over the two elected branches of government to reverse Obama's initiatives vis-à-vis Cuba. While the legal impediments of Helms-Burton and the Libertad Acts are substantial, Benjamin-Alvarado notes that the combination of heightened partisan polarization and divided government in the near future offer little to no chance of removing these legal obstacles to normalization. Benjamin-Alvarado's chapter provides a clear-eyed understanding of what is necessary for a fundamental transformation of the U.S.-Cuban relationship to take place: confidence and reliability over time. Yet the specter of the Helms-Burton Act looms large on the ability of either actor to build trust and reliability and, as a result, limits the odds of a normalization of relations between the two.

Chapter 10 addresses an equally challenging impediment to normalization in the form of unresolved property claims issues stemming from the regime's expropriation of foreign lands and business interests after the 1959 revolution. Here, Kelly, Moreno, and Witmer focus on several possible challenges posed by the taking of properties but also offer a solution, in the form of a legal framework that would benefit both sides. As the authors note, resolution of these claims involves several important issues, including documentation of such claims and how to finance the $6 billion price tag. While this thorny issue continues to be raised by ex-patriots and multinationals, resolution of outstanding claims is also important to the Cuban regime, which has faced an exponential increase in interest in properties on the island, both as a source of revenue and as a boon to the growing tourist industry that has overwhelmed the island's resources. The model presented in chapter 10 provides a solution for both sides that, if implemented, could result in increased economic development, while building trust between the two nations.

The internal legal adjustments that will be necessary for Cuba to fully engage the United States and the rest of the world are addressed by Backer in chapter 11. The focus is on three key questions. The first considers the adjustments Cuba might have to undertake if it is to engage global trade and financial institutions. The second addresses the likelihood that these reforms are possible within Cuba's current legal and economic system, given limits on political reform and external pressure to address human rights issues. The third further examines possibilities for Cuban-U.S. relations following the 1996 presidential election and developments in other regions of the world, including Europe. Backer's analysis of the limitations of the Cuban Communist Party's stated direction (as expressed in the publication of the party's Economic and Social Guidelines, or *Lineamientos*, in 2011) contrasts with the opportunities presented by the European alternative, as expressed in the EU's Political Dialogue and Cooperation Agreement (PDCA) published in 2016 (see chapter 11, this volume).

Chapter 12, considers the environmental challenges that Cuba faces in light of global climate change and domestic scarcities. Verchick and Sokol consider Cuba's goals for addressing climate change, as represented in domestic and international law and policy. The chapter also explores the role of the United States in the global climate debate, as well as how this impacts Cuban efforts to combat climate change. By addressing the opportunities and challenges that the Cuban government faces as global temperatures rise, the chapter provides valuable insight into a pressing issue for an island nation that is vulnerable to these changes.

By every measure, each of the political, economic, and legal challenges that face the U.S.-Cuban relationship has an array of potential solutions that could be explored. Yet the complex and interwoven nature of the political, economic, and legal issues facing Cuba and the United States means that solutions will likely need to address multiple issues simultaneously. Of course, as with any vexing policy problem, the pursuit of potential solutions requires that the main actors have the political will to pursue them. Whether this will is generated at the elite or mass level may impact the speed and comprehensiveness of any proffered solutions. Additionally, the authors of the included chapters have suggested a myriad of detailed options to both states. These policy prescriptions provide an opportunity to address issues that make the normalization of relations seem out of reach. Yet challenges remain.

The final chapter of this volume presents the editors with an opportunity to highlight the key opportunities and challenges that continue to face Cuba and the United States. While the potential for both states to gain from a rational and sustained rapprochement are significant, so are the challenges. By differentiating these challenges and opportunities along three interconnected dimensions—political, economic, and legal—a larger picture comes into focus. The final chapter identifies where progress is more likely between the two states and where it is less achievable. While a full normalization of diplomatic relations between the two states is probably not in the cards in the near future, there are signs that changes underfoot—in Cuba and in the United States—have the potential to have long-term implications for the two states. Here, we return to the two-level game that appears to be taking shape in both states. For instance, Obama-era changes to travel restrictions, the establishment of a tourist sector, and the presence of a growing class of *cuentapropistas*, has put a growing number of U.S. and Cuban citizens in contact with each other. This person-to-person diplomacy that is taking place may prove to be important in building the foundation for rapprochement in the future. Yet, at the state level there is surprisingly little movement on either side. Certainly, the presence of serious structural impediments to normalization have played a significant role in freezing the relations between these two states in a Cold War–era policy. Yet, movement just under that layer of ice is evident. Whether that movement yields a significant thawing remains to be seen.

PART I
THE POLITICAL DIMENSION

2
Opening Cuba—Negotiating History

Peter Kornbluh and William M. LeoGrande[*,1]

On a rainy day in December 2014, President Barack Obama gathered a small group of senior officials in the Oval Office and placed a telephone call to Raúl Castro. Sitting on a couch to Obama's left were National Security Council aides Benjamin Rhodes and Ricardo Zuniga, personal emissaries whose eighteen months of secret negotiations were about to culminate in the first substantive conversation between the presidents of the United States and Cuba in more than half a century.

Obama later told reporters that he'd apologized to Castro for talking for such a long time. "Don't worry about it, Mr. President," Castro responded. "You're still a young man and have still the time to break Fidel's record—he once spoke seven hours straight." After Castro finished his own lengthy opening statement, Obama joked, "Obviously, it runs in the family," (White House 2014b).

Despite the levity, both leaders understood the seriousness of their forty-five-minute conversation. "There was," one White House official recalled, "a sense of history in that room."

At noon the next day, the two presidents stunned the world when they simultaneously announced the dramatic breakthrough (The White House 2014); (Castro 2014). Obama repudiated fifty-five years of U.S. efforts to roll back the Cuban revolution, declaring that peaceful coexistence made more sense than perpetual antagonism. Both leaders described a prisoner exchange that had occurred earlier that morning. For "humanitarian reasons," Cuba had released Alan Gross, incarcerated since December 2009 for setting up illicit satellite communications networks as part of a U.S. Agency

* Peter Kornbluh, National Security Archive, peter.kornbluh@gmail.com; William M. LeoGrande, American University, wleogra@american.edu.

The Cuba-U.S. Bilateral Relationship. Michael J. Kelly, Erika Moreno, and Richard C. Witmer, II.

for International Development (USAID) "democracy promotion" program (Farley 2014).

Cuba also released Rolando Sarraff Trujillo, a CIA spy whom Obama called "one of the most important intelligence agents that the United States has ever had in Cuba," (Mazzetti, Schmidt, and Robles 2014). In return, Obama commuted the sentences of the last three members of the "Cuban Five" spy ring—Gerardo Hernández, Antonio Guerrero, and Ramón Labañino—imprisoned for sixteen years after they were caught infiltrating anti-Castro Cuban American groups and providing information that (the United States claimed) allowed Cuba to shoot down two planes flown into its airspace by an exile group, killing four Cuban Americans (Miroff 2015). (The other two members of the Cuban Five had been released earlier, having completed their sentences.)

But the prisoner exchange was only the beginning. Obama promised to loosen restrictions on travel and trade, and authorize telecommunications companies to bring internet services to the island. For its part, Cuba pledged to release fifty-three political prisoners and engage with the International Red Cross and United Nations on human rights and prison conditions. Most importantly, the two presidents agreed to re-establish diplomatic relations. On July 20, 2015, Cuba's foreign minister, Bruno Rodríguez, traveled to Washington to raise the Cuban flag over the former embassy on 16th Street; on August 14, Secretary of State John Kerry traveled to Havana to reopen the U.S. embassy in the sleek, modernist structure built for that purpose in 1953.

What brought about this radical change was a unique alignment of political stars: a shift in public opinion, particularly among Cuban Americans; a transition in Cuban leadership from Fidel to Raúl, followed by Cuba's slow but steady evolution toward a market socialist economy; and Latin American leaders no longer willing to accept Cuba's exclusion from regional affairs. Seizing the opportunity were a handful of dedicated U.S. legislators, well-financed lobbyists, Alan Gross's aggressive legal team, an activist pope from Latin America, and a woman hell-bent on getting pregnant.

But one factor trumped the rest: Obama's determination. He was, one top aide recalls, "a president who really wanted to do it."

All the President's Men

Obama's push to break "the shackles of the past" began shortly after his re-election, when, according to one aide, he "told us we needed to design a play to run with Cuba." By April 2013, Obama had chosen Rhodes and Zuniga to lead the negotiations. Rhodes had joined Obama's 2008 campaign as a speechwriter and was personally close to the president. "All it takes is one Google search for these guys to know that Ben speaks to the president, and has daily access, and can be a trusted back channel," explained a former White House official (Crowley 2015). Zuniga, meanwhile, had served in the U.S. Interests Section in Havana (the embassy stand-in) and as the State Department's acting coordinator for Cuban affairs (Associated Press 2014).

Over the next eighteen months, the two men met nine times with a small team of Cuban officials in various locales, from Ottawa to Rome. From the start, it was clear that before any discussion of normalizing relations could occur, both countries wanted their imprisoned citizens released.

It was a touchy subject, but one that had already been broached following the devastating 2010 earthquake in Haiti, which led to unprecedented U.S.-Cuban cooperation on disaster relief. Over the next two years, two top State Department officials—Hillary Clinton's chief of staff, Cheryl Mills, and Deputy Assistant Secretary for Western Hemisphere Affairs Julissa Reynoso—secretly negotiated with Cuban officials in Creole restaurants in Port-au-Prince, subterranean bars on Manhattan's East Side, and a hotel lounge in Santo Domingo. U.S. officials focused on freeing Gross, while the Cubans requested that the wives of Cuban spies Hernández and René González be allowed to visit their husbands in jail. (These women's visas had previously been denied because they too were suspected of being covert agents.) The Cuban position "started with 'Treat our guys better,'" says a U.S. official with knowledge of the talks, and evolved into "We want them all home." By September 2011, the Cubans had explicitly proposed swapping the Cuban Five for Alan Gross.

But U.S. officials believed that such a direct exchange would be politically toxic. Instead, they hoped their growing rapport would convince the Cubans to free Gross. As a show of good faith, they arranged for the wives of Hernández and González to secretly visit them. In exchange, the Cubans permitted Judy Gross regular visits with her husband, held in a military hospital in Havana.

"We thought this would lead to the release of Alan Gross," one U.S. official recalls. But the Cubans continued to hold out for the swap, even as the parole dates for two of their five spies neared. Eventually U.S. negotiators realized their strategy was doomed. In May 2012, Clinton received a memo from her team that stated: "We have to continue negotiating with the Cubans on the release of Alan Gross but cannot allow his situation to block an advance of bilateral relations . . . The Cubans are not going to budge. We either deal with the Cuban Five or cordon those two issues off."

The memo hit at an opportune time. Clinton and Obama had just returned from the Sixth Summit of the Americas, where they'd been chastised by heads of states furious over the U.S. stance on Cuba. "It was clearly an irritant and a drag on our policy in the region," said Roberta S. Jacobson, assistant secretary of state for Western Hemisphere affairs (Romero and Neuman 2014).

Clinton had previously pushed the White House to liberalize regulations on educational travel to Cuba, finally going directly to the president to bypass White House aides worried about political fallout. In the wake of the summit debacle, she instructed her deputy to assemble what one adviser called "the full monty" of potential actions to change Cuba policy. "I recommended to President Obama that he take another look at our embargo," Clinton recalls in her memoir. "It wasn't achieving its goals and it was holding back our broader agenda across Latin America," (Gearan 2014).

Following his re-election, Obama approached Massachusetts Senator John Kerry about replacing Clinton as secretary of state—and immediately raised the prospect of a new approach to Cuba. Kerry was receptive. As chairman of the Senate Foreign Relations Committee, he'd been a vocal critic of the USAID democracy promotion programs that financed Gross' secret missions to Cuba. Kerry had also long opposed the U.S. economic embargo, and played a key role in normalizing relations with Vietnam—a triumph he hoped to repeat with Cuba.

Still, when a new round of secret talks began in June 2013, Kerry was not privy to them (Strobel, Spetalnick, and Adams 2016). Only a handful of U.S. officials knew, among them Vice President Joe Biden, White House chief of staff Denis McDonough, and National Security Adviser Susan Rice. No one at the Pentagon was "read in." Although Kerry was eventually brought into the loop, "we kept it fairly tight on our side, and the Cubans, I think, did the same on their side," a senior U.S. official said. "We didn't want any wrench to be thrown in the gears that could complicate attempts to secure Alan Gross' release," (Morello and DeYoung 2014).

The effort at secrecy was aided by Canada, which allowed the two sides to meet in Ottawa and later Toronto. The Cubans' top priority was still getting their spies back—particularly Gerardo Hernández, who, as the leader of the Cuban Five and the broader crew of spies known as the "Wasp Network," was serving two life sentences. Zuniga and Rhodes came to the table with a more fluid approach. "We had no fixed vision of what an agreement would be," recalls a White House official knowledgeable about the talks. Instead, they wanted to "try out different formulas" to explore what could be agreed on. "We never went in thinking there would be a grand bargain."

But politically the White House was in a tricky spot. If all that came out of the talks was a prisoner exchange and a few travel and trade tweaks, Obama's initiative would not register as a serious policy change. Lifting the embargo was in Congress's hands, but restoring diplomatic ties was the one dramatic action Obama could take unilaterally (Schroeder 2014).

During the first negotiating sessions, the U.S. team had to listen to the Cubans recite the long history of U.S. depredations against the island, starting with the Spanish-American War in 1898. To old hands, it was the requisite throat-clearing to be endured before getting down to real business. But Rhodes had no prior dealings with Cuba and at one point interrupted the diatribe. "Look, I wasn't even born when this policy was put in place," he told the Cubans. "We want to hear and talk about the future," (Strobel, Spetalnick, and Adams 2016).

Historical disagreements were only the beginning. The U.S. team wasn't willing to talk about the USAID programs or Guantánamo; the Cubans weren't willing to discuss human rights or U.S. fugitives hiding in their country. "There were a lot of dry wells for us and for them," according to a White House official. Both sides were eager to talk about the prisoners, but a straight-up trade—Gross for the three remaining members of the Cuban Five—was still a nonstarter for the White House. The president had said repeatedly that Gross had done nothing wrong, was not a spy, and therefore could not be exchanged for spies. In the administration's public portrayal of Gross, he was just a development specialist attempting to bring internet access to Cuba's small Jewish community. To the Cubans, Gross was a covert operative engaged in a program to subvert their government, and the Cuban Five were patriots protecting their country against the far-right zealots of Little Havana.

To break the deadlock, the U.S. negotiators raised the case of Rolando Sarraff Trujillo, who'd been a top CIA mole inside Cuban intelligence until his arrest in the mid-1990s. Sarraff had provided the United States with information that led to the prosecution of many Cuban spies, including Ana Montes, the Defense Intelligence Agency's top Cuba specialist; State Department employee Walter Kendall Myers and his wife, Gwendolyn; and the Wasp Network—including the Cuban Five (Stein 2014).

During negotiations in Toronto in January 2014, the Americans suggested that if the ailing Gross were released on humanitarian grounds, they would swap the three Cuban spies for Sarraff. But the Cubans did not want to give up Sarraff—a double agent they considered so treacherous they'd held him in solitary for eighteen years.

Negotiations got even pricklier in May 2014, when the Obama administration announced it was swapping five Taliban leaders held at Guantánamo for Sergeant Bowe Bergdahl, a U.S. soldier captured and imprisoned by the Taliban since 2009 (Landler 2014). The political uproar in Congress and the media was intense, especially after Bergdahl was reported to have deserted his post. From the U.S. perspective, this made a similar trade with Cuba completely out of the question. The Cubans, however, figured that since Washington had traded five Taliban combatants for one U.S. soldier, the White House would eventually agree to trade their three spies for Alan Gross.

It took months of negotiations for U.S. diplomats to convince the Cubans that the only exchange the White House could abide would be trading spies for spies, namely the Cuban agents for Sarraff. Finally the Cubans relented, and talks turned to what one U.S. official describes as "a bigger package"—including the restoration of full diplomatic relations.

A Ticking Time Bomb

In defending the Bergdahl deal, Obama officials cited intelligence indicating his mental and physical health were deteriorating after five years of captivity. They faced a similarly dire situation with Alan Gross. More than four years after being arrested, Gross was despondent over the administration's inability to obtain his freedom. At one point he lost more than one hundred pounds. By December 2013, when the coauthor of this article, Peter Kornbluh (2014), visited him in the military hospital where he was held, he seemed determined to get out on his own—dead or alive. “I'm a ticking time bomb. Tick. Tick. Tick,” Gross warned during the three-hour visit, in which he alluded to a plan to break down the “flimsy” door of his cell and challenge the heavily armed guards on the other side. A few months later, in April 2014, Gross went on a nine-day hunger strike (Liptak 2014). On his sixty-fifth birthday on May 2, he announced it would be the last he would spend in a Cuban jail.

When Gross' terminally ill, ninety-two-year-old mother, Evelyn, took a severe turn for the worse in late May, negotiations became urgent (Landler 2014). Meeting in Ottawa in early June, the Cubans pushed for a quick prisoner trade, expressing their fear that Gross would kill himself when his mother passed away. U.S. officials, meanwhile, worried that if Gross died in a Cuban prison, a change in U.S. policy would become politically impossible.

Kerry reached out to Cuban Foreign Minister Bruno Rodríguez and proposed a “furlough” to the United States—Gross would wear an electronic bracelet to allow the Cubans to monitor his movements, and he would return to prison after his mother's death. “Alan promised unequivocally that he would return to incarceration in Cuba after visiting his mother at the hospital in Texas,” his lawyer Scott Gilbert recalls, “and I offered to take his place until he returned. That is how important this was.”

But the Cubans considered the plan too risky. After Evelyn Gross died on June 18, 2014, Kerry warned Rodríguez that if any harm came to Gross while in Cuba's custody, the opportunity for better relations would be lost (Landler and Gordon 2014).

Gross was in “a difficult state of mind,” Gilbert recalls. As the summer progressed, he refused to meet with officials from the U.S. Interests Section who routinely brought him care packages, and he told his wife and daughter that unless he was released soon, he'd never see them again. His lifeline was Gilbert, who pressed the Cubans to allow him to speak to Gross every day, and who traveled to Cuba twenty times to sustain his client's morale.

Stork Diplomacy

Gross was also taking regular calls from Tim Rieser, a top aide to Senator Patrick Leahy (D-Vt.). Rieser was instrumental in securing better conditions for Gross in return for one of the more unusual confidence-building measures in the annals of diplomacy—a long-distance effort to impregnate the wife of Gerardo Hernández, the jailed Cuban spymaster (Londoño 2014).

This idea was first conceived in early 2011, when the head of Cuba's Interests Section in Washington met with the State Department's Julissa Reynoso to deliver a diplomatic note stating that Cuba did not see "any solution" to the incarceration of Hernández and that his wife, Adriana Pérez, was nearing the age of forty. Cuba sought U.S. support to "facilitate" her ability to get pregnant.

After what she calls a "sensitive" meeting on the matter, Reynoso explored the possibility of a secret conjugal visit between Pérez and her husband, but efforts to arrange such a rendezvous "fizzled out" due to Bureau of Prisons regulations. Two years later, in February 2013, Pérez met with Leahy, who was visiting Cuba with his wife, Marcelle. In a Havana hotel room, Pérez made an impassioned appeal to the Leahy's to help her find a way to have a child with her husband, who had been in jail for fifteen years. "It was an emotional meeting," Leahy remembers (Londoño 2014). "She made a personal appeal to Marcelle. She was afraid that she would never have the chance to have a child. As parents and grandparents, we both wanted to try to help her. It was a human thing. It had nothing to do with the politics of the two countries," (Orsi 2014). But it would.

Leahy asked Rieser to find a solution. A conjugal visit was a nonstarter, but there was precedent for allowing an inmate to provide sperm for artificial insemination. Eventually, Rieser secured approval, and the Cubans flew Pérez to a fertility clinic in Panama.

Meanwhile, Rieser was pressing the Cubans to improve the conditions for Gross: "I wanted to make clear to them that we cared about the treatment of their people, just as we expected them to care about the treatment of ours." The Cubans reciprocated, permitting Gross to be examined by his own doctors, giving him a computer and printer, and allowing him more outdoor exercise.

As Pérez's pregnancy became obvious, the State Department asked the Cubans to keep her out of the public eye, lest her condition stir speculation that a U.S.-Cuban rapprochement was in the works. "We had given our word to keep the pregnancy and all of the process around it a secret in order not to prejudice the greater objective, which was our freedom," Hernández later explained (Granma 2015). When he landed in Cuba, state television showed him being greeted by Raúl Castro and, to the astonishment of his countrymen, a nine-months-pregnant wife (Oppmann and Perez 2015). Three weeks later, on January 6, 2015, their baby girl, Gema Hernández Pérez, was born (Redaccion Digital 2015).

"Just Do It!"

Although Leahy's "stork diplomacy" contributed to the success of the Cuba-U.S. negotiations, even he was unaware of the secret talks underway. Meanwhile, he served as the unofficial leader of a group of senators and representatives who pressed Obama and his aides for change at every opportunity. "All of us had been pushing the president when we saw him at ceremonial functions for a few seconds—telling him, 'You've got to do something on Cuba,'" recalls Representative Jim McGovern (D-Mass.).

Leahy decided that to get the attention of the president, a former legal scholar, he'd have to flesh out the legal basis to release the Cuban spies. The senator's staff collaborated with former White House counsel Greg Craig to draft a ten-page memo of options "to secure Mr. Gross' release, and in so doing break the logjam and change the course of U.S. policy towards Cuba, which would be widely acclaimed as a major legacy achievement." The document, dated February 7, laid out a course of action that would prove to be a close match with the final accord. "It was a damn good memo," Craig says.

Still, it took until May 1 before Leahy, along with Senators Carl Levin (D-Mich.) and Dick Durbin (D-Ill.) and Representatives Chris Van Hollen (D-Md.) and McGovern, finally met in the Oval Office with Obama, Biden, and Susan Rice. They urged Obama to press for Gross's release and replace the policy of hostility with one of engagement. "You said you were going to do this," McGovern reminded the president. "Let's just do it!" (Crowley 2014).

"We're working on it," Obama told them, but he gave no hint of the back-channel diplomacy then well underway.

"There was a bit of tension with the president. We're pushing him, and he's pushing back," McGovern recalls. "We were pretty aggressive." At the meeting's end, the members were not very optimistic. "We were not reassured that this was going to happen."

A New Normal

Three days earlier, a series of billboards appeared in the Washington Metro stations nearest to the White House and State Department. "Mr. President, it's time to take action on Cuba policy," read one. Another declared, "The American people are our best ambassadors. It's time to allow all persons to travel freely to Cuba." The ads, which generated significant media buzz, were sponsored by a new advocacy group, #CubaNow, which positioned itself as the voice of the younger, more moderate Cuban American community in Miami.

#CubaNow was the brainchild of the Trimpa Group, an unusual organization that matched deep-pocketed donors seeking to change policy with a political strategy and advocacy campaign. In 2003, for example, founder Ted Trimpa developed a lobbying strategy to mount a marriage-equality movement across the country financed by multimillionaire businessman Tim Gill.

Nine years later, in October 2012, Gill traveled to Cuba on a U.S.-licensed tour with a wealthy friend, Patty Ebrahimi, who was born and raised in Cuba but left with her family a year after Fidel Castro seized power. Ebrahimi chafed under the restrictions of the tour imposed by U.S. Treasury regulations. She couldn't go off on her own to visit the neighborhoods of her youth, track down family friends, or see her old schools. "The idea that I could go anywhere else in the world, including Vietnam, North Korea, or Iran, without special permission from the US government but couldn't go to Cuba without a license angered me," she recalled. As she vented her frustrations to Gill in the lounge of the Saratoga Hotel in Havana, he offered a suggestion: "You should use your money to change the policy." A few months later, he introduced Ebrahimi to Trimpa.

After conducting a three-month survey of the political landscape, the Trimpa Group reported that "the highest level of decision makers within the Obama administration" wanted change—they just needed political reinforcement to push for it. After consulting with her husband, Fred, the former CEO and owner of Quark Software Inc., Patty gave the lobby shop $1 million to finance a campaign to embolden the White House.

"My decision to take up this work was an emotional one," she later said. "We did it because we wanted to help," Fred Ebrahimi noted. "We did it because we thought we could be effective."

The Trimpa Group pulled out all the stops. It counseled Ebrahimi to make donations to key political figures such as Senate Majority Leader Harry Reid (D-Nev.) and Durbin—donations intended to gain access and "be in the room," according to Trimpa's strategic plan. The lobby shop hired Luis Miranda, who had recently left his position as Obama's director of Hispanic media, and sought the blessing of Jim Messina, Obama's deputy chief of staff, to launch a public campaign promoting a change in Cuba policy. The Trimpa team also met with key foreign policy officials. To all the players, the Trimpa Group insisted that there would be no political blowback for Democrats in Florida if Obama changed Cuba policy. To bolster that argument, they financed a series of opinion polls. One, conducted by an Obama pollster, John Anzalone, found that Cuban Americans in Florida—especially the younger generation—favored engagement. And the Atlantic Council conducted a national poll sponsored by Trimpa that found, as a *New York Times* headline (Gladstone 2014) would put it, that a "Majority of Americans Favor Ties With Cuba."

The polls were intended to "show broad support for change," "create a new normal," and "give voice to the silent majority," says James Williams, the political operative who oversaw the Trimpa Group's efforts.

Williams also had the support of groups key to the Cuba debate, ranging from funding powerhouses (like Atlantic Philanthropies, the Ford Foundation, and the Christopher Reynolds Foundation) to policy shops (the Washington Office on Latin America, the Center for Democracy in the Americas, and the Latin America Working Group) to elite think tanks (Brookings and the Council of the Americas).

On May 19, 2014, this coalition released an open letter to Obama signed by forty-six luminaries of the policy and business world, urging the president to engage with Cuba (Support Cuban Civil Society 2014). The signatories included former diplomats and retired military officers—among them former UN Ambassador Thomas Pickering—and Cuban American business leaders like Andres Fanjul, co-owner of a Florida-based multinational sugar company. But the name that attracted the most attention was John Negroponte, George W. Bush's director of national intelligence.

The same day, not coincidentally, the conservative U.S. Chamber of Commerce announced that its president, Tom Donohue, would lead a delegation to Cuba to "develop a better understanding of the country's current economic environment and the state of its private sector," (U.S. Chamber of Commerce 2014).

Soon after that, the *New York Times* launched a two-month editorial series slugged "Cuba: A New Start." (New York Times Editorial Team 2014). The weekly editorials were the work of Ernesto Londoño, who talked to administration officials, Leahy's office, and the Trimpa Group. "There was really no collusion or formal cooperation in what they were doing and what we were doing," he told Terry Gross on Fresh Air (Gross 2015). The *Times* simply saw an opportunity to push the policy it advocated forward. "We figured it was worthwhile to give it a shot."

All these forces, in other words, were marshaled to push Obama through a door whose threshold he had already crossed.

Divine Intervention

And let's not forget the pope. Even as the secret negotiations continued, members of Congress kept looking for allies to press Obama on Cuba, and provide him cover from attacks from the right. In a September 2013 meeting at Rice's office, Durbin floated a new idea: What about getting the new pope involved? As the first pontiff from Latin America, Francis knew Cuba well. After Pope John Paul II's 1998 visit to the island, Francis—then the assistant archbishop of Buenos Aires—had written a short book (Associated Press 2014) about the trip, *Dialogues Between John Paul II and Fidel Castro*. And the Vatican had credibility with Havana because of its consistent opposition to the embargo.

All parties saw the wisdom of divine intervention. Leahy sent a confidential message to Cuban Cardinal Jaime Ortega, asking him to encourage the pope to help resolve the prisoner issue. Drawing on the close ties between Obama's chief of staff, Denis McDonough, and Cardinal Theodore McCarrick of Washington, the White House also "got word to the Vatican that the president was eager to discuss this" at an upcoming meeting in March with the pope in Rome, according to Craig. And at a strategy meeting of the Cuba advocacy groups, Tim Phillips of the peace group Beyond Conflict (Beyond Conflict 2018) suggested approaching Cardinal Seán O'Malley of Boston. "We knew that O'Malley was very close to the pope," recalled Craig, who had ties to the Catholic Church hierarchy in Boston from his days as a foreign policy aide to Senator Ted Kennedy. "O'Malley had spent time in Latin America, spoke Spanish fluently, had known the pope before he became pope, and had a relationship with the pope that was unusual, certainly much, much better than McCarrick's."

In early March 2014, a small group of Cuba policy advocates, including representatives of the Trimpa Group, Phillips, and Craig, met with Cardinal O'Malley in the rectory of the Cathedral of the Holy Cross in Boston. "We explained the recent trends, the conversations with POTUS and others in the administration and Congress," Phillips recalls, "and indicated this was a historic moment, and a message from the pope to POTUS would be significant in moving the process forward." Craig brought a letter from Leahy urging the cardinal to focus the pope's attention on the "humanitarian issue" of the prisoner exchange. Leahy personally delivered a similar message to Cardinal McCarrick, and arranged for yet another to be sent to Cardinal Ortega in Havana. There now were three cardinals urging the pope—as yet unaware of the secret dialogue between Washington and Havana—to put Cuba on the agenda with Obama.

Three weeks later, Obama met the pope in his private library, a marble-floored chamber overlooking St. Peter's Square (Vallely 2014). There, they spoke for an hour under a frieze of Renaissance frescoes. Obama "told the pope that we had something going with Cuba and said it would be useful if he could play a role," according to a White House official familiar with the meeting. A few days later, Francis summoned Ortega to enlist his help.

Over the summer, the pope wrote forceful, confidential letters to Obama and Raúl Castro, imploring the two leaders "to resolve humanitarian questions of common interest, including the situation of certain prisoners, in order to initiate a new phase in relations," (Vatican 2014). To safeguard his communications, the pope sent both letters via papal courier to Havana—with instructions to Cardinal Ortega to personally deliver the message into the presidents' hands. Ortega then sent his top aide to Washington to advance his clandestine diplomatic mission. But arranging a secret face-to-face meeting with the president of the United States was easier said than done. Alerted to the problem, Cardinal McCarrick conferred with White House officials, who enlisted his help as a secret back-channel go-between. In early August, McCarrick traveled to Cuba carrying a note from Obama that asked Ortega to entrust McCarrick with delivering the pope's letter to the White House. But Ortega's papal instructions were to deliver the message himself. McCarrick left Cuba empty-handed.

Back in Washington, McCarrick worked with McDonough to arrange a secret meeting for Ortega with the president. On the morning of August 17,

Ortega gave a talk at Georgetown University—providing a cover story for his presence in Washington—and then quietly went to the White House. (To make sure the meeting did not leak, U.S. officials kept Ortega's name off the White House visitor logs.) Meeting with the president on the patio adjacent to the Rose Garden, Ortega finally completed his mission of delivering the pope's sensitive communication, in which he offered to "help in any way."

It was a convoluted process, but an unprecedented gesture. "We haven't received communications like this from the pope that I'm aware of other than this instance," a senior U.S. official (The White House 2014b) recalls. "And that gave, I think, greater impetus and momentum for us to move forward."

Open to Change?

By late October, the pope had invited the negotiators to Rome (Landler and Gordon 2014). "It was less a matter of breaking some substantive logjam but more the confidence of having an external party we could rely on," says a senior U.S. official (Richter and Kington 2014).

It was at the Vatican that the two sides hammered out their final agreement on the prisoner exchange and restoring diplomatic relations. Rhodes and Zuniga also noted Obama's intention to ease regulations on travel and trade, and to allow U.S. telecom companies to help Cuban state enterprises expand internet access. They acknowledged these initiatives were aimed at fostering greater openness in Cuba, though they delivered this message respectfully. Cuban officials said that while they had no intention of changing their political system to suit the United States, they had reviewed the Americans' list of prisoners jailed for political activities and would release fifty-three of them as a goodwill gesture," (Strobel, Spetalnick, and Adams 2016; Spetalnik, Adams, and Wroughton 2015). The pope agreed to act as guarantor of the final accord (Landler and Gordon 2014).

Obama's National Security Council met on November 6 to sign off on the details. Later that month, the negotiating teams convened one last time in Canada to arrange the logistics of the prisoner exchange.

On December 12, Zuniga called Alan Gross's wife, Judy, to the Executive Office Building to tell her the good news. Four days later, on the eve of Hanukkah, Scott Gilbert called his client to tell him he'd soon be a free man. "I'll believe it when I see it," Gross replied (Hirschfeld Davis 2014).

He didn't have to wait long: Early the next morning Gross was taken from his prison cell in Havana to a small military airport, where he was met by his wife, his attorney, and members of Congress who had worked to win his release. The prisoner exchange was choreographed so carefully that the blue-and-white presidential plane sent to bring Gross home was not cleared to depart Havana until the plane carrying the three Cuban spies touched down on a nearby runway.

Once in the air, Gross was given some of his favorite foods—popcorn and corned beef on rye—and took a call from Obama. After clearing Cuban airspace, he called his daughters to tell them simply, "I'm free," (Oppmann 2014).

At noon, Obama and Castro simultaneously announced the deal. "We will end an outdated approach that, for decades, has failed to advance our interests," Obama said. "Neither the American nor Cuban people are well served by a rigid policy that is rooted in events that took place before most of us were born," (White House 2014). Raúl Castro was more restrained, focusing on the return of the three Cuban "heroes." Normalization of diplomatic relations received just a single sentence, followed immediately by a reminder that the embargo—"the heart of the matter"—remained in place (Castro 2014).

Obama called on Congress to rescind the embargo—a policy, as he said, "long past its expiration date." But with Republican majorities in both houses and a presidential election in the offing, getting Congress to end the sanctions looks to be a lot harder than reaching an agreement with Havana. Senator Marco Rubio (R-Fla.), who led the Republican tirades against the deal, said the president gave the Cuban government "everything it asked for" and got nothing in return. "I am committed to unravel as many of these changes as possible," he added (Kiefer 2014).

While Rubio and the rest of the old-guard anti-Cuba lobby fumed, the process of normalization was moving forward. Obama officially removed Cuba from the State Department's list of state sponsors of terrorism (Schwartz 2015), and U.S. and Cuban flags were lofted over the re-established embassies in Havana and Washington.

At the Seventh Summit of the Americas in April, Obama and Castro met privately in person for the first time and reaffirmed their commitment to normalize relations. Although Castro prefaced his speech before the assembly with a fifty-minute litany of U.S. transgressions against Cuba at the end, his tone changed to conciliation and even warmth (BBC News 2015).

"I have told President Obama that I get very emotional talking about the revolution. I apologize to him because President Obama had no responsibility for this," Castro said, noting that nine other U.S. presidents could have reached out to Cuba and didn't. "In my opinion, President Obama is an honest man. I have read his autobiographies and I admire him and his life and think his behavior comes from his humble background. There, I said it."

Obama chose not to revisit old bitterness (The White House 2015): "America never makes a claim about being perfect. We do make a claim about being open to change. The United States will not be imprisoned by the past. We're looking to the future."

Obama's opening to Cuba culminated in his two-day trip to the island in March 2016 (New York Times 2016). He met with Raúl Castro, with Cuban private entrepreneurs, and with Cuban dissidents. Obama and Castro attended a baseball game between the Tampa Bay Rays and Cuba's national team, and Obama even made an appearance on Cuba's most popular TV sitcom.

The high point of the presidential visit was Obama's (2016) speech to the Cuban people, broadcast live from the newly renovated Grand Theater. "I have come here to bury the last remnant of the Cold War in the Americas," he said early in his address. Obama's central theme was how much Cuba and the United States have in common, their sharp differences notwithstanding: "The United States and Cuba are like two brothers who've been estranged for many years, even as we share the same blood." He spoke eloquently of the pain suffered by Cuban Americans forced into exile, but also of how their enduring love of country could help to build a bridge across the Florida Strait. "It is time, now, for us to leave the past behind," he said in conclusion. "It is time for us to look forward to the future together—a future of hope."

Note

1. Adapted from P. Kornbluh and W. LeoGrande, "Inside the Crazy Back-Channel Negotiations That Revolutionized Our Relationship with Cuba," *Mother Jones*, Aug. 12, 2015 (used with permission and subject to further editing), available at http://www.motherjones.com/print/280571.

3

Succession versus Transition

Michael J. Kelly, Erika Moreno, and Richard C. Witmer, II[*]

Cuba has undoubtedly had a long and, often, troubled relationship with its neighbor to the north, the United States. The Spanish-American War that freed Cuba from colonial rule was replaced with decades of direct and indirect intervention by its northern neighbor. Domestically, the island was plagued by countless interruptions in governance and the absence of democratic governing institutions and norms. By the 1950s large swaths of the Cuban public were ready to receive a strong, nationalist leader who could bring the island into modernity.

When Fidel Castro marched triumphantly into Havana on New Year's Day in 1959, he was met with substantial public support. Over fifty years later, Castro's imprint on the island remains strong. Between the slogans found throughout the island, on public walls and private spaces, and the ever-present banner of the Castro regime, it is clear that Fidel Castro's ragtag group of revolutionaries have profoundly changed the island. However, it is far less clear what the revolution's long-term legacy will be as the island veers toward a new reality: a succession from the Castro era to a new, as yet undefined, era. As Cuba undertook its governmental succession in 2018, most scholars and policy experts wondered whether the change in leadership would auger dramatic changes in policy. Further still, will the change in leadership result in changes to the regime? The answers to these questions depend, in part, on the evolving nature of domestic politics on the island, as well as its neighbor to the north. The long, and often contentious, relationship between Cuba and the United States will, no doubt, continue to play a role in understanding the range of possibilities open to the island.

[*] Michael J. Kelly, Creighton University, Ahmanson College of Law, michaelkelly@creighton.edu; Erika Moreno, Creighton University, erikamoreno@creighton.edu; Richard C. Witmer, II, Creighton University, witmer@creighton.edu.

The Cuba-U.S. Bilateral Relationship. Michael J. Kelly, Erika Moreno, and Richard C. Witmer, II.

Development of the Cuban Regime

The broader political goal of ridding the island of a corrupt and undemocratic ruler, Fulgencio Batista, was accomplished when the dictator fled the island. However, the initial governing triumvirate was, as is often the case in postrevolutionary regimes, less adept at identifying clear policy goals in the wake of the collapse of the Batista regime. It did not take long for Fidel Castro, a charismatic and effective interlocutor, to overshadow other members of the triumvirate and, in the process, begin to identify specific policies for the regime.

The first years of the revolutionary regime could easily be characterized by their lack of institution building, save for the creation of the Committees for the Defense of the Revolution (CDRs) and other organs of self-defense. Self-preservation was paramount during the immediate postrevolutionary period, as the possibility of U.S. interference was a legitimate concern, hence the emphasis on self-defense. Domestic policy goals included an ambitious agrarian reform, an emphasis on literacy, and the desire to build a new type of citizenry. These initial policy moves were strongly endorsed by the regime's lead idealist, Ernesto "Che" Guevara. However, efforts to build a "New Cuban Man" during the 1960s, which sought to simultaneously provide moral incentives for volunteerism and radically transform agriculture, stymied when the island failed to meet a self-imposed goal of harvesting ten million tons of sugar. The failure of the ten million ton goal and the capture and death of "Che" Guevara in the Bolivian highlands both steered the regime to a period of protracted pragmatism (Skidmore and Smith 2001). With the guidance of the Soviet Union and under the watchful eye of Fidel Castro, Cuba began a period of institution building during the 1970s. The regime introduced new programs to oversee agricultural production (e.g., JUCEPLAN), formed the Communist Party, and strengthened diplomatic and economic ties with the Soviet Union and its satellite states. The flurry of institution building represented a shift away from charismatic models of governance towards the creation of new sources of power and decision-making. Regular Communist Party meetings replaced the idealistic tone that characterized the immediate postrevolutionary period. Pragmatic economic policies allowed for the introduction of small-scale market mechanisms, including farmers markets.

Efforts to institutionalize the revolution were short-lived, however, and Castro returned to a more charismatic ruling style during the 1980s. The swing away from institution building was exemplified by the move toward "Rectification" in 1986. Fearing that the island nation had succumbed to a form of "ideological AIDS," Castro and the ruling elite ended promarket programs and sought to de-institutionalize many of the programs that sprung from the previous decade of innovation. The period of "Rectification" saw the rebirth of programs that supported or relied on volunteerism, in a manner reminiscent of the efforts to build a "New Cuban Man" in the 1960s. The regime sought to counteract the political and economic openings taking place in the Soviet Union during the latter half of the 1980s (Corrales 2004; Cruz and Seleny 2004; Eckstein 1980). The period of "Rectification" and its emphasis on the revolutionary creed also served to undermine potential political rivals and competitors by elevating Fidel Castro's reputation as revolutionary figure and father to a new nation (Azicri 2001). The move away from pragmatism and toward charisma and ideological fervor fed the mythology that surrounds Fidel Castro. His image is larger than life. Castro is both a living symbol of the revolutionary struggle and the savior foretold by island lore.

"Rectification," of course, gave way to the panoply of measures taken under the "Special Period," which marked the island's most severe economic and societal crisis to date following the fall of the U.S.S.R. (Perez Stable 1999). The crisis was brought on by the Soviet Union's collapse in the early 1990s and represented a severe contraction of the Cuban economy. The loss of trading partners, loans, and cheap energy reverberated across various sectors of the Cuban economy. Nutritional deficiencies, such as those that caused in excess of 40,000 cases of optic neuritis (and blindness) and the scarcity of energy and medicine were all blamed on the economic contraction (Eckstein 1986). Today, most experts have concluded that the severe economic contractions that occurred in the 1990s have been reversed as the Cuban economy rebounded.

Throughout this time, the Revolutionary Armed Forces (FAR) gained a strong foothold in Cuban society, politics, and economics. The FAR represent some of the strongest features of the regime. The military was lauded for its role in several African campaigns in the 1970s and was seen as a loyal and patriotic institution. As a reward, and under the tutelage of Raúl Castro, the FAR has increasingly taken on an important role in overseeing major sectors of the economy, including the airlines and other basic industries (Azicri 2001). Currently, the armed forces play the role of corporate player in the modern Cuban state. This position was strengthened in the years since Fidel Castro stepped down and allowed his younger brother, Raúl, to lead the island.

By the 1990s, it became increasingly clear that the island would have to find innovative ways to maintain itself, especially after having lost the support of a world power and its bloc of supporters. This meant innovation in economic affairs, and the use of some market mechanisms, as well as the cultivation of a supporting cast of potential successors. At the top of the list of successors to Fidel was, of course, his brother Raúl Castro. But, in addition to Raúl Castro there has been a small but nonetheless important group of high-profile policymakers who have played an important role in identifying and generating successors that would continue the regime. For instance, Miguel Díaz-Canel, former vice president to Raúl Castro, filled the leadership void in early 2018 when Raúl stepped down. Díaz-Canel is flanked by several key figures, including Ricardo Alarcón, former head of the National Assembly and former ambassador to the United Nations, Esteban Lazo Hernández, current president of the National Assembly, and Ana María Mari Machado, vice president of the National Assembly. Surrounding these prominent political figures are a handful of assistants and aides who will also play a pivotal role in directing Cuba in the near term. These individuals, added to the top figures of the FAR are likely to remain important in the short, medium, and long term as the island continues its political evolution.

Transition versus Succession in Cuba

Today, many elements of the U.S.-Cuban relationship remain frozen in a Cold War–era time warp. Even as the Barack Obama administration attempted to thaw the relationship by making several gestures toward the regime, the current status of the relationship still seems mired in a decades-old set of grievances. Chief among those grievances is concern regarding the nature of the Cuban regime. Not only does the nature of the Cuban regime matter for the possibility to extending discussions and a rapprochement, it is critical for reversing decades of Cold War–era policies between the two countries.

A discussion of the potential short-, medium-, or long-term political changes on the island is likely to affect the nature of the U.S.-Cuban relationship. In this regard, it is important to recognize that a range of possible future political scenarios are likely, ranging from succession (or continuation of the current regime) to a full-scale political transition to democracy. While a range of outcomes is possible, it is important to remember that not all outcomes are equally likely.

Inherent in recent legislative efforts to address the Cuban regime is the promotion of regime transition, rather than a succession to the Castro regime. The distinction between these two concepts is articulated in the Cuban Democracy Act of 1992. As well as the most recent iteration of the Commission for Assistance to a Free Cuba report issued by the U.S. State Department in June of 2006. In the following, we identify the key distinctions between these two concepts as presented throughout several examples of policy toward the island.

Transition: A government defined by the presence of regularly scheduled, free, and fair elections. Government actions promote and respect internationally accepted definitions of human rights and other democratic rights and norms.

Succession: A change in leadership within a preexisting regime. This signals a continuation of the regime while providing a means of renovating it through the installation of a new leader or leaders.

While transition suggests an interruption of the regime and the establishment of a new regime type, succession represents a change in leadership but maintenance of the regime. Although democratic governance and norms are often invoked in the broader concept of a transitional government, democracy is one of many possible outcomes. The notion that regime change would result, necessarily, in a democratic regime is often the justification for pursuing a regime change on the island. However, democracy can be defined in many different ways. Narrow definitions of democracy may simply signal the presence of elections (often referred to as electoral democracies). In contrast, fuller definitions may include the presence of governing institutions (often referred to as a procedural minimal definition of democracy) and the preeminence of civilian rule and democratic norms (often referred to as "liberal" democracies) (see Dahl 1971; Diamond 2000). While it is not entirely clear which of these definitions is sought for in the short or long term, it is evident that transition in the sense that it has been used by U.S. policymakers toward Cuba implies some form of democracy that goes beyond a simple electoral democracy; that is, it is more than the mere presence of elections. Determining the democracy quotient sought by U.S. policy is not entirely clear given the current body of legislation and policy toward Cuba. Current policy toward the island also fails to clearly state whether democracy ought to be fully consolidated before it is deemed a true transition. We will return to these themes as we discuss the range of possible short-, medium-, and long-term scenarios.

The differences between transition and succession are crucial, in large part because they reflect clear concerns among those in the U.S. policy community regarding the long-term direction of the island. However, it is important to keep in mind that just as they are conceptually distinct, so are the probabilities of seeing these scenarios in the short, medium, and long terms. In other words, the likelihood of witnessing a full-scale transition to democratic governance will vary quite dramatically from a succession. Further, these distinctions have important implications for the kinds of policies that are possible vis-à-vis the island and its relationship with its northern neighbor.

The Ties that Bind: The Libertad Act, CAFC, and the U.S.-Cuban Relationship

The distinctions between transition and succession are important for two key reasons. First, the focus on a transitional government in Cuba created a set of seemingly inextricable ties that have kept the two states at loggerheads diplomatically. The focus on forcing a change of regime in Cuba was made tangible in a series of legislative efforts undertaken by the U.S. Congress, which include the Cuba Democracy Act of 1992, the Libertad Act of 1996 (also know as the Helms-Burton Act), and the work of the Commission for Assistance to a Free Cuba Act. Second, legislative efforts bolster the normative concerns about the Cuban regime while simultaneously tying the hands of elected officials in the United States. After all, any resolution of outstanding property claims lodged against the Cuban government on behalf of U.S. citizens and Cuban expatriates is contingent on Cuba's acceptance of democratic norms and the presence of a transitional government. Legislative efforts like the Cuba Democracy Act of 1992 and the Libertad Act of 1996, in their efforts to force the island to change, have effectively limited the scope of options available to elected officials to engage in open and constructive talks, even on issues that could be beneficial to U.S. citizens and firms.

The Cuba Democracy Act of 1992 represents a major policy statement toward Cuba, and it has had profound impacts on bilateral relations ever since it was passed into law. Much like the Libertad Act, this piece of legislation was pursued and passed in an effort to prevent any rapprochement with the island without the presence of a transitional government in Cuba. The act effectively states that U.S. policy and any efforts to establish bilateral relationships between the two states are prohibited until a dramatic regime change has occurred on the island; it has had a profound chilling effect on bilateral relations. Efforts, for instance, to address fundamental legal issues surrounding property rights claims, are not possible under the current state of the Cuba Democracy Act.

The language of the Libertad Act stipulates that the United States will not negotiate with a successor government; rather bilateral negotiations can only take place after the Cuban government has seen a democratic transition. The Libertad Act also issues an indictment of the Cuban regime's human rights record along with its lack of democratic (or participatory and competitive) governing structures (see Libertad Act, section 1702.) The act states that U.S. policy toward Cuba seeks a full-scale democratic transition before the two can engage in highly anticipated discussions of issues, including trade relations and property rights resolution. Section 1703 of the Libertad Act delineates U.S. policy goals in the following manner:

- To seek a peaceful transition to democracy and a resumption of economic growth in Cuba through the careful application of sanctions directed at the Castro government and support for the Cuban people;
- To seek the cooperation of other democratic countries in this policy;
- To make clear to other countries that, in determining its relations with them, the United States will take into account their willingness to cooperate in such a policy;
- To seek the speedy termination of any remaining military or technical assistance, subsidies, or other forms of assistance to the Government of Cuba from any of the independent states of the former Soviet Union.
- To continue to vigorously oppose the human rights violations of the Castro regime;
- To maintain sanctions on the Castro regime so long as it continues to refuse to move toward democratization and greater respect for human rights;

- To be prepared to reduce the sanctions in carefully calibrated ways in response to positive developments in Cuba;
- To encourage free and fair elections to determine Cuba's political future.
- To request the speedy termination of any remaining military or technical assistance, subsidies, or other forms of assistance to the Government of Cuba from the government of any other country and
- To initiate immediately the development of a comprehensive United States policy toward Cuba in the post-Castro era.

The Libertad Act develops a series of mechanisms to promote such goals, both by punishing the current regime through the use of sanctions as well as punishing other states that do not serve to further U.S. policy toward the island. For instance, Section 1704 asserts that states deemed to be "assisting" Cuba are subject to U.S. sanctions. It goes on to define assistance as:

> [A]ssistance to or for the benefit of the Government of Cuba that is provided by grant, concessional sale, guaranty, or insurance, or by any other means on terms more favorable than that generally available in the applicable market, whether in the form of a loan, lease, credit or otherwise, and such term includes subsidies for exports to Cuba and favorable tariff treatment of articles that are the growth, product, or manufacture of Cuba; includes and exchange, reduction, or forgiveness of Cuban debt owed to a foreign country in return for a grant of an equity, interest in a property, investment, or operation of the Government of Cuba . . . or of a Cuban national.

The Commission for Assistance to a Free Cuba (CAFC), which was created in 2003 under President George W. Bush, sought to examine the potential for improved bilateral relations between the United States and Cuba. The commission issued two reports, one in 2004 and another in 2006. Both reports continue to identify a clear preference for transition over succession on the island. The 2006 CAFC report stipulates the importance of establishing a transitional government before any major changes—economic, political, or otherwise—are possible between the United States and Cuba. The CAFC report includes a section dedicated to property rights, which notes: "Perhaps no issue will be fraught with more difficulty and complexity for the Cuban Transitional Government than the status of property rights and confiscated property." (CAFC 2006, 68). Even with the rather significant incentives to resolve this issue, seeing as so many of the certified claims seeking restitution are or were large U.S. corporations, like Exxon, Texaco, and Coca-Cola, CAFC saw democratization as an essential prerequisite to beginning discussions on property rights. In fact, the 2006 CAFC report notes that "a democratically elected government, representing the will of the Cuban people, should make decisions regarding confiscated property." (CAFC 2006, 68).

While the conditions placed on U.S.-Cuban relations have their obvious merits, these legislative efforts both reduced any chances of a true restoration of bilateral relations between the two states, in part by angering their Cuban counterparts, and sharply limited the options available to policymakers in Washington, D.C. After all, it should not be surprising that reactions to these legislative efforts and the CAFC report in Havana were swift and sharply critical of the United States' efforts to violate the island's sovereignty (U.S. Department of State 2004).

Second, even if U.S. lawmakers were unconcerned with the potential for diplomatic backlash, insisting on a transitional government as a prerequisite to improved bilateral relations presents its own problems. For one, such a focus on a political change has meant that other issues, including economic ones, have gone unresolved for so long that many of the key actors have since undergone generational change. The property rights issue is particularly instructive here. In 1959, when Cuba underwent its revolutionary change and adopted a significant agrarian reform law that targeted multinational and foreign corporations for expropriation by the new Cuban regime, many of the key claimants included the United Fruit Company (UFC) and the F.W. Woolworth Co. Today, many of these large corporations have been morphed into multinationals under the banner of other parent companies or have disappeared altogether. For instance, the UFC is no longer an actor on the world stage since it was refashioned into the Dole Corporation. However, the Woolworth Co. has since disappeared as a corporate entity. The delay in a resolution of property rights claims has certainly not favored a number of corporations (and individuals) with large claims against the Cuban state.

On another level, the presence of legislation like the Libertad Act and the Cuban Democracy Act have served to bind policymakers in the United States who might otherwise see opportunities to put an end to Cold War–era grievances against Cuba. Because both laws require a complete transition to democracy before talks can begin, bilateral relations are contingent on dramatic political transformations that may be decades or generations away. After all the island would need to see the end of the current regime and a rapid replacement of the governing institutions (including the FAR), the presence of free and fair elections, and a generalized respect for human rights. The likelihood of a completed transition is hardly a sure bet in the short or medium term. While there are a host of potential political outcomes in the short, medium, and long term, it is far from assured that a completed democratic transition is in the offing. U.S. policymakers in the 1990s and early 2000s inextricably bound today's U.S.-Cuba policy to the Cold War era. Absent a radical change in Cuba or in U.S. legislative precedents, bilateral relations will remain forever trapped in that era.

Political Transition Scenarios

To inform our understanding of political transitions, we turn to a rich and varied literature on democratization in the field of political science. Here, an emphasis on several seminal works serves to highlight the manner in which succession and transition scenarios may unfold in Cuba. More importantly, we will use that body of literature to inform our understanding of the implications of a change in regime on U.S.-Cuban relations.

Since democracy can be defined narrowly or broadly, it is important to begin by first defining democratic government. As noted earlier, the most narrow definition posits the regular observance of elections as sufficient to qualify a state as democratic. An "electoral democracy" is, in many ways, far from the ideal that most associate with a fully democratic society, as it does not require the presence of institutions to support decision-making, nor does it speak to the value of contestation or citizen participation. Not only is this definition intuitively unappealing, it also tends to misrepresent the number and quality of democratic societies across the world. A fuller definition, often used in the literature on democratization comes from the work of Robert Dahl (1971). The proposed "procedural minimal" definition of democracy includes seven key criteria that are necessary to deem a polity democratic. These criteria include:

- Control over government decision about policy is constitutionally vested in elected officials.

- Elected officials are chosen in frequent and fairly conducted elections in which coercion is comparatively uncommon.
- Practically all adults have the right to run for elective office in the government.
- Practically all adults have the right to vote in the election of officials.
- Citizens have a right to express themselves without the danger of severe punishment on political matters broadly defined.
- Citizens have a right to seek out alternative sources of information. Moreover, alternative sources of information exist and are protected by law.
- Citizens also have the right to form relatively independent associations or organization, including independent political parties and interest groups.

Inherent in Dahl's definition is a concern for free and fair elections, a general respect for basic democratic rights, and the creation of a set of procedures to support democratic governance. While this definition is far more appealing than a simple electoral democracy, it does not attempt to represent fuller expressions of democratic societies. This is most evident when the "procedural minimal" definition is contrasted with the concept of a liberal democracy (see Diamond 2000). Liberal democracies are loosely characterized as polities where:

- Freedom of belief, expression, organization, and other civil rights, including protection from political terror and unjustified imprisonment.
- A rule of law under which all citizens are treated equally.
- Neutrality of judiciary and other governmental institutions.
- Open, pluralistic civil society.
- Civilian control of the military.

Thus, in contrast to Dahl's (1971) definition, which focuses on the development of procedures to support democratic governance, a liberal democracy attempts to address issues of fairness and pluralism within society as well as the importance of the rule of law and civilian supremacy. While there are many variants of this particular definition of liberal democracy, then tend to share several key aspects. Even more inclusive definitions exist that reach beyond the limits of liberal democracies by suggesting that democracies must require free and fair elections, proper government procedures, and just government policy outcomes (or "substantive" democracy). Definitions of substantive democracies suggest that citizens must have equal access to public schooling and healthcare regardless of their social class or ethnicity. This conceptualization of democracy would effectively disqualify many "procedural" democracies, like India, from the club of democratic states.

The differences that arise in categorizing states are a direct reflection of the many ways in which democracies are conceptualized in the literature. This is evident as different operationalizations of democracy are used to quantify the number of democracies across the world. Today, as scholars and policymakers actively debate the extent of democratic backsliding across the world, it is even more important that we begin any discussion of democratization with a clear understanding of the terms' meaning. Cuba remains well outside most commonly accepted definitions of democratic governance, even the most minimal definitions. Yet, democratic transition has served as the cornerstone of U.S. policy toward the island. While most of the legislation that currently shapes the U.S.-Cuban relationship dictates that democratic transition is paramount to re-establishment of relations, none of the legislation clearly articulates a set of principles or guideposts to determine if the island has met that requirement. U.S. legislative efforts emphasize free and fair elections, respect for individual human rights, and an end to the Castro family's stranglehold on the country's political institutions. These elements are consistent with many operationalizations of democracy, including the procedural minimal definitions noted earlier but not the more inclusive substantive definitions. The more far-reaching elements of substantive democratic societies are less likely to be achieved in the short run, given the longevity of authoritarian institutions on the island.

Therefore, in keeping with this general approach, and with the intent of facilitating a discussion of possible and probable political scenarios in modern Cuba, Dahl's procedural minimal definition of democracy will serve as a guide to this discussion. Since the question of whether a complete normalization of relations between the United States and Cuba still hinges on the probability that the island undergoes a democratic transition, we will address that likelihood over the near, medium, and long term. Here, the collapse of Cuba's nondemocratic system is a necessary though not sufficient prerequisite for the introduction of democracy. If elites are willing and capable of supplying a nondemocratic alternative and the masses reject democratic governance, then the island nation will continue along its current trajectory. Given some of the internal factors on the island, as well as some of the external pressures it faces from close allies, there is a good chance that this scenario will play itself out. After all, the tradition of authoritarian rule hinders the development of democratic institutions. What is more, many of the factors that usually give rise to democratic rule, including the presence of a "modern" economic structures, propitious cultural traits (Huntington 1968; Lipset 1980; Moore 1966; Almond and Verba 1966), and pressures from an active middle class (Moore 1968) are missing. Further, as Johnson and Lin note in chapter 4 (this volume) China is currently Cuba's closest and most powerful ally, and it does not have a preference for democratic governance. Nonetheless, there are a variety of potential political outcomes and structures that go beyond a continuation of the status quo. The following section develops this theme further.

The Post-Castro Era: Succession versus Transition

The adoption of democracy necessitates concerted action on the part of the elites, the masses, or both. Some have suggested that certain preconditions must be met for democracy to take root, including the presence of modern economic and social structures, a strong middle class, or a democratic political culture. Before any democratic transition is possible, the existing regime must exit the political scene. Thus, a transition is possible when a failed attempt at succession has occurred.

There are myriad models that could be used to explain the failure of a succession and the possibility of a (democratic) transition.[1] While they all have some merit, one of the most enduring and relevant models in the literature is Terry L. Karl's typology of democratic transition (Karl 1990). The value of this model is that it explicitly addresses the relative strength of the masses and members of the elite within an authoritarian setting. This model is particularly useful as it was initially employed to explain a range of transition in the Americas during the third wave of democratization in the 1980s. It is particularly useful in examining potential scenarios in Cuba because it keeps cultural and temporal characteristics relatively constant.

Table 3.1, below, presents a simplified version of Karl's typology of transitions. Central to Karl's argument is that the relative strength of the masses of the elites and the mode of transition help dictate the kind of transition that is likely to occur. Further, Karl suggests that these two

Table 3.1 Karl's Typology of Democratic Transition in Latin America

Relative Actor Strength	Mode of Transition	
	Compromise	Force
Elite Ascendant	Pact	Imposition
Mass Ascendant	Reform	Revolution

Source: adapted from Karl, Terry L. 1990. "Dilemmas of Democratization in Latin America." Comparative Politics. 23:1–21.

dimensions are useful in predicting the long-term success of that transition and its likelihood of consolidation. All of these features are important as societies must be able to make a clear choice *in favor of democracy*, not just against a specific authoritarian regime. So the adoption of democratic rules and norms must be constantly reaffirmed if democracy is to survive and be consolidated.

Where elites play the most critical role in dictating the terms of the transition to democracy two outcomes are likely: pacted or imposed transitions. Pacted transition, like those that characterized the transition in Colombia (1957), Costa Rica (1949), and Venezuela (1958), generally involved complex and consensual arrangements among previously warring members of the elite classes. Pacted transitions, on the other hand, tended to produce relatively long-lived and stable regimes, even when they effectively reduced the number of players involved in writing the rules of the democracy. Although unresolved tensions surrounding the transition process eventually contributed to social or political challenges that eventually undermined or resulted in a collapse of the party systems involved (e.g., Colombia and Venezuela), they produced far more stable democratic societies in the long run. In part, the success of pacted transitions rested on their ability to provide a large enough "buy-in" for the most powerful elements of society, often including economic and political elites and the military.

Impositions, on the other hand, suggest that the process of transition involved some level of force during the transition process. In other words, the process of writing the rules of the new democracy may have fallen disproportionately on a smaller segment of elites, such as the military. The net results were democratic regimes that included elaborate mechanisms to favor those ushered into power during the transition. This often included provisions to protect institutions, like the military, or individuals from prosecution, as well as guaranteed representation for the outgoing regime in the nascent democracy. Some have included the Chilean (1989) and Brazilian (1985) transitions as examples of imposed transitions. In both cases, the outgoing military regime was able to dictate the terms of its departure as well as the basic features of the new democracy in ways that served to protect its interests. In both cases, efforts to prosecute the authoritarian regime for human rights abuses or other excesses were undermined by constitutional and organic laws aimed at protecting the military. While impositions did not carry the same level of elite consensus that pacted transitions did, they have been somewhat successful insofar as they have provided authoritarian regimes with a viable exit strategy and incentives to allow for a democratic transition. Some might even suggest that impositions, which were far more common during the third wave, may provide the most stable and enduring forms of democratic transition in the region (Karl 1990). After all, many of these regimes were eventually able to remove many, if not all, of the protections afforded to members of the authoritarian regime. This was certainly the case for Chile, which ultimately, and famously, tried Augusto Pinochet, head of the military regime between 1973 and1989, for crimes against humanity.

Where the masses play the most critical role in sparking and guiding the transition to democracy two outcomes are likely: reform or revolution. When the masses serve as the spark but are able to forge compromise with other segments of society, including the elites, reformist transitions are most likely (e.g., Chile 1970–1973; Guatemala (1946–1954)). While this form of transition is less common than some of the elite-led processes, they have a number of benefits, including the involvement of a broader cross-section of society in the process. While this is certainly a benefit in the short and medium term, Karl notes that reformist transitions tend to include a number of features that may prove destabilizing in the long run.

Finally, revolution results where the masses trigger a transition through the use of force. These transitions are rare and volatile (see Bolivia 1950; Mexico 1917). A revolutionary scenario is the least stable of the four options for a number of reasons. Revolutions agitate the elite classes and provide very little probability of long-term compromise among sectors of society (which is often deemed essential to the building of democratic cultures). Implicit in the discussion of regime transitions is the understanding that while the masses are important in demanding change, in many respects elite acceptance of the democratic ideal is essential. In other words, elite consent for this form of political change is absolutely necessary and, in some instances, sufficient for the long-term success of democracy. This assumption is certainly not the only means by which political scientists envision the process of democratization but is a prevailing view.

In the following section, Karl's typology of transitions provides a focus for discussing the probability of a transition versus succession in Cuba. A range of potential political and economic changes that may occur in the short, medium, and long term are elaborated to provide a representative sample of the universe of possible and probable political outcomes for Cuba. While the scenarios addressed in the following section are suggestive of a range of outcomes, they are not exhaustive. Nonetheless, they are critical to understanding how the U.S.-Cuba relationship could evolve over time, given the currents constraints placed on it.

Succession versus Transition: Short-, Medium-, and Long-Term Political Scenarios

Cuba has already seen changes at the very top, starting in 2006, with the ascension of Raúl Castro to the presidency. While the line of succession from Fidel to Raúl Castro was not surprising, the timing of the succession was. Given the levels of secrecy that surrounded Fidel Castro's health, the announcement in July of 2006 took policymakers and scholars by surprise. Although the succession was initially intended as temporary, two years later, Fidel Castro made it clear that the succession was permanent. Just over a decade later, in 2016, a frail Fidel Castro implored his comrades to continue working to fulfill the promise of the communist revolution that started in 1959. Shortly after Fidel's final public appearance, the island mourned his death in April of 2016, just a month after a historic visit by U.S. President Barack Obama.

Raúl Castro ushered in a few economic changes that permitted a rapid rise in private enterprise on the island. Rules that eased the way for Cubans to set up their own businesses, often taking advantage of the influx of tourists, created a very different economic environment in Cuba, as is evident in the flourishing of entrepreneurial spirit (see, for instance, Henken's chapter 6 in this volume). There were several analogues to these entrepreneurial measures in the agricultural sector, where the state recognized small market sales and provided incentives for entrepreneurship (see González-Corso and Nova-González's chapter 5 in this volume).

In the broader scheme of events, economic policy changes undertaken since 2006 seem quite mild, especially when compared to political developments that have unfolded in the last few years. Here, a few key events take center stage: Castro's announcement of his retirement and the appointment of Miguel Díaz-Canel to the post of vice president in 2013. These two events occurred simultaneously and constituted the biggest changes that the island has seen in decades. What is more, they both provided a clear indication that the island's elite was shaping the environment to allow for some change, or alternation in power, while largely maintaining the status quo.

The announcement, in 2013, that Raúl Castro intended to step down from the presidency to allow for a succession in 2018 was important for several reasons. Castro indicated in his public statements that the intent was to allow for change at the very top of the leadership structure. The announcement was paired with the appointment of Miguel Díaz-Canel Bermúdez as vice president, which served to indicate a clear line of succession. While most observers were struck by the announcement of Raúl Castro's imminent departure and the appointment of a young successor, there are two important features to the announcement. First, it indicated a desire to renew the regime through the selection of a young, but entrenched, partisan. So, the announcement suggested a clear and orderly continuation of the regime. No major structural changes were included in the announcement even though the face of the regime was guaranteed to change. Second, and most importantly, the announcement set a precedent for presidential term limits. Raúl Castro made clear that he planned to step down after his second five-year term as president, noting that two terms should be the limit for Cuba's top executive. The presence of a term limit, even if it is only informally enforced, suggests that Raúl Castro sees value in the alternation of executive leadership. In essence, this has the potential, if employed after his departure, to weaken the executive relative to other institutionalized players in the political system, including members of Cuba's influential military (FAR). It also has the potential to continue to renew the political system on a regular basis, thereby providing it with an influx of new ideas without challenging the nature of the regime. Therefore, even with a new leader in place, Cuba may see minimal change in the regime and its policies since the president is in a potentially weaker position than members of the politburo and the military. So, unless the next Cuban executive can build a solid base of support outside of the island's current political/ military elite, there is little chance that the governments' policies will reflect anything other than the interests of the status quo. In many respects, this move signaled a direction modeled after postrevolutionary Mexico with the institutionalization of single party governance.

The ascension of Miguel Díaz-Canel Bermúdez to the vice presidency in 2013 and, eventually, as president in 2018 provided a clear signal of Raúl Castro's interest in creating a new line of succession. It also suggested that Castro has a vision for the post-Castro era. Even though we know relatively little about Díaz-Canel's policy interests, there are several important elements of his background that provide some insight into the kind of leader he might become. Díaz-Canel's relative youth indicates a desire to ensure that the regime survives by transmitting its norms and values to a new generation of leaders. There is no doubt that putting a young face on a regime birthed during the mid-twentieth century is a difficult task, but appointing a young but experienced successor is a clear effort to do just that. Díaz-Canel is an entrenched and loyal member of the Cuban Community Party, and worked his way up through the ranks of the party over a thirty-year span. So he is unlikely to upset the apple cart.

It is also important to note that Díaz-Canel does not hail from a military background. This feature alone is noteworthy given the preponderance of former war heroes and military personnel in the highest echelons of power in Havana. Díaz-Canel worked his way up the party structure, taking on posts at the provincial level and acting as the Minister of Higher Education most recently. He has kept out of the spotlight but those familiar with the vice president note a populist touch that propelled his anticorruption campaigns and his interest in modernizing the island (Trotta 2016). What is more, Díaz-Canel's relative youth suggests that he would be likely to help modernize state-run media and improve access to the internet for years to come (Trotta 2016).

Díaz-Canel's ascension to the presidency in the spring of 2018 marks him as the nation's first civilian leader in modern history. Given his tendency to avoid the spotlight, it is unclear what his policy priorities are. However, it is reasonable to assume that in the short and medium term, he is unlikely to upset the apple cart. If he remains loyal to the norm of a two-term presidency, he would have even more incentives to first consult members of the state that could exercise authority over him, including members of the political and military elite, before making any major reformist steps. Raúl Castro may well continue to observe his successor's performance up close from his position in the Cuban parliament, if his election to that body is any indication (CBS New Miami 2018). This development merely highlights the fact that even as the presidency is expected to change, the old guard elite expects to retain its presence in the key organs of the Cuban government, whether it is the FAR, the Politburo, or the Communist Party. As such, the old guard will maintain veto power over any policy changes sought by the president since it serves as the selectorate[2] for the executive.

The last decade was marked by continuity in spite of Fidel Castro's absence. There are several indications that the regime intends to keep a firm grip on its institutions of power. Díaz-Canel may result in an effective rebranding of the 1959 revolution, but he will be carefully watched by the old guard. Given Díaz-Canel's cautiousness in approaching Cuba's centers of power, there is little reason to expect a radical change from the status quo. Therefore, in the short term, it seems reasonable to suggest that the Cuban government will see the emergence of several new faces, but, aside from efforts to increase access to technology and modernize the state, there is little reason to expect dramatic political change.

In the medium and long term, however, there are several possibilities that may present themselves. Ranging from most to least likely, they include:

- Power transfer to successive political elites, with minimal change in the nation's power centers (FAR, Communist Party, Politburo). Successions are orderly with minimal fractionalization among political elites.
- Power transfer to successive political elites, with marginal change in the nation's power centers (FAR, Communist Party, Politburo), owing to generational displacement and recruitment. Successions are relatively orderly, but increasing levels of fractionalization among elites generate small fissures in the government. Potential for restrictions on the political sphere increase.
- Power transfers to successive political elites are accompanied by changes to the rules of recruitment and selection. Generational displacement and recruitment allow for orderly successions. Increasing levels of fractionalization among elites generate new wings of the Communist Party but are addressed through the regime's ability to coopt newly formed interests.

- Power transfers to successive political elites are accompanied by high levels of fractionalization. Generational displacement and recruitment create new actors with unmet demands that facilitate conflict within the regime. Unsuccessful efforts at cooptation are met with growing, vocal opposition to the slow pace of reforms. A change in the direction of the elite is possible while maintaining the same structures in place.
- Power transfers to successive political elites are accompanied by high levels of fractionalization. Generational displacement and recruitment create new actors with unmet demands that facilitate conflict within the regime. Unsuccessful efforts at cooptation are met with growing, vocal opposition to the slow pace of reforms. Potential for a radical change in the elite class increases even though the regime does not change radically.

Each of the possible scenarios maintains an authoritarian regime in place, while exhibiting varying levels of conflict among the ruling elite. Indeed, in any regime setting, a fractured selectorate can spell doom for the regime; this is especially true in authoritarian settings, where the selectorate is usually small. If the regime is unable to deliver targeted benefits to its selectorate, the likelihood of conflict and stress increases exponentially. Ultimately, the continuation of an authoritarian regime in the medium and long term rests on its ability to keep the elite happy. If the state promises too much in the way of economic reforms and cannot maintain the elite happy, it would likely trigger divisions and conflict within the regime. The manner in which that conflict is addressed by the president and other key elites (including the FAR) will determine whether the regime will adequately quell that conflict. If open conflict is met with force, the probability of a radical change in the ruling elite is high. If, however, conflict is met with some form of compromise or successful co-optation, very little would change.

In each the previously mentioned scenarios, Cuba will be sensitive to guidance from its closest political and economic allies. If a rapprochement with the United States does not occur, then it is quite possible that China will continue to exert influence on the island's political elites. As Johnson and Lin suggest (chapter 4, this volume), the China model provides the Cuban elite with a blueprint that allows the state to modernize and seek out new economic partners while maintaining a tight grip on power. The Cuban elite view their partnership with the Chinese as potentially important both politically and economically. Such a partnership provides Cuba with a chance to sidestep calls from the United States to democratize and present their public with a Caribbean analogue to the China model. As a result, political elites would find external support for continued authoritarian structures for as long as possible, seeing as the two states currently comprise the entire universe of Communist regimes in the world.

Although the likelihood of a democratic transition is a low probability, it is more likely as a long-term possibility. The possibility of democratic change is dependent on two related factors: the collapse of the existing regime and the acceptance of democratic forms of governance. There are several historical examples of regime collapses, ranging from dramatic (e.g., U.S.S.R in the early 1990s) to the bloodless (e.g., Bulgaria 1989). A collapse of the Cuban regime would require a wholesale challenge to the regime's legitimacy, likely stemming from a lack of leadership (e.g., a succession crisis) or lack of results (e.g., economic or social failures). Ultimately, the factors that precipitate a collapse of the regime could come from either a challenge from below or a challenge from the elite class. In spite of years of U.S. pressure to trigger an end to the regime, the most likely causes for a regime collapse will come from within Cuba. Thus, it is most likely that severe unmet challenges may produce a chain reaction that causes a collapse. The most important players in such a scenario are likely to come from the elite classes, as they are better mobilized than the masses (Mesa Lago and Perez-Lopez 2005). While the masses play a role in provoking or exacerbating a crisis of legitimacy on the island, they are not as likely to play a central role in dismantling the regime, mainly because of the historic weakness of independent civil society institutions. There are many well-organized groups both on and off the island, including the Association of the Defenders of Political Rights, the Cuban Commission for Human Rights and National Reconciliation, the Harmony Movement, and *Cambio Cubano*, just to name a few (Rivera 1994). There are also several high-profile critics of the regime, like Yoaní Sánchez, who could serve as the locus for mass mobilization. However, it is unclear that those varied actors can translate their organizational or communication skills to undermine the regime.

Following a regime collapse, masses or elites must make a concerted effort to choose democracy. The reasons for selecting democracy over other forms of government may rest on perceptions held by the key actors. The preference for democratic governance is also aided by the external pressure or implicit acceptance of its norms. In this regard, if the United States seeks not to re-engage Cuba on this issue, the elite class may find democracy less compelling. Likewise, if the world continues to see continued rollback in the number of democracies (see Freedom House 2017) or its perceived acceptance around the globe, then it is less likely that this form of governance is chosen.

The chances of a sustained democratic transition are most likely to come from above. As noted earlier, some of the most successful cases of transition in the region have come as a result of elite actions, either through pacted or imposed transitions. If Cuba experiences a transition, it is likely to be guided by an elite ascendant process due to the historic weakness of civil society organizations (Mesa Lago and Perez-Lopez 2005). Since little is known about the true preferences of Cuba's elite, it is hard to know if any desire for democratization exists. However, in order from most to least probable, a few scenarios are possible.

Elite Ascendant scenarios:

- Continuation of current pro-market policies spark calls for political reforms. A select number of elites craft rules for a forced, gradual transition. (Imposition)
- Continuation of current pro-market policies are accompanied by a tightening of political restrictions. Frustration with the status quo spark a desire for political reform. Strategic elites identify coalition partners to organize a gradual transition. (Pact)

In both scenarios, the elites are in charge of the direction of the transition. An imposition arises when the elites use force to direct the transition. In contrast, a pacted transition suggests some degree of compromise with other key elites. The last option also suggests a desire for an orderly exit from the existing regime.

Naturally, of course, the Cuban government could also face pressure from within. Several possible scenarios, listed from most to least probable include:

Mass Ascendant scenarios:

- Continuation of current policies, including pro-market reforms. Masses coalesce with strategic elites to begin a transition. (Reform)
- Continuation of current policies, including pro-market reforms, accompanied by a tightening of political restrictions. Masses initially

rebel but eventually coalesce with strategic elites to begin a transition. (Reform)

- Continuation of current policies, including pro-market reforms accompanied by a dramatic tightening of political restrictions. Masses fail to convince strategic elites to coalesce with them and use force to spark a transition. (Revolution)

Internal pressure from the masses could produce uncertainty in the ruling class, especially if they are unable to co-opt those segments of the population. Here, the challenge to the regime would come from outside of the regimes' selectorate and is most likely to produce a violent response from the elite, especially initially. Each scenario assumes that civil society can organize an opposition to the regime and maintain itself even in the face of retaliation from the regime. The most likely products of mass ascendant scenarios are reformist outcomes. Revolution is the least likely of all the possible transition scenarios and is less likely to be successful in producing a long-lived democratic alternative to the current Cuban regime.

Failed attempts at democratic transition are far more likely to turn on the relative strength of the regime. This means that the authoritarian regime has not collapsed nor is it in the process of collapsing. On the contrary, it suggests that efforts to move the country toward democracy were premature. It also suggests that the regime in power continues to maintain legitimacy and a monopoly on the use of force. So, crises—like the "Special Period" in the early 1990s—did not trigger a collapse because the regime maintained its legitimacy in the face of a severe economic contraction (Hawkins 2001; Nelson 1984). If history serves as prologue, there are many reasons to expect that failed transitions are more likely than successful transitions to democracy unless the state faces a truly dramatic decline in legitimacy or its ability to deliver basic services to its people.

Conclusions

While the political scenarios discussed here are hardly exhaustive, they illustrate the kinds of forces that could work for the continuation of authoritarian rule or the transition to democracy. The United States still continues to favor democratization and current legislation has limited rapprochement with the island until it has experienced regime change. However, the current political and social climate in the United States makes it unlikely that the island will experience a dramatic external push for democratization from its northern neighbor. Meanwhile, Cuba's growing relationship with China ensures that the forces of the political status quo will remain intact. External political pressure on Cuba's political elite are most likely to support a continuation of single (Communist) party rule into the foreseeable future.

Internally, the relative strength and preferences of Cuba's masses are impossible to truly know, but there is little reason to suspect that the masses plan to unseat the regime in the near or medium term. Likewise, moves by the political elite in the last five years of Raúl Castro's term as president suggest that the regime is finding ways to renew itself while ensuring the current elite's control of the levers of power. This is a perfect recipe for the continuation of the status quo into the short and medium term.

Naturally, of course, Cuba's trajectory into the foreseeable future puts it at odds with U.S. policy directives, evident in the Libertad Act and Helms-Burton. The United States has its hands tied formally by these legislative efforts. So what does this mean for the likelihood of a full restoration of relations between these two states? It means that the two states are likely to remain at stalemate. Unless the U.S. Congress finds a way to alter existing legislation that guides our relationship with Cuba, or the Cuban government transitions to democracy in the near future, all efforts at normalizing relations will remain frozen. While this may seem like a far cry from the optimism expressed under Barack Obama's presidency, even then a full normalization was not in the offing. While a stalled relationship seems less than ideal, policymakers and scholars alike can draw some solace from knowing that the two states have not regressed much further from where they were just a few years ago. In spite of some harsh rhetoric, the Republican-led administration in Washington, D.C., has not carried out any sweeping changes to U.S.-Cuban policy. This offers a glimmer of hope that relations could be normalized in the future.

Notes

1. It is important to note here that a democratic transition is one of several options. Transition to a new form of authoritarian government is also possible.
2. A "selectorate" is the group or groups involved in the selection of key leadership in any regime. The selectorate is also essential in maintaining the leadership in power.

4

The China Factor and U.S.-Cuban Relations

*Gregg B. Johnson and Zhimin Lin**

Introduction

China fundamentally supports the complete normalization of U.S.-Cuban relations. In fact, when President Barack Obama announced his intention to restore Cuban-American diplomatic relations, the spokesperson for China's Ministry of Foreign Affairs called it a "positive development," while also calling for the U.S. embargo to be lifted ". . . as soon as possible and comprehensively . . ." in accordance with the desires of the international community (Hua 2015). Similarly, *The China Daily* (2015) called the U.S. embargo a "failure" and stated, "Obama made a wise move by restoring U.S.-Cuban diplomatic ties." Likewise, China's former ambassador to Cuba praised Cuban leaders for their negotiating prowess, but warned that the restoration of relations with the United States would create "tremendous challenges and tests" for the Cuban economy (Liu 2015). China's international politics experts were also divided, with some analysts doubting the change in U.S. policy would bear fruit for Cuba and that warming relations were subject to reversal if a new U.S. administration reversed Obama's policy opening with the Castro regime (Yang and Dong 2016). Other scholars went so far as to suggest the decision to restore relations would also improve Sino-American relations (Yang 2015). Overall, the Chinese foreign policy community expressed largely positive views of U.S.-Cuban engagement, arguing it was a smart, logical move, while also expressing significant concerns for both China and Cuba. However, China's influence on U.S.-Cuban relations remains largely unexamined.

* Gregg B. Johnson, Valparaiso University, gregg.johnson@valpo.edu; Zhimin Lin, University of Macau, zhiminlin@umac.mo.

The Cuba-U.S. Bilateral Relationship. Michael J. Kelly, Erika Moreno, and Richard C. Witmer, II.

One of the major ways China may influence U.S.-Cuban relations is through its role as a model for a Cuba in transition. China underwent an enormous shift in economic policy that has led to impressive growth rates, raised the standard of living in China, and in many ways is seen as an alternative development model to the Washington Consensus. The China Model of development not only transformed China's domestic economy but also its relationship with the world economy. Furthermore, China overhauled its economy while maintaining one-party rule and improving relations with the United States and the rest of the international economic community. As such, China serves as a potential economic and political model for Cuban leaders to follow. It shows Cuban leaders that economic opening and re-engagement with the United States does not inevitably lead to regime change (Cheng 2007b; Hearn 2012b; Oppenheimer 2005).

The second major way China may influence U.S.-Cuban relations is related to Cuba's dependence on trade and investment from China, which reinforces Chinese influence on the Cuban government. During the Cold War, Cuba depended heavily on trade and investment from the Soviet Union (Katz 1983). However, the collapse of the U.S.S.R. left an enormous political and economic hole in Cuba's foreign relations—a hole that China has partially filled (Lehoczki 2012). While Cuba's political and economic reliance on China is not as strong as its reliance on the U.S.S.R. during the Cold War, the asymmetry of the relationship gives China far more leverage over Cuba than it gives Cuba over China. At a minimum, Cuban leaders are extremely familiar with the outcomes associated with the withdrawal of political and economic support of Cuba's chief international patron.

The third major way China may influence the future of U.S.-Cuban relations is through its role as a facilitator for Cuba on the international stage (Hearn 2012a; Feinberg 2011). China became the world's largest trading economy by engaging with the international economic system. It ascended to the World Trade Organization (WTO), expanded its role in the International Monetary Fund (IMF), recently founded the Asian Infrastructure Investment Bank (AIIB), and joined regional development banks in Africa, Asia, and especially in Latin America.[1] China's growing influence in these key international organizations can further facilitate Cuba's integration into the international system. If China were to facilitate the reintegration of Cuba into the international economy, this would both reassure Cuban leaders and potentially reduce U.S. resistance to Cuban membership in these key organizations.

The ability of China to act as a model, an economic patron, and an international facilitator can influence the pace and scope of change in U.S.-Cuban relations. China's leaders have clearly signaled they want Cuban leaders to increase the pace of economic reform, which would increase opportunities for trade and investment from the United States. China's recent economic slowdown may exacerbate these pressures, though they may also decrease China's leverage. However, the potential for change varies greatly with the type of leadership in Cuba. China would be hard pressed to get hard line Cuban leaders to significantly change the pace of economic reform or the pace of change in U.S.-Cuban relations. However, if more reformist elements come to power in Cuba, then China will likely play a key role not only in the economic transition but also in increasing the rate of "thaw" in the historically frosty U.S.-Cuban relationship. Regardless of the type of leadership, China is willing to provide at least minimal support to Cuba in order to maintain a socialist ally.

This chapter is laid out as follows. First, we will briefly address the history of Sino-Cuban relations in order to illustrate how China can influence Cuban policy. Second, we outline the China Model and how China's engagement with Latin America in general, and Cuba in particular, affects Cuban attitudes and policies. We argue the relationship is asymmetrical due to China's outsized role in the Cuban economy, which increases China's influence over Cuba's future. Third, we explore the details of China's role as a facilitator in international economics, the limits of facilitation, and how this influences Cuban policies. Next, we draw on the logic outlined in the previous sections to analyze the influence of China on U.S.-Cuban relations. We focus specifically on the pace of change in Cuba and the effects of a change in Cuban leadership on the likelihood of further normalization of U.S.-Cuban relations. The final section restates our main arguments and offers readers advice regarding what to look for in Sino-Cuban relations to predict changes in U.S.-Cuban policy.

A Brief History of Sino-Cuban Relations

While China is a large, heavily populated, economically powerful world power, Cuba is a geographically distant island that is small in size and population, as well as being an economically marginal player in both the world and Chinese economies.[2] While a relatively minor part of China's economic puzzle, Cuba occupies a special place in Chinese foreign relations. After the Cuban Revolution, the Sino-Cuban relationship experienced a four-year "honeymoon" from 1960 to 1964. In fact, Cuba was the first government in Latin America to switch diplomatic ties from Taiwan to the People's Republic of China, a point the Cuban state newspaper *Granma* makes routinely in stories involving Sino-Cuban diplomatic relations (Redacción International 2015). However, friendly bilateral relations plunged precipitously after the Sino-Soviet split became public and Cuba chose to side with the Soviet Union. This long deep freeze in Sino-Cuban relations reached its coldest when in the late 1970s Fidel Castro went so far as to launch personal attacks on Mao (Cheng 2007a) and in the years to follow on the architect of China's economic reforms, Deng Xiaoping (Ratliff 2004; Small and Ferrer Rincon 2008).[3] Simply put, Cuba's siding with the U.S.S.R. rather than China during the Cold War led to a deep gulf in Sino-Cuban relations.

The global reaction to China's crackdown on the Tiananmen Square protestors served as the impetus for Chinese and Cuban leaders to re-engage. Fidel Castro spoke out loudly in support of Chinese leadership. Cuba not only provided vocal support but also key diplomatic cover. China's Foreign Minister Qian had just begun a tour of Latin America when the tanks rolled through Tiananmen Square and he met stern government faces in places he did visit, while having visits canceled outright in others. However, Fidel Castro welcomed Minister Qian with open arms, providing the Chinese foreign minister a safe haven when his other Latin American visits were canceled (Cheng 2007b). Furthermore, the Castro regime offered much-needed international support for the use of force against the protestors. Coming on the heels of the Cuban foreign minister's visit to Beijing (Voice of America 1989), the Chinese government considered this state visit to mark the birth of modern Sino-Cuban relations (China View 2004).

The collapse of the Soviet Union accelerated the pace of rapprochement. Both states simply had far fewer regimes supporting one-party communism on the international stage. Cuba also lost its main economic patron, with the U.S.S.R. accounting for about 80 percent of Cuban trade for much of the Cold War and billions in annual subsidies (Farnsworth 1988; Lehoczki 2012). China provided desperately needed goods, economic aid, and investments during Cuba's Special Period, when aid and trade with the U.S.S.R./Russia collapsed. That the Tiananmen Square crisis and the collapse of the U.S.S.R. happened within two years of each other created significant incentives for Chinese and Cuban leaders to restore closer ties.

In the ensuing quarter-century Sino-Cuban relations continued to expand. China rewarded Cuba with the most significant diplomatic honor a foreign partner could expect—high-profile state visits. Chinese presidents took official state visits to Havana four times between 2001 and 2015, with only South American giant, Brazil, receiving as much high-level diplomatic attention. China visited their other four largest Latin American trade and investment partners, Argentina, Chile, Mexico, and Venezuela, only three times each (Brand, McEwen-Fial, and Wolfgang Muno 2015). Considering Chinese-Brazilian trade is nearly twenty-seven times greater than Chinese-Cuban trade (Simones and Hidalgo 2011), the number of state visits indicates Cuba's importance to the Chinese government. The diplomatic gulf that existed during the Cold War appears to be finally and fully bridged.

In addition to state visits, China and Cuba have also had frequent military contacts, though these contacts remain limited in scope. Early on in the rapprochement process, U.S. officials expressed concerns that China would lease naval bases and transfer significant military resources to Cuba, as had the Soviets. However, despite *Granma*'s emphasis on the "high level of links" between the two militaries (Prensa Latina 2017), the last three years of coverage detailed only one Chinese naval visit, a few officer exchanges, and pledges to strengthen military cooperation. Even after President Xi's visit to Cuba led to agreements for more extensive cooperation, little progress is apparent. In fact, Cuban officials withdrew a proposal to allow the Chinese navy to dock in Cuba for extended periods of time (news.takungpao.com 2015). The March 2017 meeting between China's minister of defense and the head of the Cuban military demonstrates the limited links. While vowing to expand military cooperation, no concrete agreements were announced (TeleSur 2017; The State Council 2017).

Despite limited military cooperation, Cuba still represents one of the "five golden flowers" of socialism and, as such, is deemed worthy of special support in Beijing. For example, an examination of UN General Assembly voting data shows Sino-Cuban ideal points are close together, whereas U.S.-Sino and U.S.-Cuban ideal points are much more distant (Bailey, Strezhnez, and Voeten 2017).[4] Furthermore, Sino-Cuban ideals points have moved closer together since the end of the Cold War, while U.S.-Cuban and Russia-Cuban ideal points have moved further away from each other. For Cuba, China provides not just diplomatic support and (limited) military cooperation, but is also an absolutely key economic partner. In short, the Sino-Cuban partnership represents a major diplomatic alliance for both countries, with China holding the more powerful position in the partnership. We now turn to China's role as a potential reform model for the Cuban economy.

The China Model and Its Limits

China's move from Mao's development model to Deng Xiaoping's more market-oriented, export-driven development model is well known, as are its successes (Ratliff 2004). After seeing growth fluctuate wildly during the 1960s and 1970s, Deng's reforms set China on a path to more than thirty years of uninterrupted economic expansion, even after accounting for population growth (World Bank 2016). The Chinese and foreign media use the term the "China Model" to refer to the state-led capitalist reform strategy employed by Deng Xiaoping and refined by his three successors after the 1989 Tiananmen crackdown. While media and scholars emphasize different aspects of Chinese reform, the model generally refers to four key aspects of China's reforms over the last four decades: (1) the divergent practice of allowing greater market freedom and open-door policy in foreign economic relations, but restricting political freedom; (2) the emphasis on strong, authoritarian leadership combined with elements of political meritocracy; (3) enhancing state capacity and its role in mobilizing resources for targeted goals; and (4) placing a premium on social stability at all costs (Bell 2015). Similarly, Vietnam also undertook a move to a more market-based economic development model with an emphasis on export-led growth, all while the ruling Communist Party maintained commanding power (Lehoczki 2012; Wilkinson, S 2012; Bell 2015). As such, the China Model offers a potential way forward for the Cuban government.

A key aspect of the China Model is its emphasis on export-led growth, which requires access to inexpensive and abundant primary products and expanding overseas markets in order to fuel industrialization. As a consequence, China has greatly expanded its presence in Latin America, anchoring its penetration into the historical "backyard" of the United States on economic relationships (Ellis 2014; Wu and Liu 2015). Here, China relies on a three-pronged approach to gain traction and lay the groundwork for further expansion. The three prongs are: (1) mega energy projects that tap into Latin America's most valuable resources while helping meet China's ever growing (until recently at least) thirst for energy; (2) loan-based infrastructure projects few other countries could match in scale or terms, much welcomed in region looking for foreign investment; and (3) building a network of manufacturing, service, and logistics that aims at helping lock in China's advantage in both merchandise and service exports in the region (Dominguez et al. 2006; Johnson and Wasson 2011). This strategy has worked well for China as a whole. China needed only a decade to move from minor player to major actor, to become the region's second largest trading partner, third largest source of foreign investment, and the third largest overseas contracting market for China (Wu and Liu 2012). The China Model's emphasis on state-led development was also seen as an attractive (and effective) alternative to the market-oriented Washington Consensus in many countries.

Trade with Latin America expanded at a dizzying pace. China's rapid growth offered both new markets and increased demand for those commodities exporters across Latin America (Ferchen and Garcia Herrero 2011). Similarly, Chinese-made products quickly found their way into Latin America, with China becoming one of the top sources of manufactured goods in Latin America's largest economies (Simoes and Hidalgo 2011). In fact, trade expanded so quickly that some scholars became concerned that Latin America was experiencing a period of neo-dependency (Ferchen 2011; Inter-American Development Bank 2004; Poniachik 2011) and that Chinese exports threatened Latin American manufacturing (Blazquez-Lidoy et al. 2006; Gallagher, Moreno-Bird, and Porzecanski 2008; Heine 2008; Rosen 2003). Regardless, scholars concluded that Chinese trade with Latin America had profound economic effects and these relationships gave China greater leverage in the region.

While trade with Latin America expanded, trade between China and Cuba plateaued in the late 2000s and then declined somewhat. Nearly all of Cuba's exports to China consist of sugar, nickel, and petroleum, while imports consist of a far more diverse array of products and are mostly manufactured goods (Simones and Hidalgo 2011). Given the expansion of China's trade with the rest of the region, the small size of the Cuban economy, its limited natural resources, the trade with Cuba is relatively unimportant for China's development (see Table 4.1). However, trade with China is absolutely essential for the Cuban economy. China is both Cuba's largest export destination and the largest source of imports, accounting for

Table 4.1 Sino-Cuban Economic Relations (Million USD)

Year	Total Trade*	As % of Chinese Trade with Latin America	Imports from China	Exports to China	FDI from China**	As % of Chinese FDI (stock) to Latin America	Change in FDI from China***
2006	1792.45	2.55	1264.13	528.31	5991	0.30	3037
2007	2285.71	2.22	1170.25	1115.46	6649	0.27	658
2008	2257.85	1.57	1354.81	903.06	7205	0.22	556
2009	1547.31	1.27	1547.31	972.87	8532	0.22	1293
2010	1831.51	0.99	1067.22	765.22	6898	0.16	−1635
2011	1947.81	0.81	1043.66	904.15	14637	0.27	7671
2012	1742.75	0.66	1173.58	569.17	13569	0.02	−557
2013	1879.42	0.72	1374.79	504.63	11134	0.13	−2437
2014	1395.48	0.53	1062.96	333.07	6255	0.06	−2222
2015	2216.38	0.94	1886.10	330.00	12062	0.10	4243
2016	2057.18	0.95	1783.43	273.75			

Sources: ***Annual Report on Latin America and the Caribbean (2016–17),*** pp. 393–397, 399. ***Annual Report on Latin America and the Caribbean (2015–2016),*** pp. 360–361, 366. ***Annual Report on Latin America and the Caribbean (2011–2012),*** pp. 342, 348. ***Annual Report on Latin America and the Caribbean (2011–2012),*** pp. 342, 348, 355.

Notes:

* In addition to trade, China also provided official aid. From 2003 and 2008, China provided fifteen Latin American countries with a total of forty-two "turn-the-key" project as part of official aid. Of them, Cuban received seven, mainly in the form of small hydraulic power stations farm-fishing facilities. ***China's Foreign Aid, 60 Years in Retrospect,*** p. 302.

** Stock or cumulative amount of FDI at the end of particular year.

*** Net yearly flow of FDI.

about one-fifth of both imports and exports (Simoes and Hidalgo 2011). While not as closely link as it was to the U.S.S.R. during the Cold War, China's outsized role in Cuba's trade gives Chinese leaders economic leverage, while Cuba's one true economic advantage is that it serves as a hub of transportation between China and the Caribbean. Hence, Cuba's role as an economic hub for China is roughly analogous to its role as a hub for Soviet influence in the Americas.

In addition to near exponential growth in trade between China and Latin America, China now is one of the largest sources of investment for the region. As noted previously, much of this is predicated on China's demand for raw materials and consists of investment in energy and mining, or in infrastructure projects (e.g., roads and ports) designed to get materials to market (Blazquez-Lidoy, Rodriguez, and Santiso 2006; Carmody and Owusu 2007). However, Chinese investment in the region, particularly outside industries directly related to energy production and commodities, is quite limited. Thus, while China's energy and other commodities demands produce economic benefits for states like Bolivia, Chile, and Venezuela, these investments may be volatile due to fluctuations in commodities prices and China's own economic challenges. Regardless, Chinese investment in Latin America lags behind only the United States (Armony 2012), giving Beijing considerable influence throughout much of the region. The financial meltdown in the United States and Europe during 2007–2008 and the ensuing Great Recession only enhanced China's leverage (Lehoczki 2012).

Chinese investment is particularly important for the Cuban economy, even though it represents only a tiny fraction of China's investment in Latin America (see Table 8.1). Chinese aid to Cuba is also extremely important (Hearn 2012a). China announced a number of joint ventures in typical areas of Chinese interest like mining, oil, and infrastructure, but also expanded into telecommunications, technology, and medical research (Lehoczki 2012). Cuba has also accepted credit from the Chinese in exchange for the purchase of much-needed industrial and consumer goods (Hearn 2009). Cuba's state newspaper *Granma* routinely announces Chinese investment deals, paying particular attention to investment in the medical field (AIN 2015; Peláez 2015). Much like investment and credit gave the Soviets substantial influence on the island, it also affords China substantial leverage.

At least partially due to its outsized role in the Cuban economy, Havana appears willing to alter its actions based on pressure from Beijing. For example, Cuba's famed Buena Vista Social Club was slated to play a concert in Taiwan early in 2016. However, the election of a pro-independence president in Taiwanese elections led Beijing to apply pressure to Cuba and the subsequent cancellation of the concert (San Diego Union Tribune 2016). Similarly, Cuba supported China's boycott of the 2010 Nobel Peace Prize ceremony for human rights activist Liu Xiaobo. In a more systematic analysis, Strüver's (2016) measure of foreign policy similarity places Cuba consistently in the 90th percentile in UN General Assembly voting with Chinese positions, meaning Cuba is one of China's most reliable international supporters. The combination of historical international support, trade, investment, and aid make China the single most important and potentially influential international actor on Cuban foreign policy.

The China Model, combined with Chinese trade, aid, and investment, has affected and continues to affect Cuban leaders' attitudes about reform. Fidel Castro was notoriously wary of the China Model (Hearn 2012a, 2012b; Wilkinson, S. 2012). After initially seeming to warm to the idea of a "socialist market economy" in the early 1990s, Chinese leaders repeatedly found Fidel deeply skeptical of China's reforms (Cheng 2007b). He simply seemed far more comfortable with a more Soviet-style economy. In turn, these same Chinese leaders offered veiled criticism of the slow pace of policy change in Cuba (Oppenheimer 2005). Alternatively, Raúl Castro was seen as much more pragmatic and amenable to a more market-oriented economic model (Lehoczki 2012). In 2005, he made a second trip to China to observe the changes there in greater detail and depth. After his return, he established a special unit to study China's practices. According to one Chinese scholar, some in Cuba even wanted to copy directly from the Chinese model (Wilkinson 2012). As a result of these exchanges, Cuban leaders moved from observation to implementation of economic reform, albeit on a much smaller scale than China. As a latecomer to reform, Cuba clearly picked reform measures that worked well in China and that were viewed as suitable to Cuba's conditions. For example, from an emphasis on changing the mindset of party leaders, to setting up term limits, to practicing essentially a two-track system (allowing the private sectors to grow while retaining a large public sector),[5] one can easily see the shadow of China on Cuban policy (Zou 2013).

Nevertheless, Cuba insists, at least rhetorically, on a planned economy while also allowing for the introduction of some elements of a more market-based approach. Cuba's current crop of leaders simply seems unwilling to engage in aggressive economic reforms like those found in the China Model. While the size of the private sector increased substantially, the government fails to report the relative size of the private sector in Cuba's gross domestic product (GDP) (Government Accountability Office 2016). Only three types of private sector employment is authorized, self-employed businesses (*cuentapropistas*), agricultural cooperatives, and nonagricultural cooperatives. These forms of private sector employment both limit the size of the private sector and demonstrate the limits of the regime's willingness to follow the China or even the Vietnamese models (Government Accountability Office 2016; Lehoczki 2012). Like Chinese leaders, Cuban leaders listed maintaining social stability as one of the prime considerations when deciding the direction and pace of reform (Jiang 2010).

Both as an economic model and as an economic partner China can influence Cuban leadership, but that influence on Cuba's internal policies is limited. One reason for the slow pace of change is that current Cuban leaders understand their economy is very distinct from China's of the late 1970s. China was much poorer, and had the benefits of an enormous workforce and the example of state-led development found in other parts of Asia to draw on when they launched reform (Wilkinson, S. 2012). Several scholars suggest Vietnam is a more appropriate role model for Cuban leaders, as it was a small (in population and size), largely agriculture-based economy when reforms were launched (Gabriele 2011; Lehoczki 2012). One Chinese expert suggested that one of the reasons that Cuba seemed to favor the Vietnamese model of reform more so than the Chinese model was that unlike China, Vietnam was able to launch political reform, albeit slowly, while conducting economic reform (Guo 2012). However, Cuban leaders also resist the Vietnamese model of "innovation and opening," instead preferring to call reforms in Cuba simply "change." According to one well-known Chinese expert on Cuba this reflected both the influence of Fidel and the desire by Raúl to distinguish Cuba's reforms from both China and Vietnam (Wilkinson 2012). Furthermore, Cuba represents a tiny fraction of China's Latin American economic strategy. The limits of the appeal of the China Model to current Cuban leaders, China's focus elsewhere in Latin America, and the slowing Chinese economy may limit the leverage China holds over Cuban foreign policy down the road.

While the China Model has thus far exerted limited influence on the Cuban economy, China can also act as an important economic facilitator in other areas. Cuba is far less integrated into the global economy than is China (Lehoczki 2012). China has long supported an end to the U.S. embargo in annual votes held at the United Nations (General Assembly 2014). More importantly, China has become more active in international organizations like the International Monetary Fund (IMF) and the World Trade Organization (WTO), as well as joining the Inter-American Development Bank (IDB) (Hearn 2009). Here China began to play a far more active and innovative role than its tiny share of IDB would typically indicate.[6] China's re-engagement with the international economic system and the successes it has enjoyed has resulted in China pushing Cuba to re-engage in the international economic system (Wu 2013).[7] For example, while the United

States has opposed Cuban membership in the IMF, China has supported this idea. Raúl Castro expressed interest in possibly joining an institution that is sometimes referred to as a "lender of last resort"—indicating some Cuban leaders were open to greater international economic integration (Hearn 2012a; Feinberg 2011). Interestingly, Cuba has, almost in a quid pro quo fashion, facilitated China's integration into international organizations within Latin America. In January 2014, Cuba's ambassador to China mentioned Cuba played a key role in the second Summit of Latin America and the Caribbean Community's adoption of a special statement endorsing the founding of a joint China-Latin America Forum (Lin 2014). In sum, China can facilitate the reintegration of Cuba into the international economic system, while Cuba offers China access to Latin American and Caribbean institutions.

China's commitment to act as a facilitator for the Cuban regime is bolstered by China's traditional support of Cuba's one-party state. As previously noted, the collapse of the Soviet Union caused extreme hardship in Cuba. China offered emergency support during the "Special Period" and became the source for not only investment and aid but also supplied much needed consumer and commercial goods that vanished with the U.S.S.R. Chinese-made buses ferried commuters to work, while shops were stocked with electronics and appliances manufactured in China, helping the regime limp through the 1990s and 2000s (Hearn 2012a). Again, China and Cuba combined represent 40 percent of the remaining one-party, communist regimes in the world. As the largest and most economically powerful of the "five golden flowers," China is willing to help Cuba resist Western, particularly U.S., pressure to engage in political liberalization (Lehoczki 2012). The small size of the Cuban economy has meant that China's costs of supporting Cuba are quite manageable, at least as long as China's economy continues to rapidly expand.

In sum, China and Cuba see each other as important political allies. Economically, China serves as both a key source of trade and investment, as well as a role model for economic reform without political liberalization. Furthermore, China serves as an economic liaison—helping facilitate Cuba's integration into the international economic order. For Cuba, China's support over the last twenty-five years has been invaluable. Hence, China has considerable political and economic leverage in its relationship with Cuba. Nevertheless, Fidel's lack of enthusiasm for Chinese-style economic reforms limited economic opening in Cuba since 2008. Even Raúl's more pragmatic approach has done little to speed reforms, frustrating Beijing and even the small ethnic Chinese community in Havana (Hearn 2012b). The recent slowdown in the Chinese economy will likely exacerbate tensions regarding the seemingly glacial pace of Cuban reform. The China Model may simply appear less attractive, and China may have less leverage if trade, aid, and investment from China slow in coming years. If that happens, it may reignite the deep-seated fear among Cuban leaders of a possible replay of the cost of overreliance on a senior partner in an asymmetrical relationship similar to the one they had with the Soviet Union. This will leave them with few attractive options: to reduce reliance on China at the cost of more economic hardship at home, or to look for possible off-setting partnerships that lack China's empathy for Cuba's one-party state.

China's Influence on U.S.-Cuban Relations

We contend China's political and economic support of the Cuban regime detailed in the previous section gives the Chinese government influence in Cuban decision-making. For example, the Chinese government long opposed the United States' political and economic isolation of Cuba, so it is not surprising the Cuban government likely kept Chinese leaders informed of their secret negotiations with the United States (Mu 2014). Given China's asymmetric influence over the Cuban economy and its position as a powerful political backer of the one-party state, the Chinese enjoy greater influence among Cuban government officials than perhaps any other government in Latin America, especially after Hugo Chávez's death.[8] Hence, Beijing relished the restoration of diplomatic relations with the United States and the series of steps the Barack Obama administration took to weaken the U.S. embargo (chinafocus.com 2015; Hua 2015; Sun 2015). The Chinese largely viewed the change in U.S. policy under the Obama administration as mirroring the normalization of Sino-American relations, a change that has proved vital to China's political and economic reintegration to the global political and economic system since the change first began in the 1970s. They also saw the Obama administration's moves as an important first step in a lengthy process designed to end with Cuba's full inclusion in regional and global political and economic institutions like the Organization of American States, the World Bank, and the Inter-American Development Bank. However, Donald Trump's campaign pronouncements and announced policy changes since his election have not only delayed Cuban integration, they have forced China to rethink its tacit cooperation with the United States on several regional issues, as well as issues outside Latin America such as the ongoing tensions between the Trump administration and the Kim regime in North Korea.

In the short run, China is likely to influence U.S.-Cuban relations in several key ways. First, the Obama administration's shift in policy from regime change to diplomatic engagement fits perfectly with China's foreign policy goals (Lehoczki 2012). This not only removed a point of contention between China and the United States but also freed China to place greater pressure on the Castro regime to increase the pace of economic liberalization. China long expressed frustration with the pace of Cuban reforms (Cheng 2007b), yet the crippling effects of the U.S. embargo limited the amount of pressure China was willing to bring to bear on Cuban leaders. Still, Chinese leaders long preferred a Castro-led Cuba with an unreformed, state-controlled economy to watching a repeat of the collapse of the Soviet Union. The Obama administration's abandonment of regime change as the centerpiece of the United States' Cuba policy gave China greater room to push for increased movement toward the China Model of economic liberalization without being seen as coaching Cuban leaders on political matters. From the perspective of the Obama administration, a more open Cuban economy provided opportunities for U.S.-based investment and greater person-to-person contact. Interestingly, both the Xi and Obama administrations expressed frustration with the seemingly glacial pace of economic opening. The Trump administration's partial rollback of Obama's policies opening trade, investment, and travel to Cuba lessen China's willingness to pressure the Cuban regime to engage in more aggressive economic reforms. Beijing simply has no political or economic incentives to cooperate with the Trump administration's harder line policies toward Cuba. In short, China and the United States shared similar goals for the future of the Cuban economy after the Obama administration's rapprochement, but the Trump administration's harder line on Cuba is likely to undermine President Xi's efforts to promote a more open Cuban economy.

Second, the recent slowdown in the Chinese economy may also influence U.S.-Cuban relations. One the one hand, a slowing Chinese economy means less demand for raw materials, as well as decreased foreign investment and development aid (Giles 2016). This decreases Chinese leverage in their relationship with Havana, which may undermine Chinese efforts to encourage economic liberalization in Cuba. Here, the Chinese slowdown may also indirectly undermine American efforts to re-engage with Cuba as the latter may feel less economically secure. On the other hand, a slowing Chinese economy also means Cuban leaders face even greater internal pressure to "fix the economy" or face a possible return to the worst years of the "Special Period." Furthermore, Chinese businesses, especially private businesses, increasingly seek investments with quick return and higher probability of profitability. A warmer U.S.-Cuban relationship creates expectations of a tourism boom along with greater needs for hospitality facilities, better transportation, and up-scale commodities and accommodations (such as golf courses). Several Chinese companies took steps to capitalize on these opportunities.[9] If the trend continues under the Trump administration, Cuban-American relations may see more concrete steps forward from the help of an unexpected third party whose motivation of improving Cuban economy has nothing to do with the U.S., but whose end results have everything to do with the U.S. business community. In this scenario, the Chinese economic slowdown makes American investment more attractive and reinforces U.S.-Cuban re-engagement.

Given the Chinese role, the normalization of U.S.-Cuban economic relations could enhance American leverage and facilitate Cuba's economic liberalization. The Obama administration failed to spur congressional action on U.S.-Cuban economic normalization, while unified Republican control under the Trump administration weakened prospects for additional economic engagement. However, hardliners have only partially succeeded in rolling back Obama's economic overtures, failing to fully reverse the previous administration's policy changes. This strengthens the Xi administration's resolve to support the Cuban regime regardless of China's economic slowdown.

Third, China and Cuba see each other as ideological comrades in a world with few such friends. *Granma* routinely runs stories celebrating state visits and ". . . the construction of socialism with characteristics appropriate for each country." (Gallo 2014) The state-run paper blares headlines that "Sino-Cuban Relations are at their Historic Best" with articles that celebrate China's opposition to the "cruel blockade" of the United States (Gallo 2014). The term "fraternal bond" (*el clima fraternal*) also appears regularly (Redacción Nacional 2014). These stories demonstrate the weight Cuban authorities give to their relationship with China, but also show the reader even the Cuban government sees flexibility within a one-party socialist regime. Consequently, the relationship with China gives the Cuban regime both ideological flexibility and a strong friend to rely on if economic reforms lead to domestic or international pressure for significant political reform. In combination, these reassured Cuban leaders that normalization of relations with the United States was not a direct threat to the regime, while further encouraging the types of economic reforms championed both in Beijing and in Washington, D.C.

Finally, any discussion of China's influence on U.S.-Cuban relations must address the issue of leadership change in Cuba. Despite more than five decades of U.S. policy designed to bring an end to the Castro brothers, Father Time is halfway to accomplishing what the U.S. government failed to do for over five decades. After previously announcing a temporary transfer of power to his brother due to health reasons, Fidel Castro officially stepped down from the presidency in 2008 and died in 2016. Raúl immediately replaced his brother, but even Raúl is an advanced octogenarian. The adoption of term limits ushered in the first non-Castro president in 2018, regardless of Raúl's continued good health (Lopez-Levy 2013). Hardened anti-communists and pro-engagement reformers alike agree the shadow of the Castro brothers will exert considerable influence behind the scenes. For example, Raúl is expected to remain the First Secretary of the Communist Party, and as such hold considerable sway over future policy decisions (Lopez-Gottardi 2018). However, the Castro brothers' influence will wane in the near future, despite the best efforts of the Cuban medical system.

Many news outlets accurately predicted that Miguel Díaz-Canel would serve as Cuba's president (for examples see Orsi 2013; Wilkinson 2015). When Díaz-Canel was tapped for the role of vice- president in 2013 he replaced another aging revolutionary, José Ramon Machado Ventura. While relatively little is known about the specifics of Díaz-Canel's policy preferences, his elevation to the vice presidency by Raúl Castro, his age, and his affinity for the internet (Wilkinson 2015) suggest he may adopt a more reformist tone. However, Díaz-Canel's infrequent public comments seem supportive of a more conservative approach to economic opening (Caulfield 2018). Regardless, if the new leadership is reformist in nature, it will likely accelerate the pace of reforms by incorporating the most successful aspects of the Chinese and Vietnamese reform efforts. For example, the 2008 and 2012 agricultural reforms in Cuba were far more modest than similar reforms undertaken by China and Vietnam. Perhaps not surprisingly, these reforms have produced limited results, though private sector output grew, while the state sector's output declined (Mesa-Lago 2014). Further reforms in this and other sectors could increase output and make Cuban agriculture an attractive investment target for U.S.-based agri-industries. Similarly, current housing policies limit the sale of existing homes and the construction of new housing stock, leading to one of the country's largest social policy problems. Moderate reforms to allow mortgages and possibly foreign ownership would stimulate both the construction industry and the financial sector, easing the housing crisis (Mesa-Lagos 2014). Cuban-American émigrés, real estate developers, and the banking sector would all find even modest reforms attractive. Both sets of reforms would be consistent with the China Model and would likely receive support from Beijing and warm reception from Chinese companies eager to expand globally and invest in new markets.

These types of reforms would create even greater incentive for both China and the United States to be more involved in the Cuban economy. Chinese leaders would view new, reformist leaders very favorably, given these leaders' past expressions of frustration with the sluggish pace of Cuban reforms (Cheng 2007b; Hearn 2012a, 2012b; Lehoczki 2012). Chinese leaders would not only welcome the adoption of a more "socialist market" economic system, but would also likely provide greater aid and investment in order to facilitate the transition. After all, China has a strong history of investing in one of the "five golden flowers" after one engages in "socialist market" reforms (Kubny and Voss 2010). American businesses would also react positively to reformist leadership, supporting more market-oriented economic policies (see U.S. Chamber of Commerce 2014). The further opening of the Cuban economy, even at a slow pace, would enhance incentives for American businesses to pressure government leaders to allow greater U.S. involvement in the Cuban economy. The Xi administration would be supportive of greater U.S.-Cuban economic engagement given the obvious benefits.

However, the effectiveness of this pressure will likely vary by administration. After the Obama administration normalized diplomatic relations and worked to ease economic restrictions, Congress took little action to facilitate further opening. Future Democratic administrations and most moderate Republican administrations will likely continue seeking ways to overturn or circumvent the Helms-Burton Act—a change sought by China for years. For example, a bipartisan bill to end travel restrictions earned fifty-five co-sponsors, including nine Republicans in the polarized Senate

(U.S. Congress 2017). In previous work, we predicted only an extremely conservative or reactionary Republican administration was likely to slow or reverse U.S.-Cuban economic engagement (Johnson and Lin 2016). However, even the Trump administration largely restricted its reversal of President Obama's policies to small changes in trade and travel, without abandoning the U.S. embassy in Havana.

After reacting positively to the Obama administration's rapprochement with Cuba, the Chinese response to the Trump administration's Cuba policy has been quite muted. During the Trump-Xi summit in April 2017, neither leader publicly mentioned Cuba, choosing to focus on more pressing issues like trade and North Korea (Tiezzi 2017). Similarly, after the Trump administration's announced changes on U.S.-Cuban policy the Chinese government did not issue a formal statement. The Xinhua News Agency (state-run) instead ran several stories reporting reactions from several prominent Chinese academics in the field (Xinhua 2017a, 2017b, 2017c, and 2017d; Xu 2017; Zhongpingshe 2017). These Chinese-based exports largely argued the "thunder" made by Trump during the campaign far exceeded the "storm" associated with these policy changes. They also attributed the changes in U.S.-Cuban policy first and foremost to Trump's appeal to his electoral base, rather than some sort of anti-communist ideological zeal. Neither the state-run news agencies nor the academic community has commented extensively on what the Chinese government's reaction to the Trump administration's policy changes should be. In short, the muted Chinese reaction to Trump's limited reversal of Obama's Cuban policy suggests that China is largely taking a patient approach. This does not, of course, preclude follow-up actions on the part of China should the Trump administration substantially escalate its pressure on Cuba.

In short, if reformist elements within the Cuban Communist Party come to power after the death of Raúl Castro, Chinese and American economic interests will largely coincide. Interestingly, China will be seen largely as on the same side with the United States in pushing for opening the Cuban economy to market forces. Conversely, Beijing's political support for one-party rule in Cuba may cause minor friction at times. If the death of the Castro brothers leads to the elevation of hardliners, this will complicate both Sino-Cuban and U.S.-Cuban relations. Hardliners may try to reverse even the limited reforms implemented over the last few years and return Cuba to the "bad old days" of a rigidly planned economy. Hardliners could potentially try to use the threat of regime collapse to extract greater trade, aid, and investment from China. In the past, North Korea has used this ploy to obtain support from Beijing (Chen 2015). Under such circumstances China might provide significant international support and continued economic support for Cuba much to the dismay of the United States, particularly if the regime were under threat. However, such an extreme response from China is less likely than in the North Korean case, as Cuba lacks a nuclear threat, and the regime's collapse poses nowhere near the security, economic, or immigration threat to China that the collapse of the North Korean regime would pose. Furthermore, China has shown an increased willingness to distinguish between its reform-minded socialist brethren and those that openly resist following the China Model of reform (Harnisch, Bersick, and Gottwald 2016). These latter two points suggest a new generation of Cuban hardliners would enjoy very, very limited support from Beijing at the substantive level, even if China were to avoid rhetoric criticizing hardliners in Havana.

The effects of China on U.S.-Cuban relations in the event of hardliners coming to power in Havana will depend on which of the two scenarios, reformers versus hardliners, comes to pass. If Chinese leadership is willing to tolerate the explicit rejection of the China Model in order to prop up a socialist comrade, this will limit Chinese pressure on Cuba to cooperate with U.S. administrations. This combination would likely result in a return to a pre-Obama status quo, with China and Cuba on one side and the United States on the other, particularly if the Trump administration were in power when this came to pass. This situation may occur if Cuban hardliners and a conservative/reactionary Republican administration come to power simultaneously in the near future.

However, we very much doubt the emergence of a constellation of hardliners in Havana and Washington, D.C., and unconditional support from Beijing for Cuba is likely in the near future. Beijing is far more likely to adopt a more adversarial tone with hardliners in Havana, as Beijing would chafe at the rejection of the China Model (Noesselt 2016). Consequently, China would likely hold similar views as a typical U.S. administration and nudge hardliners to act as economic reformers. In sum, whether reformers or hardliners come to power China will likely share many of the same policy preferences toward Cuba as the United States, at least as far as the Cuban economy goes. Only a complete reversal of the Obama administration's rapprochement with Cuba is likely to lead to a more full-throated expression of support for the Cuban regime. As such, China may end up acting as an unlikely U.S. partner in this new era of U.S.-Cuban relations.

Conclusions

In this chapter we argue that China plays a large role in Cuba's economy and international relations, which in turn influences current and future U.S.-Cuban relations. Our evaluation is based on an examination of the history of Sino-Cuban relations, and the dual roles of China as an economic model for potential reforms and an international facilitator for reintegration into the global economy. China enjoyed unprecedented economic expansion in the decades since the adoption of a "socialist market" development strategy and greatly expanded its influence in international organizations. Both China and the United States have pushed Cuban leaders to adopt a more open economy, albeit at a pace that frustrates both Beijing and Washington, D.C. Furthermore, without China's guidance and support since the collapse of the Soviet Union, the Castro regime's "Special Period" would likely have been much grimmer. China became Cuba's major source of trade, aid, and investment. Additionally, China has now moved into a more multifaceted framework of relations with Latin America. This shift means Cuba is no longer the only (or even a major) recipient of China's interests and money. Given the asymmetrical nature of these economic relations, this chapter argues China holds considerable leverage in its relationship with Cuba. However, Cuba's special status in overall Chinese relations with Latin America is likely to continue to ebb in importance, as other markets for Chinese trade and investment draw attention elsewhere.

In the latter portion of this chapter we argue the effects of China's leverage on Cuba influences U.S.-Cuban relations in several ways. First, the China Model affords Cuba some ideological flexibility both in enacting reforms at home and in re-engaging with the United States. Second, the slow pace of reform in Cuba frustrates leaders in Beijing. This, combined with the economic slowdown in China, creates greater pressure for Cuban leaders to open their economy to trade and investment from abroad, including from the United States. On this issue, Beijing and Washington share similar preferences regarding the Cuban economy and the direction of its future change.

Third, we argue China's experience and leverage will influence Cuba's next generation of leaders. If reformers gain influence under the Díaz-Canel administration and the Castro brothers' influence fades, we see an even greater likelihood of cooperation between Beijing, Washington, and Havana. China would support efforts to adopt a Cuban version of the China Model and such reforms would increase incentives for the United States to engage. A more open Cuban economy simply presents greater trade and investment opportunities, while the support of Beijing provides political cover to depart from past Cuban economic policies. If hardliners come to power in Havana, we predict Beijing and Washington will still usually have similar economic policy preferences regarding Cuba. Cuban hardliners could stifle or reverse the recent, limited reforms attempted under Raúl Castro. However, this would ostracize both Chinese leaders, who bristle at the explicit rejection of the China Model, and American leaders seeking rapprochement with Cuba. Only the threat of imminent regime collapse might cause Beijing to increase support for hardliners, and even then support cannot be taken for granted. In sum, even a change in leadership in Cuba will likely result in similar policies toward Cuba in both Beijing and Washington, D.C.

Only with the simultaneous elevation of Cuban hardliners and of anti-Castro hardliners in Washington, D.C., is likely to result in significant split between the two global powers. A belligerent American foreign policy may lead to a more pronounced change in policy toward Cuba in the future, yet China maintains significant leverage. The United States is far more likely to press China for help with North Korean aggression or some other international political or economic crisis then to push China away to pursue an antagonistic anti-Cuba policy. Furthermore, administrations in Havana and Beijing tend to have longer time horizons than American administrations, so even a complete reversal of Obama's policy may lead to a more measured response from both, as each knows they likely only need to wait for the next American administration to return to the Obama-era status quo.

Finally, we argue that China is likely to remain a reliable political friend of last resort for Cuba. China simply acts as an "insurance policy" against the event that improved U.S.-Cuban relations prove to be ephemeral. China successfully re-engaged with the West over the last several decades and enjoyed enormous economic and political benefits as a result. The decision of Raúl Castro and the Obama administration to re-engage after decades of animosity puts Cuba on a similar path, a path supported by Cuba's largest economic benefactor and international supporter. Hence, Sino-Cuban relations should facilitate further improvements in U.S.-Cuban relations and not the other way around.

Notes

1. China joined the Organization of American States in 2004 as permanent observer. It joined the Inter-American Development Bank in 2009. China joined the Forum for East Asia and Latin American Cooperation in 2009. China also became an observer when the Pacific Alliance was created in 2011. China has also increased its relationships with various subregional groups such as the Group of Rio, the Andean Community, and the Caribbean Community.
2. Cuba ranks as China's tenth largest trading partner in Latin America, and accounts for less than 0.1 percent of exports and imports for China (MIT 2015).
3. Deng Xiaoping was not that fond of Cuba either. In an internal speech Deng made after China's brief border war with Vietnam, he used the term "Cuba-in-the-East" several times when tried to justify China's decision. http://history.dwnews.com/news/2016-02-10/59716875.html.
4. Voeten (2013) measure ideal point estimates for all countries voting in the UN General Assembly and measure the absolute difference between countries. We restricted our analysis to the post-1990 era and found that China's average distance from all countries is 0.88. Its distance from Cuba averages only 0.74, while its distance from the United States averages 3.57.
5. Though by 2013, private sectors in China contributed to over 55 percent of GDP, while in Cuba, private sectors contributed to a little more than 5 percent with a goal of lifting the percentage to between 40 percent and 50 percent in five years.
6. China, for example, provided IDB US$2 billion in 2009 to establish a joint fund to support public and private projects, first of its kind in the Bank's history and was instrumental in a number of loans IDB approved the last few years.
7. Cuba jointed the WTO in 1995.
8. The death of Hugo Chávez, the collapse of oil prices, and the mounting troubles facing Chávez's successor have all weakened Venezuela's influence in Cuba.
9. Indeed, these Chinese companies, while showing growing optimism in expanding business in Cuba, worried that the U.S. companies would be their strong competitors given the latter's long history in the region and close proximity. http://world.huanqiu.com/exclusive/2016-05/8857103.html.

PART II
THE ECONOMIC DIMENSION

5

The Future of Cuba's Non-Sugar Agricultural Sector

Mario A. González-Corzo and Armando Nova-González[*]

Introduction

U.S. food and agricultural exports to Cuba have increased significantly since the approval of the Trade Sanctions Reform and Export Enhancement Act (TSRA) in 2000. The total value of U.S. agricultural and food exports to Cuba increased from $4.6 million in 2001 to an estimated $292 million in 2014. While U.S. agricultural and food exports to Cuba represented a negligible fraction of the island's total imports in 2001, they represent close to 40 percent of Cuba's agricultural and food imports at the present time. Despite these impressive figures, agricultural trade between the United States and Cuba has been "one-way trade," primarily due to U.S. economic sanctions. More recently, U.S. food and agricultural exports to Cuba have declined due to conditions that hinder Cuba's capacity to purchase such imports, which limits the ability of U.S. exporters to expand their sales in this important market.

The potential improvement of diplomatic and trade relations between the United States and Cuba could facilitate the expansion of U.S. agricultural and food exports to the island, as well as Cuban exports to the United States. While bilateral relations between both nations are in a state of flux at the present time, the ability to export to the United States will more than likely improve Cuba's capacity to import agricultural and food products from the United States, and contribute to higher levels of bilateral trade between both nations.

[*] Mario A. González-Corzo, Ph.D., Department of Economics and Business, The City University of New York (CUNY), Lehman College, Mario.Gonzalez-Corzo@lehman.cuny.edu; Armando Nova-González, Ph.D., Centro de Investigaciones de la Economía Internacional (CIEI), Universidad de La Habana, Cuba, armando@rect.uh.cu.

The Cuba-U.S. Bilateral Relationship. Michael J. Kelly, Erika Moreno, and Richard C. Witmer, II.

This chapter examines the evolution of U.S. agricultural exports to Cuba since the approval of the Trade Sanctions Reform and Export Enhancement Act (TSRA) in 2000. The future prospects and policy implications for U.S.-Cuba agricultural trade are also discussed, taking into account the shift in U.S.–Cuban relations initiated after December 17, 2014. Section one presents an overview of the importance of agriculture in the Cuban economy. Section two presents a detailed analysis of Cuba's emerging agricultural model, and efforts to transform this vital sector of the Cuban economy since 2007 through the implementation of policy measures such as: moderate price reforms for selected agricultural products; the transfer of idle state-owned land to usufruct farmers and cooperatives; administrative decentralization and the consolidation of state agencies and ministries dealing with agriculture; decentralization of the commercialization of selected agricultural products; and the provision of microloans to nonstate agricultural producers. Section three analyzes the evolution of U.S. agricultural exports to Cuba since the approval of the TSRA in 2000. Finally, section four discusses the future prospects for U.S.-Cuba agricultural trade under a (potential) scenario of normalized trade relations.

The Importance of Agriculture in the Cuban Economy

Agriculture is one of the principal sectors of the Cuban economy. While its direct share of the nation's gross domestic product (GDP) remains slightly below 4 percent (see Table 5.1, below), close to 20 percent of Cuba's total output is directly and indirectly dependent on agriculture (Nova González 2013). The domestic agricultural sector provides 40 percent of the country's caloric intake and 37 percent of the proteins consumed by the Cuban population (Nova González 2013).

Despite several years of labor force restructuring and the expansion of the services sector, agriculture remains one of the principal sources of employment in Cuba. In 2015, a total of 898,400 persons were employed in agriculture (Anuario Estadístico de Cuba [AEC] 2015). Even though employment in the agricultural sector declined 2.5 percent between 2010 and 2015, its share of total employment remained virtually unchanged at 18.5 percent during this period (Anuario Estadístico de Cuba [AEC] 2015).

Table 5.1 Cuban Gross Domestic Product by Economic Activity at Constant 1997 Prices (Million Cuban Pesos (CUP))

	2009	2010	2011	2012	2013	2014
Gross Domestic Product (GDP)	46,353	47,461	48,791	50,262	51,643	52,184
Agriculture	1,815	1,722	1,807	1,817	1,902	1,945
Fishing	79	60	52	55	58	59
Mining	278	298	303	309	302	300
Sugar industry	222	193	203	218	235	245
Manufacturing industries (excluding sugar industry)	6,195	6,294	6,540	6,673	6,798	6,534
Construction	2,864	2,651	2,458	2,734	2,951	2,883
Electricity and water	662	651	669	698	724	729
Transportation, warehousing, and communications	4,118	4,224	4,377	4,648	4,796	5,002
Commerce	8,374	8,537	9,004	9,485	9,837	10,158
Hotels and restaurants	2,385	2,559	2,790	2,932	3,001	3,094
Financial intermediation	1,244	1,251	1,266	1,272	1,287	1,339
Enterprise services, real estate activities	1,342	1,424	1,473	1,684	1,727	1,815
Public administration, national defense, social security	1,888	1,921	1,950	1,949	1,972	1,961
Science, innovation, and technology	203	218	235	252	262	262
Education	3,731	3,899	3,692	3,552	3,475	3,370
Public health and public assistance	7,984	8,432	8,721	8,756	8,917	9,095
Culture and sports	1,799	1,939	1,904	1,900	1,990	2,038
Other activities, communal services, personal associations	727	726	738	732	764	780
Import rights	443	462	609	596	645	575

Source: Anuario Estadístico de Cuba (AEC), 2015.

Agriculture remains as the second most important source of employment in Cuba, after *communal services*, and its share of total employment exceeds the share of the fast-growing hospitality sector, which includes commerce, hotels, and restaurants (Anuario Estadístico de Cuba [AEC] 2015).

Cuban agricultural workers are better remunerated than employees with similar skills in other sectors of the economy. Agricultural workers earned an average monthly salary of 834 Cuban pesos (CUP)[1] in 2015, which was 1.2 times higher than the national average monthly salary of 687 CUP (Anuario Estadístico de Cuba [AEC] 2015). The average monthly salary for Cuban agricultural workers increased 72 percent between 2010 and 2015, compared to an increase of 53.3 percent for the national average monthly salary during the same period (Anuario Estadístico de Cuba [AEC] 2015).

Agriculture is also a leading source of merchandise exports and foreign exchange receipts. Between 2009 and 2014, the value of Cuba's agricultural exports increased 66 percent, from 305.9 million CUP to 507.8 million CUP (Anuario Estadístico de Cuba [AEC] 2015). This was primarily caused by significant increases in the prices of Cuba's agricultural exports. However, as the data demonstrates, agricultural exports remained virtually unchanged as a share of total merchandise exports during this period. In 2009, agricultural exports represented 10.7 percent of total merchandise exports; this figure declined slightly to 10.5 percent in 2014, despite their notable growth, in terms of value, during the 2009–2014 period (Anuario Estadístico de Cuba [AEC] 2015).

Cuba's Emerging Agricultural Model

Agricultural Reforms: 2007–Present

Declining agricultural output and yields, falling labor productivity, high levels of inefficiency, the rising costs of food imports, and the deterioration of the merchandise trade balance have placed food production as one of the principal challenges confronting the Cuban economy (Hagelberg 2010). Cuba spent close to $1.9 billion on imported food and agricultural products in 2014, representing 13.6 percent of the country's total merchandise imports for that year (U.S. Department of Agriculture [USDA] 2015).

To address these challenges, transform its agricultural sector, and reduce its growing dependency on food imports, Cuba has implemented a series of economic reforms since 2007. These policy changes are an integral part of Cuba's efforts to make a gradual transition toward a new agricultural model. The most important reform policy measures include: moderate price reforms for selected agricultural products; the transfer of idle land to nonstate producers (e.g., cooperatives and individual farmers) in usufruct; the decentralization and consolidation of the state administrative apparatus in charge of agricultural policies; the decentralization of the commercialization of non-sugar agricultural products; and the provision of small bank credits and loans to nonstate agricultural producers.

Moderate Price Reforms

The initial steps to transform Cuban agriculture consisted of moderate price reforms for selected agricultural products introduced in 2007. During the first stage of this process, the state procurement agency, *Acopio*, increased the prices it paid milk producers as well as the percentage paid in convertible pesos per liter produced and delivered. *Acopio* also increased the prices paid to meat and poultry producers. The prices paid by *Acopio* for other agricultural products such as rice, meat, and poultry have increased significantly since 2007. For instance, rice prices increased from 1,931 Cuban pesos (CUP) per ton in 2007 to 6,304 CUP by the end of 2013 (Spadoni 2014). Similarly, the price paid by *Acopio* to agricultural producers for potatoes rose from 544 pesos per ton to 652 pesos per ton between 2007 and 2013 (Spadoni 2014); and the prices paid to milk and beef producers increased from 900 pesos per ton to 5,218 pesos per ton, and from 2,450 pesos per ton to 8,900 pesos per ton, respectively, during the same period (Spadoni 2014). Higher prices incentivized agricultural producers to improve their output deliveries (or sales) to *Acopio*, resulting in notable fuel savings and improved distribution to the state-operated retail store network (Nova González 2010).

Payments in convertible pesos (CUC), which are valued more highly than the CUP, to meat and poultry producers, introduced since 2007, have increased their purchasing power, allowing many of them to obtain essential agricultural inputs in recently created hard currency stores for this purpose (there are stores in 70 of the 168 existing municipalities). Unfortunately, these stores tend to offer a limited variety of inputs of about sixty-four products, supply has been unpredictable and unreliable, and prices tend to be relatively high. The increase in producers' incomes resulting from moderate price reforms introduced since 2007 have also contributed to notable improvements in producers' capacity to obtain essential inputs to further increase production (Nova González 2010). These measures constituted a direct stimulus to agricultural producers.

The approval of Resolutions 237, 238, and 239 in 2015 introduced another round of moderate price increases (for certain "fundamental" agricultural products) to stimulate production, improve the quality of agricultural products, reduce retail and wholesale prices, and eventually diminish Cuba's dependency on imported food products (Gaceta Oficial de Cuba No. 18 Extraordinaria 2015). The prices paid by *Acopio* for potatoes (collected in the fields) were raised from 45 to 65 pesos per quintal; the price paid for tomatoes increased from 100 pesos per quintal to 110 pesos per quintal; the price of beef was raised from 6 pesos and 50 cents per kilogram to 12 pesos per kilogram; the price paid for pork increased from 9,700 pesos per ton to 26,600 pesos per ton; and the price of cow milk was raised from 2 pesos per liter to 2.40 pesos per liter (Gaceta Oficial de Cuba 2015).

Transfers of Idle Land to Nonstate Agricultural Producers

Another important agricultural reform measure was the transfer of idle state-owned land (in usufruct) to cooperatives and usufruct farmers after the approval of Decree Law 259 in July 2008. Decree Law 259 incorporates some elements that were not taken into consideration in previous efforts to transform Cuban agriculture, such as the duration of transfers to natural persons (ten years, renewable leases, regardless of the type of crop harvested), and the transfers of land to legal entities such as cooperatives (Nova González 2010).

Article 15 (of Decree Law 259) stipulated that once the usufruct (or lease period) is finalized producers can receive payment or compensation from the state for *bienhechurias*, or infrastructure or physical improvements to the land and facilities used for production, with the exception of housing built by individual producers or cooperatives. This provision, however, reduced producers' incentive to make the investments required to run a successful operation and prevented them from permanently settling in their newly acquired lands (leased from the state). It also explains why most of the lease holders (or *usufructurarios*) consider themselves as transient (nonpermanent) producers. In reality, as Nova González (2008, 2010) indicates, the successful transformation of Cuba's agricultural sector requires the *recampesinización*, or the repopulation of the countryside; without significant and long-lasting increases in the quantity of farmers, technicians, and administrative and managerial personnel dedicated to agriculture, there is no guarantee and stability of a sustainable agricultural production (Nova González 2009, 2010).

The approval of Decree Law 300 in 2012 expanded the transfer of idle state-owned lands to nonstate producers (e.g., cooperatives and usufruct farmers) in usufruct. Decree Law 300 expanded the maximum number of hectares that could be transferred to nonstate producers (in usufruct) to 67.1; it also allows usufruct farmers operating under this new modality to become affiliated with cooperatives other than the Credit and Services Cooperatives (CCS). Under Decree Law 300 (2012), usufruct farmers can also associate themselves with Cooperatives of Agricultural Production (CPA) or Basic Units of Cooperative Production (UBPCs); in addition, they are allowed to use alternative channels to procure essential inputs and distribute their output, once delivery quotas with the state have been fulfilled (González-Corzo 2011).

Decentralization of Economic Decision-Making

The decentralization of economic decision-making and the restructuring of the ministries responsible for agricultural policies are key elements of Cuba's recent agricultural transformations. Cuba's emerging model of decentralized decision-making identifies the municipality as the principal actor responsible for making rational economic decisions and implementing the required strategies within its territorial boundaries. At the present time, each municipality has established a Municipal Delegation of Agriculture (169 in total), which is primarily responsible for managing the transfers of idle state-owned lands and state-owned livestock to the nonstate sector, to promote and stimulate the development of three "core" modalities of production: (1) urban agriculture; (2) suburban agriculture, which covers a span of about 10 km from the periphery of cities and urban centers; and (3) productive or conventional poles (Nova González 2010).

In 2010, the Ministry of the Economy and Planning (MEP) selected five municipalities to implement decentralized forms of economic management, focusing on import substitution, the generation of export earnings, and the food and employment problem (Nova González 2010). The MEP also implemented a series of internal reforms to consolidate and simplify the operations of the administrative entities involved in the production, distribution, and consumption of agricultural products. The first step in this direction was the unification of the Ministry of the Food Industry (*Ministerio de la Industria Alimenticia* (MINAL)) with the former Ministry of Fisheries after the approval of Decree Law 287 and Decree Law 294 in 2011.

Decree Law 287 transferred some of the functions of the Sugar Ministry (MINAZ) to the Ministry of Agriculture (MINAG) and to the MEP. The MINAG was assigned regulatory and supervisory functions such as managing land dedicated to sugar production, enforcing industrial and environmental regulations, and overseeing the commercialization of refined sugar and sugar derivatives. The MEP is currently responsible for managing state investments in the sugar sector, and the Ministry of Trade and Foreign Investment (MINCEX) is responsible for implementing export policies and managing foreign investment in agriculture. Decree Law 294 replaced the MINAZ with a holding company, *Grupo Azucarero AZCUBA*, a diversified holding company, comprised of twenty-five specialized subsidiaries, organized to manage sugar production and exports.

Decentralization of the Commercialization of Selected Agricultural Products

The approval of Agreement 6853 in 2010 authorized the commercialization (or trade) of agricultural products in roadside kiosks (or "points of sale") operated by agricultural cooperatives or state enterprises. Producers or their representatives are allowed to sell their excess output, after their quotas to the state have been met (Gaceta Oficial de Cuba 2010). They are required to pay taxes and/or fees for the use of these kiosks (or "points of sale) as stipulated by Resolution 206 issued by the Ministry of Prices and Finance. According to Resolution 206, sellers in the kiosks (or "points of sale") established by Agreement 6853 are required to pay a sales tax of 5 percent, based on their daily gross sales, plus a fee of 2 percent of the value of their reported gross sales for the use of the kiosks and related facilities, and self-employed workers (who work on these kiosks) are required to make social security contributions (González-Corzo 2013).

While the approval of Agreement 6853 in 2010 represents a step toward a more flexible system of agricultural commercialization, it contains several provisions that limit its potential. First, the entities that administer the kiosks (or "points of sale") are state-owned, which implies that the state will continue to play a significant role in the administration of these important sales venues. Second, producers that use these venues to commercialize their agricultural products must first fulfill their delivery quotas to the state at prices and amounts established by the latter. These conditions limit the autonomy of participants in the kiosks (or "points of sale") in terms of determining output prices and quantity, and are likely to contribute to imbalances between supply and demand.

The approval of Resolution 90 by the Central Bank of Cuba, Resolution 122 by the Ministry of Agriculture, Resolution 369 by the Ministry of Finance and Prices, and Resolution 121 by the Ministry of Tourism in 2011 provided the legal framework for greater decentralization in the commercialization of agricultural products. These policy measures facilitated the direct sale of selected agricultural products to tourism enterprises; authorized nonstate producers, such as cooperatives and usufruct farmers, to sell part of their output directly to such enterprises; and created a new entity, FINTOUR, S.A., to provide credit financing to tourism enterprises engaged in direct commercialization with participating agricultural producers (González-Corzo 2013).

Agricultural Credits for Nonstate Producers

The approval of Decree Law 289 and Resolution 99 in 2011 authorized the extension of agricultural credits (from state-owned banks) to nonstate agricultural producers. Decree Law 289 allowed self-employed workers and private farmers earning more than 50,000 Cuban pesos (CUP) to open a business account; it also eliminated the existing ceiling of 3,000 CUP on bank loans to natural persons, and eliminated the 100 convertible peso limits on payments by state-owned enterprises (SOES) to self-employed workers, who provided goods and services to SOES, on a contractual basis (González-Corzo 2013).

Resolution 99, approved by the Central Bank of Cuba in November 2011, authorized the extension of bank-based credit financing (up to 500 CUP) to nonstate agricultural producers (e.g., cooperatives and private farmers). Resolution 99 allows nonstate agricultural producers to obtain credit financing to purchase and repair equipment, procure inventory, and obtain other essential inputs, including the costs of replanting and reconditioning previously planted fields (González-Corzo 2013). Depending on the borrower's circumstances and the nature (or purpose) of the loan, it can be amortized using any source of income, for periods of eighteen to sixty months (González-Corzo 2013).

The "Guidelines" and the Party Congresses (2011–Present)

Cuba's gradual transition toward a new agricultural model was advanced by the ratification of the "Guidelines" (*Lineamientos de la Política del Partido y la Revolución*) after the Sixth Congress of the Communist Party on April 2011. As Nova González (2013) indicates, Cuban agriculture currently faces three unresolved issues: (1) the need to achieve the "realization of property";[2] (2) the need to recognize (and accept) the existence and role of the market; and (3) the inexistence of a systemic strategy through the productive cycle that would reflect its complex microeconomic and macroeconomic interrelations.

Several policies responses have been recommended and discussed to address or resolve these issues. These include: (1) the creation and development of input markets where agricultural producers can obtain essential inputs and supplies; (2) granting greater autonomy to agricultural producers, allowing them to decide how much output to produce, where to sell it, and whom to sell it to, based on market conditions and social requirements; (3) facilitating diverse forms of agricultural commercialization as an alternative to the state monopoly; (4) allowing agricultural producers to freely hire labor; and (5) providing new and existing agricultural producers with adequate financial and technical support (Nova González 2013b).

The Guidelines offer several proposals to address the three fundamental, unresolved issues confronted by Cuban agriculture. With regard to the creation of input markets where agricultural producers will be able to obtain essential inputs, the Guidelines indicate that such wholesale markets will be able to purchase or lease equipment, machinery, and other essential inputs, with the objective of increasing producer autonomy, limiting state intervention, and recognizing the participation of nonstate forms of production (Nova González 2013). In terms of prices, the Guidelines explicitly state that the state will retain full discretion over price regulations, and prices will be established according to the plan (i.e., prices will be centrally determined), taking into account the social and economic functions of the products and services for which prices will be centrally determined by the state (Nova González 2013). In essence, the Guidelines stipulated that prices will be centrally established in accordance with efforts to "update" the country's economic model (Nova González 2013).

The Guidelines also provided a framework for transforming the commercialization of agricultural products in Cuba. Article 183 proposed the transformation of the system of agricultural commercialization by simplifying the supply chain between producers and consumers, including the possibility of allowing producers to reach consumers through their own means (or resources) (i.e., via direct sales or commercialization) (Nova González 2013). Article 304 aimed to restructure retail and wholesale agricultural commerce through more flexible arrangements in order to simplify the linkages between producers and consumers, taking into account economic conditions and the diversification of production and property forms (Nova González 2013).

The Guidelines also included several provisions to increase producer autonomy with regard to hiring labor by considering the expansion of employment in the nonstate sector, as an alternative modality closely aligned with emerging production and property forms. In that respect, the Guidelines are closely synchronized with Resolution 32 and Resolution 33 of the Ministry of Labor and Social Security, which authorized a new form of self-employed agricultural worker and regulate labor hiring practices by cooperatives and self-employed workers (Nova González 2013).

Finally, with regard to providing new and existing agricultural producers with adequate financial support and training, Article 50 of the Guidelines identified the implementation of policies to support those activities that stimulate national production and the provision of bank credits to facilitate the expansion of the nonstate sector as its principal goals (Nova González 2013). Other policy objectives included applying a differentiated tax regime to stimulate agricultural production, the expansion of insurance programs to cover agricultural producers, and the development of specialized banking and financial services to meet their needs, including nonstate producers who received land in usufruct after the approval of Decree Law 259 in 2008 (Nova González 2013).

In 2013, as part of a gradual process to implement the Guidelines, and as part of its efforts to "update the economic model," the Cuban government introduced a new round of economic reforms. These reforms primarily focused on facilitating the expansion of agricultural sales to tourism enterprises, stimulating the direct commercialization of agricultural products, and restructuring the Ministry of Agriculture. The approval of Resolution 58 by the Ministry of Agriculture, Resolution 352 by the Ministry of Finance and Prices, and Resolution 37 by the Ministry of Tourism on September 2013 represented another step to facilitate the direct sales of agricultural products to tourism enterprises. These measures supplemented Resolution 122, which was approved in 2011. Their principal provisions included the authorization of direct sales in Cuban pesos (CUP) by all types of agricultural producers to tourism enterprises, without state intermediation, including individual (private) farmers, and the expansion of authorized products to include: fresh cut flowers, gardening services, floral arrangements, dry spices, and eggs. According to Resolution 9, prices can be directly determined by market participants. Resolution 9 also establishes the implementation of a "transaction fee" of 9 CUP for every convertible peso (CUC) generated from the direct sale of agricultural products to tourism enterprises (by all types of agricultural producers). In accordance with Decree Law 112 (2012), *Casa Financiera, S.A.* and other financial and banking institutions collected a 5 percent (sales) tax payment from tourism enterprises.

The approval of Decree Law 318 and Resolution 673 by the Ministry of Agriculture in 2013 authorized the creation, on an experimental basis, of nonagricultural cooperatives in some of the previous locations of the *Mercados Agropecuarios Estatales* (MAEs; State Agricultural Markets) in Havana, Artemisa, and Mayabeque provinces. These policy measures aim to decentralize the commercialization of agricultural products by facilitating the creation of *mercados de abastos* (wholesale markets), where agricultural producers and or authorized intermediaries can offer their products at wholesale prices. The approval of Decree Law 318 and Resolution 673 represents the implementation of *Lineamiento 181* (which basically proposed the alignment of supply and demand in agricultural markets) and *Lineamiento 183* (which focused on steps to improve the commercialization of agricultural products).[3] These measures were applied to all types of agricultural producers in the state and nonstate sectors, including a new category of intermediary officially labeled as *carretilleros* (street cart vendors).

Decree Law 318 and Resolution 673 authorized the creation of Provincial Administration Councils responsible for implementing and overseeing policies, determining the location of retail outlets and zones of operation for the *carretilleros*, and regulating direct sales of agricultural products to Centers of Social Consumption such as hospitals, schools, daycare centers, dinning commons (*comedores*), and so forth. Beef, fresh milk, coffee, selected honey products, tobacco, and cocoa are excluded. Potatoes are subject to "social consumption requirements" (defined by the state).[45] State producers (e.g., state farms and enterprises) are authorized to participate; the same applies to nonstate producers such as UBPCs, CPAs, CCSs, private farmers, and self-employed workers (a newly authorized producer category). Authorized agricultural products may be distributed in the following outlets: *Mercados Agropecuarios Estatales* (MAEs), *Mercados de Oferta y Demanda* (MOD), *Mercados Arrendados* (a newly created outlet-type leased by the state to nonstate producers), and *Puntos de Ventas* (stalls, or kiosks, located in neighborhoods, rest stops on the highway, etc.).[6]

In terms of prices, Decree Law 318 and Resolution 673 stipulate that retail prices will be set by the Ministry of Finance and Prices for fixed price products; however, producers that operate in MAEs that have been converted to nonagricultural cooperatives can set their own prices, with the approval of the Ministry of Finance and Prices. With respect to wholesale input markets, both policy measures stipulate that as an initial part of the experiment, some MAEs will be converted into *mercados de abastos*—located in the City of Havana only—which would allow enterprises and other entities to buy agricultural products directly from state and nonstate producers. Finally, cooperatives that participate in these markets are exempt from taxes for the first three months; self-employed workers can also participate, but receive a different tax treatment (as part of the efforts to prioritized cooperatives, which are considered a superior, and more socialized, property form).

The efforts to restructure the Ministry of Agriculture (MINAG) announced in early 2014 represent another important step toward a new (less centralized) agricultural model. These efforts are divided into three phases, which are still under implementation. The first phase consists of updating the MINAG budget system. Phase two considers the creation of Provincial Enterprises (*Empresas Provinciales*), and during phase three, it is expected that the Provincial and Municipal Administrative Councils will be phased out. The following measures are also planned: (1) transferring Provincial Enterprises to Provincial Administration; and (2) the consolidation of fifteen existing Agricultural Research Stations with similar institutions in the Ministry of Science, Technology, and the Environment.

Selected Performance Indicators: 2007–Present

While Cuba's goal to reduce its dependency on agricultural imports and achieve self-sufficiency in the production of non-sugar crops still remains unfulfilled, the agricultural reforms introduced in since 2007 have contributed to expansion of the nonstate sector in terms of its share of landownership. These policy measures have also contributed to higher output levels in some non-sugar crop categories, particularly by nonstate agricultural producers. This section briefly analyzes the evolution of several key agricultural indicators such as land distribution, area planted and under production, and physical output since the introduction of Cuba's (recent) agricultural reforms in 2007.

As expected, the share of Cuba's agricultural land held by the nonstate sector, which includes the Basic Units of Cooperative Production (*Unidades Básicas de Producción Cooperativa* [UBPC]), Cooperatives of Agricultural Production (*Cooperativas de Producción Agropecuaria* [CPA]), Credit and Services Cooperatives (*Cooperativas de Créditos y Servicios* [CCS]), and private farmers (*privados*), increased significantly since the onset of the agricultural reforms in 2007. The nonstate sector held 44.6 percent of the country's total surface, 46.3 percent of the agricultural land, and 76.8 percent of the land under cultivation. The relatively more autonomous CCS and private farmers held 28.6 percent of the total land surface held by the nonstate sector in 2007. The CCS held 59.4 percent and private farmers held 34.8 percent of the cultivated land in the nonstate sector in that year.

While the nonstate sector's share of the total land surface remained virtually unchanged (46 percent) in 2014, its share of the agricultural land and land under cultivation increased to 69.1 percent and 81.4 percent, respectively. Similarly, the share of nonstate land held by the CCS and private farmers also increased significantly during the 2007–2014 period. In 2014, the CCS and private farmers held 49.3 percent of the total land and 49.7 percent of the cultivated land in the non-state sector (see Table 5.2).

Between 2008 and 2015, the areas planted and under production increased in three out of the nine categories of non-sugar agricultural crops reported by the National Statistics Office as follows: *viandas* (5.8 percent),

Table 5.2 Cuban Land Distribution Based on Tenure Form, 2007 and 2014

2007		State		Non-State		
Thousand Hectares	Total	Total	Total	UBPC	CPA	CCS and Private
Total Land Surface	10,988.60	6,088.90	4,899.70	2,804.80	692.8	1,402.10
Agricultural Land	4,415.50	2,371.20	2,044.30	244.2	585.8	1,214.30
Cultivated Land	2,988.50	694.2	2,294.30	1,189.90	305.3	799.1
Noncultivated Land	3,631.00	1,677.00	1,954.00	1,258.30	280.5	415.2
Idle Land	1,232.80	627.2	605.6	465.4	73.4	66.8
2014		**State**		**Non-State**		
Thousand Hectares	Total	Total	Total	UBPC	CPA	CCS and Private
Total Land Surface	10,988.40	6,152.80	4,835.60	1,849.10	601.2	2,385.30
Agricultural Land	6,278.90	1,942.60	4,336.30	1,598.80	509.6	2,227.90
Cultivated Land	2,668.70	496.5	2,172.20	823	269.6	1,079.60
Noncultivated Land	3,610.20	1,446.10	2,164.10	775.8	240	1,148.30
Idle Land	n.a.	n.a.	n.a.	n.a.	n.a.	n.a.

Source: Oficina Nacional de Estadísticas e Informacíón (2016).

legumes (3.6 percent), and cocoa (6.8 percent). Conversely, during the same period, the areas planted and under production declined in the following crop categories, in which the state sector is the predominant producer: plantains (–4.0 percent), vegetables (–29.4 percent), tobacco (–18.9 percent), and citrus fruits (–69.6 percent) (Oficina Nacional de Estadísticas e Informacíón [ONEI] 2016).

Output in seven of the nine reported categories of (non-sugar) crops increased as follows during the 2008–2013 period: *viandas* (22.5 percent), plantains (17.4 percent), cereals (2.5 percent), legumes (20.9 percent), tobacco (14.0 percent), other fruits (27.6 percent), and cocoa (36.4 percent). These output levels, however, were significantly lower than in 1989, the last year before the onset of the "economic crisis of the 1990s" and the disintegration of the Socialist Camp and the Soviet Union in the early 1990s. By contrast, output declined in the following two non-sugar crop categories during the same period: vegetables (–9.6 percent) and citrus fruits (–70.6 percent) (see Table 5.3).

Table 5.3 Cuban Non-Sugar Agricultural Production, Selected Crops (Tons)

CROPS	2008	2009	2010	2011	2012	2013	2014	2015	% Chg.
Viandas[a]	2,150,700	2,236,000	2,250,000	2,280,000	2,337,000	2,239,000	2,507,056	2,633,618	22.5%
Roots and tubers	1,392,500	1,565,600	1,515,000	1,445,000	1,452,000	1,580,500	1,670,864	1,743,422	25.2%
Potato	196,100	278,600	191,500	165,600	130,933	106,700	53,308	123,938	–36.8%
Boniato	375,000	437,100	384,743	311,900	335,319	396,347	512,825	506,839	35.2%
Malanga	240,000	199,400	137,400	132,100	153,782	185,922	269,590	246,472	2.7%
Plantains	758,200	670,400	735,000	835,000	885,000	658,500	836,193	890,197	17.4%
Bananas	280,800	245,400	249,200	250,000	195,496	150,336	203,225	234,471	–16.5%
Plantains	477,400	425,000	485,800	585,000	689,504	508,164	632,967	655,726	37.4%
Vegetables	2,439,300	2,548,800	2,141,035	2,200,000	2,112,000	2,406,500	2,498,960	2,424,163	–0.6%
Tomato	575,900	750,000	517,040	601,000	557,100	678,000	454,112	551,007	–4.3%
Onions	128,100	131,300	111,737	143,500	118,244	126,876	112,779	107,181	–16.3%
Pepper	63,677	56,672	44,545	55,057	62,202	73,336	60,543	69,034	8.4%
Cereals	761,700	868,400	778,863	920,400	1,002,000	1,098,800	1,013,495	781,058	2.5%
Rice	436,000	563,600	454,400	566,400	641,600	672,600	584,800	418,036	–4.1%

Corn	325,700	304,800	324,463	354,000	360,400	426,200	428,695	363,022	11.5%
Legumes	97,200	110,800	80,439	133,000	127,100	129,800	135,545	117,556	20.9%
Beans	97,200	110,800	80,439	133,000	127,100	129,800	135,545	117,556	20.9%
Tobacco	21,500	25,200	20,500	19,900	19,500	24,000	19,800	24,500	14.0%
Citrus Fruits	391,800	418,000	345,000	264,500	203,700	166,900	96,810	115,384	–70.6%
Oranges	200,400	261,000	178,263	122,900	93,837	85,110	36,103	40,159	–80.0%
Grapefruit	166,100	121,500	137,660	112,000	84,741	63,979	41,421	56,268	–66.1%
Lemon	5,400	8,300	6,060	6,600	6,475	5,025	7,925	6,579	21.8%
Other Fruits	738,500	748,000	762,045	817,000	964,900	925,000	884,464	942,675	27.6%
Mangoes	228,700	269,300	203,595	185,000	286,385	285,526	177,834	260,076	13.7%
Guava	126,500	84,900	71,581	85,000	103,191	124,964	180,397	158,720	25.5%
Papaya	89,400	95,700	135,707	135,000	178,558	197,842	139,531	202,499	126.5%
Cocoa	1,100	1,387	1,709	1,510	2,027	1,425	2,188	1,500	36.4%

[a] Includes roots and tubers and plantains.

Source: Oficina Nacional de Estadísticas e Información (2016).

The fluctuations of physical agricultural output between 2008 and 2015 can be attributed to several factors, such as adverse weather conditions (e.g., drought, hurricanes), difficulties in obtaining essential agricultural inputs, existing limitations with regard to the "realization of property" (as discussed earlier), price controls, problems and inefficiencies related to the commercialization of agricultural products, insufficient warehousing and storage capacity, logistical difficulties associated with the transportation and cold storage of agricultural products, soil erosion and degradation, insufficient irrigation capabilities, and other administrative, organizational, and structural problems (Mesa-Lago 2012; Nova González 2013a; Spadoni 2014).

U.S.–Cuban Agricultural Trade: Evolution and Recent Trends

Cuba and the United States enjoyed strong economic ties before the 1959 Revolution. Close to 67 percent of Cuba's exports were destined for the U.S. market, and U.S. products accounted for 70 percent of the island's merchandise imports in 1958 (Ross 2004). Geographical proximity, close cultural and political ties, U.S. investment in strategic sectors of the Cuban economy, the structural characteristics of both countries' economies, and reduced transportation costs were among the principal reasons for close economic ties between Cuba and the United States in the 1950s.

Relations between the United States and Cuba deteriorated significantly after 1959. The United States ended diplomatic relations with the island in 1961, and it imposed a unilateral trade embargo in 1962, which severed economic ties between the two countries almost four decades. In 1963, the Cuban Assets Control Regulations was introduced under the Trading with the Enemy Act. Almost three decades later, in 1992, the U.S. Congress approved the Cuban Democracy Act, also known as the Torricelli Act, which tightened the U.S. embargo by limiting trade between foreign-based subsidiaries of U.S. multinational corporations and banning vessels that had docked in Cuban ports from docking in U.S. ports for a period of 180 days (Ross 2004).

The approval of the Cuban Liberty and Democratic Solidarity Act, also known as the Helms-Burton Act, in 1996 further tightened the U.S. embargo by requiring the U.S. president to prepare a plan for proving economic assistance to transition in Cuba, creating the legal mechanisms to sanction U.S. nationals who may be trafficking in confiscated property in Cuba, and by authorizing the U.S. government to deny visas and exclude from the United States persons who traffic in confiscated property claimed by U.S. nationals in Cuba (after 1996) (U.S. Department of the Treasury 2013). In 1999, U.S. President Bill Clinton approved changes in U.S. commercial policy toward Cuba, which allowed sales of U.S. food and agricultural products to private farmers; cooperatives; privately owned, small-scale restaurants known as *paladares*; and nongovernmental organizations (Ross 2004).

The intensification of U.S. economic sanctions, combined with the dissolution of the Socialist Camp (1989), and the disappearance of the Soviet Union (1991) dealt a severe blow to the Cuban economy, particularly its agricultural sector. As an agricultural producer, and despite incurring notable merchandise trade deficits, Cuba maintained positive agricultural trade balances during the 1990s. At the onset of the "Special Period" in 1990, Cuban agricultural exports, which consisted of food, live animals, beverages, tobacco, vegetable oil, and animal fat, totaled US$4.8 billion. However, the total value of agricultural exports, as well as total merchandise exports, declined notably after 1990 (see Table 5.4). This was mostly the result of the loss of its traditional "Socialist Bloc" export markets and the severe economic crisis resulting from the collapse of the Socialist Camp (Nova González 2006; Ritter 1994; Mesa-Lago 1993). In 1990, agricultural exports accounted for 87.5 percent of total merchandise exports; by 2002, this figure had declined to 53.2 percent (see Table 5.4).

The economic crisis of the 1990s also affected Cuba's capacity to import food and agricultural products. The value of agricultural imports declined quite notably during the most difficult years of the Special Period (1990–1993) and never recovered to 1990 levels. Cuba's agricultural production and trade were also impacted by natural disasters, particularly Hurricane Michelle in 2001, declining levels of investment, lower total factor productivity, insufficient inputs such as fertilizer and pesticides, and existing regulatory constraints and prohibitions (Comisión Económica Para América Latina y el Caribe 2000).

Table 5.4 Cuban Agricultural Trade, 1990–2002 (Thousands, USD)

Year	Imports			Exports			Trade Balance	
	Total Imports	Agricultural Imports	% of Total Imports	Total Exports	Agricultural Exports	% of Total Exports	Total Trade Balance	Agricultural Trade Balance
1990	7,416,525	903,799	12.20%	5,414,949	4,738,431	87.50%	–2,001,576	3,834,632
1991	4,233,752	879,035	20.80%	2,979,512	2,628,771	88.20%	–1,254,240	1,749,736
1992	2,314,916	530,247	22.90%	1,794,424	1,485,639	82.80%	–520,492	955,392
1993	2,008,215	496,521	24.70%	1,156,663	947,010	81.90%	–851,552	450,489
1994	2,016,821	491,378	24.40%	1,330,756	993,231	74.60%	–686,065	501,853
1995	2,882,530	651,086	22.60%	1,491,634	1,011,679	67.80%	–1,390,896	360,593
1996	3,568,997	763,986	21.40%	1,865,526	1,290,540	69.20%	–1,703,471	526,554
1997	3,987,256	800,511	20.10%	1,819,127	1,217,646	66.90%	–2,168,129	417,135
1998	4,181,192	777,438	18.60%	1,512,197	978,835	64.70%	–2,668,995	201,397
1999	4,349,090	818,864	18.80%	1,495,783	878,473	58.70%	–2,853,307	59,609
2000	4,795,613	744,167	15.50%	1,675,259	837,154	50.00%	–3,120,354	92,987
2001	4,793,235	823,553	17.20%	1,621,891	943,357	58.20%	–3,171,344	119,804
2002	4,129,453	793,631	19.20%	1,402,268	745,656	53.20%	–2,727,185	–47,975

Source: Ross, 2004, and authors' calculations.

Relaxing the Embargo through Agricultural Trade

In an effort to improve relations with Cuba and improve the lives of ordinary Cubans, President Bill Clinton signed the Trade Sanctions Reform and Export Enhancement Act (TSRA) into law in October 2000. The approval of the TSRA in October 2000 marked the beginning of a new era of U.S.-Cuba relations. Before the approval of the TSRA, the United States was virtually absent from the Cuban market; since then, despite existing Cold War tensions between the two countries, exports of U.S. agricultural and food products have turned the United States into one of Cuba's principal trading partners.

On December 17, 2014, President Barack Obama announced a series of "updated" U.S. policy measures toward Cuba, which took most observers by surprise, and shifted the U.S. approach toward the island from confrontation and isolation to calibrated engagement. One resilient aspect of Washington's updated Cuba policy since December 17, 2014, was its emphasis on facilitating the ability of U.S. economic actors (e.g., individuals, private firms, and organizations) to play a larger and more influential role in the expansion of Cuba's emerging nonstate sector. According to "Fact Sheet: Charting a New Course on Cuba," published by the White House on December 17, 2014, "(these) policy changes make it easier for Americans to provide business training for private Cuban businesses and small farmers, and provide other support for the growth of Cuba's nascent private sector." Furthermore, "additional options for promoting the growth of entrepreneurship and the private sector in Cuba will be explored."

To achieve these goals, the principal elements of this new U.S.-Cuba policy approach included:

1. The expansion of authorized travel by U.S. citizens to Cuba under twelve existing categories.
2. Facilitating remittances to Cuba by U.S. persons by increasing authorized remittances levels from $200 to $2,000 per quarter, eliminating specific license requirements for remittances to support the development of private businesses in Cuba, and no longer requiring remittances forwarding agencies to have a specific license.
3. Authorizing expanded commercial sales and exports from the United States of certain goods and services to empower the emergent nonstate sector in Cuba. (U.S. suppliers will be authorized to export

certain building materials for private residential construction, goods for use by private-sector Cuban entrepreneurs, and agricultural equipment for small farmers. The objective is to make it easier for ordinary Cuban citizens to have access to certain lower-priced goods to improve their living standards and gain greater economic independence from the state.)

4. Facilitating authorized transactions between the United States and Cuba by authorizing U.S. financial institutions to open correspondent accounts at Cuban financial institutions to facilitate the processing of authorized transactions, permitting the use of U.S. credit and debit cards by travelers to Cuba, and revising the definition of the statutory term "cash advance" to specify that it means "cash before transfer of title" in order to provide more efficient financing of authorized trade with Cuba.

On September 18, 2015, the U.S. Treasury Department and the Department of Commerce announced a series of (new) amendments to "further implement President Obama's 2014 announcement related to the easing of Cuba sanctions." The additional revisions to the Cuban Assets Control Regulations and Export Administration Regulations became effective on September 21, 2015, and include the following provisions to further facilitate travel to Cuba for authorized purposes: expand the telecommunications and internet-based services general licenses, authorize certain persons subject to U.S. jurisdiction (including individuals, entities, and organizations) to establish a business presence in Cuba (e.g., an office, branch, or other similar facility) to facilitate authorized transactions, allow certain U.S. persons to open bank accounts in Cuba, facilitate financial transactions, including remittances or transfers to provide financing for private businesses, authorize U.S. persons and entities to provide goods and services to Cuban nationals residing outside Cuba, and facilitate the expansion of authorized activities such as the provision of legal services, imports of gifts, and educational activities.

While there were a number of notable changes that resulted from the directives of 2015, much of the agricultural sector was still operating under the TSRA of 2000, which authorized the sale and export of certain food, medicines, and medical equipment to Cuba but strictly prohibited the import of agricultural products from Cuba. The TSRA also sanctioned the extension of credit financing to facilitate U.S. agricultural exports to Cuba and prohibited the provision of U.S. government programs to support exports to the island (American Society of International Law 2001). Even though the changes in U.S. policies toward Cuba implemented since December 17, 2014, opened a new chapter in diplomatic and commercial relations between the two nations, the U.S. trade embargo remains in place, and bilateral commerce between Cuba and the United States continues to operate under a series of constraints and limitations.

Despite these limitations, U.S. agricultural exports to Cuba have expanded significantly since 2001.

As Table 5.5 demonstrates, between 2001 and 2008, the total value of U.S. agricultural exports to Cuba increased from close to $5 million in 2001 to $685 million in 2008 (their peak year). U.S. agricultural exports to Cuba reached an average annual value of $320 during the 2001–2008 period. Cuban imports of U.S. agricultural and food products reached their peak in 2008; in that year, the United States accounted for nearly 33 percent of Cuba's agricultural and food imports. In 2008, the total value of Cuba's imports of agricultural and food products from the United States increased 59 percent, compared to 2007.

These trends can be attributed to several factors. In 2008, Cuba was affected by three major hurricanes, Ike, Gustav, and Paloma, resulting in significant losses in agricultural output and damaging a notable part of the infrastructure. According to Messina (2008), 3,414 tobacco curing barns were destroyed and 1,590 tobacco storage barns were damaged in Pinar del Rio Province. Poultry production was affected nationwide. Eighty percent of the banana and plantain plantations were knocked down by hurricane-force winds, representing an estimated 350,000 banana and plantains trees. An estimated 50 percent of the coffee plantations in Central Cuba and 100 percent of the coffee plantations in the eastern part of the country were destroyed (Messina 2008). Some 135,000 tons of citrus fruits were lost, and 10,000 hectares of vegetables and tubers were destroyed (Messina 2008).

Between 2007 and 2008, Cuba's agricultural output (for selected non-sugar crops) declined as follows: *viandas* (–9.2 percent), roots and tubers (or horticultural crops) (–6.3 percent), corn (–11.4 percent), tobacco: (–15.4 percent), and citrus fruits (–16.4 percent) (Messina 2008). However, the increase in the value of agricultural and food imports from the United States in 2008 was also driven by higher global agricultural commodity prices. In terms of volume, U.S. agricultural and food exports to Cuba

Table 5.5 U.S. Agricultural Exports to Cuba by Commodity or Product (Million USD)

Year	Total	Poultry & Products	Oilseeds & Products	Grains & Feeds	Dairy & Products	Horticultural Products	Cotton, Linters, & Waste	Livestock & Meats	Sugar & Tropical Products
2001	4,574	1,959	0	2,327	288	0	0	0	0
2002	139,814	23,713	61,952	51,879	336	1,067	0	721	146
2003	247,571	37,755	113,010	92,220	341	2,760	572	652	261
2004	383,870	62,192	89,421	186,733	28,951	10,218	2,922	1,999	1,085
2005	346,044	58,563	80,406	148,970	30,284	11,286	1,593	10,129	565
2006	320,847	44,480	89,609	128,392	13,156	23,858	395	15,408	149
2007	431,187	78,079	114,620	224,127	711	4,677	664	8,181	128
2008	685,453	139,431	141,170	369,367	15,665	4,727	1,855	13,198	40
2009	525,259	144,565	135,215	218,004	2,946	9,683	562	13,432	852
2010	349,303	108,919	83,692	127,049	2,645	9,812	0	16,070	1,116
2011	352,781	100,162	69,843	150,666	3,965	12,253	4,038	10,248	1,606
2012	459,477	160,494	104,128	171,449	5,632	4,974	3,116	9,495	189
2013	350,150	146,188	108,740	82,681	2,473	996	0	9,072	0
2014	286,428	147,787	97,906	37,639	1,415	367	0	1,314	0
2015	148,818	77,758	65,437	4,944	412	267	0	0	0

Source: U.S. Department of Agriculture (USDA), Global Agricultural Trade. System GATS 2016.

grew 11 percent between 2007 and 2008, compared to the aforementioned growth rate of 59 percent in terms of value.

The value of U.S. agricultural exports to Cuba has declined significantly since 2008 (see Table 5.5). These trends can be attributed to several economic, political, and strategic factors. In 2007, Cuba's state-owned agricultural and food importing agency, ALIMPORT, notified the U.S. government that it would substantially reduce purchases from U.S.-based companies due to a lack of effort by U.S.-based companies in obtaining changes in U.S. policies and regulations pertaining to agricultural exports to the Island (Economic Eye on Cuba, December 2015). U.S. agricultural and food exports to Cuba during the 2009–2015 period were also hindered by the Cuban economy's limited ability to generate the foreign exchange receipts (or hard currency) necessary to pay for higher volumes of U.S. agricultural and food products in cash. The direct financial support (in the form of favorable terms of credit, subsidies, etc.) offered by Cuba's principal trading partners—such as Venezuela, China, Brazil, and Vietnam, as well as Canada, the European Union, and Mexico—also contributed to the decline of U.S. agricultural and food exports to the Cuba during the 2009–2014 period. U.S. agricultural sales to Cuba during this period were also impacted by the Cuban government's decision to give preference to purchases (and imports) from state-owned enterprises from countries with closer diplomatic and economic ties with the island.

In terms of specific commodities or product categories, it is worth noting that the rankings (as percentages of the total) of U.S. agricultural exports to Cuba have fluctuated notably since 2001. As Table 5.5 indicates, between 2004 and 2012, grains and feeds represented the largest category, in terms of value, followed by poultry, oilseeds, livestock and meats, dairy products, horticultural products, sugar, tropical products, and seeds. Corn, wheat, and rice accounted for the bulk of U.S. grains and feeds exports to Cuba during the 2001–2008 period. While corn exports have increased substantially since 2001, wheat and rice exports have declined since 2008. U.S. rice exports to Cuba have basically disappeared since 2008 due to increased competition from Vietnam, which has replaced the United States as Cuba's principal rice supplier. Increased wheat imports from Canada and the European Union have displaced U.S. wheat exports since 2010.

In the poultry category, broiler meat and turkey exports to Cuba have grown significantly since 2001. U.S. exports represent an estimated 80 percent of total Cuban poultry imports, and poultry and poultry products (mainly broiler meat) accounted for 52.2 percent of the total value of U.S. agricultural and food exports in 2015 (Table 5.5). The relative importance of U.S. poultry and poultry products as a share of Cuba's agricultural and food imports can be primarily attributed to three principal factors: (1) increases in the demand for poultry as a principal source of protein; (2) the competitive advantage enjoyed by U.S. producers; and (3) the inability of Cuban producers to meet national demand. Increases in household incomes associated with the expansion of self-employment in the nonstate sector since 2010 also contributed to higher demand for agricultural and food imports. U.S. exports of oilseeds, particularly soybean cake and meals, as well as soybeans, have also increased notably since 2001. Soybean patties, *picadillo de soya*, have emerged as one of the principal sources of protein distributed to the Cuban population (at subsidized prices) through a rationing system since 2002. In 2002, U.S. soybean exports to Cuba were valued at $62 million, accounting for 44 percent of the total value of U.S. agricultural exports to the Island. While its share of the total value of U.S. agricultural and food exports to Cuba remained unchanged at 44 percent, the value of soybean exports increased 5.5 percent to $65.4 million in 2015 (Table 5.5).

U.S. exports of dairy and dairy products to Cuba have increased significantly since 2001; their share of the total value of U.S. agricultural and food exports to the island has experienced notable variations, particularly between 2004 and 2008. As Table 5.5 illustrates, exports of nonfat dry milk accounted for a large share of total U.S. dairy exports to Cuba during this period. Exports of nonfat dry milk represented 92 percent of U.S. dairy exports to Cuba in 2004, 98 percent in 2005, 95 percent in 2006, 0 percent in 2007, 85 percent in 2008, 0 percent in 2009, and 18 percent in 2010, the last year in which Cuba imported nonfat dry milk from the United States (see Table 5.5).

U.S. exports of livestock and meats to Cuba have also increased significantly since 2001. Livestock and meats exports accounted for a significant share of the total value of U.S. agricultural and food exports to Cuba during the 2004–2013 period, but have declined since 2014 (Table 5.5). Historically, pork has dominated this category. Pork exports represented 73.7 percent of the total value of U.S. livestock and meats exports to Cuba in 2002; this figure reached its peak of 92 percent in 2011 and 2012, primarily due to pent-up demand, insufficient domestic production, and higher world prices. By 2013, the value of pork exports to Cuba as a percentage of the total value of U.S. agricultural and food exports declined to 54 percent, and, by 2015, U.S. pork exports had basically disappeared as domestic production recovered and imports from other countries increased.

Even though U.S. agricultural and food exports to Cuba have increased substantially since the approval of the TSRA of 2000, the U.S. share of Cuba's total agricultural and food imports has declined significantly since 2008. In 2008, imports from the U.S. represented 33 percent of Cuba's total agricultural and food imports, in terms of dollar value (see Table 5.6, below). This figure declined to 15.2 percent in 2014. By contrast, imports from the European Union accounted for 8.5 percent of the total in 2008, but increased to 23.1 percent in 2014. Agricultural and food imports from Brazil increased slightly, from 16 percent of the total in 2008 to 18 percent in 2015. Similarly, imports from the rest of the world increased from 42.6 percent to 43.6 percent during the same period (Table 5.6).

Future Prospects

Even though it accounts for approximately 5 percent of GDP, through its strong linkages with other sectors and positive "spillover effects," agriculture plays a significant role in the Cuban economy (Nova González 2013a). Cuba's agricultural sector is an important source of employment, a major consumer of raw materials, intermediate, and finished goods, and one of the country's principal generators of renewable energy (Nova González 2008). Since the economic crisis of the 1990s, due to the disappearance of the Eastern European Socialist Bloc and the former Soviet Union, Cuban agriculture has been affected by declining production levels, higher external sector dependency, and increased hard currency expenditures to finance growing agricultural imports (Nova González 2013a; González-Corzo and Nova González 2013).

Since 2007, the Cuban government has implemented a series of economic transformations to increase domestic agricultural production and reduced the country's dependency on agricultural imports and is food and agricultural vulnerability. These include moderate price reforms, transfers of idle state-owned lands (in usufruct) to nonstate producers, moderate price reforms, the decentralization of decision-making and the commercialization of selected agricultural products, the consolidation of several ministries responsible for agricultural policies and regulation, and the provision of small agricultural credits to nonstate producers (Mesa-Lago 2012;

Table 5.6 Cuban Agricultural Imports by Region, 2001–2014 (Million USD)

Year	United States	European Union	Brazil	Rest of the World	Total
2001	5	217	57	310	589
2002	140	193	37	279	649
2003	248	224	23	257	752
2004	384	149	58	379	970
2005	346	154	103	516	1119
2006	321	153	141	455	1070
2007	431	165	171	620	1387
2008	685	176	330	885	2076
2009	525	149	166	473	1313
2010	349	246	288	618	1501
2011	353	338	385	710	1786
2012	459	348	377	504	1688
2013	350	369	326	812	1857
2014	286	434	340	820	1880
		AVERAGES			
Average (2001–2014)	349	237	200	546	1331
Average (2001–2008)	320	179	115	463	1077
Average (2009–2014)	387	314	314	656	1671
		SHARE OF THE TOTAL (%)			
Year	United States	European Union	Brazil	Rest of the World	Total
2001	0.80%	36.80%	9.70%	52.60%	100.00%
2002	21.60%	29.70%	5.70%	43.00%	100.00%
2003	33.00%	29.80%	3.10%	34.20%	100.00%
2004	39.60%	15.40%	6.00%	39.10%	100.00%
2005	30.90%	13.80%	9.20%	46.10%	100.00%
2006	30.00%	14.30%	13.20%	42.50%	100.00%
2007	31.10%	11.90%	12.30%	44.70%	100.00%
2008	33.00%	8.50%	15.90%	42.60%	100.00%
2009	40.00%	11.30%	12.60%	36.00%	100.00%
2010	23.30%	16.40%	19.20%	41.20%	100.00%
2011	19.80%	18.90%	21.60%	39.80%	100.00%
2012	27.20%	20.60%	22.30%	29.90%	100.00%
2013	18.80%	19.90%	17.60%	43.70%	100.00%
2014	15.20%	23.10%	18.10%	43.60%	100.00%

Source: USDA/GATS (2016), and authors' calculations.

Spadoni 2014). So far, the most significant of these reform measures has been the transfer (in usufruct) of idle state-owned lands to cooperatives and usufruct farmers after the approval of Decree Law 259 in 2008 and Decree Law 300 in 2012 (Nova González 2013a).

Official statistics suggest that these reform measures have (thus far) produced mixed results (recall Tables 5.2, 5.3, and 5.4). Using 2008–2015 data, we conducted a simple linear regression to analyze the relationship between agricultural production (the dependent variable) and the area planted and under production (the independent variable). Our analysis produced a correlation coefficient (R^2) of 0.774, suggesting a strong (positive) linear relationship between these two variables. Our regression results also showed a coefficient of correlation (R^2) of 0.599, indicating that close to 60 percent of the variation of the dependent variable (i.e., agricultural production) around the mean can be explained by the variation in independent variable (i.e., the area planted and under production). Our findings, which were statistically significant ($p < .05$), also suggest that one of the measurable effects of Cuba's recent agricultural reforms appears to the reallocation of agricultural land to the production of selected crop categories, as the country advances toward a new agricultural model.

Existing material, regulatory, and financial constraints have limited the effectiveness of Cuba's recent agricultural reforms and its efforts to achieve agricultural and food self-sufficiency. This represents an opportunity for expanded U.S. agricultural and food exports to Cuba. Given their similarities, in terms of demographics and per capita incomes, a comparison of U.S. agricultural exports to the Dominican Republic and Cuba during the 2012–2014 period provides a useful method to estimate the potential for U.S. agricultural and food exports to Cuba under a scenario of normalized trade.

Table 5.7, below, highlights several important differences and similarities between U.S. agricultural exports to Cuba and the Dominican Republic, which can have meaningful implications for the prospects of U.S. agricultural trade with Cuba, if relations between the two countries were normalized. While grains and feeds represent a significant share of U.S. agricultural exports to both countries during the 2012–2014 period, it is worth noting (as mentioned earlier) that wheat exports are an important component of this category in the cased of the Dominican Republic, but in the case of Cuba are virtually inexistent. Corn represented 75 percent of Cuba's grains and feeds imports from the United States during this period, indicating that under normalized trade relations U.S. wheat exports to Cuba can potentially gain market share (Table 5.7).

Animals and animal products are another important category of U.S. agricultural exports to Cuba and the Dominican Republic, with chicken and pork accounting for significant shares of the total, both in terms of value and volume (Table 5.7). However, there are notable differences between Cuba and the Dominican Republic in this category that underscore potential opportunities for higher U.S. exports to Cuba under normal trading conditions. For instance, as Table 5.7 indicates, beef and veal represented 17.3 percent of total U.S. agricultural exports to the Dominican Republic between 2012 and 2014, compared to less than 1 percent in the case of Cuba. Given Cuba's insufficient beef production levels, the deteriorated condition of its beef cattle herd, the likelihood of increased domestic demand for beef as more Cubans join the emerging nonstate sector, and the comparative advantages enjoyed by U.S. beef producers, the Cuban market is likely to provide U.S. beef producers with opportunities to expand their market share.

Turkey meat and nonfat dry milk are other important categories of animal and animal products in which U.S. exporters and producers can potentially expand their Cuban market share under normalized trade. Recall, as noted in Table 5.7 earlier in this chapter, turkey and nonfat dry milk represented 4.6 percent and 12 percent, respectively, of the average annual value of U.S. animal and animal products exports to the Dominican Republic between 2012 and 2014. In the case of Cuba, by contrast, turkey accounted for a mere 0.68 percent of the average annual value of U.S. exports of animal and animal products during the 2012–2014 period, and nonfat dry milk exports virtually disappeared.

Another category in which U.S. exports can potentially increase their Cuban market share is oilseeds and oilseed products. Table 5.7 shows that in the case of the Dominican Republic soybean meal and soybean oil account for the bulk of U.S. exports of oilseeds and oilseed products. Similarly, in the case of Cuba, soybean meal and soybeans are the principal commodities imported from the United States in the oilseeds and oilseed products category. However, as Table 5.7 demonstrates, when compared to Cuba, the volume of U.S. exports of oilseeds and oilseed products to the Dominican Republic is significantly larger, suggesting the possibility of increased U.S. market share under normalized trade.

Table 5.7 U.S. Agricultural Exports to the Dominican Republic and Cuba (Annual Averages, 2012–2014)

	Exports to the Dominican Republic, Value (Thousands USD)	Exports to Cuba Value (Thousands USD)
Total	1,149.64	365.255
Animal and animal products	233.699	161.192
Beef and veal	40.351	0.041
Pork	40.7	4.331
Chicken meat (fresh or frozen)	21.156	148.925
Turkey meat (fresh or frozen)	10.84	1.112
Nonfat dry milk	28.131	0
Cheese	19.961	0
Other animal and animal products	72.56	6.783
Grains and feeds	331.272	97.257
Wheat (unmilled)	158.847	0
Corn	67.43	72.869
Prepared foods (cereals, cereal products)	35.828	0
Brewing or distilling dregs or waste	0.271	14.055
Mixed feeds	1.469	10.279
Other grains and feeds	67.427	0.054
Fruits and preparations	34.322	0.973
Apples (fresh)	15.363	0.104
Other fruits and preparations	18.959	0.869
Fruit Juices	13.029	0.015
Vegetables and preparations	46.85	0.09
Dried beans	24.302	0
Other vegetables and preparations	22.548	0.09
Oilseeds and products	292.231	103.584
Soybean meal	186.78	59.371
Soybean oil	64.918	0
Soybeans	0.345	44.083
Other oilseeds and products	40.188	0.13
Tobacco (unmanufactured)	89.898	0
Essential oils	10.315	0
Sugar and tropical products	20.337	0.063
Other horticultural products	50.553	1.029
Other agricultural exports	27.137	1.052

Source: Zahniser et. al. 2015.

The normalization of agricultural trade between the United States and Cuba also offers the potential for U.S. rice producers to gain market share (McMinimy 2015). Cuba has the highest rice consumption per capita in the Western Hemisphere, but at the present time, it imports close to 50 percent of its annual rice consumption, estimated at 435,000 tons (Zahniser et al. 2015). Vietnam supplies close to 70 percent of Cuba's rice imports, and the remaining 30 percent is imported from Brazil (Zahniser et al. 2015). Cuba's dependency on rice imports has been caused in part by insufficient production, mainly caused by insufficient access to essential inputs, difficulties in commercialization, supply-chain constraints, and adverse climatic events (e.g., droughts and hurricanes).

In 2014, rice output reached 423,000 tons (milled basis), representing an increase of 18 percent from the production levels reached during the 2000–2001 harvest (Zahniser et al. 2015). Since 2010, the area dedicated to rice production has averaged 203,000 hectares annually, compared to 144,000 hectares during the previous five year period (Zahniser et al. 2015). However, compared to other rice producers in the Western Hemisphere, Cuban rice production suffers from relatively low yields. Between 2009 and 2014, Cuba's rice yield averaged an estimated 2.8 metric tons per hectare, compared to 4.7 per hectare in the Dominican Republic, 4.4 per hectare in Nicaragua, and 3.5 per hectare in Costa Rica (Zahniser et al. 2015).

Cuba's relatively high per capita rice consumption and its inability to satisfy domestic demand provide a potential opportunity for increased U.S. market share (McMinimy 2015). It is estimated that, under normal trade relations, U.S. rice producers can gain 20 percent to 30 percent of the Cuban rice market, representing between 90,000 and 135,000 metric tons, valued between $40 million and $60 million (McMinimy 2015). However, the potential gains for U.S. agricultural producers resulting from normalized relations with Cuba extend beyond rice and the principal agricultural products highlighted in Table 5.7. The total value of U.S. agricultural exports to Cuba could potentially reach $1.2 billion annual, within five years after the elimination of existing financing and travel restrictions, placing Cuba at a similar level as the Dominican Republic as a destination for U.S. agricultural exports (McMinimy 2015).

At the present time, despite the policy changes announced by the United States in December 2014 and in September 2015, the prospects for increased U.S. market share of Cuban agricultural imports are hindered by several limiting factors. Prohibitions on credit financing for U.S. exporters limit their ability to obtain financing to expand their sales of agricultural products to Cuba. Restrictions against U.S. government support programs for U.S. exporters conducting business in Cuba limit their ability to participate in government support programs (e.g., the Market Support Program and other technical and financial assistance programs offered by the U.S. Department of Agriculture, and other branches of the U.S. government), direct payments to farmers or agricultural producers, price supports through government purchases and store, subsidies for crop insurance, export subsidies, and so forth. Current prohibitions regarding U.S. tourists and visitors to Cuba have a constraining effect on Cuba's demand for agricultural imports, thereby, reducing the potential size of the market (and hence the market share of U.S. agricultural producers). Finally, the existing general ban on U.S. merchandise imports from Cuba limits the ability of Cuban producers to generate the necessary foreign exchange receipts to purchase U.S. agricultural products and agricultural inputs.

The Cuban economy also faces several barriers that limit its ability to (substantially) increase agricultural imports from the United States. The most significant include: (1) its limited ability to generate (or earn) hard currency to pay for agricultural imports (in cash); (2) existing regulations requiring all U.S. agricultural imports to be processed through state-run ALIMPORT; (3) the relatively low (real) purchasing power of Cuban households and individuals; and (4) existing limitations on foreign direct investment in Cuba's agricultural sector.

From the U.S. perspective, several policy measures could be implemented to facilitate the expansion of U.S. agricultural exports to Cuba. A potentially beneficial initial step should be the elimination of existing restrictions on U.S. travel and tourism with regard to Cuba. Given the geographic proximity between both countries, the relatively high quality of U.S. agricultural products, and the comparative advantage enjoyed by U.S. producers, increased U.S. tourism to Cuba is likely to contribute to notable increases in Cuba's demand for U.S. agricultural imports.

The authorization and expansion of direct banking and financial services between U.S. and Cuban institutions, and the provision of credit financing for U.S. exporters doing business in Cuba is another important step toward the normalization of agricultural trade. To influence Cuban demand for U.S. agricultural products and inputs, thereby contributing to the expansion of U.S. agricultural exports to the island, Cuban merchandise and service exports to the United States should be allowed. This will likely provide export-oriented Cuban enterprises, production cooperatives, and privately owned small and medium-sized enterprises with opportunities to enter the lucrative U.S. market and earn the necessary hard currency to finance their purchases of U.S. capital goods, finished products, and services—including agricultural inputs, technology, and technical support services.

Under a possible scenario of normal trade relations, increased bilateral trade between Cuba and the United States offers an attractive potential for both countries. Normalized bilateral trade relations between the two countries offers several key benefits for U.S. agricultural exporters wishing to increase their share of the Cuban market. The United States enjoys a clear geographical advantage compared to other competing suppliers of agricultural goods. Increases in U.S. tourists and visitors to Cuba, as well as increases in Cuban household incomes due to the expansion of the nonstate sector, could potentially drive up demand for U.S. agricultural products such as: pork, poultry, meat products, and processed foods. Given the competitive advantage enjoyed by U.S. producers and their geographic and logistical advantages, some additional agricultural products in which their Cuban market share can potentially increase also include: rice, dairy products, grains, grain feeds, and soy-related products.

Barring any drastic policy reversals in Cuba, the reduction, and eventual elimination, of existing U.S. restrictions will likely have a positive impact on U.S. agricultural exports to the island. As Cuba continues to "update" its economic model through the reduction of the excessive state paternalism of the past, increased economic decentralization, and the implementation of market-oriented economic reforms, the nonstate sector's share of the economy is likely to increase. The expansion of the nonstate sector is expected to result in higher household income (at least for some sectors of the Cuban economy) (Kornai 2008). This will increase the country's demand for imported food, agricultural products, and essential agricultural inputs such as fertilizers, equipment, and machinery. The expansion of international tourism, including American visitors in the not-too-distant future, would also contribute to increases in Cuba's demand for food and agricultural imports, providing U.S. producers with a unique opportunity to further penetrate and expand their market share in the Cuban market.

Notes

1. Cuba employs a dual currency regime, the CUP (peso) and CUC (convertible peso). Both are called pesos but the CUP is a currency that is used by Cuban nationals while the CUC (convertible peso) is used by tourists and is valued at a higher rate than the CUP (peso). This system means that goods and services can br priced in CUP or CUC with the intent of maintaining affordable consumer goods for Cuban nationals .
2. The concept of the "realization of property" refers to the right of producers to have complete autonomy in determining output levels, choosing the final destination of their output, and determining its price; and having the ability to directly access input markets to obtain the essential inputs to close the productive cycle (Nova González 2013).
3. The term *Lineamientos* refers to the *Lineamientos de la Política Económica y Social del Partido y la Revolución*—or the "Social and Economic Guidelines of the Party and the Revolution" (commonly referred to as the Guidelines)—approved by the Sixth Congress of the Communist Party of Cuba on April 18, 2011. The Guidelines are the framework that broadly delineates Cuba's economic policies since the Sixth Party Congress.
4. Social consumption refers to the portion of agricultural output subsidized by the state and allocated to centers of "social consumption," such as hospitals, schools, and work places.
5. Social consumption refers to the portion of agricultural output subsidized by the state and allocated to centers of "social consumption," such as hospitals, schools, and work places.
6. The retail agricultural outlets operated by the Youth Work Army are excluded from Decree Law 318, and will continue to operate as in the past.

6

Between the "Party Line" and the "Bottom Line"[1]

El Proyecto Artecorte and the Virtuous Circle of Entrepreneurial Solidarity in One Old Havana Neighborhood

Ted A. Henken[*,2]

> I realize I'm not going to solve all of the world's problems. But if I can solve problems in the little piece of the world where I live, *it can ripple across Havana.*
>
> —Gilberto "Papito" Valladares, Cuban social entrepreneur and *cuentapropista*, as quoted by President Barack Obama, March 22, 2016 (emphasis added)

Introduction: Self-Employed but in "Solidarity"

On March 22, 2016, during his historic visit to Cuba, President Barack Obama celebrated the accomplishments of Cuban entrepreneurs on both sides of the Florida Straits during his remarks to the Cuban people delivered from the stage of Havana's Alicia Alonso Theater. "In a global economy, powered by ideas and information, a country's greatest asset is its people," he argued. "In the United States," he added, "we have a clear monument to what the Cuban people can build: it's called Miami." Obama

* Ted A. Henken, Baruch College, City University of New York, YumaTed@gmail.com.

The Cuba-U.S. Bilateral Relationship. Michael J. Kelly, Erika Moreno, and Richard C. Witmer, II.

then pivoted from this celebration of Cuban-American ingenuity to make a similar point about the well-known "resolve" and "inventiveness" of Cubans on the island. "Here in Havana, we see that same talent in *cuentapropistas*, cooperatives, and old cars that still run."

Obama then publicly celebrated the pioneering work of Cuban social entrepreneur Gilberto "Papito" Valladares, a man who until that moment was largely unknown even in Cuba outside of his own small Old Havana neighborhood, Santo Ángel. "Look at Papito," Obama recommended, "a barber, whose success allowed him to improve conditions in his neighborhood." Highlighting Papito's own philosophy of local enterprise development and social responsibility, Obama went on to quote the barber's own words: "I realize I'm not going to solve all of the world's problems. But if I can solve problems in the little piece of the world where I live, *it can ripple across Havana*" (emphasis added). He concluded by holding up Papito's hopeful example of what the barber himself has described as a community project of "entrepreneurial solidarity,"[3] arguing that it was in line with his administration's own historic shift toward entrepreneurial engagement and empowerment. "That's why our policies focus on supporting Cubans," he insisted, "instead of hurting them."

Most past studies of Cuban entrepreneurship (referred to by the Cuban government as *trabajo por cuenta propia* or "self-employment")[4] to date have focused either on a single industry or set of industries (such as private *paladar* restaurants, bed and breakfasts, or shoe manufacturing) (Henken 2002; Jackiewicz and Bolster 2003; Taylor and Zuberi 2015; Ritter and Henken 2015; Mulet Concepción 2016; Henken and Vignoli 2017), on state policies applied to the sector broadly across the entire island (Peters 2012; Vidal Alejandro and Pérez-Villanueva 2010, 2012; González-Corzo and Justo 2014; Henken and Vignoli 2016; Feinberg 2016; Scarpaci, Henken, and Ritter 2016), or on the experiences and opinions of a cross-section of *cuentapropistas* themselves (Mesa-Lago et al. 2018). Likewise, these studies have largely understood this emergent economic sector as Cuba's very limited, homegrown version of what would simply be considered private enterprise in other contexts.

In contrast, this chapter describes and analyzes one of the relatively underexplored potentialities of Cuba's emergent private enterprise sector: that which Papito, cited above, calls "entrepreneurial solidarity" (*emprendimiento solidario*) and has alternatively been labeled "social entrepreneurship," the "social and solidarity economy," or "socially responsible enterprise"[5] by the handful of scholars who have studied its emergence within Cuba's unique sociopolitical context (Betancourt and Sagebien 2013; Betancourt 2014, 2015, 2016, and 2017; Cuba Posible and D'Angelo 2016; D'Angelo 2012, 2016a, and 2016b; Sagebien and Betancourt 2014; Sagebien and Leenson 2015; SRELDC 2013). Most simply, these overlapping terms go beyond a singular focus on the financial bottom line and include the social outcomes and environmental impacts of economic activity in their definition of entrepreneurial "success." They also factor different forms of "sustainability" into their business models and typically seek to alter the standard top-down management culture of private enterprise making it more participatory, collaborative, and democratic.

This chapter investigates this topic thorough a case study approach that focuses on a single Old Havana neighborhood (Santo Ángel), tracing the efforts of Papito Valladares's grassroots community project there (*El Proyecto de Desarrollo Integral Comunitario Artecorte*, hereafter simply *Artecorte*) to marry: (1) economic development (via private entrepreneurship as a licensed *cuentapropista*) with (2) social responsibility (via a variety of community development initiatives) and (3) cultural preservation (through an important alliance with Office of the City Historian). In short, *Artecorte* embraces an ethic of contagion over competition, combining bottom-line-oriented private enterprise with neighborhood uplift, community outreach, and collaborative synergy—alternately independent from or in sync (and occasional partnership) with the government's "party line." Given the unique, even unprecedented nature, strategy, and success of *Artecorte*, this chapter seeks to uncover the lessons that the project can teach other community-based entrepreneurial initiatives on the island, questioning how sustainable and broadly replicable it is given the special circumstances of its origins and development and the unique charisma of its founder and special connections of its key institutional sponsor (IPS 2017; Cuba Posible and D'Angelo 2016).

Entrepreneurship, Social Entrepreneurship, and Socially Responsible Enterprise

Before exploring the concepts of social entrepreneurship and socially responsible enterprise, a brief comment on the concept and nature of entrepreneurship itself—and its role in the process of development—is appropriate. In 1730, Richard Cantillion coined the term "entrepreneur" to identify the unique risk-bearing role that freelancers play in economic development. To the idea of risk, other theorists added a uniting, coordinating, organizing, and supervising function (Say 1847). In this sense, an entrepreneur is one who combines various inputs (such as land, labor, and capital) in order to produce a product, retaining the profit as a reward. Joseph Schumpeter (1974) expanded our understanding of entrepreneurship further by stressing the innovative role of the entrepreneur as a "creative destroyer" leading to economic growth and development (Brouwer 2002; Wu 2011).

The contribution of entrepreneurship to the process of economic development is clear from the above description. Entrepreneurs are a dynamic force in an economy, envisioning the possibilities of new types of economic activity and doing everything necessary to put into effect their visions. As a result, entrepreneurs give birth to new enterprises, new economic activities, and new sectors in an economy. They promote the process of learning and adapting to changing circumstances as technology changes, as markets evolve, and as policies change. Presumably, an entrepreneur can operate in any arena of human endeavor. More often, however, the entrepreneur is understood to be the essential motor, idea generator, efficiency ensurer, and "connective tissue" in the economic realm. Of course, the concept *social* entrepreneurship takes these same traits and activities and applies them beyond an exclusively economic realm that includes what has been called the "triple bottom line" of financial, social, and environmental development (Betancourt and Sagebien 2013; Betancourt 2016).

The foregoing depiction of entrepreneurship is all positive. However, for entrepreneurship to operate in this type of constructive, pro-developmental way, the proper institutional environment (a system of laws, a regulatory environment, and basic political and economic stability) has to exist. In pathological circumstances—in the absence of law and order, a reasonable judicial system, and political stability, or in a context where economic monopolies (state or private) and corruption predominate—entrepreneurship may become deformed, criminalized, or simply impossible. In systems with vast and complex regulations and restrictions, entrepreneurs may become preoccupied with "rent-seeking" of various sorts, all of them relatively unproductive, and they may dissipate their entrepreneurial energies in endless bureaucratic maneuvering and red-tape manipulation. When law and order break down or when government policy makes entrepreneurial activities illegal or stigmatizes them as illegitimate,[6] entrepreneurship may be forced underground and become criminalized through mafia-like racketeering organizations or through official corruption. Therefore, entrepreneurship alone is a necessary but insufficient factor in the generation of economic development. Instead, it must operate within a supportive, legal, and orderly institutional and regulatory environment.[7]

Clearly, such a supportive environment did not exist in Cuba before Raúl Castro became president in 2008, after which he kicked off a series of era-defining economic reforms aiming to grant more autonomy to the country's still dominant state enterprises as well as allowing greater space to the so-called "nonstate sector," which includes Cuba's *cuentapropistas* and a new crop of nonagricultural cooperatives. Since 2010 and roughly parallel to the gradual unfolding of new pro-reform regulations always instituted in Raúl Castro's famous and oft-repeated phrasing, *sin prisa pero sin pausa* (without haste but also without pause), a small group of academics, community activists, and government officials on the island have sought to promote entrepreneurship, spread awareness about the benefits of social entrepreneurship, and discover whether "[t]he country's emerging market enterprises, though hampered by serious constraints, could provide a laboratory for the application of socially responsible business models" (Sagebien and Leenson 2015, 59). Highlighting Cuba's peculiar hybrid version of a mixed economy along with the government's expressed intention of "updating" socialism and making it more efficient, productive, and sustainable, these scholars tend to reject the more common term "market socialism" (*socialismo de mercado*) (as now exists in China and Vietnam) and instead describe Cuba as having or aiming to achieve "socialism with markets" (*socialismo con mercado*) (Sagebien and Betancourt 2014).

However, in promoting the concept of social entrepreneurship, the expansion of socially responsible enterprises, and the growth of the social and solidarity economy more generally, these policy-oriented scholars and community activists remain a minority. They recognize that they are fighting against the current of Cuba's rigid political culture and centralized bureaucratic system of management (Betancourt 2017). For example, Betancourt and Sagebien note that "it remains to be seen whether in practice an economy with a vertical and centrally planned tradition like Cuba's can develop consultative and inclusive styles of management that encourage the solidarity economy" (2013). In fact, the related concepts of the "social and solidarity economy", "socially responsible enterprise", "inclusive markets development", and "local development" are all relatively new if not completely unknown in the context of Cuban enterprises (private or public).[8]

Terms like "corporate social responsibility" are familiar as corrective measures employed to make the "free market" more socially just in capitalist countries. But Cuba is not a capitalist country. Indeed, one could argue that the original raison d'être of embracing state socialism as the Cuban Revolution's form of economic organization was in fact aimed at building just such a "social and solidarity economy" made up of "socially responsible" state enterprises, which would implicitly place social priorities over economic ones and people over profits. If this were the case, then Cuban socialism would already exhibit an intrinsic social (and environmental) responsibility based on social inclusion, citizen solidarity, and sustainability, and thus have no need to develop the explicit terms or corrective remedies associated with "social entrepreneurship," "socially responsible enterprise," or the "social and solidarity economy."[9] However, Betancourt also indicates that the managers of these Cuban state enterprises do not enjoy the bottom-up managerial or financial autonomy that would allow them to "allocate part of [enterprise] revenue toward social or environmental actions that are not explicitly contemplated in the national Economic Plan" (2014, 2).

To wit, Betancourt quotes directly from the government's 2011 "Guidelines for Social and Economic Policy," a document which anchors Raúl Castro's economic reform plan aimed at updating Cuban socialism by making it more efficient, productive, and sustainable. "In Cuba's socialist society," the document promises, "no one will go unprotected." It also guarantees that "economic entities of all forms of management will be subject to a regulatory framework that takes into account the established norms of social and environmental responsibility." However, this is again a decidedly "top-down" form of socially responsible enterprise "based on external norms and regulations established by the government, not as a voluntary, discretionary initiative, managed by the firm as a form of stakeholder engagement" (Betancourt 2014, 2). Thus, in Cuba there is a palpable tension between the "party line" that bureaucratically mandates social responsibility as an implicit (and decidedly "top-down") part of the state-owned enterprise sector under state socialism on the one hand, and any autonomous, self-managed, "bottom-up" projects arising from civil society that seek to make social and environmental goals an explicit part of the so-called "triple bottom line" of the newly resurgent private and cooperative economic sectors on the other.

Self-Employment in Cuba: From the "New Man" to the "Economic Man"

In 1965, in one of his most influential essays, "Socialism and Man in Cuba," the Argentine-born Che Guevara, then serving as the Cuban Revolution's minister of industry, argued:

> [W]ork must acquire a new status. Human beings-as-commodities cease to exist, and a system is installed that establishes a quota for *the fulfillment of one's social duty*. [. . .] Work no longer entails surrendering a part of one's being in the form of labor power sold, which no longer belongs to the individual, but becomes an expression of oneself, *a contribution to the common life* in which one is reflected. [. . .] [O]ne truly reaches a full human condition when no longer compelled to produce by the physical necessity to sell oneself as a commodity. [. . .] That will be communism. (Guevara 2005 [1965], emphasis added)

Following Guevara's powerfully expressed ideological stance on work under Cuban socialism no longer being a commodity but "the fulfillment of one's social duty" and "a contribution to the common life," Cuban entrepreneurship was abolished by Fidel Castro in 1968 as part of his so-called "Revolutionary Offensive." From then on, it was illegality (i.e., the black market and underground economy) that shaped the development of Cuban entrepreneurship until the crisis of the 1990s forced the leadership to enact a series of pro-market reforms, among which was the liberalization of a limited number of preexisting underground entrepreneurial practices, now bureaucratically christened *trabajo por cuenta propia*, or *cuentapropismo*.

Indeed, entrepreneurship has an elastic history in revolutionary Cuba. It has undergone oscillating phases of decreased or increased relevance, vigilance, legality, and legitimacy, which coincide with what Cuban-American economists Carmelo Mesa-Lago and Jorge Pérez-López have identified as a series of "idealist" and "pragmatist" cycles of economic policymaking (2013). After the Revolutionary Offensive wiped out virtually the entire remaining private sector in 1968 (then made up of some 58,000 small and microenterprises), the government allowed a very limited experiment in "self-employment" to begin in 1978 legalizing just forty-eight quite marginal, private occupations for freelancers. However, most of these were run out of business once again during the "Rectification Campaign" that began in 1986, as a reaction against the perceived growth of inequality, the concentration of wealth in private hands, rising prices in the private sector, and the corrosive influence of the Soviet Union's twin policy reforms *perestroika* and *glasnost*.[10]

Following the collapse of the Soviet Union, between 1989 and 1993 Cuba lost 35 percent of its GDP and over 75 percent of the country's imports and exports; this dramatic contraction in economic activity threw nearly 20 percent of the island's labor force out of work and dealt a near-fatal blow to the island's iconic sugar industry. As if under siege of war, Cubans were forced to make major sacrifices, including a sudden contraction in caloric intake, drastically reduced access to basic goods and services, and major cuts in electricity and public transportation. Reacting to these macroeconomic shocks, President Fidel Castro attempted to avoid talk of an impending "economic crisis" or "structural adjustment" à la Latin American neoliberalism, and instead euphemistically declared a "special period in peacetime" to begin on August 30, 1990. Still, the special period amounted to a Faustian bargain aimed at neutralizing the Revolution's most severe economic crisis by seeking to ensure its survival at the risk of unleashing the unpredictable consequences of pro-market reforms, such as increased economic inequality, ideological compromise, and a weakening of central control.

Though Castro initially attempted to limit reforms to foreign investment and international tourism, he was soon forced to significantly liberalize the domestic economy when the initial external opening toward international tourism and foreign investment proved insufficient to stabilize the economy. While these changes did eventually staunch the economic hemorrhaging and inject a new socioeconomic complexity into Cuban reality, they were never intended as a transition to capitalism. Despite these intentions, the widespread introduction of market mechanisms—which included reopening private farmers' markets, reorganizing agricultural cooperatives, allowing foreign remittances, legalizing the use of the U.S. dollar, and licensing and significantly expanding self-employment—had a twofold effect on entrepreneurship: (1) it legalized what already existed underground and (2) fueled its expansion as a marginally legitimate way for Cubans to *resolver* and *inventar* (i.e., come up with inventive, often illegal solutions to the unending challenges of economic survival during the special period). In other words, the emerging regulatory framework during the 1990s was a de facto acknowledgment both of the pervasiveness of previously criminalized forms of economic agency and of the government's inability to deter their growth since underground entrepreneurs were picking up the slack left behind as the state sector contracted, allowing themselves, and ironically the socialist system, to survive.[11]

As a result, economic pragmatism overtook political idealism and *cuentapropismo* was grudgingly re-legalized and significantly expanded in 1993 legalizing 117 occupations, which grew to 157 by 1997. However, this was justified by Fidel Castro himself as a "necessary evil." Thus, while this expansion of *cuentapropismo* was an obliged administrative response to a multitude of homegrown, mostly illegal, survival strategies developed by Cubans from all walks of life, past ideology regarding the nature, purpose, and value of work—as expressed above by Guevara—proved difficult to reconcile with *cuentapropismo*'s new lease on life. Indeed, the special period was characterized by a decidedly ambivalent approach to entrepreneurship whereby legalization went hand in hand with marginalization and rigid control—thus intensifying *cuentapropismo*'s pathological aspects instead of promoting it as a potential economic resource for Cuba's future. In other words, while *cuentapropismo* was de jure "sanitized," it remained de facto *satanizado* (demonized): hampered bureaucratically; repressed through excessive taxation, regulations, inspections, and closures; and cast politically as beyond the moral pale of a "revolutionary" and still nominally socialist society.

By the early 2000s, the government had instituted policies that ran many of these small enterprises out of business or back underground, and officially ceased to issue new licenses in 40 of the total 157 legal self-employed occupations—all as part of Fidel Castro's ideological swan song known as "The Battle of Ideas." This negative approach to entrepreneurship contributed to the generalized distrust of legal institutions among Cuban entrepreneurs and the prevailing culture of illegality in Cuba. As a result, the total number of licensed *cuentapropistas* dropped from a peak of 209,606 in January 1996 to 149,000 by January 2004, and remained at that level for the subsequent six years before Raúl Castro shelved Fidel's "Battle of Ideas" and changed economic policy once again in the second half of 2010.

This on-again, off-again cycle of pragmatic opening and ideological closure hinted at a more fundamental and potentially corrosive shift from Guevara's 1960's "New Man" (*el hombre nuevo*) to the entrepreneurial "economic man" (*homo economicus*) of the 1990s and beyond. Indeed, while Guevara long promoted voluntary labor in Cuba as a way to prioritize moral over material incentives and thus more effectively create the "New Man" and move toward the construction of full-blown communism on the island, this tactic bore diminishing returns after 1990. In part, this was due to the diminishing rewards (carrots) that could be provided to such "volunteers" during years of pronounced scarcity. However, the punishments (sticks) designed to encourage voluntarism met with decreasing effectiveness as well-making "voluntary labor" not so voluntary after all.

In July 2011, Cuban authorities decided to get rid of the last elements of such programs by suspending the Student Work Brigades, the Forces of Pioneer Action, and the University Social Work Brigades. The supremely brief and simple reason given publicly in the youth-oriented national newspaper *Juventud Rebelde* for this turnabout speaks volumes about the official shift in mentality toward work in today's Cuba: It was found that "recent campaigns showed an unequivocal and unfavorable correlation between expenses and returns."[12] Finally, in July 2018 as Cuba announced plans to enact a new constitution, citizens were informed that the goal of achieving communism would explicitly eliminated from the new Magna Carta even if the *Partido Comunista de Cuba* would remain the country's exclusive legal "single party" (*partido único*) and retain its "leading role" as the "superior guiding force of society and the State" (Granma 2018a; Escobar 2018; Rojas 2018).

Raúl Castro's Economic Mambo: Two Steps Forward and One Step Back

The Cuban government's decision to shelve the most important elements of the revolutionary tradition of voluntary labor dovetails with President Raúl Castro's relaunching of *cuentapropismo* in late 2010 through an official list of 178 "liberated" self-employed occupations (subsequently expanded to 201). Indeed, this unprecedented move communicated that self-employment was not only "here to stay," but it was also placed at the very center of Cuba's new economic development plan, which—it was repeatedly emphasized—sought not to abolish socialism in a transition toward capitalism, but to "update" and "perfect" it as part of achieving greater economic efficiency, productivity, and prosperity under the Revolution. In a radical effort to address a bloated public sector, staggering underemployment (too many people hired but little for them to do at their assigned jobs),[13] and reduced productivity of the state apparatus, the government aimed to slash the public sector by 1.8 million by the year 2013: terminated workers were to be re-employed in the nonstate sector, with *cuentapropismo* initially slated to absorb the lion's share. As a result of these measures, the total number of registered *cuentapropistas* reached beyond half a million for the first time after mid-2015, more than 100,000 of whom were actually licensed employees of other private enterprises (14ymedio 2017a, 2017b; García 2017), something both unthinkable and expressly illegal prior to 2010 (even if the 1976 Cuban Constitution continues to anachronistically ban private sector employment).

This shift toward the "economic man" has also been a key part of the new social contract between the Cuban state and its worker-citizens, whereby pay would no longer be based on need but on the quality and quantity of work performed. Indeed, as president between 2008 and 2018, Raúl Castro was fond of criticizing egalitarianism as a grave error leading to economic dysfunction, lack of efficiency, low productivity, and freeriding—something he famously ridiculed as "a form of exploitation—that of the good worker by the lazy one." On the one hand, this new economic orientation assured Cubans that "in a socialist society no one will be abandoned" by the state—though some Cuban workers have certainly felt as such given the unprecedented layoffs and cuts in many long-sacrosanct subsidies and social services. On the other hand, a set of Communist Party–approved guidelines ratified the principle that "socialism means equality of rights and opportunities, not egalitarianism." Work was declared "simultaneously a right and a duty" that "should be remunerated based on quantity and quality." However, these guidelines only made official something Raúl had become fond of repeating since becoming president in 2008: "We must erase forever the notion that Cuba is the only country in the world where you can live without working" (Castro 2008, 2010a, 2010b; Guidelines 2010).

Thus, for the first time under the Revolution, *cuentapropismo* has become a vehicle to resignify the nature of work—from a "party-line" sacrifice meant to pave the way for the establishment of genuine communism to a "bottom-line" profit for the individual or family unit; that is, from Che's *hombre nuevo* back once again to the *homo economicus*.[14] Furthermore, in the years since late 2010, Raúl Castro sought to put flesh on the bone of his elder brother's now-infamous admission to American journalist Jeffrey Goldberg in a rare moment of economic candor in that Cuba's economic model *ya no funciona ni para nosotros* (no longer works even for us) (Goldberg 2010). Indeed, just weeks following Fidel's grim assessment, on September

24 Cuba's Communist Party newspaper *Granma* published an article that celebrated *cuentapropismo* as "much more than an alternative" to the state sector, publicly banking on it to both absorb laid-off state workers and lead the reversal of the economy's long-flagging efficiency and productivity. "We aim," the article boldly declared, "to distance ourselves from those concepts that condemned self-employment to near extinction and stigmatized those who practiced it legally in the 1990s" (Martínez Hernández 2010).

While the expansion of self-employment can be celebrated given its expansion of economic freedom and productivity, the provision of job opportunities, greater productivity and efficiency, and a markedly higher quality of goods and services for those who can afford them,[15] it is also curious that the Cuban government has embraced it historically only during times of economic crisis when it could no longer provide enough jobs, goods, or services for the people. Indeed, this is one of the mantras most commonly repeated in the official press when justifying the downsizing of the state sector and the expansion of "on-your-ownism" (Krauze 2015): The state must "lighten its load" so it can focus only on the fundamental elements of the economy. Given such a context, Cuban workers can be forgiven for concluding that Raúl Castro's much trumpeted economic reforms, constant calls for greater productivity and efficiency, and sharp criticisms of Cuba's "inflated state payrolls, bulky social spending, undue gratuities, and excessive subsidies" (2010a) are simply fancy words for the state's abandonment of its historic commitment to them under the Revolution.

At the same time, Cuba's successful *cuentapropistas*, the embodiment of *homo economicus* on the island today, often find themselves in the frustrating position of being counted on to supplement the moribund state sector by providing nonstate employment, high-quality goods and services, and economic productivity and efficiency, on the one hand. While on the other hand, they continue to be denied any "legal personality" (*personalidad jurídica*) as true business enterprises, bear an increased tax burden the more workers they hire, and are legally prohibited from accumulating "private concentrations of wealth or property" (Gómez Armas 2017). That is, while Cuba's *cuentapropistas* may be individually licensed to operate as freelancers (i.e., *personas naturales*), "Cuban law does not recognize the private enterprise [itself] as a legal entity." And without "legal status as a private mercantile enterprise, [. . .] they cannot open a bank account or sign contracts" (Betancourt 2014, 5).[16]

Muddying the already opaque waters of "entrepreneurial Cuba" even further, the second half of 2017 saw a series of ominous signs, public declarations, and legal decrees that froze in place the continued growth Cuba's private sector representing a veritable bucket of cold water poured over the island's expectant but always wary entrepreneurial class. First, in July 2017, just weeks after Cuba's National Assembly approved the Communist Party's decision to move forward on granting small and medium-sized capitalist enterprises (SMEs) a legal personality, Raúl Castro made headlines by openly criticizing the "irregularities" commonly found among private enterprises and Cuba's new crop of nonagricultural cooperatives (Hernández 2017; Gámez Torres 2017a). Indeed, in his speech to Cuba's National Assembly in late July 2017, Castro expressed his displeasure with the supposedly high-flying lifestyle of some successful private business owners. "Criminal acts have been committed," he declared. "There are reports of cases where the same person has two, three, four, and as many as five restaurants . . . Someone who has travelled abroad more than thirty times. Where did he get the money? How did he do it?" (Rodríguez 2018; Ferreira 2018).[17]

Then, on August 1 Cuba's Labor Ministry published Resolution No. 22 that froze the issuance of new licenses in twenty-seven occupational categories, justifying the measure with the argument that already existing self-employment regulations were insufficient and that the sector would now "require better order and control." Until that was achieved, new licenses in many of the most popular and lucrative private sector occupations would be unavailable. These included bed and breakfasts, private *paladar* restaurants and cafeterias, private real estate and rental agents, auto repair shops, party planners, shoemakers, private language and music teachers, and computer programmers. While the "freezing" of licenses for these occupations would be temporary, the resolution also included a list of five other occupations (such as the wholesale and retail sale of produce, pushcart produce sales, and CD-DVD sales) for which it would no longer be possible to apply for licenses at all (Gaceta Oficial 2017; Puig Meneses 2017; Gámez Torres 2017b).

On top of this significant legal "pause" in the growth and consolidation of Cuba's private sector, during the summer of 2017 a number of well-known and highly successful private businesses were raided and shuttered, and their inventory seized for carrying out economic activities beyond the scope allowed by their licenses. This coincided with the release of a video of a private meeting of Communist Party officials with then First Vice President (and now President) Miguel Díaz-Canel ominously railing against the supposedly counter-revolutionary orientation of Cuba's private sector, the independent digital media, and the normalization of relations with the United States, which he reminded his listeners continued to plot the "political and economic conquest" of the Revolution.

Dashing the hopes of some that Díaz-Canel was only pandering to old guard regime hard-liners as he anticipated succeeding Castro as president (which he did in April 2018), the December 2017 National Assembly meetings ratified the need for tighter regulations on Cuba's private sector. It was announced that henceforth private entrepreneurs would no longer be allowed to obtain more than a single license and that cooperatives would be limited to operating only within their home province. This effectively gutted the innovative business strategies of some entrepreneurs who had simultaneously run *paladares* and/or bars together with bed and breakfasts under the same roof and others who had operated the same cooperative across multiple provinces. Salaries for cooperative leaders would also be capped, and contracts between state tourism enterprises such as Havana Tours and private *paladares* (where they often take tourists for meals) would be limited to a total value of $75,000 per year (LeoGrande 2017; The Economist 2017; Frank 2017; Recio 2018).

Then, in the closing days of February 2018, *Reuters*' Cuba correspondent Sarah Marsh published an exclusive describing a 166-page internal government report drafted the previous summer by a special economic reform commission that aimed to "increase state control over the private sector and curtail private enterprise" (Marsh 2018a; Consejo de Ministros 2017). These measures would go significantly beyond the freeze that had been implemented the previous August and added specific detail to the measures announced by economic reform Czar Marino Murillo at the National Assembly in December. "Dated Aug. 3, 2017 and signed by Marcia Fernández Andreu, deputy chief of the secretariat of Cuba's Council of Ministers," the detailed report recommended the elimination of the loophole that had allowed some successful restaurateurs to skirt the limit of just fifty seats per establishment by obtaining more than a single *paladar* license. In the future, each individual or household would be limited to a single license. More broadly, Marsh reported that "the document calls for a new division under the Ministry of Labour to administer and control self-employed work." It is also expected that the current list of 201 private sector occupations will be given a major overhaul with the new number of occupational categories falling below 125 (Marsh 2018a; El Toque 2018).

Sensing that the "new rules" supposedly aimed at "perfecting the exercise of self-employment" being drawn up in secret by the government would likely do more harm than good in terms of the flexibility and prosperity enjoyed by Cuba's emergent entrepreneurial sector, a group of forty-three licensed *cuentapropistas* delivered a private letter on August 21, 2017, addressed to the Minister of Labor and Social Security (MTSS), Margarita Marlene González Fernández, seeking to initiate a dialogue where they could share their concerns. While they agreed among themselves to keep the letter itself private so as to increase the chances of actually being heard by the minister, the group's informal spokesperson, Oniel Díaz Castellanos, eventually summarized the contents of the letter in a Facebook post on December 14 of that year given that by then more than seventy days had passed without any word from the Ministry despite the fact that sixty days is the legal limit for an official response to a citizen petition (Recio 2017). "We want to be heard and taken into account," Díaz wrote. "We will continue insisting" (Díaz Castellanos 2017).

Díaz then listed the six proposals the group hoped to discuss in their meeting with the minister so they could participate in formulating a policy that would overcome the main bottlenecks that hampered the optimal development of Cuba's entrepreneurial sector:

1. facilitate access to wholesale inputs,
2. allow commercial imports,
3. overhaul the tax system so it better reflects the actual conditions of the national economy,
4. replace the long and exceedingly specific list of permitted self-employment activities with a much shorter "negative list" of prohibited activities based on "national, political, economic, or environmental interests,"
5. create a formal mechanism to allow ongoing dialogue between policymakers and *cuentapropistas*, and
6. implement a legal framework for SMEs in Cuba—that is, provide private businesses with a path to obtaining a legal personality (*personalidad jurídica*) (Díaz Castellanos 2017; Recio 2017).

Amazingly, Díaz updated his timeline just over two weeks later in early January 2018 reporting the good news that he and Marta Deus, another leading private entrepreneur, did in fact have a two-hour meeting with high-ranking MTSS officials on December 28 where they were able to raise all their concerns. He considered it a successful meeting, where "both sides spoke with transparency and listened with interest; an encounter of agreements and disagreements." He ended his post with the promise: This is "a space we intend to enlarge and defend" (Díaz Castellanos 2018a; Recio 2018).[18]

"The Revenge of the Jealous Bureaucrat": New Rules for Cuba's *Cuentapropistas*

Six months later on July 9, 2018, when the official party newspaper *Granma* announced that the government had finally concluded its deliberations and would issue a new 129-page draft of self-employment regulations the next morning (based largely on the earlier privately circulated 166-page draft), it did so with the explicit claim that "the contents of the norms respond . . . to requests from self-employed workers themselves" (Granma 2018b; Castro Morales 2018). However, this justification (Orwellian in itself given the actual content of the regulations described in the following) was mixed with the unmistakable message that the government's idea of *perfeccionamiento* remained much more about bureaucratic order and control than the facilitation, integration, and support envisioned by Díaz's list of proposals. Indeed, apart from a slight adjustment that will allow a greater deduction of business expenses before taxes and a streamlining of the list of allowed occupations (regrouping the original 201 categories into 123), the new rules are totally silent on the most urgent concerns of Cuba's *cuentapropistas*. That is, nothing is said about expanding access to inputs or wholesale pricing, nothing on the right of *cuentapropistas* to import commercial inputs or export their goods and services, nothing on converting the exceedingly complex and detailed list of allowable occupations into a simpler "off-limits" list of banned ones, nothing on allowing professionals to work in the private sector in their professions, nothing soliciting further feedback from or dialogue with *cuentapropistas*, and nothing outlining special legislation that would finally grant private Cuban SMEs legal personality (Gaceta Oficial 2018; Auge 2018; Feinberg and Padrón Cueto 2018).

The government's deafening silence on all these key issues was not lost on Díaz himself, who penned a scathing op-ed in the independent digital newspaper *OnCuba*, where he blasted state bureaucrats for missing the forest of "private sector support and incorporation" due to its overriding paranoia about the trees of "limiting and repressing the growth" of an entrepreneurial sector that might contribute to social inequality, the private concentration of wealth and property, or the empowerment of a fledging middle class. "The authorities have insisted that they are satisfying some of the requests of *cuentapropistas* themselves," he writes. "However, those [measures] asked for with shouts and which would have a greater impact, continue to shine by their absence."[19] Entitled, "New Regulations for Private Sector: More No's Than Yes's," the essay also points out that while the word "no" appears a total of 243 times in the regulations (almost two times per page!), their authors missed a golden opportunity to change their philosophy from trying to micromanage the private sector with ever more layers of red tape to announcing a clear, structural shift toward the dynamic support for and engaged dialogue with the private sector. To wit, Díaz quips that they could have started by saying "no" to the initiative killing list of allowable occupations (that makes all others illegal by default) and replacing it with a "negative list" that would "give free reign to Cubans' creativity and drive to resolve their economic problems and contribute with products, services, and greater tax revenue to the nation" (Díaz Castellanos 2018b).

Perhaps the most telling assessment of the government's "massive compendium of tough new regulations" for the private sector came from Brookings Institution Cuba watcher Richard Feinberg and Cuban journalist Claudia Padrón Cueto who summarized them simply as "the revenge of the jealous bureaucrat" (Feinberg and Padrón Cueto 2018; Whitefield 2018). More concerned with restricting private wealth accumulation and controlling successful competition from innovative and newly prosperous *cuentapropistas* than with poverty alleviation, investment stimulation, or job creation, the mostly nameless bureaucrats behind the new rules seem motivated by the selfish desire to protect the moribund if monopolistic state enterprise sector and the eminently political aim to prevent the rise of a moneyed middle class. Indeed, "the very ministries that stand to lose market shares," they note, "are [now] in charge of approving licenses in their sector."

Those searching for a glimmer of good news among the new regulations were forced to celebrate as a kind of pyrrhic victory the fact that new licenses in the twenty-seven previously frozen, high-end occupations would indeed be activated again—but only after another five months of waiting (on December 7, 2018) in order, in the words of *Granma*, "to permit the creation of conditions to carry out an effective ordering [of the rollout], with total adherence to the law" (Granma 2018b). *Granma* also reported that as of the end of May 2018 the total number of licensed *cuentapropistas* had reached a record 591,456 (making up 13 percent of the island's labor force), up from 157,371 in October 2010, when the initial reopening of the sector began. The new law also includes strong antidiscrimination language aimed at protecting a number of vulnerable groups in the private sector, requires that the hiring of private sector employees must now include a labor contract between parties, and allows the owners of private homes to rent them out to legal entities, such as state enterprises or agencies (Gaceta Oficial 2018; Auge 2018; Weinstein and Rodríguez 2018).

On the downside, however, the new regulations explicitly ban a number of heretofore common *cuentapropista* practices and increase taxes as well as legal sanctions for any violations of the law, including for the first time the definitive loss of one's license and the seizure of one's place of business itself (usually the owner's residence) in the most severe cases (Gaceta Oficial 2018; Auge 2018). Some of the innovative, cost-saving, and diversification strategies now off limits to Cuban entrepreneurs include holding more than a single license (for a single person or a single household) mainly to prevent violations of the absurd fifty-chair limit for *paladares*; doing business with foreign entities (such as private bed and breakfasts commonly do with international tourism companies or individual Cuban programmers do for foreign tech firms); having a relative or friend stand in as the nominal business owner (known colloquially as a *testaferro* in Cuba) to permit the development of brands, chains, and franchises; or running private schools, academies, or full-fledged real estate agencies under the guise of self-employment (Díaz Castellanos 2018b; Muñoz Lima 2018; Rodríguez 2018; Frank 2018).

Interestingly, the private childcare businesses that have quickly spread across the island over the past eight years have been allowed to remain but now will have to contend with a laundry list of astoundingly specific regulations that not even state-run nurseries have to follow. For example, they must "allocate at least two square meters per child, have no more than six children per attendant, and be outfitted with pristine bathroom facilities described in exquisite detail" (Feinberg and Padrón Cueto 2018).

According the Mimi Whitefield of the *Miami Herald*, they must also guarantee that each child is provided with "personal toiletry items [including] a comb, toothbrush, bath towels, hygienic towels, cutlery, and mugs"—each one bearing the child's name. And the regulations even specify that "the hooks for their towels must be a minimum of 20 centimeters apart" (Whitefield 2018).

Still saddled with a mentality that sees Cuba's emergent Cuban entrepreneurial class as fundamentally at odds with its vision of *cuentapropistas* as marginal, survival-oriented, family-based freelancers, government bureaucrats insist that overly ambitious entrepreneurs are violating the "essence and spirit of self-employment, that consist in [individual] workers daily exercising the activity for which they are authorized." Indeed, Cuba's Vice-minister of Labor and Social Security, Marta Elena Feitó Cabrera, explicitly argues: "There are workers who have a café and at the same time have a license as a manicurist or for an auto repair shop, or to make and sell shoes. This is not possible. In practice, it is a single owner who has many businesses" not what was intended for a *cuentapropista* (Gámez Torres 2018; Castro Morales 2018).

In order to properly prevent such violations of *cuentapropismo*'s "essence and spirit," the *Gaceta Oficial* also announced that a new licensing procedure would take effect on December 7, now requiring a detailed written application, a visit by inspectors to the proposed place of business, and a sworn declaration attesting to the licit origin of all business equipment and financing for the venture. Moreover, higher-end *cuentapropistas* will now be required to set up business accounts at state banks, which they will have to use for all business-related transactions and which must carry a minimum balance of the equivalent of three monthly tax payments. The tax exemption that had existed for an enterprise's first five employees will be eliminated, and on top of that, Cuba will become one of the few countries on earth to impose a progressively onerous pay scale on businesses the more workers they hire (Torres 2018a). That is, any business with between eleven and twenty employees will have to pay those workers three times the average wage, a rate that increases to six times the average wage for more than twenty workers (Gaceta Oficial 2018; Castro Morales 2018; Auge 2018). To this is added an especially invasive and censorious Ministry of Culture regulation (Decree No. 349) that aims to ensure the "proper application of the cultural policy of the revolution" in the private sector (Auge 2018; Gaceta Oficial 2018). This measure will ban independent artists and musicians from performing in private businesses such as restaurants, bars, or nightclubs without prior approval, licensing, and oversight by the state entity to which they "belong." The Decree also applies to authors, painters, and other artists who attempt to sell their work without prior state authorization and outlines punishments for artists who use "violent, sexist, vulgar, or obscene language," who violate copyright, and even for those who play their music too loudly (Gámez Torres 2018; Feinberg and Padrón Cueto 2018).

This major pushback against the free development of self-employment and the larger private sector in Cuba is quite ironic given that it has come to a head just as Raúl Castro—the driving political force behind the opening to microenterprise since 2008—has stepped aside as president. In fact, while it is quite common to hear Cuban entrepreneurs privately complain that Raúl Castro's entrepreneurial reforms did not go far or fast enough (much more *pausa* than *prisa*), this new counter-reform indicates that at least some of the other powerful members of Cuba's Communist Party—including the new fifty-eight-year-old President Miguel Díaz-Canel himself it seems—fear that Raúl's free market reforms went too far, too fast (Álvarez 2018; Torres 2018a). Indeed, while many had expected that pro-market reforms would deepen with the presidential succession into a post-Castro era, perhaps a retrenchment is in store instead.

It is also worth noting that a quick scan through the twenty-odd legal resolutions and decrees included in the compendium of new self-employment laws published in the *Gaceta Oficial* on July 10 reveals that the five central Decree Laws issued by the Council of State were in fact signed, sealed, and delivered by then President Raúl Castro in February and March *before* Miguel Díaz-Canel succeeded him in April. Díaz-Canel signed only one of the twenty Decrees, No. 349, which requires private artists to respect Cuba's "cultural policy" as described earlier. This indicates first that Raúl Castro has been both the architect of an unprecedented opening toward self-employment *and* a "law-and-order" General-President who values order and control above all else. It also reminds us that grand pronouncements about Cuba finally entering any post-Castro era may be quite premature.

The economic logic of reform has run up against the political and ideological logic of the status quo. Party officials likely feel that the uncontrolled growth of the private sector directly threatens their bureaucratic and political power regardless of how much it contributes to the growth of the economy (Estado de Sats 2018). This is the conclusion reached in various published analyses of the government's entrepreneurial rollback by Ricardo Torres, a leading young economist at the University of Havana's Center for the Study of the Cuban Economy (Torres 2018a, 2018b). "It's no longer an ideological prejudice," he has said, "here we have a political calculation of not empowering certain sectors within the country which one day could question the reigning political power" (Muñoz Lima 2018). Furthermore, others within the government likely view the pockets of undeniable prosperity generated by successful private enterprises not with a capitalist's satisfaction but with a socialist's disapproval as it paves the way for (or simply reveals) Cuba's rising inequality (Frank 2018). To this legitimate worry, others have retorted: "I strongly believe that socialism should fear poverty more than it fears wealth" (Ferreira 2018).

Proyecto Artecorte: "Something More Than Money"

Instead of the usual approach of private business (in any part of the world) as defined in competitive, zero-sum terms, *Artecorte* approaches private enterprise development in Santo Ángel with a collaborative, "win/win" approach that is built on relationships of synergy with a variety of neighborhood partners all of whom benefit from their mutual success (Valladares and Condis 2016; Valladares 2017).[20] Indeed, in his own profile of Papito, tellingly entitled, "The Individual Entrepreneur and Social Engagement" (*El emprendedor individual y la obra social*), journalist Fernando Ravsberg incredulously demanded to know whether Papito understood that his sponsorship of a hairdressing school was "creating your own professional competition." "No," Papito shot back, "what I'm doing here is multiplying my own dream" (Ravsberg 2016). Papito further expanded on his unique "entrepreneurial solidarity" approach in our interview:

> Enterprising together [*emprender juntos*] is the key to success in what we do. [. . .] For us, *the success of one business guarantees the success of its neighbors*. Many customers come looking for different services for which there are many options. However, in most cases, instead of preferring to consume a single business, they try different things each time they visit. That gives us the guarantee that *each customer of one business is a potential customer of another one*, which from another perspective could be seen as its competition.

> At the same time, in a country with such serious supply-chain problems, maintaining good relationships with our neighbors[21] insures mutual support. Let's say I have a restaurant that sells beer. Instead of competing against me, a similar business will let me know where beer is available or lend me some other scarce supply. *I'll return this favor later*, guaranteeing that neither of us misses out on potential customers due to Cuba's chronic scarcity.
>
> Of course, this is very difficult to understand outside of Cuba's unique context. But it is an important part of who we are. (Emphasis added.)

Born on December 22, 1969, Papito started his first job at seventeen in 1987 working as a state-employed barber. Admitting he was a poor, directionless student, he quickly took to the barber trade. His skill gave him pride in his work, which in turn provided him with a focus and purpose in life and a way to serve his community. His talent and enthusiasm allowed him to quickly rise within the state sector, where he eventually landed a choice job as a barber at one of Cuba's premier hotels, the *Hotel Habana Libre* (formerly known as the Havana Hilton). This was in the mid-1990s just as international tourism was reintroduced to the island's economy as a partial solution to the crisis of the special period. Apart from this position that presumably allowed Papito access to hard-currency tips, he had already become interested in celebrating the traditions of the barber trade through social outreach by traveling the country and providing free haircuts in public parks while demonstrating his tonsorial skills to local residents.

Despite his successes as a state-employed barber, as the 1990s came to a close Papito decided to make a go at becoming self-employed in 1999 by setting up a barbershop in his own Santo Ángel home, a third-floor walk-up. Although he now jokes that in hindsight it seems an insane business plan to locate a new business in such a hard to reach place, at the time operating from his own home was his only legal option. Moreover, there were virtually no other *cuentapropistas* working in this faded, crumbling section of Old Havana, far from the tourist-trafficked public plazas near Obispo Street. On the one hand, he would have little local competition; but on the other hand, he feared he would struggle to attract a customer base (either Cuban or foreign) willing to venture off the beaten path to his door perched atop a series of steep, narrow staircases. However, even from these early days, he was energized both by his family's economic need to find a stable source of income during a critical time, and his continued desire to combine his love for the sartorial arts with a celebration of their cultural history in Cuba. Soon after he opened the doors to his private business, he also launched Cuba's first and still only home-based barber museum and art collection (also co-located in his home and humorously named *Hasta el último pelo*, a Cuban colloquialism roughly meaning "Until the last straw").

His success during these early years created a growing international reputation that led to his being invited to an international hairdressing forum in Mexico in 2007. However, since at the time he was still required to obtain an exit visa to travel abroad, he became embroiled in a bureaucratic fight with local authorities. "They treated me badly, like I was a counter-revolutionary," he remembered, "as if my desire were to emigrate, when really all I wanted was to represent Cuba at an event where no Cuban had ever been before" (Cuba Posible 2016, 13). Given the bitter taste this difficult struggle left in his mouth, he decided the time was not right in Cuba for his project of social entrepreneurship to flourish. He did not return to Cuba after the event in Mexico and remained living there for the next two years (exactly the outcome that Cuban authorities most feared). However, in 2009, as the prospects began to improve in Cuba for entrepreneurial projects like his, he decided to return to Old Havana and pick up where he had left off. As Papito explained to the editors of *Cuba Posible*:

> The head of the Office of the Historian of Old Havana, Eusebio Leal tracked me down and convinced me to return. I did, taking up once again everything that I had started before. In the end, I am from here and I deeply believe in what I do; this is why I try to defend it and why I know the impact it can have for this moment and for the future of the country (Cuba Posible 2016, 13).

It turns out that prior to the major relaunch of self-employment in the fall of 2010, Raúl Castro had authorized a series of pilot projects of economic liberalization in Cuba's retail sector, starting first with private taxis in 2009 and later adding barbers and hairdressers in early 2010 (Peters 2010a, 2010b, and 2010c). "In what appears to be the start of a long-expected revamping of state retail services by President Raúl Castro," announced *Reuters* correspondent Marc Frank in April 2010, "Communist Cuba is turning over hundreds of state-run barber shops and beauty salons to employees across the country." (Frank 2010). While this shift did not have a direct impact on *Artecorte* given that it was already private, such changes did make a difference when combined with later liberalizations of self-employment announced in the fall, allowing business owners like Papito to legally hire employees for the first time since 1968 and to rent out spaces other than their own homes to set up shop. Indeed, Papito admitted that the first change allowed him to "come out of the shadows" and officially register the handful of employees with whom he had long been working informally.

Thus, it was only after returning from Mexico in 2009 at the urging of Leal and in the context of the expansion of self-employment during 2010 that Papito's long-incubating cultural and entrepreneurial project began to really transform itself into a true "social enterprise" of local development and community uplift. In subsequent years, Papito deepened his alliance with the Office of the City Historian (OH), which has served as the key, sine qua non institutional facilitator for everything that has blossomed for *Artecorte* since. This includes *Artecorte*'s free barber school, which is housed in a storefront owned by the OH, allowing the project to use it for free. The OH also provided funding and logistical support for *Artecorte*'s transformation of the final, northern-most block of Aguiar Street into a pedestrian mall now better known simply as *El Callejón de los Peluqueros* (Barbers' Alley). This is where Papito's barbershop, the school, and the bulk of the neighborhood's other new private businesses are located.

More recently, *Artecorte* expanded its public-private partnership strategy by refurbishing a long-abandoned public park together with the OH (which permitted use of the space) and a group of students from Havana's Superior Institute of Design (ISDI), rechristening it *Barbeparque* (or Barber Park). The park includes a special area for children's haircuts and is filled with slides, swings, and seesaws, all designed by ISDI students as a school project to resemble various tools of the barber trade such as scissors, combs, and razors—all produced and paid for by the OH. While the park is free to access, it is able to sustain itself through an ingenious arrangement with a number of locally trained *cuentapropistas*: two are barbers who graduated from *Artecorte*'s own school and now earn their living giving children haircuts there. Another is an ex-con who sells ice cream. Together they are responsible for paying a local elderly man to keep the park clean while the OH covers additional custodial costs (Rosales 2016).

While this is perhaps the most elaborate, successful, and easily recognizable public-private partnership launched by *Artecorte* to date, their many other neighborhood improvement projects include partnerships with Cuba's National Association for the Deaf and Hard-of-Hearing (ANSOC) to train young deaf students for careers in hairdressing, a bartending school provided for local youth through the sponsorship of Havana Club rum (Cuba's leading joint venture between Cuba Ron and the French multinational Pernod Ricard), weekly live music and dance sessions provided free of charge for residents of a nearby home for the elderly by the self-employed musicians who work in the restaurants on the *Callejón*, and a series of free after-school workshops for local youth in archeology, arts and crafts, and responsible use of alcohol all run by volunteer teachers (Sagebien and Leensen 2015, 59; Cuba Posible and D'Angelo 2016, 11–12).

All this community activity and social outreach has not detracted from the success or energy devoted to private enterprise in the neighborhood. On the contrary, it has served as an anchor for sustainable community development by turning the area into a cleaner, safer, more prosperous neighborhood, and therefore more attractive one for entrepreneurs in search of a promising location where they can launch their own businesses. Indeed, this was just the vision Papito had when he began his focus on community entrepreneurship.

> What sets us apart from other entrepreneurs is the fact that we aim to connect actors from all sectors of society (private and public, religious and cultural, etc.), so that we can *work together for the common good*, which is nothing more than developing our neighborhood in every way possible, while simultaneously generating social, cultural, educational, environmental, and economic benefits for everyone.
>
> The natural evolution of our project is the definitive proof of the important relationship between Cuban culture, economic development, and social relations. [. . .] Backed by enthusiastic entrepreneurs who were in search of *something more than money* [. . .], our work gradually brought together cultural and economic efforts that were linked by ever broader and more complex social relationships, giving birth to the results we have achieved today.
>
> The example of *El Callejón de los Peluqueros*, which was initially only used as a space for cultural activities but has become *home to more than a score of private businesses*, is living proof of this synergy. (Emphasis added.)

Indeed, while Papito's barbershop that opened in 1999 was likely the first licensed *cuentapropista* enterprise in the neighborhood, as of August 2016 there were twenty-three different private businesses located just on the one block pedestrian section of *El Callejón*. Within the larger eleven-square-block area north of *Calle Chacón* that makes up the Santo Ángel district, there are 194 private businesses employing a total of 976 people. Of these 194 businesses, 133 are bed and breakfasts that cater to the tourist market, 34 provide food services, 21 are related to the sale of Cuban arts and crafts, and the other 6 provide various other services. These numbers come from an internal study of the local economic impact of its programs carried out by *Artecorte* in conjunction with a team of academic researchers in mid-2016. Enterprise growth has continued to be robust in the year since then. However, beginning the following summer the neighborhood began to suffer a notable stagnation as a result of the new, more restrictive policies toward the private sector issued by the Cuban government (as described previously). Unfortunately, this internal entrepreneurial freeze has been exacerbated by an equally severe external one imposed on travel to and economic engagement with Cuba by the Donald Trump administration.

Artecorte's dynamism is drawn both from the local community and the private sector, but combines these with a variety of innovative alliances with the public sector as well. That is, it is not organized from the top down (following an imposed "party line"), or from the outside in (with the "bottom line" dictated by outside investors or shareholders), but from the ground up. This strategy dovetails nicely with what Betancourt and Sagebien recommend about the application of successful socially responsible enterprise (SRE) and *economía social y solidaria* (ESS) (social and solidary economy) development models from other contexts to Cuba.

> The experiences of ESR and ESS throughout the world demonstrate that civil society should be the main actor in the formation of enterprises with the state playing essentially a facilitating role. Cuban directors and planners should resist the temptation to directly control and intervene in the non-state sector and entrepreneurs should enjoy autonomy.
>
> "Instead of being 'top-down,' the management paradigm should be 'bottom-up.'" (2013, 64)

Of course, this hands-off, bottom-up approach that prioritizes the efforts of an autonomous civil society does not preclude the use of strategic alliances of the kind *Artecorte* has developed with the OH. Indeed, Papito has gone beyond this key initial alliance to develop others with entities of local government, various universities, think tanks, and associations (such as the Center for Psychological and Sociological Research and the previously mentioned ISDI and ANSOC). *Artecorte* has also begun to partner with various state-owned or joint venture enterprises and even most recently with foreign entities such as the Swiss Agency for Development and Cooperation (González 2016). "The objective," Papito insists, "is not to rise up with the flag of self-employment, but instead to work all together, the [state] institutions and the non-state sector. The day that we no longer speak of [separate] sectors, we will have won." (Cuba Posible 2016, 5).

Incubator or Anomaly?: Lessons for the Future of Social Entrepreneurship in Cuba

This chapter examines the meaning, function, and possible future(s) of entrepreneurship in Cuba. Within the larger process of Raúl Castro's unprecedented economic reforms and in the midst of a historic move toward "normalization" of relations with Cuba begun under the Obama administration, we ask: How is entrepreneurship being reconfigured from within by Cubans themselves? What effects will that reconfiguration have in shaping the popular response to the oversimplistic either-or model of a mere party-line "updating" of socialism on the one hand versus an implicit "transition" to bottom-line capitalism on the other?

What was—and is—the meaning of entrepreneurship in the Cuban context, especially from the perspective of entrepreneurs themselves? Do they see themselves as playing a part in the "perfecting" of Cuban socialism, as pioneers for the eventual establishment of an SME sector, as inventive survivalists without any particular ideological claim or aim, or as innovators in community-oriented "entrepreneurial solidarity" that eschews the often divisive capitalist and socialist labels but actively seeks out public-private and international partnerships aimed at achieving local economic development and community empowerment?

This focus on entrepreneurship acquires more urgency (and demands deeper analysis) in the rapidly changing context of U.S.-Cuba bilateral relations following the historic thaw initiated on December 17, 2014, culminating in the establishment of diplomatic relations and the opening of embassies on July 20, 2015. Indeed, President Barack Obama's "empowerment through engagement" policy explicitly targeted Cuba's emerging entrepreneurial class as agents of change following Raúl Castro's 2010 private sector liberalizations, described previously. Obama even explicitly cited Papito's *Artecorte* project as an example of "where hope begins" in his historic speech to the Cuban people. However, the new economic possibilities that opened up for Cuban entrepreneurs and between them and their potential American investors, partners, and patrons during 2015 and 2016 have been thrown into great doubt (if not placed into deep freeze) by four subsequent developments.

First came the stagnation of Cuba's economic reforms and a new reticence on the part of the Cuban government toward a broader, deeper, and more rapid opening toward the private sector. This retrenchment became especially evident on the island during the surprisingly defensive and robustly nationalistic April 2016 Seventh Party Congress, which followed directly on the heels of President Obama's state visit in March of that year (and seemed to take the form of a pointed rebuttal to it). As argued previously, based on the new self-employment regulations issued in summer 2018 and set to take effect on December 7, what was a retrenchment now threatens to become a full-fledged counter-reform for Cuban entrepreneurs given the "breathtaking picture of the scope and footprint of suffocating contemporary Cuban bureaucracy," according to the sharply worded assessment of Cuba's new cuentapropista rules from Paul Hare, former British ambassador to Cuba (Frank 2018).

The second development was the unexpected election of Donald J. Trump as U.S. president in early November 2016. This was followed quickly at the end of November by the historic passing of Cuba's longtime maximum leader, Fidel Castro. Finally, came the equally historic transfer of executive power from Raúl Castro to Miguel Díaz-Canel in April 2018 (a succession originally planned for February), signaling the denouement if not necessarily the end of the nearly sixty-year Castro era. How does each of these "wild cards" impact U.S.-Cuban relations and the unprecedented opening toward the entrepreneurial sector on the island begun under Raúl Castro in 2008?

To address these questions, this chapter focuses on a particular site: Old Havana's Santo Ángel neighborhood and its independent, grassroots community development project *Artecorte*. The initial success, extraordinary public recognition from President Obama, and subsequent positive press coverage of the *Artecorte* project has certainly risked calling undue attention to itself and potentially provoking the ire of some of the "jealous bureaucrats" mentioned previously. However, Papito's unique business philosophy that combines local economic development via private enterprise with community outreach, neighborhood solidarity, and cultural preservation has channeled most of the government attention they *have* received into a series of innovative public-private partnerships that have provided essential institutional support making this particular entrepreneurial project quite unique. But should we understand *Artecorte*'s pioneering uniqueness an asset or a liability given that its special orientation and insertion in Old Havana is predicated in part on relations of reciprocity and bureaucratic support unlikely to be found in Cuba outside the once impregnable walls of the city's *Centro Histórico*, much less in Cuba's other major cities or far-flung provinces? In other words, to return to Papito's own hopeful claim cited in this chapter's opening epigraph, can *Artecorte*'s success as a social entrepreneurial pioneer "ripple across Havana" and even throughout the island?

The fact is that *Artecorte*'s grassroots success as an enterprise incubator in Santo Ángel has been possible to a large extent because it overlaps considerably with the Office of the City Historian's Master Plan for the revitalization of Old Havana. *Artecorte* has also benefited from the charisma and unique personal relationship between Papito, a man with deep community roots who has slowly earned the trust of his neighbors, and City Historian Eusebio Leal, someone who has long enjoyed equally vital connections and bona fides both from the residents of *La Habana Vieja* and within state institutions. However, this anomalous situation has recently become quite tenuous given Leal's declining health and the recent takeover of the Office of the Historian's lucrative and heretofore largely autonomous mercantile company Habaguanex by the Cuban military (Escobar and Pentón 2016; García 2016; CiberCuba 2016). This is to say nothing of the potential negative impact on Habaguanex in particular and commerce in Old Havana more broadly that Trump's new measures that ban American trade with and patronage of a long list of Cuba's military-, security-, and intelligence-related enterprises.

Still, even if the OH weren't facing such a pair of immediate existential crises, the alliance between *Artecorte* and the Office of the Historian will be hard to replicate elsewhere given its informal, context-dependent, and personality-driven nature, despite continuing efforts by the Office of the Historian to find and support other Papitos and *Artecortes* in the district. While there are certainly various projects of social outreach sponsored by other private businesses in Old Havana and indeed throughout the island, *Artecorte* seems to stand alone in its deeply organic and fully integrated approach that has successfully married entrepreneurial acumen with social, cultural, and environmental commitments and connections. It also has been a pioneer in establishing alliances with a multiplicity of state, academic, corporate, and nonprofit entities, a dynamic innovation rarely replicated elsewhere. University of Havana economist Luis Alberto Barreiro Pousa, who has studied *Artecorte*'s unique and successful approach, argues:

> In the Historic Center there really are no other experiences like *Artecorte*. Although there are other projects that, because of their social impact, are sometimes considered examples of "Solidary [*sic*] Economy" (*Economía Solidaria*) they really are not.[22] All these initiatives contribute both to the cultural and social sustainability of Old Havana, but they incorporate the philosophy of "Social Economy" in a circumstantial manner within their daily activities *not* as part of the structural logic of their management model. (Barreiro Pousa 2018)

However, the San Gerónimo University College (Havana) economist Rafael Betancourt, quoted extensively previously, has a slightly more positive take on the question of *Artecorte*'s uniqueness replicability. He argues that the project is far from being an anomaly and that in fact there are many other examples of solidarity enterprises in Cuba's private sector and especially among its agricultural cooperatives. The problem, he contends, is that no serious, systematic study has been undertaken of the social and solidary economy (SSE) phenomenon in Cuba. "What makes *Artecorte* unique," he posits:

> is (1) it is the only case that has been thoroughly documented and presented nationally and internationally, (2) Papito has managed to "*contagiar*" [infect] many neighbors, thus creating a neighborhood SSE ecosystem, and (3) it has reached out to and engaged the international tourism market through Airbnb, domestic web pages, and the state travel agencies. (Betancourt 2018)

One other hard to replicate element behind *Artecorte*'s success in Old Havana is the backdrop of the Master Plan of Old Havana. This one-of-a-kind overarching plan for Cuba's premier historic and architectural district has provided the Office of the Historian with an extremely unique level of political autonomy and legal and financial prerogatives that are unheard of elsewhere in the country (Cuba Posible and D'Angelo 2016, 12). Indeed, when questioned about the sustainability and replicability of the Santo Ángel success story outside of Old Havana, Papito maintains on the one hand that "our model is completely sustainable and replicable in other communities," while also emphasizing that this is the case only "as long as it is accompanied by an institution that supports the project and helps guide the steps needed to bring it to fruition." However, the fact is that few other institutions like the OH exist outside of Old Havana with the same administrative autonomy and financial resources to "support" and "guide" projects with similar "entrepreneurial solidarity" commitments as those of *Artecorte*.

Given the Trump administration's June 2017 announcement from Miami's "Little Havana" explicitly aimed at "canceling" and "rolling back" what Trump himself has called Obama's "bad deal" with Cuba, we can expect that such aggressive and isolationist policies toward the Cuban government will also harm the island's fledging entrepreneurs. While some had hoped for a Cuba policy driven by a deal-making businessman interested in creating American jobs and economic prosperity. Instead, we have witnessed a distracted and ill-informed demagogue pandering to the Cuban-American hard right with isolationist and vindictive policies based on scant knowledge of or curiosity about the Cuban economy or the complex role of the emergent private sector within it. The antagonistic history of U.S.-Cuban relations suggests that any pressure from Washington to exact "concessions" from the Cuban government based on U.S. "demands" that it reform its internal policies either in the area of human rights and democracy or speed up its opening toward private enterprise or the internet will backfire (LeoGrande and Kornbluh 2015; Marsh 2018b). When under external threat or pressure—especially from the United States, the nation the Cuban government perceives to be its historical nemesis—Havana has always reacted by "circling the wagons" and restricting political and economic rights and civil liberties in a defensive crouch aimed at defending Cuban national sovereignty and preserving the Revolution. As the age-old Spanish refrain has it: *En una plaza sitiada la disidencia es traición* (In a house under siege, dissidence is treason).

It was just such logic that motivated the Obama administration to radically alter long-standing U.S. policy toward Cuba, eschewing isolation and impoverishment aimed at regime change for a policy of engagement and empowerment aimed at facilitating the growth of economic independence and civil society on the island. If, as the African proverb puts it, "when the elephants battle, the grass suffers," the hope was that ceasing to directly battle the Cuban government with so much aggression might allow the grass of independent Cuban civil society to gradually regrow (Hoffmann 2015). This is precisely what Obama was aiming for when he spoke the words, "the United States has neither the capacity nor the intention to impose change on Cuba," during his speech in Havana. However, the pointedly defensive and arguably paranoid reaction of the Cuban government following President Obama's very effective soft-power charm offensive during his March 2016 state visit indicates that basing predictions of Havana's internal policies on whether U.S. policy is more or less engaging or aggressive is not always helpful.

Obama's youthful charisma, approachable manner, mixed racial origins, and multicultural pedigree surely endeared him to the vast majority of the Cuban people. However, these same qualities combined with his unapologetic public advocacy for what he called "universal human rights" simultaneously left the Cuban leadership profoundly spooked. Now with a new president in the White House who can be counted on to consistently provoke and directly attack the Cuban government, once again making explicit the imperial intent to impose change on Cuba from Washington (i.e., regime change), Cuban leaders may be thankful to once again have a convincing northern Goliath against whom they can rally the waning revolutionary ire of a tired populace while playing the role of an aggrieved Caribbean David. Ironically, Trump's bizarre strategy that aims to "impoverish the Cuban people, so that they may be freer" (in the sharp phrasing of Cuban economist Ricardo Torres) dovetails nicely with the Cuban government's own political and ideological resistance to a greater economic opening and can help it justify its own economic "pause" on the private sector as a necessary defensive measure in the face of foreign aggression (Torres 2017).

Under Raúl Castro, the Cuban government has repeatedly declared that what it insists on calling the "nonstate" sector will gradually expand *sin prisa pero sin pausa* (without haste but without pause), while remaining a decidedly secondary supplement to what will remain a dominant centrally planned and state-owned socialist economy. While Deng Xiaoping may have kicked off China's own economic revitalization under the Communist Party with the pungent slogan: "To get rich is glorious!" Cuba's own

Communist Party continues to explicitly restrict the private concentration of wealth or property. Thus, while we can expect that an aggressive Trump policy that rolls back or conditions parts of U.S. economic engagement on Havana's "good behavior" will be counterproductive and indeed economic injurious for Cuban *cuentapropistas*, it does not follow that continuing or deepening Obama's policy of engagement will necessarily increase economic freedoms on the island at least in the short term.

This is so because it is Havana's own continued and myriad restrictions on the private sector (not to mention its ongoing suppression of fundamental political rights and civil liberties)—sometimes referred to as the "internal embargo" (or *auto-bloqueo*) (Henken and Ritter 2014, 2015)—that present the greatest obstacle to entrepreneurial success on the island, not U.S. policy embodied in the still existing embargo. Ironically, neither the recent death of former President Fidel Castro nor the transfer of state power from Raúl Castro to his much younger hand-picked successor Miguel Díaz-Canel (both epoch-making events for the island) will in and of themselves lead to faster or deeper economic reforms that benefit Cuban entrepreneurs. This is the case because change in leadership does not necessarily mean change in policies, especially when Raúl Castro's administration openly claims to be "updating socialism" and justifies the timid economic opening by quoting the largely meaningless if not outright Orwellian words of his big brother Fidel: "Revolution is changing everything that should be changed." Until this change explicitly includes clear and defensible rights to private property and a recognized "legal personality" (*personalidad jurídica*) as business enterprises for today's so-called *cuentapropistas*, Cuban entrepreneurs will remain largely powerless against arbitrary state power now a decade after the start of Raúl Castro's economic reforms in 2008 and even after Díaz-Canel's "successor generation" assumes power and issues a new Constitution.

Notes

1. The title of this chapter paraphrases Sagebien and Leenson's observation that Cuba's economic reforms are unlikely to be linear, and instead "will be punctuated by fits and starts—and by occasional retreats. In Cuba, after all," they quip, "the 'party line' is still more important than the 'bottom line'" (2015, 60).
2. I would like to thank Gilberto "Papito" Valladares for responding to my questionnaire about *Artecorte* and Camilo Condis for providing useful comments on an

earlier draft of this chapter. I'd also like to recognize Archibald Ritter and Gabriel Vignoli for their collaboration on past projects, cited in the references, which form part of the theoretical foundation for this work.

3. I translate Papito's Spanish phrase *empredimiento solidario* as "entrepreneurial solidarity" both here and in my title. However, it could also be translated as "solidary [*sic*] entrepreneurship" as it is related to the better known concept *economía social y solidaria* (ESS, or "social and solidary economy," SSE—sometimes also written "social and solidarity economy") described later and defined in footnote 8 *infra*.
4. While the government term *trabajo por cuenta propia* is most commonly rendered in English as "self-employment," such a translation fails to capture the sense of separation, abandonment, and even stigma felt by many Cuban *cuentapropistas* I have interviewed in the past twenty years. As one Cuban entrepreneur recently indicated to me: "I think the importance of the term is that it was completely made up by them and that they recognize us as 'we're on our own,' like 'no strings attached,' 'separated from them.'" For this reason, a better translation for *cuentapropismo* would perhaps be "on-your-ownism" (Krauze 2015).
5. As Rafael Betancourt explains in his article "Corporate Social Responsibility in Cuba": "The terms 'corporate social responsibility' (CSR), 'corporate citizenship,' 'sustainable business' (SB), and 'socially responsible enterprises' (SRE) are little known in Cuba, beyond limited academic circles and, in general, are seen as foreign, not appropriate to the national context" (2016, 2). As used here, corporate social responsibility is synonymous with socially responsible enterprise (*responsabilidad social empresarial*), though perhaps the second term is more appropriate to Cuba's private microenterprise (*cuentapropista*) sector since "corporate" implies foreign multinationals or large domestic private firms of the kind that do not exist on the island.
6. Even under the current economic reforms launched by Raúl Castro in 2008, which give unprecedented space to would-be Cuban entrepreneurs, one never hears political leaders or the state media use the words *empresario, emprendedor* (entrepreneur), or *sector privado* (private sector) to refer to the island's nascent microenterprise sector. Instead, they are described with the euphemistic terms *cuentapropista* (self-employed worker) and *sector no-estatal* (nonstate sector). And while the Communist Party has approved "small and medium-sized private enterprise" in theory, existing legislation including the latest self-employment regulations issued in July 2018 are completely silent on granting legal personality (*personalidad jurídica*) to private businesses, forcing all private entrepreneurial activities to don the regulatory straight jacket of *cuentapropismo* (Monreal 2018; Nieves Cárdenas 2018). Cuban blogger Yoani Sánchez highlighted this dilemma by stating: "Among the most glaring euphemisms of recent years is 'self-employed worker' . . . it's prohibited to say 'entrepreneur'" (2013). Likewise, when introducing a group of five young Cuban businesswomen at the Association for the Study of the Cuban Economy's (ASCE) annual conference in summer 2014, they insisted on being presented to the public not as *cuentapropistas* but instead as *emprendedoras*, because the latter term highlighted their grassroots ingenuity, resourcefulness, and market savvy (ASCE 2018).

7. For greater elaboration on these and related points about Cuba's changing state policies toward small enterprise, entrepreneurship, and informality, see chapter 2, pp. 23–30 in *Entrepreneurial Cuba: The Changing Policy Landscape* (Ritter and Henken 2015), from which the preceding section is drawn.
8. The social and solidarity economy carries out business activities in order to achieve social and environmental objectives and have traditionally taken the form of cooperatives, mutual benefit societies, associations, nonprofits, and foundations. Socially responsible enterprises are individual businesses that aspire to social and environmental goals—often called social enterprises. It is a form of management defined by its ethical and transparent relationship with all stakeholders. Inclusive markets development is an effort to extend markets and their benefits to the poor and marginalized, often led by international development agencies in tandem with national governments, private sector financial institutions, and local or national civil society organizations. Local development "extrapolates the impact derived from economic growth in a specific territory. It goes beyond generating economic wealth, integrating social commitment as a means to make the most of local assets, potential, and vocations, beginning with the design of a participatory action plan and a model of governance based on shared management" (Betancourt 2015, 2–3; Betancourt and Sagebien 2013; Sagebien and Betancourt 2014).
9. Betancourt has reiterated this same point elsewhere by arguing that under the Cuban Revolution:

    > social responsibility and solidarity constitute–theoretically—the *raison d'être* of economic activity, promoted top-down by the central government in an economy with strong predominance of the State sector. The term used in Cuba to characterize our system is "socialist economy", not "social and solidary [*sic*] economy", despite its coincidences. This model was created by the State through its socio-economic and political system, central planning and state-owned enterprises. The enterprises have social objectives that are implicit, rarely explicit or defined by its managers and workers. (2014, 2)

10. At the time of this mid-1980s campaign, officially named "The Rectification of Errors and Negative Tendencies," Cubans liked to joke that Castro's unique version of (or reaction against) Soviet perestroika was *la espera estoica* (the stoic wait) (Pérez-Stable 2011).
11. As a result, such inventiveness at solving life's many daily supply problems has gradually embedded itself as a "way of life," or fundamental part of Cuban culture so that today Cubans tend to think that stealing resources from one's state job or illegally selling things on the ubiquitous black market are legitimate ways to make a living. President Obama openly recognized this fact of daily life in his March 2016 speech to the Cuban people when he said, in Spanish, *el cubano inventa del aire* (Cubans invent out of thin air), a quip that was met by hearty, knowing applause from the Cuban audience.
12. The original reads: "*Las campañas más recientes enviaban señales inequívocas: desfavorable correlación gastos-aporte*" (Álvarez 2011).

13. This situation led in Cuba to a bitter quip already deeply embedded in the lore of employment under Soviet communism: "We pretend to work and the government pretends to pay us."
14. This situation recalls the popular joke about socialism (very similar to one Russians used to tell about communism) that made the rounds in Cuba following Raúl Castro's turn back towards the market in late 2010. "Question: What is socialism? Answer: The longest and most painful path from capitalism to capitalism."
15. In some cases, the expansion of the private sector has also driven down prices. However, because of extensive subsidies and price controls in the state sector combined with chronic material scarcity and a dual currency system where a good portion of the private sector operates in hard "convertible" currency, prices for most goods and services available in Cuba's private sector are very high relative to the state sector.
16. Summary documents published a month following the Seventh Party Congress, which took place on April 2016, indicated that "micro-, small-, and medium-sized private enterprises" would be "recognized as legal entities" (*personas jurídicas*) (Concepualización 2016, 32). However, it took Cuba's National Assembly more than a year to actually approve this decision, which it finally did on June 1, 2017 (Gómez Armas 2017). It remains to be seen exactly whether, when, and how this change will be implemented in practice (with no indication of movement toward such a legal implementation by August 2018), despite the issuance of major new self-employment regulations on July 10, which are set to take effect on December 7 (Gaceta Oficial 2018). It is also unclear the extent to which this legal change will ease the burdens of Cuba's private sector entrepreneurs, many of whom currently run SMEs without legal protection and under the pretext that they operate "on their own" as *cuentapropista* freelancers.
17. One of the ironic things about this statement is that it stands in such stark contrast to one Castro gave to the same body in late 2010, just as he was relaunching *cuentapropismo* and trying to get his cadres in the Party and government to change their mentality toward it and its practitioners:

    > If self-employment constitutes another alternative of employment [. . .] what the Party and government should do in response is first of all facilitate its management and generate neither stigmas nor prejudices toward [*cuentapropistas*], much less demonize them. This is why it is fundamental to modify the negative existing assessment many of us have toward this kind of private work. [. . .] The steps that we have been taking and will continue to take in the opening and flexibilization of self-employment are the fruit of profound meditations and analysis and we can assure you that this time there will be no going back (Rodríguez 2016; López 2011).

18. On a more humorous but equally penetrating note, as of summer 2018 if you Google the phrase *medidas del gobierno cubano* (measures of the Cuban government), the first link that appears is a post of the same title on the blogger platform *Medium* by the Cuban telecom engineer and media activist Norges Rodríguez. Posted on December 28, 2017, the article is written in the dry, official argot of a typical Cuban

government announcement and describes a veritable wish list of long-awaited, thoroughgoing reforms that Cuba has supposedly decided to launch starting on February 1, 2018. Before hinting at fundamental changes to Cuba's migration, agricultural, telecommunications, mass media, and democratic participation policies, the post begins with a lengthy description of key changes to its *cuentapropista* policies, which echo those recommended here by Díaz Castellanos and his colleagues: "This group of measures has as its objective of overcoming once and for all the economic crisis that has affected the country for nearly the past three decades and countering the impact of U.S. regulations that affect Cuba in its commercial and financial dealings." Turning to self-employment, the post states:

> Considering the importance that self-employment has for the country's development, the Ministry of Labor and Social Security, after study and analysis that began on August 1, 2017 when the granting of licenses was halted, approved today a resolution that eliminates the concept of "permitted activities" and elaborates a list of sectors of the economy that can only be managed by public enterprises or entities which include health services, education, electricity, mining, water and sewage, and other utilities as listed in Resolution 1228 of 2017. One of the innovations of this measure is that starting on February 1, *cuentapropistas* will be able to obtain a legal personality, have direct commercial dealings with both state and foreign enterprises, import commercial products, and expert their goods and services." (Rodríguez and Norges 2017).

After listing three other measures with equally convincing detail, Rodríguez informs his readers that they should follow an embedded link to learn the full extent of the government's decision. To the great amusement of some of his readers (and provoking the ire of others for having been taken in by his ruse) the link takes them to the Wikipedia page for *Día de los Santos Inocentes* (the Cuban equivalent of April Fool's Day in the United States), which takes place on December 28 each year.

Indicating the pent-up demand for such fundamental reforms as those described in the post, Rodríguez's playful ruse soon took on a life of its own. According to him, the link to the article was shared over 20,000 times on Facebook, while many others cut and pasted the article on their Facebook timelines inadvertently omitting the final link to Wikipedia, thus eliminating the final "Gotcha!" punch line and converting the post from a practical joke into a kind of "fake news" for other readers. On *Medium* itself, the article has been viewed more than 255,000 times and read 133,000 as of August 12, 2018, still garnering an average of 1,500 views each month more than six months after its initial publication. Rodríguez even reports that in the early months of 2018 the post left the exclusively virtual realm of the internet and entered the largely offline Cuban realm of the street with people printing out the list of reforms on scarce parchment and passing it from hand to hand in a number of Cuban barrios (Rodríguez and Norges 2018).

19. Díaz also laments that the likely result of the new measures would be to simply push a greater portion of Cuba's struggling *cuentapropistas* out of business or into *clandestinidad* (Cuba's extensive black market and informal economic sector). To underline this, via Facebook he shared an ingenious graphic penned years earlier

by Cuban cartoonist René de la Nuez that depicted a brief conversation between a pair of Cubans. The first man whispers to the second, ". . . Pues yo voy a pasar a la clandestinidad" (. . . Well, I'm going underground). Prompting the second man to respond, "¿Política?" (The political underground?). Frustrated, the first man then retorts: "No, hombre, económica" (No, man, the economic underground) (de la Nuez 2018).

20. The full transcript of the interview on which this profile is based is available in English at *Cuban Counterpoints*, "A Good Hair Day in Old Havana," March 6, 2017. The original Spanish interview was published by *14ymedio*, "El éxito de un negocio garantiza el éxito del negocio vecino" March 24, 2017. Additional background information on the history and development of *Artecorte* presented here is based on the following sources, all cited in the bibliography: Alcalá 2010; Cortés 2012; AFP 2015; Jara 2015; Sagebien and Leenson 2015; Beoto 2016; Cuba Posible 2016; *Cuba Posible* and D'Angelo 2016; Ravsberg 2016; Rosales 2016; Valladares and Condis 2016; Whitefield 2016; Padrón Cueto 2017; Iglesias and Valladares 2017; Fernandes 2017; and Henken 2018.
21. Before I published the English translation of my interview with Valladares, I shared it with his assistant Camilo Condis, who, unlike Papito, is fluent in English. Although Condis approved of the translation with the quip, "As long as you don't change any of our words it's the same to us [if you publish it in] *El Nuevo Herald* or *Granma*," he did ask that I change my original translation of the phrase, *una política de buen vecino*, from "good neighbor policy" to something less suggestive of U.S. imperialism. According to him, every Cuban school child learns about Franklin D. Roosevelt's "Good Neighbor Policy" not as signifying an important shift toward more respectful dealings with Latin America, but as a bitter exercise in doublespeak since it involved U.S. meddling in Cuban presidential politics in 1933 and led to the rise of military strongman Fulgencio Batista. Thus, here the phrase is translated simply as "maintaining good relationships with our neighbors."
22. Barreiro Pousa specifically mentions the following projects: Adelaida y el Ojo del Ciclón, Barrio Habana de Belén, La Moneda Cubana, Imagen 3 de Prado, La Casa Gaia de la Plaza Vieja, Alas de Mariposas de San Isidro, and Teatro y Audiovisual de Belén. Camilo Condis, one of Papito's main outreach coordinators at *Artecorte*, also noted that a number of other private businesses in Old Havana have special social or community outreach programs which have been active in the past. These include the restaurants El Divino (outreach to the elderly and work with community children), La Guarida (a program of cooking classes for children), La Moneda Cubana (a low-cost food service training program for youth), and Café Ajiaco (a training program for young chefs that it offers in collaboration with ArteChef, The Association of Cooks of Cuba). Likewise, the jewelry store Rox 950 has a jeweler training program for young people, and the design store Clandestina and the tattoo parlor La Marca both offer free children's workshops. Finally, the bike shop VéloCuba offers free assistance with wheelchairs for the disabled (Condis 2018).

7

Success Characteristics of Market Entry in Cuban Tourism

Janet L. Walsh[*]

Papers and magazines are full of enticing ads and information about visiting Cuba. Alumni associations, professional organizations, tour operators, and cruises tout the excitement, fun, and historical opportunities for visiting Cuba. Anyone interested in Cuba as a destination for tourism or business will find the following study of Cuba market entry in the tourism business useful and interesting. This study was finalized at the end of 2016 and updated in 2018 with additional research and information. This study is based on eighteen of the ninety-one organizations operating in the tourism business in Cuba as of 2015. It provides a detailed, in-depth look at the tourism industry's challenges and opportunities in Cuba market entry.

Cuba is an emerging market with eleven million people, a growing demand for products and services, and a government open to foreign direct investment (FDI) (Economist Intelligence Unit 2014; Feinberg 2013; Solorza 2016). To acquire hard currency to pay global bills and strengthen the Cuban economy, global FDI in the tourism industry has grown under the leadership of Cuban President Raul Castro (Smith and Walter 2016) and represents a critical aspect of economic development in the post-Castro future (Carty 2009).

The importance of tourism in Cuba is clear given the expected 3.8 million visitors in 2018 (Caribbean Tourism Report Q1 2018). This number is likely to increase in future years as well. Conversely, although the ten-year trajectory of U.S.-Cuban relations has been toward making it easier to travel and do business in Cuba, the U.S. administration of Donald Trump in November 2017 moved to reinstitute restrictions on tourism

[*] Janet L. Walsh, Birchtree Global, LLC, walsh@birchtreeglobal.com.

The Cuba-U.S. Bilateral Relationship. Michael J. Kelly, Erika Moreno, and Richard C. Witmer, II.

and market-entry activities by American companies (Jordan, Boley, Knollenberg, and Kline 2017). As of 2018, travel to Cuba by U.S. citizens is permitted only for family visits; journalistic, religious, and educational activities; professional research and meetings; public performances; support for the Cuban people and humanitarian projects; official government business; and export/import or the transmission of information or information materials (United States Embassy in Cuba 2018).

U.S. citizens wishing to travel to Cuba do so primarily under the travel category "Educational activities and people-to-people exchanges" (United States Department of the Treasury 2018). The category is relatively broad. Travelers are required to have "a full-time schedule of educational exchange activities that will result in meaningful interaction between the travel and individuals in Cuba" (United States Department of the Treasury 2018). As such, Americans traveling to Cuba have to go as part of organized trips such as people-to-people exchanges (United States Department of the Treasury 2018). Under the Barack Obama administration these rules were relaxed, permitting "self-certifying" travel to Cuba, meaning it was not necessary to be part of a regimented, organized group, but under the Trump administration, "self-certification" is not permitted (Jordan, Boley, Knollenberg, and Kline 2017).

Educational companies in the United States and abroad have capitalized on the growing interest in Cuba as a travel destination and recently imposed limits on individual travel. Much of this has come in the people-to-people travel market where companies from the United States continue to legally operate tours in Cuba (US DoT 2015). This specialized type of tourism must meet current government criteria and does not allow typical tourist activities such as lying on a beach and soaking up the sun while drinking colorful cocktails festooned with tiny umbrellas. Travel must be purposeful and include a full agenda of meeting Cuban people to understand specific aspects of the culture.

In addition to the recent 2017 limits on U.S. citizens visiting the island, the tourism industry in Cuba has been negatively affected by the breakdown in Venezuelan oil subsidies. As a result, Cuba faces a shortage of oil to power tourist infrastructure and businesses, including hotels (Fletcher 2017). While fuel shortage affects the tourism industry, it also serves to underscore the need for Cuba to develop a sustainable source of hard currency, such as the tourism business. Hurricane Irma in September 2017 further strained the island's infrastructure by damaging properties and facilities important to the tourism industry (Caribbean Tourism Report Q1 2018).

Companies wishing to invest in Cuba's tourism industry and other businesses can access the call for investment by the Cuban government (CEPEC 2015). Yet for those wishing to invest, there are currently no studies or available data about the performance of Cuban market-entry strategies. Similarly, detailed case study information describing the specific steps taken by successful Cuba market-entry companies is not found in the literature as companies working in Cuba are reluctant to reveal their competitive business strategies, or violate the U.S. embargo put in place by laws such as the Helms-Burton Act (1996) (DeGeorge, Tweed, and Donville 2014; Frank 2013; Lamrani 2012; Price 2016; Spadoni and Sagebien 2013). As a result, little specific research information exists to guide businesses interested in foreign direct investment in the Cuban tourism industry.

To close this information gap, the author conducted a qualitative case study to examine market-entry strategies, challenges, opportunities, and organizational actions of eighteen tourism businesses operating in Cuba. The eighteen tourism businesses were a subset of ninety-one, non-Cuban businesses operating in the tourism industry in Cuba for at least two years, as of January 31, 2015. From the master list of ninety-one, businesses were contacted until a representative sample of eighteen was achieved. To further develop the reliability and validity of the study, additional in-depth interviews were conducted in June and July of 2015 with the presidents and company leaders of ten of the representative eighteen tourism companies. Follow-up research was conducted in the fall of 2018 updating the information.

By illustrating how successful tourism industry companies entered the Cuban market and achieved sustainability, potential investors can learn from these experiences to build and fine-tune their own market-entry strategy (Matysiak and Bausch 2012). For those interested in the Cuban economy, this research presents additional insight into the factors that facilitate and inhibit business entry into the Cuban market. Furthermore, this study may narrow the gap between Cuba as a potential location for FDI and the specific actions necessary to establish business operations in Cuba. These actions may include how companies adapt to the political and economic challenges, establish legal entities, attract customers, manage financing challenges, and oversee human resources. This information may be of particular interest to tourism-related businesses as relationships with Cuba continue to evolve and improve (DeGeorge et al. 2014; Rainsford 2014).

What follows is a review of the market-entry literature and theories behind foreign direct investment. This allows the reader to categorize the actions of the study participants and see the tourism industry in a way that allows for better analysis and understanding of past, current, and future tourism business activities. An explanation of the study data and methodology is included, which allows the reader to better understand the conclusions and results. The results are presented at the end of the chapter.

When leaders of organizations consider beginning a new business in a foreign country, they may do so to maximize profits, to attain long-term, sustainable company performance, to achieve stakeholder satisfaction, and/or for altruistic, personal satisfaction (Paunescu 2013). However, the way in which companies make decisions on market entry is often the result of nonsystematic and ad hoc decision-making, rather than an analysis of theoretical options (Górecka and Szalucka 2014; Marchi et al. 2014; Musso and Francioni 2014). Organizational leaders may not have specific theories in mind as they globalize their businesses, however, the underlying theories of FDI help codify and add context to firm activities. Understanding the theories of FDI and examining the way other businesses globalize helps organizations new to Cuba market entry consider the implication of their actions in light of similar organizational patterns.

In this study there were four theories of FDI that represented the actions of the tourism companies entering Cuba. They included first-mover advantage (McMillan 2015; Murray et al. 2012), foreign direct investment theory (Blonigen and Piger 2011; Hymer 1976; Trapczynski 2013), internationalization theory (Brida, Driha, Rodriguez, and Scuderi 2015; Mura, Grublova, Gecikova, and Kozelova 2011), and the behavioral theory of FDI (Cyert and March 1963; Harlan 2014). These four key theories as they apply to market entry by the tourism companies are described in more detail following.

First-Mover Advantage

A key consideration faced by hotel and tourism companies is whether or not to move into the market before competitors to obtain first-mover advantages. In this study, first-mover advantage categorized the Cuba market entry actions of the tourism firms that entered Cuba. There are pros and cons to establishing an organization in Cuba with a first-mover advantage. First-mover advantage explains why firms may seek to gain advantage or to secure the best properties (McMillan 2015; Murray et al. 2012). Early movers in the hotel industry can capture favorable locations. Sol-Melia International from Spain, for example, has operated in Cuba for twenty-five years, managing twenty-seven properties as of 2015 (Melia Hotel International 2015; Nessler 2015). In addition to Sol-Melia International, Barcelo, Iberostar, NH, Accor, and Pestana have existing development interests in high-end hotel properties of the same caliber found in other Caribbean locations (Nessler 2015). So, these firms have an advantage in working in Cuba.

Airbnb has achieved a first-mover advantage in Cuba (Airbnb 2015; Nasr 2015). However, there are challenges, including technology limitations in Cuba, payments to Cuban homeowners, providing support and training for homeowners, and addressing pricing, advertising, and feedback (Airbnb 2015; Nasr 2015). Despite these obstacles, companies that have successfully transitioned into the Cuban market have an established presence and momentum. These advantages are further magnified by limits on U.S. citizens' ability to stay in hotels with connections to the Cuban government.

Educational experiences and people-to-people exchanges (US DoT 2015) are another area in which tourism business have achieved first-mover advantages. These travel activities are proliferating in Cuba (US DoT 2015). Early first-mover organizations in this business have developed a robust network of Cuban professionals to provide experiential activities and have developed experience working with Cuban government institutions. This is an area that is poised to grow in the future as U.S. government restrictions on travel impact this sector less than others.

Yet, being a first mover does not guarantee a firm's longer-term survival. For example, in seeking golf course development in Cuba, two top Coral Capital executives were accused of spying. Despite finding the accusations unproven (The Economist 2012; Freeman 2013; Vasilak 2015), company leaders were expelled from Cuba, and the project was turned over to a Hong Kong investment company, Beijing Enterprises Holdings, with no apparent golf course experience (Beijing Enterprises Holdings 2015).

First-mover advantage, however, is sometimes advantageous and sometimes not (Kalyanaram, Robinson, and Urban 1995). Shankar Carpenter and Krishnamurthi (1998) suggested innovation by late movers could overcome first-mover advantages. For example, companies entering the market establish relationships and pathways of doing business that can be used by subsequent businesses. Optimal timing in market entry rather than necessarily being first may provide a better advantage (Murray et al. 2012). Given that Cuba's political and economic environments are evolving (Economist Intelligence Unit 2015; Feinberg 2014), advantages gained from a first-mover strategy may not be retained over time as the country changes (Delios and Makino 2003; Wang, Yubo, and Xie 2010).

First-mover advantages in the hotel and tourism industry in Cuba are also affected by the decisions made by the managers in the business. If an organization does not make good decisions with respect to contracts with Cuban leaders, negotiations with employee representatives, ownership, and financing, the value of the project could be compromised (Murray et al. 2012). Thus market-entry timing as well as company structure and size of the investment may affect company success (Brida et al. 2015; Murray et al. 2012).

Foreign Direct Investment Theory

The theory of foreign direct investment (FDI) was the second type of market-entry activities by the tourist businesses in this study. FDI theory can be used to describe the way in which companies invest outside of their home country (Blonigen and Piger 2011; Forte and Moura 2013; World Bank 2015). FDI theory has three key elements: (1) investment made by a resident of one economy in another economy; (2) investment of a long-term nature or lasting interest; and (3) investor has a significant degree of influence on the management of the enterprise (UNCTAD 2015). Since the global economic crisis of 2007, the pace of globalization has increased as companies seek profit in new markets (Berend 2014; Costello and Costello 2012; Morfessis and Malachuk, 2011; Zhonghou and Yan 2013). From the macro view, the theory of FDI helps explain why companies seek to invest and profit in Cuba.

FDI can be viewed as market-driven (economic size or location), resource-driven (locating and using natural resource assets), or efficiency-driven (human resources in country or country infrastructure) (Blonigen and Piger 2011; World Bank 2015). For example, Okafor's (2015) economic study revealed U.S. FDI was enhanced when education, training and skills acquisition, inflation targets, trade openness (especially in the natural resource sector), corruption control, and political stability were promoted by the host country. From the tourist industry perspective, Cuba has natural resource assets that foreign investors seek, including attractive beaches, abundant ecotourism, a vibrant cultural heritage, beautiful scenery, and a highly educated workforce (Cabello et al. 2012). Cuba also has a locational advantage of being only ninety miles or a forty-minute flight away from the city of Miami, Florida. With the expansion of flights to Havana and an increase in cruise ship dockings, the country is easily accessible to the rest of the U.S. market as well.

Other factors positively influencing FDI include country stability, the level of corruption, political environment, and financial stability (Forte and Moura 2013). Foreign firms benefit from a stable macroeconomic and political environment that creates low inflation and respect for property rights, as well as efficient regulatory and predictable policy environments (Forte and Moura 2013). When uncertainty is high, multinational companies may prefer high-commitment entry modes as a way to reduce uncertainty and increase growth options (Lia and Rugman 2007). This suggests that a success characteristic of FDI in Cuba is likely to depend on the structure of the legal and financial environment provided by the Cuban government. Birchtree Global's (2014) market-entry research illustrates the importance of market-entry structural components. For example, the effect of U.S. sanctions on Cuban FDI reduces U.S. investment and contributes to the structure of legal and financial infrastructure that investors must consider. Yet negative effects are largely offset by a corresponding rise in FDI from other countries (Lektzian and Biglaiser 2014). Importantly, these countries have determined that the political and economic environment is conducive to investment regardless of U.S. concerns.

The theory of FDI, as interpreted by Hymer (1976), suggests companies will engage in foreign investment if they have advantages not possessed by domestic competitors. Hymer (1976) theorized that if FDI is to occur, there must be some market imperfection motivating the investment, that is, structural imperfections in the market create advantages (Barclay 2000). The market imperfections in Cuba include the inability of the government to grow enough food to meet demand, the lack of oil, limited hard currency and few domestic competitors to outside firms (Economist Intelligence Unit 2015). To offset these problems, Cuba does have beaches and culture that are exploitable resources with development of hotel and tourism industries. Trapczynski (2013) summarized research on FDI by noting the underlying rationale of firm expansion is the maximization of firm performance. Cuba currently possesses few challengers to outside firms wishing to maximize profit.

The pathway for hotel and tourism industries to expand into Cuba includes domestic owners selling to foreign buyers, establishing sales operations in Cuban locations, creating subsidiary business operations, franchising, buying existing businesses, or participating in joint ventures (Talluri 1998). Typical new market strategies include managing an existing hotel or extending a franchise license to an independent Cuban business (McMillan 2015). The Sol-Melia hotel chain, for example, has successfully partnered with Cuban hotel management organizations to extend their brand in the country (Melia Cuba Partners 2015). Cuba also signed a hotel and tourism investment collaboration agreement with Trinidad and Tobago to develop infrastructure and train workers ("Cuba, Trinidad & Tobago . . ." 2015). As a result, Cuba has developed a pipeline for trained hospitality workers who facilitate the management of foreign hotel brands (Nessler 2015). This collaborative approach seems especially attractive to the Cuban government.

Internationalization Theory of the Firm

The internationalizing theory of the firm describes the differences between small and large firms in FDI (Mura et al. 2011). This is an important distinction in Cuban FDI because the size of firms entering a market affects the firm's ability to enter new markets successfully (Mura et al. 2011). Companies seeking advantages from FDI are not uniform in their characteristics as businesses differ in size, industry, type, and experience. McMillan (2015) noted firms that are small and medium-sized might have certain advantages during Cuba market entry. The process of internationalization for these smaller firms may also be different than in large firms (Brida, Driha, Rodriguez, and Scuderi 2015; Mura et al. 2011). The smaller companies may differentiate themselves on product quality, marketing, and customer service, while focusing on product and innovation (Brida et al. 2015; Mura et al. 2011). Small firms also do not pose a threat to the Cuban economic and political structure (Birch 2015). However, smaller companies must overcome the challenges of smaller economies of scale, limited financial resources, less market knowledge, and enterprise staffing concerns (Altinay, Chatoth, Harrington, and Ottenbacher 2014).

A challenge for any company interested in internationalizing is obtaining accurate information about the potential risks and rewards. Companies of all sizes have access to general information about Cuba from multiple sources, such as the World Bank, United Nations, or Cuban government sites. Industry information is also available from professional organizations and academic research. However, prohibition of U.S. companies doing business with Cuba as a result of the Helms-Burton Act, 1996 (Price 2016), and the protection of company strategic advantages (Melia Cuba Partners 2015; Melia Hotels 2015; Spadoni and Sagebien 2013) limit the knowledge that can be easily obtained. A more comprehensive understanding of a new market would come from detailed and accurate local information and knowledge (Mura et al. 2011). For U.S. firms, travel restrictions make this challenging.

Behavioral Theory of the Firm

The behavioral theory of the firm explains how companies sort through the decisions to be made, sometimes with limited information, when entering a new market (Cyert and March 1963; Harlan 2014). Given the limited knowledge about Cuba market entry to U.S. organizations, it was thought decisions by firm leaders might be made with less than full knowledge. Investing in human resources, physical assets, and organizational capabilities was shown to improve decision-making and ability to respond to future events.

In Cuba, minimizing transaction costs and real option value creation is not done with perfect knowledge. As a result, a go-slow approach may help companies gather knowledge on the market and develop business as more information on product viability is obtained. Esencia Group (2014), for example, has been working for several years to develop high-end vacation properties in Cuba, which they view as a positive investment of their time and finances given the lack of current services in this market niche.

Foreign Direct Investment in Cuba

Among government leaders in Cuba there is strong political will to develop and maintain a strong, sustainable tourism industry on the island (Laitamaki, Lisandra, Tada, Liu, Setyady, Vatcharasoontorn, and Zheng 2016), but historically the Cuban government has been inconsistent in their FDI policies. For example, when the Cuban economy is contracting, FDI is welcomed, but when the economy is stronger, FDI is less popular (Birch 2015). This is understandable as Cuba's emphasis on a socialist political and economic structure is not negotiable, while economic reforms are justified through pragmatic or temporary exigencies to achieve specific, short-term results (Birch 2015). For example, as of 2015, microenterprises such as Airbnb and renting a room in a home are tolerated because they ease the burden of Cuba's government in the care of its citizens and do not pose a threat to government ideology (Pineiro 2013), and hard currency is needed. Conversely, while larger enterprises are welcome, there are restrictions on capital, ownership, location, and type of business. These government restrictions often discourage larger investors (Feinberg 2013).

Problematic for larger firms is that they typically exploit resource advantages in the host country to benefit from their investment in international expansion (Matysiak and Bausch 2012). In comparing FDI in Jamaica and Cuba, Reiter (2006) noted that Jamaica's liberal economic system allowed company leaders to pursue their corporate self-interests, often conflicting with Jamaican social interests. In Cuba, however, the economic system is structured to advance social and political concerns, not corporate interests (Reiter 2006). Firms wishing to exploit Cuba's resource advantages require approval from the high governing body the Council of State, which includes the Cuban president and key sector leaders (CEPEC 2015). Further, as noted by Li, Wong, and Luk (2006), governmental preference for specific industries affects the ease by which foreign businesses can engage in international joint venture partnerships. Thus, companies contemplating market entry into Cuba should consider the cost and benefits and the future financial returns given restrictions imposed by the Cuban government.

FDI in the Cuban tourism market is a key component in the development of Cuban economic self-sufficiency (Feinberg 2013; Oficina National de Estadistíca e Informacíon 2015). While approval for certain investments in tourism industries must come through the Council of Ministers, headed by the Cuban president and department ministers (CEPEC 2015), the tourist industry is finding this a navigable venture. Airbnb, for example, has been very successful in quickly penetrating the Cuban market to take advantage of the opportunity to serve travelers (Airbnb 2015; Nasr 2015). Individual homeowners in Cuba, with the appropriate authority from the government, can join the Airbnb network (Nasr 2015). The success of Airbnb highlights the opportunities that exist if political and economic obstacles can be overcome.

The literature noted FDI in Cuba was challenged by Cuban political and economic infrastructure (Burbach 2013). FDI in Cuba is also impacted by many of the same factors that limit foreign investment in other countries. An added impediment for U.S. and international firms, the U.S. embargo, affects supply chains, infrastructure services, banking, and finance (Martinez 2015). Within this context, the tourism industry has been promoted by the Cuban government (CEPEC 2015), yet little research exists that provides a descriptive analysis of success characteristics of FDI in the Cuban tourism industry. It is this question, "what are the attributes of firms that have overcome the barriers to market entry and FDI in Cuba?" that provide the rationale for the study.

Successful Market Entry in Cuba: Study Background

In the study presented here, market entry is defined as the individual steps taken by businesses to register, license, operate, and manage an organization in a foreign location (UNCTAD 2015). The tourism industry is defined as organizations whose purpose is to accommodate, entertain, and/or operate tours for individuals or groups who are outside of their normal environment (Smith 2015; The Tourism Society 2016; UNWTO 2015). Using this definition an in-depth search of tourism companies was compiled from public sources. A total population of ninety-one firms were identified as operating in Cuba for at least two years as of January 30, 2015. From this list, a representative sample of eighteen were studied. From the representative sample of eighteen, a total of ten executives were selected and interviewed in-depth (see Table 7.1).

The definition of success in market entry in this study was based on market longevity. Longevity was selected as best representing the ability of a firm to enter and remain in the Cuban market rather than a specific financial metric. Financial measures that were accurate and obtainable were

Table 7.1 Phase 1 Study Population

Name	Country of Origin	Primary Activity	Size*
Academic Arrangements Abroad	U.S.	Educational Activities	Small
Auburn Travel	U.S.	Educational Activities	Medium
Axis Hospitality	Canada	Hotels	Small
Cross Cultural Journeys	U.S.	Tours	Small
Cuba Educational Travel	U.S.	Tours	Small
Cuba Group Tours	Australia	Tours	Small
Cuba Travel Network	BVI	Aggregated services	Small
Cuba Ventures	Canada	Aggregated Services	Small
Distant Horizons	U.S.	Tours	Small
GoNext	U.S.	Tours	Small
Iberostar Hotels	Spain	Hotels	Large
Insight Cuba	U.S.	Tours	Small
Melia Hotels	Spain	Hotels	Large
Paragon	U.S.	Tours	Small
Road Scholar	U.S.	Tours	Small
Sunwing	Canada	Aggregated services	Medium
Vox	Canada	Hotels	Medium
Y'alla	U.S.	Tours	Small

Note: Small = < 20 people; medium = 20–100 people; large = > 100 people.
Source: Author's elaboration.

difficult to find. Longevity in the market, however, is often used as a measure of market-entry success, particularly for smaller business, often described as having fewer than five hundred employees (Small Business Association Office of Advocacy 2015).

Critical components of market entry were identified from the literature and the World Bank's doing business database (World Bank 2014). The interview questions for the ten company executives were constructed and validated by subject matter experts and academic professors experienced in interview data collection. All interview participants signed informed consent and confidentiality documents, and permissions were sought from applicable country ethics boards. Interviews were conducted by phone, recorded, and transcribed by a professional transcription service. Participants were provided with a copy of the interview transcript and asked to validate the transcript accuracy. If required, corrections were made until the participants confirmed the accuracy of their statements.

Five types of data were collected during this research: interviews, discussions, public data, government data, and nongovernmental organization data. The data-analysis processes followed Creswell's (1998) established methods for collecting and analyzing data from participants in a case study. Creswell's (1998) emphasis on chronological order and the treatment of patterns in the data provided a good fit for this case study. The internal and external validity of the study was enhanced by multiple reviews of the study, two data-collection databases, data triangulation, and keeping an audit trail.

A constant comparative analysis process was conducted using a customized computer program (Glaser and Strauss 2007) to compare information from the ten interview participants and publicly available documents from the eighteen representative sample companies. The combined research from all sources revealed rich, contextualized information that described organizational market-entry actions. Comparing information from multiple sources revealed similarities and differences in approaches to market entry with emerging ideas and points of emphasis showing similarities among participants, particularly in terms of patterns of success characteristics for Cuban tourism market entry. From the analysis, five themes emerged, which are discussed in the following section.

Study Results

Research results showed the underlying theoretical motivation for existing tourist companies in Cuba was first-mover advantage (44.44 percent), where early entry in the emerging Cuban market provided financial and structural advantages; theory of FDI (27.77 percent), where corporations sought to expand their market and generate profit in Cuba; internationalization theory (22.22 percent), where smaller and midsized companies use structural advantages to enter the Cuban tourism market; and the behavioral theory of the firm (5.55 percent), which suggests investment into human resources, physical assets, and organizational capabilities improved decision-making and ability to respond to future events. In contrast, interviewed participants and public data provided by members of the study described the

U.S. embargo as a primary constraint in market entry. According to study respondents, the embargo hampered capital acquisition, banking, supply-chain movement of goods and services, and internet interface, and negatively affected investment in property, infrastructure, and equipment.

Understanding the way in which the Cuban government and agencies conducted business was also challenging. All participants commented on the length of time it took for the Cuban government to render a decision on investment, and the practice of collective decision-making on the part of the Cuban bureaucracy as challenges.

Companies overcame these challenges by developing relationships with the Cuban government, their home government, service, and supply-chain providers. For U.S. companies, obtaining a license to do business in Cuba was required, but the U.S. government provided little support for market entry. Private management companies provided some market-entry support. Non-U.S. companies worked with their bilateral chambers or government agencies in Cuba as well as their home country, which they found helpful. Results showed organizations adapted to market-entry challenges by developing new relationships, adapting to the environment, focusing on product differentiation, as well as giving back to the Cuban people and country. Table 7.2, below, summarizes the organizational responses to market-entry challenges and opportunities.

Table 7.2 Primary Organizational Response to Market Entry and Challenges

Responding to Challenges	Responding to Opportunities
Established relationships	Partnered with government and hotels, developed new relationships
Adapted	Worked to provide better booking arrangements
Worked directly with management companies	Used vertical integration strategies
Set up operations in different countries	Incorporated sustainability
Used product differentiation	Curated experiences for tourists
Provided multiple experiences	
Deepened relationships by giving back	
Market positioning	
Changed pricing strategy	
Promoted understanding	
Changed booking strategy	
Gave back to the communities	

Source: Author's elaboration.

Adaptability was found to be a core capability that allowed companies entering the Cuban market to succeed in doing business on the island. This need for adaptability could be seen in the increasing demand for Cuba travel experiences and a limited supply of hotel rooms and guides, which put pressure on the cost of market entry and Cuba as a destination. Study participants found tipping and training facilitated the performance of staff. Challenges aside, Cuba was found to be a safe location in which to do business and travel, with corruption and ethics not major concerns to market entry. For example, Canadian travelers choose Cuba as a tourist destination mostly because if its affordability (Sarrasin, Arseneault, and Boivin 2017). Cuba's reputation as a low-cost tourist experience was found to be appealing to businesses looking to enter the market as well.

The quickly changing business environment in Cuba means an increasing range of organizations are starting to become active in the tourism industry. Findings from this study provide baseline data for those organizations should the U.S. market become open, and should they choose to market to U.S. residents. For those organizations, it would be wise to pursue the adventure travel market initially, as it is those travelers who are most interested in coming to Cuba within the next year. However, as time passes, those organizations should target more mainstream tourists who may be more comfortable with a Cuban tourism product that has shifted to cater to the U.S. market. The challenge facing the American tourism industry is that while new policy and travel products have made it easier to travel to Cuba, the perception that Cuba is "off limits" may persist among potential U.S. residents (Jordan et al. 2017). As the tourism industry has changed and adapted to the sociopolitical climate over the past sixty-five years, it is expected that it will do so in Cuba as well. Looking forward, unrestricted travel from the United States to Cuba has the potential to change both the tourism product and the sense of place of American tourists in Cuba. However this may be short-lived as a variety of popular media outlets have recently published stories discussing the desire of many travelers to visit Cuba before "Americans ruin it" (Orsi 2015). Another option for longer-term growth is Cuba's emphasis on medical services and healthcare. This has resulted in it being a destination for "medical tourism" activities, which accounted for 10 percent of its total national gross domestic product (Majeed, Lu, Majeed, and Shahid 2018). This would be an opportunity for American businesses to expand into the market as well.

Despite the opportunities that currently exist, unique cultural and environmental experiences customized to the tourist interests require well-trained guides, accommodations, and meals that may not be easy to develop, although English language classes have expanded on the island. Also concerning are the challenges presented by cultural heritage and biosphere tourism, which is currently concentrated nearer to Havana. In contrast, unique UNESCO sites and biospheres in central and eastern Cuba, such as Camaguey, Baracoa, and Santiago de Cuba, can be included as tourism expands to communities throughout the island (Laitamaki et al. 2016).

Given the context of the Cuba tourism market, five themes emerged from the research. Importantly, these themes were common across all participants and provided insights into Cuba market entry.

Theme 1: Limitations for entry. A review of the literature indicated the opportunity to invest in Cuba was described in attractive investment terms (CEPEC 2015), but U.S. companies faced limitations (Feinberg 2012; Guerra 2015; Laitamaki et al. 2016; Price 2016; Sheldon 2008; Sullivan 2014; Villaverde 2010; Wylie 2012). This study's findings are in line with the literature as U.S. embargo constraints for all companies included obtaining financing, dual currency, ownership of property, and operating costs (Sullivan 2014; US DoT 2016; Wylie 2012). This did not stop market entry, particularly if infrastructure investment in Cuba was limited. Participants noted overcoming these challenges resulted in a competitive advantage for their firms, which is in line with the theoretical expectations noted earlier.

Theme 2: Relationships are critical. All companies in this study mentioned the development of relationships with Cuban government, service, and supply-chain providers as critical to market-entry success. Maintaining and enhancing relationships with officials responsible for these services was noted as important for the mutual exchange of information, ideas, and education, and to enable access to resources. Relationships with service providers were critical in developing secure supply chains. Relationships, it was noted, were not established quickly. It took time, years in some cases, to develop a trusting relationship with Cuban officials and supply-chain providers. Establishing relationships with Cuban social and environmental organizations was also mentioned as helpful to market entry. Giving back to Cuban organizations established an outside company's good intentions in contributing to the welfare of the people and the environment.

Theme 3: Consider the customer. As Smith and Walter (2016) noted, the Cuban government has financial challenges, and the Cuban people have the lowest disposable income in the world (World Bank 2016). A key finding of this study was the financial importance of identifying the "paying customer." Participants identified foreign tourists, U.S. tourists, and some Cuban government projects as viable customer targets. Tourism businesses were considered especially attractive in Cuba because the paying customers were generally foreigners and not Cuban.

Theme 4: Crafting a unique business strategy. This study found creating a business strategy that works in Cuba required a unique business model. Feinberg (2014) noted the Cuban government is constrained financially and operationally, while owning all the means of production (Wilson 2014). The Cuban political system and property ownership are unique, and most market-entry companies did not have specific, reproducible, strategy experience in this environment. Market-entry strategies that worked in other countries did not work when directly applied to Cuba market entry. Thus, crafting a business strategy that worked in Cuba required a new approach, one that required building better interpersonal relationships.

Theme 5: Adaptability is a necessity. Because there is little information about Cuba market entry (Feinberg 2012; Laitamaki et al. 2016; Sheldon 2008; Villaverde 2010), study participants all concurred that adaptability is a core competency. Study participants mentioned being patient, solving supply-chain problems, market shortages, connectivity, changing government strategy, modifying offerings, and adaptability to changes in the Cuban environment as key market-entry competencies. These skills are also required to provide a consistent customer experience.

In contrast to the five important themes identified for market entry, activities noted by participants as secondary in importance help illuminate the differences in Cuba market entry as compared to other countries. In some ways this was the most interesting part of the study. For example, although market entry in foreign countries includes legal, tax, and human resources infrastructure issues (World Bank 2016), only one participant reported Cuba market entry was slightly constrained by corporate tax strategy, nor were tax benefits for doing business in Cuba a factor in market entry. Similarly, the legal structure was not a factor in market entry for most study participants (as they did not own property in Cuba), although some reported minor difficulty with home-country or Cuban market-entry legal paperwork. Ownership of private property was mentioned as a possible impediment to in-country investment because of property ownership disputes from pre-1960 (Martinez 2015; Price 2016). Companies thinking of investing in a building or property were conscious of potential pre-Revolution property ownership disputes.

The employer/employee relationship in Cuba was not considered an impediment to improving the performance of employees. The relationship of the company with the Cuban government that provides the employees is similar to the relationship with a labor union in that the company deals with an intermediary in the management of human capital. Companies generally worked around this challenge by offering nonstatutory benefits such as tips, education, or travel opportunities, which were effective in incenting the workforce. The well-educated Cuban workforce was considered a strong benefit of working in Cuba.

All study participants considered Cuba safe for travelers. Normal travel precautions were mentioned because Cuba lacks good roads and has some food safety issues, but Cuba was considered a very safe country in which to work or visit. While the Cuban government may constrain free speech and protest policies, study participants reported no concerns of safety for guests or businesses in Cuba. However, this does not mean the threat of deportation, fines, and property appropriation does not exist in the tourism industry because the Cuban government has not always positively interacted with tourism companies (The Economist 2012; Freeman 2013; Vasilak 2015). Similarly, the ethics of doing business in and with Cuba was not considered an impediment to market entry. Organizations entering the Cuban market found there to be few issues with unethical behavior. One company executive reported an expectation of "consideration," but this was the exception.

Discussion

The objective of this research was to add to the scholarly body of information on Cuba market entry by examining the market-entry strategies, challenges, opportunities, and actions of tourism businesses operating in Cuba. The study found the theoretical underpinnings of market entry were less important than the relationships developed between inbound companies and Cuban officials. Whether to facilitate better relations with Cuban officials or a commitment to philanthropy, study participants noted positive results arising from organizational leaders who developed a personal interest in Cuba, and in response, provided support to Cuban organizations and causes. Market entry was constrained by the U.S. embargo on multiple levels, including obtaining a license (for U.S. organizations), difficulty attracting financing, banking, access to markets, advertising, transportation, and technology platforms. These constraints, however, were not sufficient to limit organizations from achieving market entry. In fact, overcoming these challenges gave market-entry companies a competitive advantage. Similarly, a lack of internet access, the state-driven employee/employer relationship, tax strategies, and legal infrastructure did not constrain market entry.

Adaptability was found to be a core capability that allowed Cuba market-entry companies to succeed in doing business in Cuba. This need for adaptability could be seen in the increasing demand for Cuba travel experiences and a limited supply of hotel rooms and guides that put pressure on the cost of market entry, and the not inexpensive nature of Cuba as a destination. Study participants found tipping and training facilitated the performance of staff. Challenges aside, Cuba was found to be a safe location in which to do business and travel, with corruption and ethics not a concern in market entry.

The Cuba market-entry literature indicates an increase in investment opportunities in Cuba (Holmes 2010; Price 2016). Investment opportunities have been increasing for U.S. companies (Pickrell 2014), but some restrictions have been brought back by U.S. President Donald Trump in 2017. The 2017 dispute over the medical problems suffered by U.S. diplomatic staff have also caused relations between Cuba and the U.S. government to become strained, although not ruptured ("Trump reverses certain steps . . ." 2017).

Li et al. (2006) noted that collaboration was an efficient way to obtain services, gain support, and understand the market. This study found a similar understanding in that collaborating or entering business relationships with Cuban-based or destination management businesses was a common step taken by study participants. Adaptability was also a key step used by organizations entering the Cuban market, with changing pricing strategies to offer a range from very low-cost to higher-cost experiences a strategy pursued by some of the smaller organizations. Some organizations adapted their strategies to better relate to their Cuban partner organizations, while adapting booking strategies helped companies find new customers and work around the restrictions of the U.S. embargo.

Application of Research Finding to U.S. Companies

Embargo restrictions continue to prohibit most U.S. business in or with Cuba (Sullivan 2014; Wylie 2012), but U.S. companies may find these research results of interest, particularly as U.S.-Cuban relations begin to thaw (Ahmed and Davis 2015; Associated Press 2015; Cohen 2015; Davis 2015; Levy 2013). Rather than relying on the limited published information about the challenges and opportunities of establishing business with Cuba (Feinberg 2012; Guerra 2015; Laitamaki et al. 2016; Price 2016; Sheldon 2008; Villaverde 2010), this study sought to provide both theoretical and empirical information with practical illustrations companies need to guide their decision-making (Shoujun and Rui 2013). From the study findings, the following nine key questions may help frame the decision to pursue entry into the Cuban tourism market:

- Who is the customer? What is the commercial objective of doing business in Cuba?
- How will the company be paid, and how financially secure is the payee?
- How will the organization obtain financing and capital for a Cuban investment?
- How will the company send and receive payments?
- To what extent does the investment depend on limited resources, such as well-trained guides, hotel rooms, popular destinations, and well-structured supply chains?
- To what extent does the investment depend on the cost and availability of Cuban labor?
- To what extent does the company know and understand the Cuban way of doing business?
- How long is the company prepared to wait for payment and/or a government decision?
- To what extent is the company prepared to consider investing in the Cuban people and environment?

Companies thinking of entering the Cuban market to achieve first-mover advantage should be aware of first-mover advantages and disadvantages and craft a business strategy accordingly. Being adaptable, building relationships, considering who is the customer, and building good supply chains are paramount.

If companies are thinking about their resources and Cuba, and want to leverage those resources as with FDI theory, they should consider the incentives to overcoming market-entry limitations. This will likely include a focus on overcoming limitations to entry, building relationships, targeting non-Cuban customers, crafting a strategy, and remaining adaptable.

Small firms should consider the lessons learned from the international theory of the firm. They may be able to leverage their size to achieve advantages in specific operations. They may look to provide specific experiences that larger firms would have trouble acquiring. Smaller firms may wish to leverage their adaptability. Larger firms may wish to consider the way in which their size and resources can be used to acquire specific resources.

Finally, in examining the behavioral theory of the firm approach to Cuba market entry, companies who wish to enter the Cuban market despite limited information should be prepared to make a long-term investment in developing infrastructure, relationships, and market understanding. Firms that are willing to invest given these parameters should consider continuous evaluation and follow-up investments as options for profitability increase.

Companies who find their market-entry strategy falling into these patterns should consider the five themes arising from this research. Market-entry strategy should consider the limitations of Cuba market entry, understand who the paying customer will be, know that relationships matter in Cuba, craft an appropriate market-entry strategy specific to Cuba, and remain adaptable.

Finally, adding to the uncertainty of Cuban business opportunity has been the political transitions in both Cuba and the United States. In Cuba, the appointment of Miguel Díaz-Canel presents an unknown with regard to the direction of the Cuban economy. In the United States, President Donald Trump has modified U.S. policy toward Cuba, although these changes have not been major. How these two leaders address business relations may greatly impact the entry of U.S. companies into Cuba—or not, depending on the amount of policy change.

8

A Political Economy Approach to U.S. Normalization Policy Toward Cuba

Obama and Trump

Roger R. Betancourt[*,1]

In this chapter, five contributions are made to advance understanding of U.S.-Cuba relations. First, empirical evidence is provided on outcomes with respect to the flows of persons, goods and services, and capital between Cuba and the United States. While the evidence stresses the last decade, it goes back to the 1990s when feasible and relevant. Second, policies and their implementation by both the U.S. and Cuban governments are viewed as the actions of political agents that provide opportunities and challenges for these outcomes to fluctuate over time in pursuit of a variety of goals. Third, these outcomes are treated as responses of U.S. and Cuban entities and residents as economic agents to the policies and their implementations by the two governments. Fourth, throughout the chapter, interactions between different policies within each country as well as between the two countries are analyzed in terms of their impact on actual outcomes. Finally, in the last substantive section the role of political factors in the two recent U.S. administrations is highlighted to bring out interactions between political and economic dimensions and to illustrate the policies explicitly or implicitly adopted by the Donald Trump administration.

Before starting on the individual sections, some general comments on the approach taken will help the exposition. A political economy approach is characterized by including in the analysis two features of government actors as decision makers affecting the economy. First, government actors as

* Roger R. Betancourt, University of Maryland, Betancou@econ.umd.edu.

The Cuba-U.S. Bilateral Relationship. Michael J. Kelly, Erika Moreno, and Richard C. Witmer, II.

economic agents have self-interests that may or may not coincide with those of the governed. This is true in both democracies and nondemocracies. Hence, in the context of U.S.-Cuba relations, it applies to both governments. Second, even in cases where the interests of government actors and of those they govern coincide perfectly, there are potential deviations between announced policies and the actual outcomes of those policies as a result of implementation issues. Once again, in the context of U.S.-Cuba relations, this gap between objectives and realizations applies to both countries. I will emphasize throughout the deviations between announced policy and its implementation while mentioning convergence of government and citizens' interests far more sparingly and only when appropriate in the context of a particular discussion.

Economists' analysis of the gap between announced policy and implemented policy at the micro level has been characterized as requiring the adoption of three different roles in these evaluations: scientists, engineers, and plumbers, in Duflo's (2017) terminology. The scientific role relies on economic theory or on a specific model to derive a logically expected outcome of a policy at an abstract level; the engineering role introduces additional aspects that may affect outcomes upon implementation with varying degrees of rigor; and the plumbing role introduces idiosyncrasies and behavioral patterns arising at the implementation level that are difficult to describe rigorously in general terms but that can determine whether expected outcomes reflect those intended by the policy. While the policies considered here are macro policies, they can be evaluated in similar terms.

Just as indicated previously, we concentrate on the gap between announced policies and their implementations, that is, on engineering and plumbing aspects that lead to actual outcomes differing from expected ones. For instance, with respect to macro policies, the engineering issues often arise from general equilibrium and strategic interaction effects that are ignored at the scientific level often on the grounds of simplicity. Similarly, these engineering aspects require a number of adaptations for implementation as a result of idiosyncrasies or of behavioral patterns of economic or political agents that can be characterized as plumbing needs. These idiosyncrasies and/or behavioral patterns are the same as what existing literature in politics and economics characterizes as principal-agent problems, for example, between any ruler and any bureaucracy that implements his or her policies. This chapter attempts to incorporate these engineering and plumbing issues throughout the chapter.

Facts on the ground are a useful starting point for policy analysis in general because to understand where we are going, it is useful to know where we are coming from. For instance, evidence and perspective on Barack Obama's policy and its effects can provide insights on Trump's announced policy (The White House Press Office, June 16, 2017), as well as on its implementation both with respect to what changed and what did not change. In the context of U.S.-Cuba relations, however, Obama's Cuba normalization policy is also useful because it was focused primarily on the embargo either explicitly or implicitly.[2] The latter has three dimensions from an economic "scientific" viewpoint: flows of persons, flows of goods and services, and flows of capital across the two countries. I consider each dimension separately in the next three sections.

Notwithstanding the prior discussion, the embargo has important noneconomic but equally "scientific" aspects in terms of political interests of policymakers that affect and interact with the economic dimensions in determining outcomes. The discussion of these issues occupies a single section that also serves to illustrate the actual policies adopted by the Trump administration explicitly or implicitly. A succinct conclusion highlights the two main explicit changes between Obama's and Trump's normalization policy for the reader's convenience.

Flow of Persons between Cuba and the United States in Recent Years

The flow of persons between countries takes two main forms: migration and tourism. In the case of U.S.-Cuba relations, migration was for many years mainly a one-way flow from Cuba to the United States, while tourism has become a two-way flow in recent years. Hence, I begin by providing evidence on the nature of these flows as well as brief commentary on accompanying events associated with these flows and interactions between different types of flows. Six types of flows are explicitly discussed: three types of immigration flows into the United States, that is, as formal permanent residents, as informal visa-less aliens, and as a special category of political refugees; emigration flows out of Cuba; and two types of "tourists" or temporary flows, that is, Cuban "tourists" to the United States and U.S. "tourists" to Cuba.

Data on a numerically and politically important type of migration flow from Cuba to the United States that are captured in U.S. immigration statistics provide a useful starting point. Table 8.1 presents data on the number of Cubans admitted to the U.S. as lawful permanent residents between 1998 and 2016. These numbers reflect two entirely different types of influences. The first influence reflects the decisions of Cubans in the United States at a particular time to become U.S. permanent residents. These individuals could have come in originally as refugees, or under a wide variety of nonimmigrant visas (B-1 or B-2, for example), or illegally as visa-less aliens. If at some point in their lives they decided to apply for permanent U.S. residence, they would show up in Table 8.1 in the year in which the status was granted.

A second influence reflects Cubans admitted to the United States directly as lawful permanent residents. These individuals would include those claimed by their relatives in the United States, for example, granted U.S. permanent resident status while in Cuba, as well as those admitted under the U.S.- Cuba Migration Accord of 1994–1995. This Accord required the United States to take in a minimum of 20,000 Cuban immigrants a year as lawful permanent residents. U.S. immigration officers select these immigrants by lottery from a pool of participants. The last lottery, held in 1998, identified about 500,000 Cubans potentially eligible to come.

The data in Table 8.1 have two characteristics: a high degree of variability, reflecting numerous influences determining Cubans becoming permanent residents, as well as a trend. The average of the numbers between 1998 and 2006 is much lower than the average between 2008 and 2016. The Accord and policy factors affecting its implementation are the main determinants of the trend. More specifically, the arrival of the Obama administration in 2008 is associated with the higher average of lawful permanent residents over the 2008–2016 period. It also generates increases for each ten-year period between 1998 and 2006.

While association does not mean causation, there is no doubt that the flow of Cuban lawful permanent residents into the United States increased substantially during the Obama years. Institutional analysis suggests that policy outcomes depend on formal rules as well as on informal ones prevailing at the time of implementation. Hence, Obama's well-known views on Cuba policy before his own election are likely to have had an impact

Table 8.1 Cubans Admitted to the United States as Lawful Permanent Residents, 1998–2016

Year	Number Admitted
1998	17,750
2000	20,831
2002	28,272
2004	20,481
2006	45,614
2008	49,500
2010	33,573
2012	32,820
2014	46,679
2015	54,396
2016	66,156

Source: Department of Homeland Security, *Yearbook of Immigration Statistics*.

on these numbers, including those generated by the consequences of the Migration Accord as well as those generated by the more recent granting of B-1 and B-2 visas associated with Cuba's liberalization of its migration law on January 13, 2013.

One of the reasons for the variability in the number of Cuban immigrants becoming lawful permanent residents is the result of individuals arriving at different times deciding to change their status in any one year. We also have data on the number of arrivals of visa-less Cuban immigrants in each of the last twelve years from the work of the Center for Immigration Studies (Luna 2016; Krogstad 2017). These visa-less Cuban immigrants are those admitted into the United States under the policy popularly known as "wet foot, dry foot," which is associated with the implementation of the Migration Accord. They are not to be confused with those admitted into the United States directly as part of the category of refugees.

Table 8.2 provides the numbers of visa-less Cuban aliens admitted yearly during the period 2005–2016. Interestingly, this table has the same features as the previous one: substantial variability as well as a trend. Nonetheless, there are significant differences. First, these characteristics occur over an annual period rather than a biennial one. Second, the trend is very marked toward the end of the period. While the variability depends on many factors,

Table 8.2 Visa-less Cuban Aliens Admitted to the United States, 2005–2016

Year	Number Admitted (at all U.S. entry points)
2005	9,064
2006	10,431
2007	13,064
2008	14,276
2009	7,504
2010	7,487
2011	7,821
2012	12,240
2013	17,696
2014	24,279
2015	43,154
2016	56,406

Source: Luna (May 2016) and Krogstad (January 2017) for 2016.

including individual decisions to migrate through risky mechanisms, for example, homemade rafts (*balseros*), the trend is easier to explain and associate with one specific policy. The year 2013 is the beginning of secret negotiations between Cuba and the United States on normalization of relations.

Among the reasons the Cuban leadership began negotiations with the Obama administration were the deterioration of the economic situation despite their reforms, officially approved in 2011, fears of Venezuela imploding after Hugo Chávez's death in March 2013, and a failure to find oil through deep-sea exploration drilling of four zones in the Gulf of Mexico by the end of 2012 (Betancourt 2016). While there can be arguments as to the extent of awareness by the Cuban population of the last two issues, the population was certainly aware of the first one. Indeed, experientially it would have been even more aware than the Cuban leadership. The Cuban Standard Economic Trend Index (CSETI), an indicator of the performance of the Cuban economy, reveals a negative trend starting in August 2013 and continuing throughout 2014 (Vidal Alejandro and Hernández Catá 2016, Figure 1).

Official announcement to seek normalization of relations took place on December 17, 2014. Table 8.2 reveals a doubling of visa-less Cuban immigrants in the two-year period 2014–2016. Hence, its association with normalization policy is extremely strong. This effect is a striking (probably unintended) general equilibrium and interaction effect of Obama's normalization policy. Indeed, if the objective of Obama's normalization policy had been to increase Cuban migration into the United States, one could not ask for a more resounding success based on Tables 8.1 and 8.2. The year 2016 saw more than 66,000 Cubans become U.S. lawful permanent residents and more than 56,000 Cubans admitted into the United States as visa-less aliens. These figures represented a 42 percent and a 31 percent increase, respectively, over the previous year.

Nevertheless, a dramatic change in policy took place on January 12, 2017: namely, the Obama administration eliminated the wet foot, dry foot policy.[3] A plausible explanation for this new policy is that these substantial increases in migration were unattractive to the Obama administration and its perception of the interests of the Democratic Party. In the short run, changing an international treaty was difficult, and it would have been ineffective in controlling the outcome. On the other hand, the wet foot, dry foot policy could be changed by executive order and its effect would be immediate in reducing new flows to almost zero. Furthermore, exposés of abuses of the policy had already led to denunciations by a Cuban-American Republican senator from Florida who was seeking changes in implementation. He was praised by the *Sun Sentinel* in an editorial for this activity (January 8, 2016). Republican opposition to the policy change, if any, was unlikely to be uniform.

While those admitted as visa-less aliens could continue to apply for the category of refugees immediately, having it granted at the discretion of the immigration officer working their case was a low probability event. The numbers in Table 8.3, below, suggest, when compared to those in Table 8.2, that there was a far higher level of difficulty for Cubans to be directly admitted into the United States with the status of refugees. Table 8.3 provides the figures for Cubans admitted into the United States directly as refugees during the period 2004–2016.

One subtle aspect of the wet foot, dry foot policy change of 2017 is as an illustration of the strategic interaction effects of policy changes. One would expect the numbers of visa-less migrants coming from Cuba to the United States to be substantially reduced from 2017 onward, since the

Table 8.3 Cubans Admitted to the United States as Refugees, 2004–2016

Year	Number
2004	2,980
2005	6,360
2006	3,143
2007	2,922
2008	4,177
2009	4,800
2010	4,818
2011	2,920
2012	1,948
2013	4,205
2014	4,062
2015	1,527
2016	354

Source: Department of Homeland Security, *Yearbook of Immigration Statistics.*

Trump administration's normalization policy officially maintains this policy change, and its enforcement efforts in this general area have been more Draconian than the Obama ones were. As mentioned in connection with Table 8.2, above, undertaking the uncertain act of migrating by Cubans was made much easier by a change in Cuba's migration policies in 2013. Yet elimination of the wet foot, dry foot policy meant that doing so after January 2017 would lead to migrants ending up in detention centers with low probabilities of being admitted to the United States as refugees. This is likely to reduce the number of Cubans that will end as visa-less aliens in Table 8.2, and the Trump implementation policies are unlikely to increase substantially the numbers observed in Table 8.3. Of course, this assertion assumes other factors underlying the data in Table 8.3 remain stable without major changes in 2017 and in future years.

An interesting coupling of strategic interaction and general equilibrium effects arises as a result of Cuba's own policy changes with respect to migration in January of 2013 coupled with its announced reforms in the spring of 2011. Table 8.4 presents net migration data from Cuba's statistical agency. Several observers writing in the ASCE blog (Ernesto Hernández-Catá, February 2016; Luis R. Luis, February 2017) have pointed to a change from net emigration to

Table 8.4 Cuba's Net Migration Flows, 2011–2016

Year	Number
2011	−39,263
2012	−46,662
2013	3,302
2014	1,922
2015	−24,684
2016	−17,251

Source: Oficina Nacional de Estadística e Información (2016, Table 3.21).

net immigration in 2013 and 2014 and speculated on its causes: methodology, coverage, demographic revolution, statistical blip, or mystery.

Simpler economic explanations are available. Cuba's migration decree of January 2013 lowered the costs of emigrating substantially, directly and indirectly. Anyone who left in 2012 could take advantage of the lower indirect cost by returning and leaving again with permission to stay abroad without loss of citizenship privileges for two years (renewable twice) instead of one year. The internal economic reforms were starting to be implemented, and those returning could leave again at lower direct and indirect costs if unhappy with the situation. By 2015, it was clear to many observers inside and outside the island that despite the process of normalization of relations with the United States, the reforms were proceeding very slowly. Indeed, even Raúl Castro characterized the process as "slowly but surely" (*sin prisa, pero sin pausa*). Thus, it is neither mysterious nor surprising that in 2015 emigration out of Cuba once again dominated immigration into Cuba by a substantial margin. Either emigrants viewed the "slowly" as a contradiction of the "surely," or their rate of time preference was inconsistent with the pace implied by the "slowly." The numbers for 2016 support this view.

Migration flows are not the only person flows among countries. There are also nonimmigrant flows arising due to a variety of reasons. The two best-known reasons are tourists and "temporary" workers of one kind or another. These reasons fall in the category of B-2 nonimmigrant visas in the United States. Moreover, in the case of Cuba-U.S. flows, nonimmigrant visas are primarily tourist visas. Table 8.5 provides information on the number of Cuban nonimmigrants admitted to the United States with B-2 visas between 2007 and 2016. In contrast to Tables 8.1–8.3, Table 8.5 exhibits less variability across the years and a steadier upward trend. In similarity with Tables 8.1 and 8.2, however, there is a substantial jump in the last three years, and the largest numbers were recorded in the last two years reported in the table—that is, during two full years of implementation of normalization policy under the Obama administration.

Incidentally, some of these B-2 visa holders might also be counted in Table 8.2 under three circumstances: if they chose to overstay their B-2 visa, if they lied about having one in order to stay in the United States, or if they claimed political persecution. A noteworthy feature underlying the numbers in Table 8.5 is that the recent increase in the number of tourists, which resulted from Cuba's immigration reform in January 2013 together with normalization of relations by President Obama in December 2014, includes very different types of tourists. Some tourists are individuals who come to visit family members residing in the United States. Other tourists are *cuentapropistas* (small business owners) or their agents, who come to purchase goods and materials for their businesses on the island. Still others are "undercover" immigrants who come to stay permanently, taking advantage of the wet foot, dry foot policy and the benefits afforded by the Cuban Adjustment Act. Finally, the remainder come for diverse reasons associated

Table 8.5 Cuban Nonimmigrants Admitted to the United States with B-2 Visas, 2007–2016

Year	Number Admitted
2007	11,237
2008	15,130
2009	17,047
2010	23,745
2011	18,593
2012	21,197
2013	34,615
2014	43,737
2015	52,215
2016	52,735

Source: Department of Homeland Security, *Yearbook of Immigration Statistics* (Table 26, various years).

with their roles in Cuba's society, for example, dissidents, artists, and well-to-do members of the nomenclature.

The flow of persons moving in the other direction, that is, from the United States to Cuba, consists of two types: Cuban-Americans and non-Cuban-American (NCA) U.S. citizens. On the U.S. side, restrictions on Cuban-Americans traveling to the island were lifted systematically by the Obama administration since 2009. Restrictions on NCA U.S. citizens were lifted informally but more systematically during Obama's second term and especially after the normalization process started in December 2014. On the Cuban side, their statistical office provides information on arrivals for two categories of persons from the United States: members of the Cuban diaspora (*Comunidad Cubana en el Exterior*) and U.S. citizens. The former is composed mainly of Cuban-Americans: Cuba does not classify Cuban-Americans as U.S. citizens even if they have proof of citizenship through a U.S. passport. Perelló (2016) reports the number to have been 292,692 in 2015. That is 75 percent of the Cuban diaspora total for that year reported in Table 8.6, below, together with the numbers for NCA U.S. citizens.

Increases in tourist visits during the two years of full normalization under Obama were far higher for NCAs than for the mainly Cuban-American diaspora. For instance, the change for the 2014–2016 full normalization period was about 68 percent of the number of U.S. citizen tourists in 2016. By contrast, the change for the Cuban diaspora during the same period was

Table 8.6 Tourist Arrivals in Cuba by Country of Origin, 2008–2016

Year	Cuban Diaspora	U.S.
2008	n.a.[1]	41,904
2009	n.a.[1]	52,455
2010	375,431	63,046
2011	397,873	73,566
2012	384,181	99,052
2013	373,371	93,420
2014	361,210	92,325
2015	390,111	162,972
2016	427,477	284,252

[1] Not available.

Source: Oficina Nacional de Estadística e Informaciǿn (2014; 2015; 2016), *Anuario Estadístico de Cuba*, Table 15.3; years 2012–2016, Table 15.6.

about 16 percent of the total number in 2016. Assuming that the proportion of Cuban-Americans in the diaspora remain the same as it was in 2015 during the 2014–2016 period, one can derive a plausible expectation of the impact of Trump's normalization policy on tourists visits. While the impact will be negative for both types of tourist visits, one would expect the biggest impact on tourist flows to fall on NCA U.S. citizens for several reasons.

First, at the formal level Trump's normalization policy remains the same for Cuban-Americans, but it became more restrictive for NCA U.S. citizens. The latter must now provide evidence of belonging to one of the twelve allowed categories of visitors rather than self-declaring that they do belong to these categories. Second, at the implementation level, the new climate in the United States created by the Trump policy (discouraging individual visitors) interacting with its requirements to ensure that tourist dollars do not flow to companies associated with the Cuban military or party hierarchy (which are difficult to enforce and avoid) will be deterrents for both NCA U.S. visitors and Cuban-American ones. Since the former grew far more rapidly during Obama's normalization (four times as fast, according to our estimates mentioned previously), they are also likely to decline more rapidly in the absence of family or affective motivations for the visits. Finally, implementation could be tightened informally through plumbing effects in the form of barriers through the Treasury Department licensing, which would affect mainly NCA U.S. citizens, and immigration officers' attitudes toward returning visitors, which would affect both.

Incentives for a decrease in both types of tourist visits as well as in Cuban tourists to the United States are magnified by a recent event. Namely, the withdrawal of a substantial number of U.S. personnel from the embassy in Cuba for medical reasons of a somewhat mysterious origin. It was officially ordered in September 2017 (https://cu.usembassy.gov/end-ordered-departure-u-s-embassy-havana/). While the ordered withdrawal was ended in March 2018, the U.S. embassy in Cuba continues to operate with a restricted number of personnel. This affects the issuing of visas to Cuban tourists and less directly the encouragement to all tourists from the United State through the security and convenience provided by a fully operating embassy. With respect to tourism from Cuba to the United States, there is likely to be a decrease in numbers for two additional reasons. First, tourists coming in as undercover immigrants have their path legally blocked by the abolition of the wet foot, dry foot policy. Second, the financial costs of visits to the United States are high, especially relative to Cuba's official average income, and less likely to be affordable unless current economic conditions in Cuba improve substantially.

Summing up, the various types of person flows between Cuba and the United States have exhibited significant oscillations in response to a variety of policy changes and their implementations in both countries despite the embargo. For the immediate future, however, one would expect these oscillations, except perhaps for the refugee category, to be on the downward side. In the long term, it would not be surprising if all the other types of person flows were to resume an upward course with one exception: visa-less Cuban aliens. The end of the wet foot, dry foot policy has become a bipartisan American policy.

Flow of Goods and Services between Cuba and the United States

Most of the statements by proponents and opponents of the embargo can find some support and relevance with respect to the flows of goods and services. Proponents can point to the limitations of Cuba's economic system, and opponents can point to areas where the system has either overcome its limitations or the effects of the embargo have been so extreme that it is difficult to attribute them to any economic system. The first exception is with respect to the flow of "export" services to tourists in Cuba and of professional services of various types—for example, medical experts, sport trainers, and military personnel—to the rest of the world.[4] The second exception is with respect to the exports of goods to the United States. We discuss first the flow of goods between the two countries and subsequently the flow of services.

One of these prominent exceptions highlighting the effect of the embargo is Cuba's exports of goods to the United States. It provides a useful starting point to a discussion of the flow of goods between the two countries due to its simplicity. These exports have remained at zero in each of the last twenty years (US Census, 2017 Trade in Goods with Cuba). This fact experienced a change in January 2017 (Delgado 2017; Vinik 2017) when a shipment of Cuban marabú charcoal made by a private cooperative was allowed to enter the United States as a result of Obama's normalization policy. Coabana Trading/Holdings LLC is the U.S. company that imported the marabú into the United States (Alonso 2017) and to whom the grandfathering provision of Trump's normalization policy would apply. It confirms the difficulty in arguing that Cuba has no comparative advantage in any good that could be imported by the United States no matter how inefficient its economic system.

More generally, it is useful to look at Cuba-U.S. trade in terms of its aggregate pattern with respect to imports. Cuban imports of manufactured and agricultural goods peaked in 2008 and had not recovered by 2014. Cuba's imports from the United States were mainly agricultural products, amounting to 95 percent to 99 percent of total imports during the period 2005–2014 (Colby-Oizumi 2016, 19). The general pattern of aggregate imports during the period was similar for the United States as for Cuba's other main trading partners, regardless of composition (Colby-Oizumi 2016, Figure 1). Table 8.7, below, provides details for the period 1998–2016 on Cuban imports of U.S. goods. Succinctly put, the table shows a great deal of variability with no trend evident. Just as indicated earlier, exports of goods remained constant at zero until 2017. Under Trump's normalization policy there is no reason to expect significant deviations since embargo provisions on goods and services have not changed much except for a hard-to-enforce list of enterprises that American visitors should not patronize and American firms should not transact with.

Cuba's trade in general has been characterized by a predominance of service exports relative to goods and a predominance of goods imports relative

Table 8.7 U.S. Trade in Goods with Cuba (Cuban Imports from the United States), 1998–2016 (Million USD)

Year	Value of Imports
1998	3.6
2000	7.0
2002	145.9
2004	404.1
2006	340.5
2008	711.5
2010	363.1
2012	464.5
2014	299.1
2016	247.2

Source: U.S. Census Bureau, *International Trade Statistics, Trade in Goods with Cuba.*

to services. The two main components of service "exports" have been professional services and tourist services. Revenues from professional services such as doctors and others are difficult to estimate as they involve a variety of essentially barter agreements linking exports of professionals by Cuba and imports of oil in the case of Venezuela and/or payments for the professional services partially to the Cuban government and partially to the individual whose services are exported. Moreover, these professional services exports do not involve the United States in any significant fashion. Cuba's data on tourist revenues, however, are easily available. Table 8.8, below, presents the figures for the period 2012–2016.

While these tourist revenues include income generated by all visitors classified as tourists, U.S. citizens plus Cuban-Americans represented 13 percent of all visitors in 2015. Moreover, they probably represented a substantially higher percentage of the tourist revenues as their expenditures would include what Cuban-Americans purchase for family members and friends while in Cuba. This interpretation is supported by the declining trend between 2012 and 2014 and its reversal for the period 2015–2016 when relations were restored and normalization was at its most extensive level. A detailed chronology of the relaxation of restrictions is available (Sullivan 2017). One would expect tourist revenues from the United States to decrease as a result of Trump's normalization policy and its reversal of travel relaxations.

Summing up, the flows of goods and services between Cuba and the United States have been limited both by the embargo restrictions (as well as the inability to obtain trade financing which will be discussed in the next section) in the case of goods and by the nature of the economic system in

Table 8.8 Cuba's International Tourism Revenues, 2012–2015 (Billion Cuban Pesos (CUC))

Year	Revenue
2012	2.613
2013	2.608
2014	2.546
2015	2.819
2016	3.069

Source: Oficina Nacional de Estadística e Información, *Anuario Estadístico de Cuba* (2016, Table 15.15).

the case of services where the barter system employed by Cuba with respect to professional services is a far greater hindrance in trading with the United States and other liberal democracies than with nondemocracies or illiberal ones. In the short term, no change in the situation is likely to occur; in the long term, changes with respect to goods seem more likely than with respect to services other than tourism, at least in the absence of far more profound reforms in Cuba than what has taken place in the last seven years.

Flows of Capital between Cuba and the United States

It is in terms of restricting a variety of capital flows that the U.S. embargo has been most effective in terms of impacting the Cuban economy directly and indirectly. Not surprisingly, in this area of capital flows, Trump's normalization policy has been to maintain the restrictions that prevailed during the Obama administration before restoring relations, while grandfathering the minor relaxations that took place in this area after restoring relations to prevent injuring business interests created during that two-year period. For expositional purposes, it is helpful to review the variety of items encompassed by the term "capital flows."

Financial flows between countries involve a variety of different mechanisms: short-term arrangements, such as trade credits and short-term loans secured in various ways; long-term ones, such as foreign direct investment and development loans and grants from countries or international financial institutions; and mixtures of short- and long-term items, such as repatriation of profits, interest payments, and remittances. On the one hand, in the case of some of the items listed, embargo restrictions have been as effective as the trade embargo on export of goods from Cuba to the United States we discussed in the previous section. On the other hand, at least in the case of remittances, these limits were systematically relaxed during Obama's first term and eliminated during the second one as a result of normalization policy. Trump's announced normalization policy has continued this practice, at least formally. We will consider each type of mechanism separately.

Many countries, if not most, subsidize exports in various forms, and the provision of trade credit to institutions in other countries to finance their imports of a country's goods has become commonplace. In the United States, imports from other countries without developed legal and financial institutions were normally financed through the Export-Import Bank of the United States (EXIM). Of course, without loans from EXIM, exporters from these countries would have to find other alternatives. In Cuba's case, the direct impact of the embargo is that Cuban institutions have to pay for U.S. imports with cash or use private finance rather than pay with loans guaranteed by EXIM. One could argue that the inability to rely on trade credit from the United States could be a potential reason for the variability of Cuba's imports from the United States observed in Table 8.7. It must be noted, however, that the embargo restriction on private sector finance was relaxed by the Obama administration in January 2016 (Hirschfield Davis 2016) with not much of an effect visible in Table 8.7. Ability to pay and credit worthiness are also important in obtaining trade credit.

Among the long term mechanisms that have impacted Cuba the most with respect to capital flows is the inability to obtain loans or grants from the international financial institutions (IFIs) in which the United States plays an important role in terms of substantial voting power, namely, the International Monetary Fund, the World Bank, and the Inter-American Development Bank. The Helms-Burton Act, which was passed in 1996, requires the U.S. directors at these institutions to vote against any loans or grants to Cuba. Even if the United States would not provide capital flows directly to Cuba, it could do so indirectly through these institutions, but this option is closed to the U.S. government. To provide some perspective on what Cuba forgoes in terms of capital flows from IFIs: the Dominican Republic, with 10.6 million inhabitants, obtained $5.957 billion in disbursements from the Inter-American Development Bank in 2016 (Inter-American Development Bank Annual Report 2016, Table 1); Cuba with 11.1 million inhabitants obtained zero.

Foreign direct investment (FDI) is another important source of long-term capital flows for many countries. Direct and indirect embargo restrictions have impacted Cuba significantly. Once again, however, it is doubtful Cuba would have received substantial FDI flows from the United States under its current economic system even in the absence of the embargo. Indeed, an economist sympathetic to the lifting of the embargo has provided a thorough report on the challenges and opportunities facing foreign direct investment in Cuba in a monograph sponsored by the Brookings Institution (Feinberg 2012). More recently (2016), the same author quotes Everleny Pérez Villanueva, a highly regarded Cuban economist, as the source of an estimate for an accumulated amount of FDI over the period 1990–2009 of $3.5 billion. He also provides estimates of FDI for other countries from various sources over the same period (Table 8.3) (https://nacla.org/article/foreign-investment-new-cuban-economy), which can be used to estimate the opportunity cost to Cuba of not being able to tap into FDI.

Briefly put, the Dominican Republic received $17 billion in FDI from all sources over the same period (1990–2009); Cuba has received zero from the United States even after normalization. Incidentally, the figure for the Dominican Republic includes U.S. FDI. In a recent year (2013), total FDI flow into the Dominican Republic was $1.991 billion, and the U.S. component was $0.3735 billion or about 19 percent. If we apply the same percentage to the cumulative $17 billion, it would be $3.73 billion, which implies non-U.S. FDI in the Dominican Republic of $13.77 billion. The latter figure is still almost four times as much from sources other than the United States as Cuba has received during the same period.

Lack of FDI in Cuba has happened for a variety of reasons, many if not most of which fall in the categories described by Feinberg in his 2012 piece and are largely unrelated to the U.S. embargo. Furthermore, the situation in terms of FDI flows has not changed that much in the more recent period despite the guidelines (*lineamientos*) or reforms, a new foreign investment law, and the creation of the Mariel Economic Development Zone (ZEDM). For instance, Luis (2016) has estimated FDI figures for Cuba during the 2009–2015 period. FDI was $0.438. billion in 2013, the largest annual amount during the period. It had decreased to $0.129 billion by 2015.

Similarly, a recent evaluation of the ZEDM by the Havana Consulting Group and Tech (Morales, June 2018) describes its five-year progress (since 2013) as a collapse because: only ten projects have become operational, with twenty-five in process; only $1.191 billion has been invested against an expected $12.5 billion; and only 4,888 jobs have been created directly by FDI as opposed to the hundreds of thousands created by self-employment. The reasons behind the poor performance put forth by Morales (2018) are similar to the ones emphasized by Feinberg (2012). Another factor, however, must be mentioned in this context. Namely, the most important private company expected to play a key role in ZEDM investments, a Brazilian construction and engineering company (Odebrecht), became limited in its ability to do so due to its getting caught in the Lava Jato corruption scandal in Brazil. The latter has led to indictments and convictions of former presidents in Brazil ("Lula" Da Silva, and Dilma Roussef, respectively) and the resignation of one (Pedro Kuczynski) in Peru.

Most short-term and long-term capital flows into Cuba from the United States and aligned institutions have been restricted by the embargo. Normalization policy under Obama had a very limited impact on ameliorating their effects for a variety of reasons. For instance, many of these reasons in the case of FDI are related to the rigidity of Cuba's bureaucracy in performing tasks required for approval or in providing ancillary operational services and are unrelated to the embargo. In the case of official long-term flows, for example, the legal restrictions are impossible to avoid and difficult to change for political reasons. Trump's normalization policy does not change the formal embargo restrictions, has had a limited impact on implementation, and has had no impact on the ones stemming from the operation of Cuba's bureaucracy. Nonetheless, an exception to all these limited impacts is provided by one type of capital flows: remittances. The latter are a substantial component of capital flows between countries. Indeed, they have become a main source of capital flows from high-income to low-income countries in the twenty-first century, and the U.S.-Cuba flows are no exception.

Perhaps the most important source of official data on remittances worldwide is the World Bank (Migration and Remittances Factbook 2016). Unfortunately, the country table for Cuba (p. 109) has no entry data on remittances. Nevertheless, a variety of sources have tried to construct estimates over various periods. One of the most often cited source of estimates is the Havana Consulting Group. In a recent analysis (April 2017) by its president, Emilio Morales, estimates for 2011–2016 are provided. Table 8.9 below reproduces them. An idea of the importance of these numbers for the Cuban economy can be gathered from the fact that revenues

Table 8.9 Remittances to Cuba, 2011–2016 (Billion USD)

Year	Remittances
2011	2.295
2012	2.605
2013	2.834
2014	3.129
2015	3.354
2016	3.445

Source: The Havana Consulting Group. Cuba Trade, April 27, 2017: Figure 1.

from total exports between 2011 and 2015 ranged from 5.87 billion Cuban convertible pesos (CUC) to 3.35 billion CUC, according to the *Oficina Nacional de Estadística e Información*(ONEI 2016). Or, that remittances exceed tourist revenues in four of the five corresponding years in Tables 8.8 and 8.9. Moreover, in 2015, they do so by over half a billion CUC (http://www.cubatrademagazine.com/analysis-cuba-remittances-shifting-pattern-cuban-emigration/).

Incidentally, the data given above only include cash remittances. Estimates by the Havana Consulting Group, cited in the previously mentioned analysis, adding the value of remittances in kind, led to a total value of $6.85 billion in 2015. The increase in remittances is also associated with the increase in Cuban migrants to the United States documented in Tables 8.1 and 8.2. Indeed, the Havana Consulting Group estimates a loss of about $1 billion in remittances during 2017 as a result of the reduced number of migrants due to the Obama administration's elimination of the wet foot, dry foot policy in January 2017. On the other hand, they also estimate in a more recent study an increase in remittances due to the fact that the lack of banking facilities through U.S. institutions has led most commercial transactions through self-employment involving U.S. entities to rely on the same channels used for remittances (The Havana Consulting Group, March 3, 2018).

One consequence is an expected increase in the amounts of cash through these channels. Unfortunately, the numbers may now represent a totally different phenomenon that has little to do with traditional views of remittances and a lot to do with the lack of financial institutions in the United States willing and able to engage in financial transactions with Cuban institutions. Trump's normalization policy prohibiting transactions with institutions associated with the Cuban military does not affect remittances directly, since the list of 180 explicitly forbidden entities includes hardly any Cuban financial institutions, as can be seen in this link: https://www.state.gov/e/eb/tfs/spi/cuba/cubarestrictedlist/275331.htm. But it does so indirectly because of the uncertainty it creates in the United States and the lack of Cuban financial institutions designed to engage in financial transactions with foreigners. Most relevant for the present discussion, it provides incentives for using traditional remittances channel for new modes of transactions, including some encouraged by the Trump policy, such as rentals in homes that are contracted through Airbnb.

Summing up, embargo restrictions on capital flows have been the most effective ones in terms affecting outcomes of U.S.-Cuba relations, with one exception: remittances. The main reason, of course, is that restrictions on the latter for Cuban-Americans were not applied as widely or were not tightly enforced during most of the Obama administration. Moreover, they were eliminated as a result of Obama's normalization policy in the last two years of the administration. Trump's normalization policy in this area has been a continuation of Obama's with respect to Cuban-Americans but not with respect to NCA U.S. citizens.

Non-Economic Dimensions and Their Interactions with the Economic Dimension

Politicians have private interests which they often wrap up around lofty purposes. With respect to Cuba, President Obama's normalization policy was driven or inspired by his desire for a lasting legacy resulting from his two terms as president, his vision of the embargo as a failure expressed during his 2008 campaign, and the curious claim that normalization as a prelude to lifting of the embargo would lead to regime change from authoritarian to democratic even with the same people in charge. This claim seemed to appeal to Obama's liberal base despite the obvious evidence that it does not happen provided by the experiences of China and Vietnam over the last forty to fifty years.

What about normalization policy under Trump? The formal announcement appealed to Trump's base as well as to broader themes selected by President Trump, which may or may not be connected to what is actually happening. Even within the conservative base, normalization policy accommodates a broad variety of perhaps conflicting interests. Moreover, the Cuban- American community, for whom this issue matters a great deal, is also heterogeneous with respect to different aspects of the policy, with well-defined patterns for some such as the wet foot, dry foot policy. For example, the pattern for the latter differs substantially by migration arrival date.[5] In practice, normalization policy is also likely to incorporate Trump's perceptions of himself as a master dealmaker, such as his expressed views during his presidential campaign that the United States got nothing or very little in return from the concessions already made to Cuba, and the somewhat curious claim that he would seek concessions that would protect human rights. The latter is curious in terms of the logic in explaining why it makes sense to do so in Cuba but not in Saudi Arabia.

With the previous discussion as a background, Cuba's normalization policy in the Trump administration follows along three major fault lines. First, a formal reversal of the Obama policy did not take place in two important areas. One, official relations and activities such as the opening of the U.S. embassy in Havana and visits by U.S. government officials for a wide variety of purposes. Of course, the purposes, for example, increasing the flow of goods and services, need not and most likely will not be the same as in the previous administration. Two, changes in the Helms-Burton Act that would require action in the form of new legislation by Congress. The costs of reversals in these two areas are high politically and in the time and resources that would need to be spent on the effort. In contrast, the benefits of doing so are low, perhaps even marginally negative economically and strategically relative to the status quo. Thus, the major economic "scientific" aspects of the embargo remain the same with respect to legislation or treaties affecting the three mainly economic outcome dimensions of the previous sections.

Second, many of the features of Obama's normalization policy could be reversed at low cost, if desired, in a manner similar to how they were implemented, namely, through executive orders and implementation directives (administrative regulations). Hence, Cuba's normalization policy in the Trump administration has developed following a piecemeal approach. The latter modifies, or not, any policy supported by an executive order or implementation directive based on the perspective of its impact on the interests and goals of the Trump administration, its supporters, and private interest groups lobbying the administration. Those areas selected for change have been announced with fanfare as validating the pursuits of laudable goals from some vantage point, for example, decreasing resources flowing to the military and the party elites and protecting human rights. Those areas selected to remain the same as in the Obama administration were announced with less fanfare, for example, wet foot, dry foot policy.

Third, many aspects of implementation of policy arising from explicit directives, executive orders, or legislation depend on the actions of agents in the bureaucracy. These officials may interpret the formal policies in ways consistent with the intentions of policymakers or deviating from them, wittingly or unwittingly, for a wide variety of reasons or circumstances. This is true of all policies in general. This behavior follows from the principal agent problem, and it can also be described as a ubiquitous plumbing problem of policy advice which is usually ignored even in Duflo's appeal to economists to become plumbers. In sum, at the macro policy level examined here, the main issues lie within the second fault line identified above and their interactions with the three economic dimensions of the policy discussed in earlier sections. That is, on what one might call consequences of the engineering aspects of the policies.

An illustration of a most interesting engineering aspect of Cuba's normalization policy in the Trump administration is one that did not change from Obama's: namely, their adoption of repeal of the wet foot, dry foot policy as their own. This policy associated with the implementation of the Migration Accord in 1995, was originally announced on January 12, 2017, effective immediately by the Obama administration (https://obamawhitehouse.archives.gov/the-press-office/2017/01/12/record-press-call-cuba-policy-announcement). It was reiterated as U.S. policy in the June 2017 announcement of the Trump administration. One reason given by the Obama administration in the announcement was the substantial increase in the number of visa-less aliens from Cuba admitted into the United States after the normalization announcement (which is documented in Table 8.2 and already discussed in the section, "Flow of Persons between Cuba and the United States in Recent Years"). The Obama announcement left in place other aspects of the Migration Accord, including the yearly minimum number of at least 20,000 permanent residents to be admitted into the United States from Cuba.

What the announcements did not mention, however, was the potential consequences for remittances over the next three or four years already discussed in the section, "Flows of Capital between Cuba and the United States." Keeping the policy unchanged is consistent with the anti-immigrant stand adopted by the Trump administration. Moreover, the potential consequences of decreases in remittances to Cuba as a result of the well-known finding that the number of migrants sending remittances decline with distance from year of arrival was not highlighted either in the Obama administration announcement of change or in the Trump administration announcement of no change. Yet in the future, the role of a substantial decrease in the number of potential migrants and its effect on remittances might be important in negotiations with the Cuban government in a variety of settings, for example, with respect to accepting deportees trying to enter illegally that are also part of the Migration Accord and were left in place by both announcements. While this policy could reduce the amount of money available to Cuba from migrants' remittances, identifying these effects with the data currently gathered could be difficult given the changes in capital flows and their measurement discussed at the end of the previous section.

Finally, the wet foot, dry foot policy allowed substantial and widespread fraud and abuse of the refugee provisions denounced by a broad segment of those who became aware, including Cuban-American legislators, as mentioned earlier. Hence, it was either low cost politically and most likely a benefit for the Trump administration to adopt repeal of the policy as their own. Ironically, an Obama administration argument for the abolition of the policy was that now Cubans were being treated like every other immigrant group. This argument was, of course, not mentioned by the Trump administration in its official announcement of normalization policy. A number of other less contentious policies were also left in place by the official Trump announcement. For instance, those related to cruises, to Cuban-American travel and remittances, and to limits on the value of tobacco and rum that could be brought into the United States from Cuba trips, as well as the grandfathering of contracts already signed, as mentioned before.

General equilibrium effects of policies and strategic interactions illustrated by migration and remittances in international settings are engineering considerations that often affect macroeconomic policies.[6] For instance, they also arise with respect to restrictions on the use of trade credit to finance exports from the United States to Cuba and embargo compensation issues. For example, agricultural interests have been working on a bill that would allow financing by private sources in exchange for paying an excise tax on agricultural sales to fund payments of certified claims of expropriated property (Gámez-Torres 2017).

Since the Cuban government has tried to make compensation for costs of the embargo a required item in negotiations about compensation for expropriated properties, this potential bill would allow the Trump normalization policy to be tough on Cuba and at the same time permit an increase in U.S. agricultural exports to Cuba. Whether it would get enacted by Congress, however, is a different issue. At this point it just provides another illustration of how a policy change could generate general equilibrium effects between goods flows and capital flows as well as strategic interactions effects if non-economic considerations led to their enactment by Congress.

Concluding Remarks

One of the main policy changes actually adopted by the Trump administration is limiting doing business with the Cuban military by both tourists and firms. It is an attractive policy goal for a variety of laudable reasons, especially signaling concerns about human rights. By the very nature of the Cuban economy, however, it is nearly impossible to do a substantial amount of tourism in Cuba's hotels and resorts without doing business with the military. GAESA, a conglomerate controlled by the military, is heavily involved in domestic air travel and tourism enterprises, including hotels, restaurants, and stores. For instance, the Cuban military recently took over Habaguanex, which controls hotels, restaurants, and stores in Old Havana. The latter is one of the main tourist attractions in Cuba. Habaguanex has over 20 hotels in Havana in the list of 180 Cuban forbidden firms. This is good news for Airbnb and Cubans with rooms to rent but less so for tourists and the hotel industry in Cuba.

Another major policy change adopted by the Trump administration is that individual travel for American tourists who are not Cuban-Americans will be far more limited than under Obama's normalization policy. A list of relaxations on travel and remittances for both types of tourists under Obama between January of 2015 and October of 2016 is available (Sullivan 2017, 26). Using Table 8.6 figures, these relaxations led to an increase in travel by NCAs during these two years of 104 percent per year. By contrast, the increase in travel by Cuban-Americans during these two years was 12 percent per year. This estimate generously assumes that all of the increase in travel came from Cuban-Americans, in contrast to the Perelló (2016) estimate of 75 percent of Cuban diaspora travelers being Cuban-Americans in 2015 reported earlier. Perhaps the most significant travel restriction reimposed by the Trump administration in the November 2017 implementation of normalization policy is the elimination of the individual people-to-people travel category under self-declaration (De Young 2017). It reintroduces licensing for this group category and the need for documentation for all travelers.

Succinctly put, over the next few years one should expect a significant reduction in travel to Cuba by NCA U.S. citizens and from Cuba by Cuban citizens as a result of the change in normalization policy from Obama to Trump. In addition, trade with and investments in Cuba by most U.S. firms will remain at low levels except for a few special cases, for example, Airbnb.

Notes

1. This chapter significantly updates an earlier paper on the general topic of the Trump administration potential Cuba policy. Comments on the earlier paper by Luis R. Luis, John Devereux, and Jorge Perez-Lopez continue to benefit this chapter. Comments on the present version by Richard Witmer have substantially improved the exposition, especially for the benefit of nonspecialists. Any errors new or old are the sole responsibility of the author.
2. Background on embargoes, the history of Cuba's embargo, and the positions taken by various economic agents and policymakers in Cuba and the United States are available in an earlier paper (Betancourt 2013). An important insight from that paper is that statements true about one economic dimension are often false or irrelevant about the other two. Thus, in general, it obscures rather than enhances our understanding to lump them together.
3. One interpretation of this policy change would be that it was intended to make it difficult for the incoming Trump administration to reverse normalization policy without clashing with its anti-immigrant position. An alternative one would be that it was a parting gift to the Cuban government, which had long argued that the wet foot, dry foot policy was a provocative incentive designed to stimulate Cubans to migrate to the United States. Both seem far-fetched.
4. The "export" services label is used to emphasize that tourist revenues play the same role as goods exports and exports of professional services in terms of providing foreign exchange to any economy.
5. The Cuban-American community is very heterogeneous in its attitude toward normalization and attitudes can be segmented by time of arrival of cohorts in the United States, according to a recent FIU Cuba Poll (conducted in October 2016). Recent arrivals (post-1995) are most favorably inclined toward Obama's normalization policy, including the wet foot, dry foot policy prior to its abolition, but less likely to be able to vote because they have not become U.S. citizens. Prior arrivals (post-1982 and pre-1982) were unfavorably inclined toward Obama's normalization policy and increasingly so the more distant in time their U.S. arrival date. Not surprisingly, they also were more likely to be U.S. citizens (https://cri.fiu.edu/research/cuba-poll/2016-cuba-poll.pdf).
6. Unforeseen factors also generate substantial effects of this type. For instance, the medical reasons leading to evacuation of U.S. embassy personnel mentioned earlier are now expected to prevent fulfillment of the Migration Accord annual commitment allowing a minimum of 20,000 Cubans as permanent residents due to the lack of processing capacity (Cancio Isla 2018).

PART III
THE LEGAL DIMENSION

9

The Ghost of Helms-Burton

Necessary Course Corrections on the Path to Normalized U.S.-Cuban Relations

Jonathan C. Benjamin-Alvarado[*]

ghost
gōst/*noun*
1. an apparition of a dead person that is believed to appear or become manifest to the living, typically as a nebulous image.
"*the policy was haunted by the ghost of the cold warrior.*"

Introduction

This chapter will investigate the daunting structural policy challenges that face the United States and Cuba in their effort to advance their bilateral diplomatic and economic affairs owing largely to the draconian conditionality codified in the Cuban Liberty and Democratic Solidarity (Libertad) Act of 1996 (aka the Helms-Burton Act). The act imposed significantly harsh conditions that can only be lifted by an "act of Congress." Given the highly partisan and divided nature of executive and legislative branches of the U.S. government, it remains uncertain as to whether Congress will allow progress in the normalization process to move beyond the limits of executive action. The chapter combines subject matter expert interviews and content analysis of print media, policy statements, and analyses to identify the limits of executive action, policy rollback, and policy horizon points as they relate to the integrity of the conditions on normalization contained in Helms-Burton. To achieve this, the analysis will explore the constitutional limits of executive action in this case, the intention and durability of Helms-Burton, and its impact of the evolving state of U.S.-Cuban relations. The

[*] Jonathan Benjamin-Alvarado, University of Nebraska, Omaha, jalvarado@unomaha.edu.

The Cuba-U.S. Bilateral Relationship. Michael J. Kelly, Erika Moreno, and Richard C. Witmer, II.

chapter concludes by identifying and exploring the concrete steps that must be undertaken by the Congress to dismantle Helms-Burton, and under what conditions that might occur. It is perhaps akin to trying to exorcise a ghost or apparition that haunts the living, in spite of the fact that it is a distraction to the work at hand. After a brief recap of the December 2014 Barack Obama Cuba Initiative, and the subsequent June 2017 Donald Trump executive order, I introduce the legal and policy requirements necessary and sufficient for achieving the long-sought-for normalization between these neighbors and erstwhile regional partners. I also will discuss the "trust and rapprochement equation," a corollary to the structural component of the normalization process that looks at the elements of attitude, behavior, and concrete outcomes drawn from the ongoing set of negotiations separate from but no less integral to the normalization process than the institutionalized elements of Helms-Burton.

Three Years On

On December 17, 2014, U.S. President Barack Obama announced that the United States was going to significantly expand its policy toward Cuba. Specifically, the new approach stated that prior policy had "failed to accomplish our objective of empowering Cubans to build an open and democratic country." The Obama administration at that time initiated steps to accomplish the following: the re-establishment of diplomatic relations; improve travel and remittance policies to increase people-to-people contact; expand the travel opportunities for American citizens in support of Cuban civil society, including the creation of general license to travel in twelve categories; expand sales and exports of U.S. products to Cuba; loosen the import restrictions of Cuban goods; and allow U.S. telecommunications firms access to the Cuban market (U.S. State Department 2014). This was bolstered by parallel initiatives to authorize direct flights from U.S. cities by commercial air carriers and a record number of an estimated 500,000 Americans visiting the island in 2015 (Watts and Brodzinsky 2015). In celebrating the one-year anniversary of the policy engagement, U.S. Charge d'Affaires at the U.S. embassy in Havana Jeffrey DeLaurentis ticked off the "successes" of the past year's engagement, noting that concrete progress had been made in the following areas: removal of Cuba from the State Sponsors of Terrorism List; the re-establishment of diplomatic relations and reopening of embassies in both countries; the continuing work of the U.S.-Cuba Bilateral Steering Committee, including work on marine environmental standards, law enforcement and counter-narcotics, mail, and claims; global health initiatives; travel, commerce, internet, and telecommunications; and Cuba's facilitation of the Colombian peace talks. He noted the increased authorized travel (60 percent increase in 2015), commerce, and the flow of information to the island. But he also noted that "normalization will not happen overnight" and significant areas of disagreement including property claims, fugitives from the United States, and human rights issues still exist, on which he commented, "we have started the process of exchanging views with Cuba and expect to continue in the next year" (U.S. Department of State 2015). It is concisely captured by the idea that the initiative was "a strategic shift from the policy of isolation and regime change . . . to a more flexible policy of mutual respect and cooperation" that essentially "required an more diverse coalition of stakeholders to support and sustain it."[1]

In spite of the significance of the diplomatic opening, there still remained significant and vexing issues that would undeniably test the mettle of diplomats and policymakers as they worked through the process of normalization. Included are perhaps the most complex and perhaps intractable elements of the process: migration and brain drain (according to a study from Pew Center, this was a 78 percent increase in 2015, and a 30 percent in 2016);[2] political reform; commercial relations and finance; the trade embargo; property disputes and compensation; and the status of the Guantánamo Bay Naval Base. It is important to note that most of the areas of progress, while important, do not address the core elements of what constitute the U.S. economic embargo against Cuba and the constituencies impacted.[3] Moreover, making a quick appraisal of the public discourse around the normalization of relations with Cuba, few if any of these analyses, commentaries, and opinions addresses the centrality of resolving the requirements of the Helms-Burton Act, although they are integral to any and all realistic effort at normalization.

It is ironic then that the Obama administration had been all but silent regarding any engagement with Congress to initiate the formal process of addressing the requirements of the Helms-Burton Act codified in Sections 205, 206, and 207. In those sections of the law, it stipulates that the president must submit reports to Congress demonstrating that Cuba has satisfactorily met the requirements and factors for determining the following: when the Cuban government is a transition government;

when it possesses a democratically elected government; and the satisfactory settlement of outstanding U.S. claims to confiscated property in Cuba.[4] It is only in a short statement buried in the last paragraph of the statement from the Department of State, that the administration called on Congress to end the embargo. As mentioned, the broader discourse almost universally contains little or no mention of Helms-Burton conditionality. Even in the case of the passage of the Omnibus Appropriations Bill of December 17, 2015, James Williams, president of the pro-Cuba normalization coalition, Engage Cuba, stated that it was notable that the coalition "successfully worked hard to prevent any rear-guard riders in the omnibus that would slow the momentum of normalization with Cuba that is now underway."[5] It could be implied that the common approach of pro-normalization advocates, by and large, is marked by a noticeable lack of any mention of the Helms-Burton Act. This is perhaps the distillation of a policy approach of "erosion" to the foundational elements of Helms-Burton until some point when there will be sufficient congressional support or disinterest in adhering to and upholding the legislative requirements for lifting the embargo. Other seasoned Cuba analysts are optimistic regarding the recent changes and point to the centrality of Helms-Burton as perhaps the biggest impediment to normalization. An American business leader contends, "It has been positive and good publicity, but the core of the embargo continues as strong as before. And it is all under the big question: when will Cuban reform and change to suit the United States. That is nothing more than the continuation of the same policy that has proven so unsuccessful for over 50 years."[6]

In light of these issues, the operative question from this stage of the exploration becomes:

> *After the significant policy changes undertaken by the Obama and Trump administrations, under what conditions in Cuba will the process of transition be satisfactory enough to U.S. lawmakers to begin the process of either intentionally "chipping away" or the outright dismantling the embargo against Cuba by legislative action?*

The requirements codified in Helms-Burton are daunting for three critical reasons:

- The detailed and specific conditionality under which the determination of a "transition" and "democratically elected" government satisfies the standard set forth in Helms-Burton.
- The extent to which the hyperpartisanship and intensity of Cuban-American legislators continues to hold sway on the arc of U.S. policy vis-à-vis Cuba, and
- The process of engendering confidence-building measures between the United States and Cuba leading to a successful process of rapprochement. This can be viewed as the respect for the sovereignty and legitimacy of the standing regime in Cuba and its system of governance. It can be argued that until such time as there is a level of confidence and reliability in the negotiations of the central and ancillary elements of the relationship will a level of trust be insufficient enough for a full normalization to occur.

This was further problematized with the election of Donald J. Trump to the presidency of the United States as it creates questions regarding key elements of the U.S.-Cuban relations, including the following:

- How willing will the Trump administration be to revisit key provisions of the Cuban Adjustment Act, that for over fifty years now have allowed most Cubans to receive preferential treatment in the immigration process upon arrival on American soil? As the administration seeks to transfer its campaign rhetoric to policy, it will be interesting to see if this critical piece of Cuban-American policy interests can be preserved, even after the rescinding of the preferential treatment of Cubans arriving from the island by President Obama in January 2017. If not, it remains to be seen how much this might cost Trump politically, if anything at all, in Florida and elsewhere;
- What elements of the Obama opening can effectively be rolled back by the Trump administration? Some of the concessions granted by the 2014–2015 policy changes were designed to soften the opening to Cuba as a means of garnering support and building confidence for some of the non-negotiable elements of the embargo and its possible removal, including the expansion of political and human rights on the island, in addition, to establishing the foundation for deeper economic ties. This also considers the large investments already made by

companies such as the Starwood Group, Verizon, and U.S. air carriers that began daily flights to Cuba in the fall of 2016; and

- Realizing that in the large spectrum of U.S. foreign policy interests, Cuba is small change. This allows us to note that perhaps one of the larger reasons why U.S. policy has remained relatively the same for the past sixty years is that it does not cost the United States anything to maintain its hard line. Unlike with the Middle East, China, or Russia, there is no imminent threat to U.S. foreign policy interests because Cuba has remained stable over that time. Owing to the Cold War promise not to directly interfere in Cuban affairs and the stable nature of the Cuban regime, the United States literally has no reason to change its policy. Even with the passing of Fidel Castro and the departure of President Raúl Castro, with the transfer of power being smooth and peaceful as expected, and with the regime holding firm to its overriding Cuban socialist principles, perhaps trimmed around the edges, there is no reason to expect that anything should change.

The Limits of Executive Action on Cuba

Given the very public nature of the Cuba Initiative undertaken by the Obama administration in December 2014 to redirect the course of U.S.-Cuban relations, and the subsequent foray by the Trump administration in the Cuban policy quagmire, it is important to note the scope and limits of executive action in the arena of foreign policy matters and the extent to which those actions conform to and deviate from previous executive acts. Moreover, it will also shed some light on the degrees of freedom that President Donald J. Trump might enjoy as he enters the second half of his term.

Within the social science literature, the conventional wisdom suggests that U.S. presidents use executive orders when legislation is too difficult to pass in the face of an opposition Congress. Previous work suggests that strategic presidents do use executive orders and proclamations to circumvent an oppositional or hostile Congress, but not if they are likely to be overturned by Congress (Deering and Maltzman 1999). The use of executive orders reflects both the ability to achieve and to maintain preferred changes to the policy status quo. Other work has discovered that the vast majority of this type of executive action involves presidential authority under congressionally delegated powers of international trade and in coordination with (but largely independent of) Congress (Rottinghaus and Maier 2015). Moreover, the predominate trend of presidents is to steer clear of national security and foreign relations matters when it comes to issuing decrees, proclamations, and directives, unless it is highly coordinated with congressional allies.

Here it is important to note that the president's authority to impose, modify, or remove sanctions and conditionality is a constitutionally delegated authority, and Congress retains the power to affirm, modify, or revoke that delegated authority. It is the modification of that delegated authority that Congress has pursued in case of the economic relationship between the United States and Cuba, most visibly through the Cuban Democracy Act, the Libertad Act (Helms-Burton), and the Trade Sanctions Reform and Export Enhancement Act, as well as through various appropriations bills that presidents have signed into law (Fisk 2014). In this way, all presidents since Bill Clinton have been constrained in exercising executive action to change U.S. policy save for the matters that have made up most of the 2014 Obama initiative, with the notable exception of the "wet foot, dry foot" migration policy in place until January 2017.

Perspectives on the Integrity of Helms-Burton

> *If there is one country where Congress has spoken and spoken repeatedly and clearly, it is Cuba. You can like it, you can dislike it, agree with it, disagree with it, you can tell your congressman what you think, and please do . . . But the path to removing sanctions is with and through the United States Congress.* —Daniel Fisk (2014)[7]

As a matter of public discourse, the speed (or lack thereof) of the normalization of relations between the United States and Cuba has been met with much conjecture as to how soon or when Americans will yet again "set up shop" in Havana. The 2014 Obama initiatives have been relatively successful, but when taken into consideration under the conditions for the effective removal of the embargo, the progress specific to this issue has been marginal. In fact, most if not all of the steps taken in 2014 were, in essence, available to President Obama the day he took office in 2009. Like the lifting of some travel restrictions in 2011, the steps were an effort to facilitate dialogue between Cuba and the United States on a number of issues.

Central to any discussion of transition in Cuba, and the appropriate response of the United States to changes on the island, the process of recognition and any subsequent successor regime will be scrutinized under the requirements and factors for determining whether Cuba "qualifies" as a transition and/or democratically elected government as codified in the Helms-Burton law. In determining whether a transition government is in power in Cuba, Helms-Burton directs the president to take into account the extent to which that government, among other things:

> . . . a transition government in Cuba is a government that—has legalized all political activity; has released all political prisoners and allowed for investigations of Cuban prisons by appropriate international human rights organizations; has dissolved the present Department of State Security in the Cuban Ministry of the Interior, including the Committees for the Defense of the Revolution and the Rapid Response Brigades; and has made public commitments to organizing free and fair elections for a new government.[8]

Furthermore, in reporting to Congress, the president is required take into account the extent to which that Cuban government

> . . . is demonstrably in transition from a communist totalitarian dictatorship to representative democracy; has made public commitments to, and is making demonstrable progress in—effectively guaranteeing the rights of free speech and freedom of the press, including granting permits to privately owned media and telecommunications companies to operate in Cuba; permitting the reinstatement of citizenship to Cuban-born persons returning to Cuba; assuring the right to private property.[9]

And is

> . . . taking appropriate steps to return to United States citizens (and entities which are 50 percent or more beneficially owned by United States citizens) property taken by the Cuban Government from such citizens and entities on or after January 1, 1959, or to provide equitable compensation to such citizens and entities for such property.[10]

Helms-Burton adds: "It is the sense of the Congress that the satisfactory resolution of property claims by a Cuban Government recognized by the United States remains an *essential condition* for the full resumption of economic and diplomatic relations between the United States and Cuba."[11] While Helms-Burton formally wrote into law the linkage between compensation and normalization of relations, this linkage had long been present in U.S. policy toward Cuba.

Richard Feinberg's analysis of the just compensation issue suggests a feasible yet perhaps controversial and contentious solution:

> Conceivably, the opening Cuban position—to negate U.S. claims with Cuba's counter-claims and call it a wash—could prevail, and no compensation funds would be required. Or Cuba could propose reverting to its law 851 (1960) whereby it nationalized many properties of U.S. nationals and offered compensation via long-term bonds bearing 2 percent interest, contingent upon the removal of U.S. trade barriers (the valuation of U.S. properties would have to be agreed upon).[12]

It suggests that the aggrieved parties could receive nothing for their claims or be forced to settle for compensation that may be only "pennies on the dollar." In either scenario, there could be deep disagreement and/or counterclaims. Under the requirements of Helms-Burton, the agreement between the parties would still be subject to the approval of Congress under the terms established in Title II, Section 207.

Moreover, when one considers that there still remains a likelihood that one, if not both, chambers of Congress will remain under the control of the Republican Party for perhaps the next two election cycles after 2016, the pro-normalization camp still faces a formidable task given the exacting nature of the Helms-Burton requirements. One can even conjecture that the Republican Party's ability to hold congressional control will remain intact until at least the 2022 election cycle because of the masterful[13] and surreptitious manipulation of the 2011 reapportionment process that produced an almost ironclad majority for Republicans in the House of Representatives (Winburn and Wagner 2010; Daley 2016).[14]

It is hard to imagine, especially with a Democratic administration in the White House, that the kind of negotiation and bargaining needed between the executive and legislative branches will be possible given the extremes of discord and mistrust within and across the domestic U.S. political party system. This is exacerbated under the present contest, where there has been so much inconsistency and lack of coordination thus far with the Trump agenda as it relates to foreign policy initiatives even with Republican control of the executive and legislative branches of the government. Within this view, the process of normalization is almost a purely domestic debate with regional implications and marginal national security implications. It also reflects the limits of presidential prerogative that has been ceded to Congress under Clinton in 1996, and remains the dominant feature of U.S. policy toward Cuba.

In response to this approach, I queried a small number of senior Cuba policy analysts about the likelihood of the policy progressing beyond the margins toward a de facto legislative dismantling of the embargo.[15] By and large there was a growing impatience on the part of the American analysts with what was viewed as a lack of adequate response on the part of the Cuban side to the significant outreach advanced by the Obama administration in the past three years. Yet, on-the-ground changes in Cuba have been profound, but in most cases do not address the core objectives and requirements of U.S. policy or, better yet, the codified requirements of the Helms-Burton law. What we can ascertain at this time is that there will be continuity because of the changes that have been evident throughout the governing tenure of President Raúl Castro. This includes the reintroduction of private property, the expansion of opportunities for private enterprise, and new and younger faces occupying leadership positions in Cuban society. While a part of the necessary process of transition to a successor regime, these initiatives are in all likelihood insufficient to meet the standards required by Helms-Burton. Even with the elevation of Miguel Díaz-Canel to the Cuban presidency in 2018 upon President Raúl Castro's retirement, we still have little indication of what type of transition and change that it will augur. We still have little concrete evidence of who the members of the Díaz-Canel inner circle are, and what direction they will decide to pursue.

Impact on the Future of U.S.-Cuban Relations

Given this exploration, we can suggest that in spite of the meaningful and symbolic overture toward the normalization of relations between the United States and Cuba, we have perhaps reached an impasse that will not curtail the progress made thus far but will significantly impede the lifting of the embargo until such time as it is being debated on the floors of Congress. In that light, any president may well keep a hand on the tiller of a course toward improved commercial relations, but it does little to address the key requirements of the Helms-Burton Act. The expansion of commercial airline service directly to Cuba has enabled more Americans to travel and explore the island, but the 2015 burst of tourists revealed that Cuba was almost at its capacity in handling the rush that resulted. Now there is doubt as to whether the upward trend can continue given pall over legal travel to Cuba articulated in 2017 by new Trump regulations. Uncertainty about Cuba travel came after a record year for tourism in the country: 4 million tourists visited in 2016, a 13 percent increase from 2015, and the Cuban Ministry of Tourism previously projected a further increase to 4.1 million visitors in 2017.

Furthermore, it lays bare the reality that the current commercial model that supports Cuba's growing tourism sector is in need of significant overhaul. Virtually all inputs into the sector have to be imported, from the food to the bath soap and from printer paper to the construction materials, furniture, and paint. The dearth of manufacturing capacity is a hostage to the weak and threadbare financial base of the Cuban economy. It points to perhaps the crucial element of the U.S. embargo that is the most effective and has had the most pronounced impact on Cuban daily life—that of a policy of economic and technology denial that makes the cost of doing business in Cuba prohibitively high on the island and has compelled the Cuban leadership to continually take shortcuts and go down ideological "rabbit holes" in its attempt to stave off complete economic disaster.

What has resulted is a barely functioning socialist economy in transition that only recently has created small beachheads for capitalist market enterprises as a desperate and last-ditch effort because of the continuing distorted performance of the island's economy. Is it enough to assuage the fears and demands of the Cuban people? That is still to be determined, but in general, Cuba remains in a static position of not moving forward significantly on its effort to grow the economy, all while its infrastructure continues to crumble underfoot (Benjamin-Alvarado and Petrow 2012). As both Castro brothers leave the scene, it will be important to ascertain what the guiding principles of the successor regime will be, and how willing it will be to address, discuss, and negotiate the transition to a post-Castro system of governance under the yoke of Helms-Burton. Given this scenario, we next explore some of the elements that could facilitate the promise of, and process of normalizing bilateral relations between these neighbors.

Trust in a Time of Ambiguity

Regardless of the structural impediments that essentially block the formal normalization of relations between Cuba and the United States, there has been plenty of public conjecture as to which of the myriad actions taken on behalf of the United States will trigger the type of response and opening that American policymakers are seeking. Some elicited high levels of promise that have yet to be delivered upon by the Cubans. Consistently, Cuba policy observers are looking for more concrete evidence that the U.S. entreaties are being viewed as legitimate and are being met with a legitimate response or concession. The previously mentioned "successes" of the first year of the Obama engagement in some respects can be viewed as working at the margins insofar as they do not directly address the core elements of the conditionality of Libertad Act for normalization.

The U.S.-Cuban Rapprochement Trust Equation

$$\frac{c+r}{T} = \textbf{Confidence Plus Reliability over Time}$$

What is becoming more apparent is that normalization by decree or executive action is perhaps only a precursor to a broad process of healing the Cold War rift between neighbors that manifests itself attitudinally, behaviorally, and institutionally on both sides. In conceiving and developing the "rapprochement trust equation" I considered that only recently have American and Cuban government officials begun the formal and intimate discourse of diplomacy that covers the spectrum of issues important to both. The discussion of telecommunications, banking, migration, and compensation for expropriated properties, for example, are each an iteration of *confidence* in and *reliability* of each other to see the negotiations through to a mutually satisfactory outcome. As such, they begin to build a bank of experiences over time that raises the prospects that the two sides can begin to build a process that works for both. In terms of the Cuban perspective on these changes, it is clear that under Raúl Castro's leadership that there was significant movement toward a better relationship with the United States, but few if any of the structural requirements and factors for the determining whether or not Cuba was a "transitional government" or a "democratically elected government" were part of the discourse.

It is this that excited the media, policy observers, and the general public, and with each new initiative and change in the status quo ante anticipation grew for a more significant breakthrough in the relations between these neighbors. Yet given the high standards set out in the Helms-Burton Act, the requisite congressional support for addressing the requirements is all but absent at the time of this writing, and it appears that until a significant event such as the retirement of President Raúl Castro in 2018, that there will be little in the way of congressional movement on the issue. As a consequence of this perspective, both sides might view the "slow-go" nature of the present bilateral discussions as a necessary precursor to broader discussions that could assist in the process of building confidence between the two sides and would allow for frank discussions and debate over the future. This could be complicated by the potential of some ham-fisted effort on the part of the Trump administration to wrest the mantle of power and dominance in the relationship, potentially forcing a retrenchment or reversal (partial or complete) of transition already seen in Cuba. The process of reconciliation lies primarily in the hands of the Cuban regime and the extent to which it feels secure that engagement with the United States does not compromise regime control in terms of its sovereignty and ability to manage the eventual process of transition and change on the island.

Moreover, as the historical legacy of American dominance in the Caribbean is a powerful impediment to building broad legitimacy among the masses and a growing number of regimes in the region owing to the harsh economic nationalist and populist stances that the Trump administration has taken on regional trade, immigration policy, and the "war on drugs," among other national security issues, it perhaps would make it less likely that reconciliation of any sort might occur under the prevailing a set of circumstances.

As David A. Lake states,

> The security provided by the United States mostly protects elites from their own people . . . the United States is not providing valuable services

> but it is often the primary threat to their well-being, at least to compared to any ideal world in which wealth and power are distributed in more egalitarian ways.[16]

All this has transpired in light of growing evidence of mass opinion on both sides of the Straits of Florida, revealing more favorable opinions of the United States and Cuba, and the path toward normalizing relations. In 2016, 63 percent of Cuban-American residents in South Florida opposed continuing the U.S. embargo against Cuba. That opposition rose to 72 percent among Cuban-Americans ages 18–59, and to 79 percent of those having arrived since 1995. A large majority (69 percent) supported the decision taken by the Obama administration to open diplomatic relations with Cuba, with younger respondents even more strongly backing the policy shift (87 percent).[17] This reflects national polls in 2017, where a majority of all Americans (51 percent to 46 percent) now view Cuba favorably, having completely flipped national opinion, whereas in 1997, 81 percent of Americans viewed Cuba unfavorably, and only 10 percent held a favorable opinion.[18] These findings are similar to recent public opinion polls conducted in Cuba, where 55 percent of Cubans say that the normalization of relations between the governments of Cuba and the United States will be mostly good for the people of Cuba.[19]

Ironically, given the present stance of the Trump administration toward Cuba, rather than creating an impetus on the part of the Cubans to make the prescribed changes of government policy that would satisfy the conditionality of the Libertad Act, it has facilitated a retrenchment of sorts on the part of the Cuban government. Cuba observers state, "The Trump Administration has given Cuba's hardliners an unexpected gift: the old enemy is again at the door."[20]

They add,

> For Cuba's hardliners, this has been a godsend. The intense ideological battles unleashed by . . . Obama . . . have since intensified, and given the hardliners, once again, the "I told you so" hand. The Americans have proven once again to be unreliable and unpredictable, and are only interested in Cuba's collapse. Obama's "Trojan Horse" has been followed by a very detectable one.

This among other factors lends credibility to the assertions advanced in the U.S.-Cuban Rapprochement Trust Equation as it appears that what little progress had been made by the Obama initiative has been all but erased and reshaped by the actions of the Trump administration that directly impact the expansion of trade relations that accompanies the chill in diplomatic relations in the wake of the mysterious medical maladies that affected members of the international diplomatic community in Havana since early 2017.[21] This is clearly evident in the major Cuba policy initiative launched in 2017, the National Security Presidential Memorandum—Strengthening the Policy of the United States, and creation of the Cuban Internet Task Force, that ostensibly "examines the technological challenges and opportunities to expanding internet access and freedom of expression in Cuba."[22]

This signals that whatever trust and confidence might have been engendered by the 2014 thaw in relations is now gone, and the hope for a mutually agreed-upon path to normalization is dead for the time being. This is also now clearly demonstrated in the actions (or inactions) on the part of the Cuban regime, where a policy analyst notes:

> The Cuban government is still dominated by the fear that a more open economy for its citizens with lead to a greater dependence on the United States, a condition that has created a Gordian knot between both countries and a profound divide between the Cuban government and its citizens.[23]

What is most troubling in the short term is the ambiguity that now exists between the United States and Cuba, as the island enters perhaps one of the most monumental changes since 1959, with the departure of Raúl Castro from the helm in leadership in Cuba, there will no longer be either of the Castro brothers in the government, and a shrinking cadre of the founding revolutionaries of the regime. With the ascension of Miguel Díaz-Canel into the presidency, will the retrograde hardliners win the day, or is there a glimmer of the type of change that the people of Cuba have been clamoring for might come to pass? And, under what conditions might the United States choose to loosen or relax the conditionality of the Libertad Act sufficiently enough to engender a mutually agreed-upon process of rapprochement and normalization across the Straits of Florida?

Conclusions

At the outset of this exploration, the following question was posed:

> After the significant policy changes undertaken by the Obama administration, and now, with the prospects of a more hardline approach to Cuba under the Trump administration, under what conditions in Cuba will the process of transition be satisfactory enough to U.S. lawmakers to begin the process of either intentionally "chipping away" or the outright dismantling the embargo against Cuba by legislative action?

The requirements codified in Helms-Burton are daunting for three critical reasons:

- The detailed and specific conditionality under which the determination of a "transition" government satisfies the standard set forth in Helms-Burton.
- The extent to which the hyperpartisanship and intensity of Cuban-American legislators continues to hold sway on the arc of U.S. policy vis-à-vis Cuba, and the engendering of confidence-building measures between the United States and Cuba, leading to a successful process of rapprochement.

It can be argued that until such time as there is an acceptable level of confidence and reliability in the negotiations on the central and ancillary elements of the relationship, progress will be of a stop-and-go nature and may never reach a full accommodation of the objectives of each of the sides. But the specter of Helms-Burton, much like a ghost, or even worse a curse, will continue to haunt the process of negotiation because of the requirements of the law that would trigger the consideration of ending the embargo. This is in and of itself the critical component of improving relations between the states, as it raises the question of the sovereignty and self-determination of a national government and its ability to legitimate its rule on the island. There is little debate as to whether the core human rights and democratic values and elements of Helms-Burton are valid, but the question that legislators and policymakers will inevitably debate is whether or not the bar is too high for Cuba, in a transitional phase of leadership after the departure of the Castro brothers, to reach. It also raises the questions as to whether some of the requirements of Helms-Burton can be sufficiently scaled back to allow for some reward to the Cubans during the transition phase. This is to acknowledge that in the past decade Cuba has undergone a radical transition. Neither Castro brother is in a position of leadership in the Cuban government, Fidel having passed away and Raúl retiring from the presidency, the state control of the economy has been scaled back, the opportunity for independent economic self-determination for some Cubans has expanded, and we have seen growing bilateral commercial relations in critical areas of the economy.

The potential of movement toward normalization in this case is not unique, but there are significant barriers, impediments, and obstacles that remain in place, and it will be interesting to see if the improvements at the margins are sufficient enough to move the debate toward the central task of removing the embargo. While the onus of change sufficient enough to trigger a full dismantling to the embargo lies with Cuba, the United States will still play a significant role setting the stage for the process to unfold. Should it desire a soft landing in the transition process, it may also be compelled to soften its insistence that all elements of Helms-Burton be satisfied prior to moving toward full and permanent normalization of relations. That remains to be seen.

Notes

1. An excellent analysis of the impact on key U.S. constituencies pushing on normalization and those with the most to gain can be found in Ted Piccone, "U.S.-Cuba Normalization: U.S. Constituencies for Change," *Idees d'Ameriques*, No. 10 (Autumn 2017/Winter 2018. Accessed at http://journals.openedition.org/ideas/2017).
2. Jens Manuel Krogstad, "Surge in Cuban Immigration to U.S. Continued through 2016," *Fact Tank—Pew Research Center* (January 13, 2017). Accessed at http://www.pewresearch.org/fact-tank/2017/01/13/cuban-immigration-to-u-s-surges-as-relations-warm/.
3. Ibid. Piccone (2017/2018).
4. This process is clearly laid out in Section 6062 of *Cuban Liberty and Democratic Solidarity (Libertad) Act of 1996. See* Pub. L. 104-114, 110 Stat. 785: 22 U.S.C. §6021-6091, at section 6062 and 6063.
5. Press release, "Omnibus Passage Signals Continued Bipartisan Support for Normalization of U.S.-Cuba Relations." *Engage Cuba*, December 18, 2015. Accessed via the internet at http://www.engagecuba.org/press-releases/2015/12/18/

omnibus-passage-signals-continued-bipartisan-support-for-normalization-of-us-cuba-relations.

6. Kirby Jones, quoted in "Will U.S.-Cuba Relations Thaw Further in 2016?" *Latin America Advisor*, January 5, 2016. P.4. Accessed via the internet at https://www.thedialogue.org/.
7. In "Executive and Legislative Pathways to Removing Sanctions," *The Cuban Embargo: Policy Outlook After 50 Years*, Occasional Papers. Number 8. Dean Rusk Center, University of Georgia School of Law. (Spring 2014), p. 35.
8. Pub. L. 104-114, 110 Stat. 785: 22 U.S.C. §6021-6091, at section 6064.
9. Pub. L. 104-114, 110 Stat. 785: 22 U.S.C. §6021-6091, at section 6065.
10. Pub. L. 104-114, 110 Stat. 785: 22 U.S.C. §6021-6091, at section 6065 (b)(2)(D).
11. 22 U.S.C. § 6067 (d).
12. Richard Feinberg, *Reconciling U.S. Property Claims in Cuba* (Brookings Institution: Washington, D.C., December 2015). Pg. 40.
13. Public opinion polling as of February 2018, estimates that the Democratic Party holds a 46 percent to 40 percent advantage of the generic ballot, based on polls that ask people which party they would support in a congressional election. *See* "Who Is Winning the Race for Congress?" *Five Thirty Eight* (February 15, 2018). Accessed at https://projects.fivethirtyeight.com/congress-generic-ballot-polls/?ex_cid=rrpromo.
14. In 2010, the Republican National Committee launched an aggressive redistricting project called REDMAP. Essentially, under this project, party functionaries drew district line. They had at their disposal detailed census results, precinct-level voter tallies, and a cloud's worth of consumer choices guaranteeing Republican control of state house and the U.S. Congress. The result is a system described as "so rigged that it hardly matters anymore who's running for office." *See* David Daley (2016), Ratf**ked: The True Story Behind the Secret Plan to Steal America's Democracy (New York: W.W. Norton, 2016).
15. Analysts from the Atlantic Council Adrienne Arsht Latin America Center, the Brookings Institution Latin American Initiative, the American Security Project, the International Republican Institute, the U.S. Embassy Havana, Universidad de La Habana, the Cuban journal, *Temas*, and independent Cuban scholars were asked in open-ended interviews in December 2015 if they thought that the Obama initiative was sufficient enough to overcome the inertia that has marked the past relations and move both sides to an accommodation of disputes, discontents, and mistrust that still exist.
16. David Lake, "Presidential Address: International Legitimacy Lost? Rule and Resistance When America Is First." *Perspectives on Politics*, Vol. 16, No. 1 (March 2018), p.12.
17. *2016 FIU Cuba Poll: How Cuban Americans in Miami View U.S. Policies Toward Cuba* (Florida International University: Miami FL, 2016). Pp. 10, 12–13.
18. *Cuba/Gallup Historical Trends* (February 2017). Accessed February 5, 2018 at http://news.galup.com/poll/1630/Cuba.aspx.

19. This favorable view is tempered by the finding that more than half of the Cubans polled say they would like to move away if given a chance, Of those, nearly 7 in 10 say that they would want to go to the United States. *See A Rare Look Inside Cuban Society: A New Survey of Cuban Public Opinion*. NORC (University of Chicago) March 2017. Pp. 8, 13. Accessed at http://www.norc.org/Research/Projects/Pages/survey-of-cuban-public-opinion.aspx.
20. Paul Hare, Senior Lecturer at Boston University, quoted in "Which Economic Ties Are Most Critical for Cuba?" *Latin American Advisor* (January 18, 2018). Pg.3. Accessed at http://www.thedialogue.org.
21. It should be noted that numerous U.S. intelligence agencies, along with the high level of cooperation from the Cuban government, have been unable to find the causes and sources of the illnesses that have affected members of the international diplomatic community. The lack of a definitive cause and effect of these maladies remains problematic, as essentially, there is no known weapon, no known perpetrator, and no known crime for these acts.
22. "National Security Presidential Memorandum (NSPM-5) Strengthening the Policy of the United States" (Public Notice 10178), *Federal Register*, Vol. 82, No. 202 (October 20, 2017).
23. Jorge Sanguinetty, Chairman and Senior Advisor at DevTech Systems, quoted in "Which Economic Ties Are Most Critical for Cuba?" *Latin American Advisor* (January 18, 2018). Pg.3. Accessed at http://www.thedialogue.org.

10

U.S. Property Claims in Cuba

Michael J. Kelly, Erika Moreno, and Richard C. Witmer, II[*]

Introduction

The settlement of property claims by U.S. citizens against the government of Cuba stands as a primary impediment to the improvement, and eventual normalization, of relations between the United States and Cuba. While current and future administrations will decide U.S. policy toward Cuba, the resolution of property settlement between the two states is perhaps best understood not simply as a goal itself, but rather as a means for encouraging and sustaining a stable, free, democratic, and economically prosperous future for the citizens of Cuba. The property settlement issue should thus be considered more than an opportunity to appease American and Cuban-American claimants and rather as an opportunity to dialogue, plan, and cooperate in the process of re-establishing and deepening diplomatic and economic ties between the two countries. To better understand how this process might occur, it is necessary to explore the underlying property rights issues as well as the context that will help shape future interaction between the two countries.

Central to the dispute over property rights is finding a solution to this complex, ongoing problem that has remained unsolved for nearly sixty years. In this chapter we provide a brief overview of the problem, including the number and size of the outstanding property claims by U.S. citizens and the instrument created by the U.S. government to identify, certify, and catalog existing claims. We then outline a proposed solution that will provide relief for American claimants while also recognizing the sovereignty of Cuba, considering the reality of current use of claimed property by Cuban citizens, and acknowledging the financial limitations of the Cuban

[*] Michael J. Kelly, Creighton University, School of Law, michaelkelly@creighton.edu; Erika Moreno, Creighton University, erikamoreno@creighton.edu; Richard C. Witmer, II, Creighton University, witmer@creighton.edu.

The Cuba-U.S. Bilateral Relationship. Michael J. Kelly, Erika Moreno, and Richard C. Witmer, II.

government that poses an obstacle to the settlement of property claims while proposing a possible solution to this impediment.

Background

In the years following Fidel Castro's seizure of power in Cuba in 1959, the Cuban government undertook a campaign to nationalize the property of U.S. citizens and corporations, as well as that of citizens of other nations. The seizure of property was not limited to foreign nationals and included Cuban citizens on the island as well. The property confiscated by the Castro government included real estate, personal possessions, stocks, bonds, business inventory, and other property owned by American citizens and businesses. At the time of the expropriation of property for use and control by the regime, nearly 6,000 assets, valued at just over $1.9 billion, were owned by U.S. citizens and subsequently nationalized by Castro's government. Today, current valuations place these claims in excess of $7 billion (Foreign Claims Settlement Commission 2018).[1]

In response to the taking of property held by U.S. citizens and corporations, Congress established the Cuban Claims Program to identify and process the claims of Americans who had their property confiscated in Cuba. Given that the expropriation occurred in the first few years of the Castro regime and that U.S. nationals and lawmakers were concerned with addressing the issue while evidence and information on property was "still fresh and available," the Cuban Claims Program was established in 1964 as Title V of the International Claims Settlement Act of 1949 (Pub. L. 88-666, approved October 16, 1964, 73 Stat. 1110, 22 U.S.C 1643). With the addition of Title V, the Foreign Claims Settlement Commission was created and charged with considering the claims of American citizens against the government of Cuba for losses resulting from the nationalization, expropriation, intervention, or other taking of property by the Cuban government. Title V also included a provision for the loss of life resulting from the actions of the Cuban government. American citizens were given a deadline of January 1, 1967, to present evidence to the commission, which would then determine if the claim was valid. During the course of the commission's work, it was determined that adjudication of claims received after the deadline would be permitted. All claims in the initial adjudication process were decided by July 6, 1972, the date that legal authority for the first commission to decide claims ended. Nearly forty years after the establishment of the commission, Secretary of State Condoleezza Rice initiated a Second Cuban Claims Program in 2005, which lasted for six months, beginning on February 13, 2006, and ending on August 11, 2006. Importantly, the Cuban Claims Programs were intended only for U.S. national claimants. The program did not include Cuban exile community claimants that were citizens of Cuba at the time of expropriation but later relocated to the United States, nor Cuban claimants still in Cuba (Foreign Claims Settlement Commission 2018).[2]

The protection of U.S. nationals' claims against Cuba was further addressed in Title III of the Cuban Liberty and Democratic Solidarity (Libertad) Act of 1996 (Pub. L. 104-114). Here the law provides a sense of Congress that "the satisfactory resolution of property claims by a Cuban Government recognized by the United States remains an essential condition for the full resumption of economic and diplomatic relations between the United States and Cuba" (Cuban Liberty and Democratic Solidarity (Libertad) Act of 1996).[3] To protect the claims of U.S. nationals, the Libertad Act further addresses the buying and selling of property confiscated by the Cuban government by providing for monetary damages to property owners whose property certified by the Foreign Claims Settlement Commission is trafficked by individuals or governments.

While firmly established in U.S. law as part of Title V of the International Claims Settlement Act of 1949, as well as the Cuban Liberty and Democratic Solidarity (Libertad) Act, the resolution of property right claims presents a number of challenges as well as opportunities as the U.S.-Cuba relationship moves forward. Among these challenges is creating a mechanism that can be used to resolve outstanding property issues that protects the interest of two sovereign nations while also addressing the needs of American citizens with claims to property in Cuba. Fortunately, a model created by legal and political scholars that may serve as a template for resolving property claims is currently available. Importantly, this model proposes a process that will handle small claims in an expedited manner while also providing a way forward on larger, more complex claims. It also requires both the U.S. and Cuban governments to work together to create and implement the legal structure for addressing existing property claims. Finally, the creation of a joint Cuban-U.S. template for handling property claims may serve as an opportunity to build trust that can be extended into other areas of a renewed, burgeoning relationship between the two countries.

Claims Settlement Model

On October 1, 2005, Creighton University was awarded a grant from the U.S. Agency for International Development (USAID) to develop a model for a property claims settlement mechanism between Cuba and the United States. The goal of the project was to create a template that could be used to address outstanding property claims by U.S. citizens following Cuba's transition to democracy. Importantly, the proposed model for property claims resolution responds to a key feature of the Cuban Liberty and Democratic Solidarity Act, noted earlier, that property claims be resolved as a precondition to the U.S. government lifting the economic embargo against Cuba. With the lifting of the embargo an important step in the normalization of relations between the United States and Cuba, the settlement of property claims is a vital first step to moving relations between the two countries forward. This chapter is an overview of the Report submitted to USAID and provides an updated analysis of the challenges and opportunities that property rights play in Cuba-U.S. relations (Borchers, Kelly, Moreno, Pearlstein, Witmer, and Wunsch 2007).[4]

Property Claimants

We begin by noting the universe of property claimants against the Cuban government. Here each group addressed in the model—which consists of three groups: U.S. National Claimants, Cuban Exile Community Claimants, and Cuban Claimants still in Cuba—provides opportunities to build trust as both sides work to resolve policy claims. The first group, U.S. National Claimants, have certified their claims through the Federal Claims Settlement Commission (FCSC), a part of the U.S. Department of Justice. The FCSC's primary mission regarding Cuba was to determine the validity and amount of loss for U.S. nationals resulting from the nationalization, expropriation, intervention, or other taking of property by the Cuban government, and compile that information for use when property settlement occurs.[5] The right of American claimants to be compensated is a widely recognized right, traditionally supported by international law. For example, see *Shahin Shane Ebrahimi v. Government of the Islamic Republic of Iran*, Award 560-44/46/47-3, Iran-U.S. Claims Tribunal (Oct. 12, 1994).

Importantly, the two-party FCSC claims certification process covered property lost by U.S. nationals only, which are reported in Table 10.1 as certified claims. Furthermore, the FCSC certification process denied claims that did not meet the statutory requirements for certification (i.e., non-U.S. nationals at the time of expropriation, failure to establish loss within statutory period, lack of available evidence/failure to meet threshold of proof, etc.), which are reported in Table 10.1 as denied.[6] These denied claims are unlikely to be revisited as part of the settlement process.

Table 10.1 reports the size of the certified and denied claims class. Here we see that of the 10,175 claims filed, 7,028, or 69 percent, were certified by the FCSC. These 7,028 certified claimants were U.S. citizens at the time of expropriation, and they, or their heirs, are central to resolving property disputes before full diplomatic, economic, and legal relations can be restored. As a result, certification of a claim by the FCSC provides an opportunity for claimants to pressure the U.S. government to come to an agreement with Cuba to settle these long-held claims, or conversely, work to secure additional compensation should they feel any agreement is not sufficient to cover their outstanding claim. Similarly, the certification of these claims provides an incentive for Cuba to address these claims before normalization can occur. As outlined later, we have created an instrument for resolving these outstanding claims that respects the certified claimant as well as the Cuban and U.S. governments. Importantly, we include both the certified and denied claimants in Table 10.1 and in subsequent tables to provide insight into the size and scope of property rights claims in Cuba.

The second group of property claimants encompasses Cuban expatriates currently living in the United States. Because they were Cuban at the time of the expropriation of their property, the FCSC process did not cover their

Table 10.1 Description of U.S. Nationals' Claims as Determined by the Foreign Claims Settlement Commission[1]

Disposition	Number
Certified	7028
Denied	3146
Total Claims Filed	10175

[1] One claim is labeled as "pending," according to FCSC. It is not included as certified or denied.

Source: FCSC.

declaration of expropriation. It is expected that this group will assert claims against the Cuban government for their nationalized property. It is also likely that they will pressure political leaders in the United States to resolve their property claims before the restoration of relations can occur. Given the concentration of Cuban expatriates and their heirs in Miami and surrounding areas of south Florida, this pressure is likely to impact future property rights discussions between Cuba and the United States. As noted later, because of their political influence, their interests are expected to be part of any settlement process, and as such, they are included in the proposed settlement mechanism. Unfortunately, data on the size and type of their claims is not currently available.

The third group of concern is Cubans living in Cuba with property claims against the Cuban government. While this is an internal matter for a future Cuban government, any resolution of property claims must not negatively impact the Cuban population; otherwise, it may adversely affect and undermine the legitimacy of the settlement process. We believe that there will be an opportunity, as part of the settlement of property claims for U.S. citizens, for the Cuban government to address settlement claims by Cuban citizens as well. This may be vital, as ongoing conflict over land ownership could serve as a destabilizing force in a democratizing Cuba. The expansion of Cuban-run lodging for tourists that is currently available via Airbnb, as well as other small businesses that have emerged with the expansion of tourism, further complicate future settlement claims.

Table 10.2 provides additional information on the type of claimant that came forward during the claims process. A few important numbers are apparent. First, an overwhelming number of claimants are individuals rather than businesses or corporations. This includes 8,970 (88.2 percent) of all claimants and 6,076 (86.5 percent) of claimants certified by the FCSC. In contrast, corporations of various types make up a much smaller number and percentage of total applicants, 1,193 (11.6 percent), and certified applicants, 914 (13.3 percent). While there is some information on the types of corporate claimant, most of the corporations fall into the other category, making identification of a particular industry difficult to assess with FCSC data.

The data in Table 10.2 is also helpful in understanding the scope of the FCSC process as it provides information on the number and percentage of claims that were submitted and certified. With over 10,169 claims submitted and 7,026 certified (six and two, respectively, were missing in the data), under 70 percent of all claims met the standard of evidence required by the FCSC.

Table 10.2 Description of U.S. Claimant Class: All Claims and Certified Claims and Type of Claimant[1]

Claimant Type	All Claimants	Certified Claimants
Individual	8970 (88.2)	6076 (86.5)
Corporation: Bank	45 (0.5)	28 (0.4)
Corporation: Export-Import Bank	2 (0.0)	2 (0.0)
Corporation: Cattle Ranches	1 (0.0)	1 (0.0)
Corporation: Mining	1 (0.0)	0 (0.0)
Corporation: Sugar	11 (0.1)	8 (00.1)
Corporation: Insurance Company	32 (0.3)	31 (12.4)
Corporation: Other	1101 (10.8)	874 (88.2)
Joint tenants	1 (0.0)	1 (0.0)
Partnership	1 (0.0)	1 (.0)
Other	4 (0.0)	4 (.0)
Total Identified Claimants	10169	7026
Missing	6	2
Total	10175	7028

[1] Percentage of column total in parentheses.
Source: FCSC.

While the number of claims are important to understand the size and scope of the problem facing the Cuban and U.S. governments, three additional tables are helpful in identifying specific information on the type, amount, and location of property claims. The first, Table 10.3, provides information on the type of loss. The second, Table 10.4, provides information on the size of the claims, while Table 10.5 provides information on the location of reported claims.

As noted in Table 10.3, most of the losses, 4,924 or 70 percent, incurred by U.S. claimants were in the form of securities, with debt/mortgage a distant second at 680 or 9.7 percent. Real property claims, including improved real estate at 603 or 8.6 percent, land 332 or 4.7 percent, and buildings 4 or .1 percent, accounted for just over 13 percent of all certified claims. This is important as stocks, bonds, and other forms of securities, as well as debt and mortgages, bank accounts, and other monetary interests generally constitute a financial loss rather than physical property loss. Thus, resolving

Table 10.3 Description of U.S. Claimant Class by Type of Loss[1]

Loss Type	All Claimants	Certified Claimants
Land	430 (4.7)	332 (4.7)
Debt/Mortgage	789 (8.7)	680 (9.7)
Securities	6488 (71.2)	4924 (70.1)
Improved Real Estate	747 (8.2)	603 (8.6)
Bank Account/Cash	108 (1.2)	93 (1.3)
Personal Property	263 (2.9)	204 (2.9)
Corporate Assets	153 (1.7)	131 (1.9)
Merchandise/Stock Inventory	26 (0.3)	17 (0.2)
Personal Injury/Death	5 (0.1)	4 (0.1)
Pension	18 (0.2)	17 (0.2)
Buildings	5 (0.1)	4 (0.1)
Other	76 (0.8)	5 (0.1)
Total Identified Losses by Type	9108	7014
Missing	1067	14
Total	10175	7028

[1] Percentage of column total in parentheses.

Source: FCSC.

Table 10.4 Amount of Property Claims[1]

Value of Claim	Certified	Denied	Total
$10,000 or Less	5224	2688	7912
More than $10,000	1721	440	2161
Total	6945	3128	10073

[1] Not included in Table 10.4. are 101 observations coded as missing and 1 coded as pending. The addition of these 102 observations equals the 10,175 as reported in Table 10.1 and elsewhere.

Source: FCSC.

nearly 90 percent of all certified claims will not involve improved real estate or land and will likely result in a financial settlement.

Information on the monetary amount of both certified and denied property claims is reported in Table 10.4. Here we divide claimants into two categories based on amount of the claim: $10,000 or less and more than

Table 10.5 Location of Property

Location of Property	All Claimants	Certified Claimants
Havana, Cuba	545 (54.8)	521 (55.0)
Oriente, Cuba	73 (7.3)	68 (7.2)
Camaguaey, Cuba	51 (5.1)	49 (5.2)
Isle of Pines, Cuba	244 (24.6)	232 (24.5)
Las Villas, Cuba	32 (3.2)	31 (3.3)
Pinar del Rio, Cuba	26 (2.6)	24 (2.5)
Matanzas, Cuba	24 (2.4)	22 (2.3)
Total Identified Losses by Type	994	947
Missing or Not Physical Property	9180	6081
Total	10175	7028

Source: FCSC.

$10,000. This distinction provides insight into the size of the claimant classes for small, $10,000 and under, and large claims that are greater than $10,000. Because three-quarters of the claims are relatively small at $10,000 or less, we anticipate a fairly quick settlement process, resulting in financial compensation for these claims. Conversely, larger claims will likely need to be adjudicated before an equitable settlement can be reached. The different legal process for small and large claims is explained later.

The final table, Table 10.5, provides information on the location of property claims. Not surprisingly, we find that over half of all property is located in Havana, while nearly a quarter of all identified physical property is located in the Isle of Pines. Other locations, while much smaller in number, suggest that property claims are distributed across the island. Importantly, because just over 10 percent of all, as well as certified claims, are real estate or land, we find the number of missing cases not identified in the table reflects a point made earlier that most lost property is in a form other than real estate or land.

As this data shows, there is great diversity in the number of certified and denied claims, in the size of claims, in the varying types of property, and in their location. As a result, any mechanism proposed to resolve these outstanding claims must consider this diversity. Furthermore, while their numbers are not large as a percentage of total certified claims, real estate and land present a challenge for resolving property claims. Similar concerns about the challenge of resolving claims larger than $10,000 or more are likely as well.

Finally, given the diversity of size, type, and location of claims certified by the FCSC, any settlement mechanism must have as part of its mission a consideration for innocent third-party owners of property, especially those who currently occupy real estate and land, claimed by U.S. nationals. Furthermore, the rights of Cubans living in the United States or Cubans living in Cuba will also likely need to be part of any settlement process as lingering doubts about property rights will continue to constrain foreign direct investment and efforts of non-Cubans, and especially U.S. businesses, seeking business partnerships on the island. The proposed settlement process described later addresses these important issues. The solution put forward is compensation for those seeking resolution of their claim rather than removing current occupants from their property. While this may not meet the expectations of some claimants, the reasons for this solution are noted in the following section.

A Proposed Tribunal for Cuba-U.S. Claims

In this section we describe the recommendation made in the *Report on the Resolution of Outstanding Property Claims Between Cuba and the United States* (Borchers, Kelly, Moreno, Pearlstein, Witmer, and Wunsch 2007) Importantly, the proposed tribunal is a natural fit for a Cuban government in transition as well as a government in the United States that seeks to protect its citizens' interests while facilitating the settlement of outstanding property claims. The resolution of outstanding property claims is also necessary as U.S. companies are unlikely to support economic development, nor be granted the opportunity to engage in economic activities in Cuba, until property issues are resolved.

The property claims model proposed includes two judicial mechanisms. The first is a bilateral Cuba-U.S. Tribunal (Tribunal) established by treaty or executive agreement between the U.S. and the Cuban governments. The jurisdiction of the Tribunal would cover property claims of U.S. nationals that have been certified by the Federal Claims Settlement Commission.

Establishing the Cuba-U.S. Claims Tribunal via bilateral treaty or executive agreement between a successor government to the Castro regime and the United States will help establish the legitimacy of the mechanism in both the countries. This is enhanced by its international legal capacity as an arbitral body and by the limited scope of the tribunal, which is to resolve outstanding property disputes between the two countries and their nationals. Other political and economic issues will be addressed in a different venue.

Specifically, the proposed model calls for a nine-member tribunal with three members selected by the Cuban government, three members selected by the U.S. government, and an additional three members selected by the six members appointed by the Cuban and U.S. governments. The Tribunal's interpretive powers will include authority to promulgate rules of procedure and the power to order interim measures of relief. In addition, the body will apply international law to resolve the claims before it, all awards will be final, binding, and fully enforceable within Cuba and the United States, and the filing of claims will be limited to one year from the time of the establishment of the Tribunal. Cost of the Tribunal will be borne equally by both countries, and if necessary, the United States will assist a new Cuban government in meeting its obligations by loan or will assist in obtaining a loan from international financial institutions on favorable terms.

The Tribunal will also consider three sets of claims based on the claims' valuation as determined by the FCSC. Small claims include all claims valued at $10,000 and less, while medium claims are more than $10,000 but less than $250,000. Large claims are those remaining claims valued in excess of $250,000 at the time of expropriation.

As part of the effort to settle claims efficiently, the Tribunal will streamline small claims of $10,000 or less in a more administrative rather than adversarial process. Such an approach may prove attractive to many claimants, even if they perceive their claims to have a value prior to expropriation over $10,000. In the small claims process, the burden of proof is reduced with certification by the Foreign Claims Settlement Commission as sufficient documentation, the procedures less formal than in medium and large claims, and the remedy is limited to monetary payments rather than a return of property. The use of financial settlement in lieu of specific restitution of property is recommended, as the potential transaction costs of specific restitution, including the return of land, domiciles, personal property, and other assets, would generally be higher than those for money damages (Levmore and Stuntz 1990). As reported in Table 10.4, above, the number of FCSC-certified small claims suggest they will be the most common type at just less than 90 percent of all certified claims. As a result, providing a streamlined settlement process is the most efficient resolution possible in this class and will help hold down the aggregate costs and time necessary to resolve any settlement process.

For medium and large claims valued at more than $10,000, the government may choose to compensate claimants through restitution when feasible, monetary payments, or by alternative remedy offered by Cuba in the form of development rights, tax credits, rights in government-owned property, or other remedies designed to promote foreign investment if the claimant agrees. The notion of giving claimants alternative remedies of this sort is not unique to this context and has proved successful in other claims settlement mechanisms (Prohaski 1998; Travieso-Diaz 1996).

There are a number of important distinctions between the mechanisms to resolve claims of $10,000 or less and larger claims. The first is that small claims will be resolved with a pro claimant standard where the tribunal is required to take due regard of difficulties of proof and valuation and draw all reasonable inferences in favor of the claimant. The standard for medium and large claims is less pro claimant and requires the tribunal to draw only appropriate inferences in favor of the claimant.

A second distinction is the appointment of hearing officers, who shall have the power to act for the tribunal in cases involving small claims. These officers will act in accordance with the rules of established arbitration and will require written submissions and documentary evidence rather than an oral hearing or live testimony, unless the hearing officer determines in-person testimony is necessary. In such cases, all steps practicable will be taken to minimize inconvenience for the claimant. For medium cases, the process becomes more formal as the stakes are higher and the remedies more complex. Here, involvement of a member of the tribunal is prudent to oversee the proceedings of these cases. Importantly, members of the tribunal overseeing medium-sized cases will have the discretion to refer the case to the full tribunal for resolution. Claimants are also afforded the right to appeal to the full tribunal in these cases as well. Here the full tribunal will review the appeal and decide whether to review the case with a majority of tribunal members necessary for further review.

For cases larger than $250,000, the complexity and potentially controversial nature of the claims make adjudication a less desirable choice for resolution. Instead, the tribunal will work to provide an opportunity for the parties to structure alternative, collaborative, dispute resolution processes that result in economic development and the advancement of mutual prosperity of the parties involved. These alternative dispute resolution models will likely include mediation that facilitates resolution in a mutually beneficial way. Should mediation fail to resolve a large claim, arbitration or a hybrid mediation/arbitration model is preferred. Finally, in the most contentious cases that mediation and/or arbitration are unable to resolve, three members of the tribunal will oversee the case. It is expected that the inclusion of three members will ensure neutrality as the makeup of the panel will include a nonaligned member from a third nation. As with medium claims, a full tribunal review is possible if a majority of the tribunal agrees to hear the case.

The second judicial mechanism proposed is a Cuban Special Claims Court (Court) constituted as an independent chamber of the Cuban national judiciary. International law recognizes Cuba as retaining jurisdiction over claims of expropriation by persons of Cuban nationality at the time of the taking. This describes a large portion of the Cuban-American exile community in Miami. Established in the same way as the Tribunal, via treaty or executive agreement, the sole purpose of the Court would be to exercise jurisdiction over and resolve property claims from the Cuban-American exile community. Here, the Cuban government in consultation with the United States would appoint the twelve-member court, of which no more than half of the members could be of the same nationality. The Court will have authority to promulgate rules of procedure (separate and apart from the other organs of the Cuban judiciary) and will follow the arbitration rules promulgated by the UN Commission on International Trade Law in 1976. In addition, cases will be decided on the basis of civil law, particularly as derived from the Spanish Civil Code of 1889.

Like the Tribunal, the Court will also review cases based on size of claim with small claims, again $10,000 and less, receiving monetary compensation as part of a streamlined process. For medium and large claims, monetary compensation through restitution is suggested where feasible. Where the property is currently nonresidential, alternative remedies may be offered by the Cuban government in the form of development rights, tax credits, rights in government-owned property, or other remedies designed to promote foreign investment by Cuban exiles. The Court is encouraged to pursue alternative remedies in consultation with the claimant.

As noted earlier, the notion of giving claimants alternative remedies of this sort is not unique to this context and has proved successful in other compensation systems (Prohaski 1998; Travieso-Diaz 1996). Furthermore, in order to expedite the processing of large claims, the proposed process requires that they undergo a period of mandatory good faith mediation before seeking resolution by the Court. Finally, all claims must be presented to the Court within two years after it is established.

The third set of potential claimants that may be addressed as part of the property rights process is Cuban claimants in Cuba. While the United States has no jurisdiction in this matter, the settlement of these claims will be important for Cuba-U.S. relations as it is unlikely that economic development and U.S. investment will proceed in areas where property ownership remains contested. Perhaps as important, it is unlikely that Cuban citizens who have a legitimate claim for compensation for property expropriated by the regime will remain acquiescent if they see payments being made to U.S. citizens and former Cubans who left the island to live abroad.

In sum, there currently exists a road map for the creation of an instrument to settle claims of U.S. citizens, Cubans at the time of expropriation who have left the island, and those who have remained in Cuba but also lost property. This is important, as a mechanism to address property rights settlement is vital to normalization of Cuba-U.S. relations.

Cuban Counterclaims

Settlement of property claims in Cuba will likely be impacted by Cuba's response to the ongoing U.S. embargo. Beginning in 1992[7] and passing in every UN session since that time, the United Nations has adopted a nonbinding resolution calling for an end to the U.S. economic, commercial, and financial embargo. The resolution, which relies on the Charter of the United Nations and international law for justification (United Nations General Assembly 1992), has been used by the Cuban government to justify counterclaims against the United States. A recent report issued in 2018 by the Cuban government suggests the accumulated harm caused by the blockade over six decades to be at least $134,499,800,000, with the most recent yearly total about $4,321,200,000 (Cuba's Report 2018). While it is unlikely that the United States will agree to compensate Cuba for either amount, the UN resolution, and subsequent Cuba report on accumulated financial damage, provides a counterclaim for Cuba to pursue in any negotiation.

Discussion

While the compensation of illegally expropriated property claims is a vital element in normalizing cross-strait relations between the United States and Cuba, the reality is that a half-century of planned economies under the Castro regimes has left the island impoverished. Consequently, several elements have been built into the instruments creating the Tribunal and the Court to mitigate both the real and perceived negative impact that it might have on the Cuban economy—especially from the perspective of the Cuban population, who may harbor resentment at compensation being secured for foreign interests and for those who left Cuba. First, investment in the Cuban economy is encouraged instead of monetary compensation or property restitution. Second, innocent third parties currently occupying confiscated property are protected in their property rights—restitution that removes the current residents will not occur in those instances. Third, financial assistance to the Cuban government specifically earmarked for this process is called for. This will come either directly from the U.S. government or foreign financial institutions; thus, Cuban assets will not be diverted from assistance to the Cuban people for meeting property claim awards.

The model for property claims settlement between Cuba and the United States put forth in the Creighton Report is one in which the short-term interests of the claimants are addressed simultaneously with the long-term interests of normalized Cuba-U.S. relations, stabilized post-embargo circumstances in Cuba, sustainable foreign investment in the Cuban economy, and direct and indirect benefit to the Cuban people. Moreover, the interests of all claimant classes are addressed in furtherance of decreasing cross-strait turmoil and mending Cuban-American–Cuban relations.

Additionally, property interests of claimant parties are recognized and addressed with compensation, restitution, or mediated investment awards while the property interests of innocent third parties in Cuba are also recognized and protected. Nobody on the island will be turned out of his or her home. Yet nobody with a verifiable claim of property confiscation will come away without recompense.

The model for property claims settlement offered in the Report considered a host of previous property claims processes and is the best, most legitimate, and most efficient means that Creighton University considered for adoption. The twin goals of maximizing the pool of stakeholders likely to opt into this process while minimizing a disruptive effect during Cuba's transition (eliminating the property issue, boosting foreign investment, and benefiting the people of Cuba) have been met by this model if it is adopted and properly implemented.

Finally, the vital importance of cultural understanding as a key element in making such institutions workable ones cannot be overstated. Infusing not only the bench but also the registrar's bureaucracy with cultural sensitivity is vital to avoiding further political and legal problems which cause considerable delay and require more expensive adjustments later. This includes giving a spectrum of Cuban representatives, whose culture the United States recognizes as internally and geographically heterogeneous, as much leeway as possible in running the Court and the Tribunal.

Notes

1. *See* the Foreign Claims Settlement Commission completed programs page for Cuba at https://www.justice.gov/fcsc/claims-against-cuba. Accessed March 9, 2018.
2. Ibid.
3. *See* Title III Section 207 (d) of Pub. L. 104-114, the Cuban Liberty and Democratic Solidarity (Libertad) Act of 1996.
4. The full report can be accessed at https://www.researchgate.net/publication/228262665_Report_on_the_Resolution_of_Outstanding_Property_Claims_between_Cuba_and_the_United_States.
5. Information on the FCSC can be found at http://www.usdoj.gov/fcsc/.
6. Dismissed claims represent a third class of claims. These claims were opened by the FCSC on behalf of known U.S. property owners. When the claimants failed to appear before the commission or provide sufficient evidence to proceed, the cases were dismissed. These claims may be reasserted as part of the settlement process; however, they were not analyzed as part of the report.
7. The question of was first addressed on November 13, 1991, in Decision 46/407. The resolution on the necessity of ending the U.S. embargo was deferred for further consideration until the 47th UN session in 1992.

11

Reintegrating Cuba into the Global Economy

Stasis and the European Alternative

Larry Catá Backer[*]

The Anticipated Shape of Cuban Reform and Reintegration: Expectation and Disappointment

"I have come here to bury the last remnant of the Cold War in the Americas." These were the words that appeared to reverberate most strongly from the Gran Teatro de la Habana Alicia Alonso in the historic "Habana Vieja" section of the city on March 22, 2016, as then President Barack Obama, on the first state visit of a sitting U.S. president since the presidency of Calvin Coolidge in 1927, addressed the Cuban people (Obama 2016a). This state visit appeared to cement the reality of efforts to normalize relations between the United States and Cuba begun with a declaration to that effect by both states on December 17, 2014 (Obama 2014). It was a moment when many in the global community thought that one could imagine the reintegration of Cuba into the global economy. That expectation was grounded on the anticipation that the United States would move forward to dismantle the legislative and administrative rules that together constituted the U.S. embargo on Cuba (Backer 2004, n.174). It was also grounded in the prospect of substantial concessions by the Cubans respecting an opening up of the economy. This was summarized nicely in President Obama's press conference in Havana on March 21, 2016: "And just as I continue to call on Congress to lift the trade embargo, I discussed with President Castro the steps we urge Cuba to take to show that it is ready to do more business, which includes

* Larry Catá Backer, Pennsylvania State University, Lcb11@psu.edu.

The Cuba-U.S. Bilateral Relationship. Michael J. Kelly, Erika Moreno, and Richard C. Witmer, II.

allowing more joint ventures and allowing foreign companies to hire Cubans directly." (Obama 2016b). The door then appeared open to Cuban integration within the global economy. There was an anticipation of the return to the Organization of American States (OAS), and Cuba joining the International Monetary Fund (IMF) and World Bank. As well there was anticipation of a greater Cuban role in the World Trade Organization (WTO), from which Cuba never left but within which Cuba had been relatively unengaged (Jones 2017).

But by 2018, these prospects had changed dramatically. The election of Donald Trump to the U.S. presidency altered the landscape of U.S. policy toward Cuba. These changes culminated in a well-publicized initiative to roll back the steps toward normalization and reintegration that had been declared just months before by former President Obama (Trump 2017). At the same time, the European Union itself was roiled (Booth and McAuley 2018) by the decision of the United Kingdom to seek withdrawal from the European Union in the aftermath of the so-called Brexit Referendum (Goodwin and Heath 2016; Hobolt 2016). Simultaneously, China and its partners announced the One Belt One Road initiative along with the establishment of a multilateral development bank, the Asian Infrastructure and Investment Bank, that was expected to operate on a model distinct from that of the IMF and the World Bank, and ultimately to displace the IMF (Chow 2016).

This chapter will seek to answer the question: What internal Cuban legal adjustments will be necessary for Cuba to enter into a fully normalized relationship with the United States and the rest of the world? That raises three distinct questions made necessary by the profound changes that have occurred between the time U.S. Cuban normalization reached its high point in early 2016, and the changes in the world situation starting with the U.S. 2016 election and its aftermath. The first question centers on consideration of the adjustments Cuba might have to undertake if it is to embed itself within the structures of global trade and finance. To that end, the chapter analyzes the legal changes Cuba would need to undertake to join international financial institutions and global and regional trade organizations as then shaped by international conditions emerging after 2016. The second question examines the extent to which Cuba is disposed to consider these possible reforms. Against the objective of socializing Cuban legal and economic practices with global norms, this chapter will critically assess the extent to which the current Cuban sociopolitical framework can produce these modifications and the consequences for such limitations, including with respect to the limits of political reform and the relevance of human rights norms in the construction of economic legal and governance structures. The third question then examines what may be possible in the aftermath of the U.S. presidential election of 2016 and other global changes, including the emergence of a Chinese alternative to national embedding in global trade. These have considerably changed the terrain within with the consequences of U.S.-Cuba normalization can be considered. The examination considers the value of the European Union's strategic initiative, the Political Dialogue and Cooperation Agreement (PDCA), as a viable basis for Cuban reintegration in the global economy.

The U.S. Opening and the Expectat ion of Conventional Reintegration Models Applied to Cuba

With the global community watching, what President Obama appeared to promise during the course of his state visit to Cuba in March 2016, was opening up of sorts, and an invitation to Cuba to rejoin the global economic community. The way toward integration was offered on terms similar to those applied to other Marxist-Leninist states, notably Vietnam and China (Obama 2014). But there was a price of sorts—a movement toward the embrace of Western-style civil and political rights as a basis for the move toward more efficient and globally compatible market-driven economic organization. Just as the Cuban leadership was reassured that it need not fear the government of the United States, so it was urged, by Mr. Obama, to fear its own people less:

> I want you to know, I believe my visit here demonstrates that you do not need to fear a threat from the United States. And given your commitment to Cuba's sovereignty and self-determination, I'm also confident that you need not fear the different voices of the Cuban people and their capacity to speak and assemble and vote for their leaders. In fact, I am hopeful for the future, because I trust that the Cuban people will make the right decisions (Obama 2016a, "We will not impose our political or economic system on you.").

All of this played well within governing circles of global economic policy in states, enterprises, and civil society. And, indeed, between 2014 through the first week of November 2016, there appeared to be a growing and self-evident understanding among these elites in discussions among themselves, that it was both necessary and inevitable to prepare Cuba for its reattachment to global production using the traditional toolkit of hard and soft law at the international level to adjust Cuban internal law and policy (cf. Abbott and Snidal 2000; World Bank 2000). The template was already well developed in the work of international financial institutions in disciplining and providing technical assistance (Barnett and Finnemore 2004; Doornbos 1995). These were buttressed by well-developed programs of conditionality in sovereign lending developed to better manage transitions of economic policy and the structures of the domestic legal orders necessary to implement and administer them (Santiso 2011; Nanda 2006); these appeared especially well developed in Africa (Harrison 2004).

Key among these would be the key multilateral development banks—the World Bank and International Monetary Fund, and perhaps the Inter-American Development Bank (Feinberg 2017). "Cuba was an original member of the World Bank but never borrowed from it. Fidel Castro rejected the World Bank early on in the Revolution, withdrawing Cuba's membership in 1960. The Bank returned Cuba's capital subscription, clearing all accounts. Membership in the World Bank would be contingent upon Cuba joining the IMF" (Feinberg 2017; World Bank 2012). The politics of membership produced some speculation to that effect after 2014 (Morris 2014: "Politically, it would make sense for the IDB to play the lead role in engaging with Cuba, with much stronger regional representation than is found in the World Bank's global governance model. An economic reform agenda stands a better chance if it is viewed as coming from the region rather than imposed from outside the region."). And, indeed, playing the regional card in trade and finance has some appeal to Cuba.

The reforms necessary for joining these multilateral development banks would have created the expectation for Cuba to conform to their well-understood reform templates; like following a recipe from a well-regarded cookbook—even with some flexibility to take account of local conditions (Ban 2014). It would start with a number of analyses (from the legal, policy, economics, and political perspectives) of the legal changes that Cuba would have to implement in order to join international financial institutions and global and regional trade organizations (cf. Gurrea Martínez and Mesa

Tejada 2016b). This analysis, in effect, would invert the relationship between the sources of popular democracy (however tenuous in this case) with the administrative-managerial machinery of transnational organizations whose rules would be subject to negotiation only at the margins (Backer 2016b).

For a little while, at least, then, the question among elites was to map the necessary changes to the Cuban domestic legal order, the technical assistance required to instill global consensus on good governance, and the behavior expectations to securely couple the Cuban to the administrative cultures of the global economy (Esty 2006). Whatever the changes, change was coming and necessary to align Cuban legalities to global consensus expectations (Gurrea Martínez and Mesa Tejada 2016a). These were made necessary by the inevitable changes in Cuban political leadership (Centeno 2017). Key areas of analysis would center on Cuba's private property laws (Peters 2014); its corporation/business association laws (Gurrea Martínez and Mesa Tejada 2016b; Backer 2004, 2013); its approaches to rule of law (a sensitive and politically charged area, e.g., Patallo Sanchez 2003), and necessary modernization of a Cuban commercial code already intimated in the *Lineamientos* (2011) beyond the laws enacted for the protection of foreign investors (Republic of Cuba Ley 118, 2014). These would be compared to and compare to "industry standard"—Organisation for Economic Cooperation and Development (OECD) consensus approaches to the organization of domestic law consistent with their principles of governance and operation, perhaps best exemplified by legal systems within the European Union and in the United States (American Law Institute 2012), as well as the U.S. Convention on Contracts for the International Sale of Goods (United Nations Commission on International Trade Law 1980). And yet these market-based reforms have long been anticipated (Betancourt 1998).

Ordinarily, to these would be added further requirements necessary for membership under the regimes of the World Trade Organization. Cuba remains a member of the WTO, but has not been much engaged (Jones 2017). Were it to be reintegrated within conventional pathways of global production, there could be regulatory consequences as the additional layer of conformity around the template of consensus rules, expectations, technical assistance protocols, and regulatory toolkits around accession to the World Trade Organization (Marceau and Trachtman 2014) could find application in actions by or against Cuba in that body. The effect might be similar to that experienced in accession (see, e.g., World Trade Organization 2006 (Vietnam)). The challenge and promise of this process was taken as a matter of faith, and science. As was noted in May 2018 relating to the ongoing negotiations for the accession of Kazakhstan by WTO Deputy Director Alan Wolf:

> Another difficult accession process as that of China, because of its size, and the complexity of the modifying tens of thousands of laws and regulations to qualify for WTO membership is. Through a 15-year accession process, China did integrate substantially into the world trading system. That integration was and is a test of the world trading system due to the degree of transformation required and the dramatic growth of China as a strong participant in world commerce. (Wolff 2018)

These accession-related issues, or at least their consequences, become more important—as template for expected responses of the domestic legal order—as Cuba might choose to use the WTO as a venue for more aggressive efforts to weaken the U.S. embargo.

Political change might come as well as there was some thinking about the need for Cuba to rejoin regional trade organizations other than its key membership in the *Alianza Bolivariana Para los Pueblos de Nuestra América* (ALBA) (Backer and Molina 2009). Thus, it would be important to also examine what internal legal changes must be undertaken in Cuba in order for it to rejoin the Organization of American States (OAS) and, by extension, the Inter-American Commission on Human Rights. The current language discussing Cuba's readmission states, "On June 3, 2009, the Ministers of Foreign Affairs of the Americas adopted Resolution AG/RES.2438 (XXXIX-O/09) which resolves that the 1962 Resolution that excluded the Government of Cuba from its participation in the Inter-American system, ceases to have effect in the Organization of American States (OAS). The 2009 resolution states that the participation of the Republic of Cuba in the OAS will be the result of a process of dialogue initiated at the request of the Government of Cuba, and in accordance with the practices, purposes, and principles of the OAS." Yet those efforts would have to be tempered by the importance of understanding the consequences of the fractured nature of regionalism in Latin America. More specifically, even as the OAS remains an important venue for certain purposes among Western Hemisphere states, it remains a difficult forum for Cuba precisely because of its jurisprudence on human rights and its reading of the democratic obligations of states. Moreover, Cuba may find in alternative venues a more congenial place from which to embed itself in conventional regional politics and policy (Main 2011). This is particularly true with respect to the Association of Caribbean and Latin American States (CELAC) (CELAC 2011).

Equally important was the sense that Cuba would have to adjust to substantial changes in the global consensus about the role of human rights consideration in economic activity (Backer 2015). There was a sense that the process of greater embedding in global production would bring with it the responsibilities of conforming to global consensus norms respecting human and labor rights. Those changes would apply with equal measure to activities within Cuba undertaken in conjunction with global enterprises and with respect to Cuban economic activity outside of Cuba (Backer 2015). By enmeshing Cuban economic activities in the web of private and transnational governance structures, change would be both necessary and inevitable—the price that Cuban authorities would have to pay (like other developing states) for access to global commerce and finance (Backer 2015).

Lastly it would be expected that Cuba would join in international arbitration frameworks since both the United States and Cuba have already signed the UN Convention on the Recognition and Enforcement of Foreign Arbitral Awards (United Nations 1958), though Cuba is not a party to the International Centre for Settlement of Invesstment Disputes (ICSID) Convention. While exploration of that option was likely on the playbooks of some, it would have been difficult to imagine for Cuba, especially in the face of occasional but substantial opposition from developing states in similar straits (e.g., Boeglin 2013; Kalia 2017; cf. Blue Bank Int'l & Trust 2017 (separate opinion of Christer Söderlund)). And indeed, by 2016, Cuba had a well-structured system of about ninety-three or so investment treaties with global reach, especially so with respect to Latin American and European states. The lingering issue revolved around takings, and that remained something of a challenge given the substantial differences in view on that point between the Cubans and their trading partners (e.g., Infante and Samra 2016). All of these changes were to inform the shape of the U.S.-Cuba bilateral trading arrangement that was to emerge from the aggregation of these changes.

But all these calculations changed and changed dramatically in November 2016, when Donald Trump was elected president of the United States just a short while after the June 2016 Brexit referendum and the subsequent determination of the United Kingdom to withdraw from the European Union. Those events were themselves preceded by the Seventh

Congress of the Cuban Communist Party meeting in April 2016 (Delgao Legon 2016), at which the reforms initiated in *Lineamientos de la política económica y social del partido y la revolución* (Economic and social policy guidelines for the party and the revolution) (Partido Comunista Cubano (PCC) 2011), approved during the Sixth Congress of the PCC (Granma 2011), appeared to be slowed or reversed. After 2016, the PCC embraced a policy that appeared to substantially insulate Cuba from global norms (Sanchez Serra 2017; Backer 2018a). Those policies—the *Conceptualización del modelo económico y social Cubano de desarrollo socialista y Plan nacional de desarrollo económico y social hasta 2030* (Conceptualization of the Cuban Economic and Social Model and the National Economic and Social Development Plan through 2030) (PCC 2016) gave notice of an intention to preserve the contemporary Cuban system with changes at the margin (Frank and Rathbone 2017).

By the end of 2017 much had changed, and that altogether too brief moment when it was plausible to think in terms of reform in Cuba to reintegrate it into the global economic community had effectively passed. From the first, the Cuban state had made it clear that going forward it would not enact comprehensive changes to its domestic legal order to satisfy the tastes of international finance, nor would it be in a hurry to plug into those conventional production chains. It would make changes, to be sure, but only under carefully controlled conditions and limited to special zones where effectively the state could insulate itself against contagion by global (capitalist) norms (Marcheco 2013), focused for the moment on the Special Economic Zone around the Port of Mariel (Whitefield 2017). The Chinese and Vietnamese model of market-based socialism was rejected and with it any likelihood of normalizing engagement with global commerce (Backer 2016a). Cuban socialist law would remain true to its conventional moorings (cf. Azieri 1980). But by 2017 there had been little progress. "Cuban authorities, so insistent upon national sovereignty and state autonomy, are not accustomed to having personnel from multilateral organizations combing over their internal accounts, no less offering advice on a broad range of delicate issues. Then there is ideological reluctance." (Feinberg 2017a: "In addition, the Cuban government fears U.S. influence in the IMF and World Bank.").

Any comprehensive bilateral trade agreement between the United States and Cuba appears more elusive than ever. It fell victim to retrenchment on both sides and to the fallout from the "affair of the sonic weapons attack" (cf. Backer 2016–2018)—that followed the accusation by the United States that its diplomats and others in Cuba had been the subject of "mysterious attacks—apparently linked to high-pitched sounds . . . Havana has denied any involvement in the incidents. In a Dec. 22 [2017] speech in the Cuban parliament, Castro accused the United States of fabricating 'pretexts' to justify the return to 'failed and universally rejected policies.'" (Grogg 2018). However, cooperation in areas of mutual interest continues (Sesin 2018).

> Cuba still refuses to re-join the OAS, however, ostensibly citing Venezuela's mistreatment in a forum that is, in Havana's words, an "instrument for imperialist domination." Political positions aside, the Cuban government probably realizes that joining the body means having to abide by its rules, which includes at least a formulaic commitment to democracy and elections, and accepting the inter-American human rights provisions. (Krepp 2017).

The OAS, for its part, has not remained silent about the need for deep political reform in Cuba (Gámez Torres 2018). That may not matter, as regional states might be abandoning the OAS in favor of "the Association of Caribbean and Latin American States (CELAC) as a vehicle for political dialogue. This is the body that brings together every independent nation in the Americas other than the U.S. and Canada and is now seen by many nations, including China, as a viable alternative to the OAS." (Jessop 2018). Cuba's Communist Party has indicated a preference for focus on ALBA and CELAC for the advancement of regional integration (PCC 2016 § 325). Cuba hosted the 2014 CELAC Summit, and CELAC has established mechanisms for regional cooperation with the European Union, China, Korea, and the Gulf Cooperation Council (CELAC, Welcome, n.d.). While an object of CELAC is to reduce U.S. influence in the region, its relations with the European Union may continue to produce the sort of pressure to adapt to global consensus standards that would be compatible with U.S. interests as well. The EULAC Focus research project, funded under a grant from the European Union, is designed to reinvigorate the EU CELAC strategic partnership through 2020 (EULAC Focus 2016).

Critically, as well, the landscape for multilateral lending has been changing dramatically since the U.S. presidential visit to Cuba in 2016. With the emergence of China's One Belt One Road initiative (Gao 2018) and its coordinated multilateral development mechanism, the Asian Infrastructure and Investment Bank (AIIB) (Reisen 2015), the need to conform to the requirements of traditional public multilateral development facilities has diminished. Obama administration officials have been cited as warning that the AIIB lending could "fail to meet environmental standards, procurement requirements and other safeguards adopted by the World Bank and the ADB, including protections intended to prevent the forced removal of vulnerable populations from their lands." (Reisen 2015, 6). More important, perhaps, Reiser points out that the effect of competition among multilateral development banks reduces their ability to extract concessions, including changes in a borrowing state's domestic legal order.

For Cuba, these events change the calculus of reintegration in a profound way—it now has a choice it did not have before: to follow the Chinese path to integration, or to continue to align with the conventional approaches. Neither is particularly palatable. The Cubans rely on China, but they do not embrace Chinese market-based socialism (Backer 2016a). On the other hand, the West and the liberal market-driven cultures of conventional multilateral development banks hold no special allure for Cuba either. Both would represent compromise. And for the moment, it appears the Cubans believe they may not need to compromise with either, except at the margins and to the specific goals of eroding the U.S. embargo and of providing sources of cash for the continuation of the Cuban Marxist project insulated from the currents of market-driven governance elsewhere (cf. Fraga 2017 (e.g., with respect to the objectives of bilateral and regional trade)). As the next section suggests, the PCC has banked on their ability to avoid the need to conform to either regime by adopting a system that may appeal enough, at the margins, to allow Cuba to forge its own path—one that permits it to remain outside global production but able to take advantage on its own terms.

The Cuban Capacity for Reform

The path that Cuba intends to follow is not difficult to discern. Nor has that path been hidden from view. Rather, Cuban intentions in the economic, political, and social field have been broadcast widely, and its approach to and rejection of reintegration along the lines of the expectations of market-driven globalization have been made quite clear. The 2016 Seventh PCC Congress was used to introduce the conceptual documents that describe, in some detail, the Cuban approach to their own internal political and legal organization, as well as the principles that will guide their economic development. These, quite clearly, suggest a rejection of market-based principles as a foundation for political or economic organization. They suggest an unwillingness to broadly open the state to market forces without the strong intermediation of the state and its officials, and they reject the possibility of incorporating international standards except to the extent that they can be naturalized into the Cuban economic and political culture. What the results of the Seventh PCC Congress, and subsequent actions of the Cuban state, have made clear is that while the Cuban state apparatus is eager to find ways of reintegrating the state into the global economy, Cuba is not eager at all to permit such integration except at the state-to-state or state-to-foreign entity level. Deep integration of the Cuban private economy with global networks will remain a highly controlled and marginal feature of the Cuban reintegration plan.

At the 2016 Seventh Congress, the tone was set by the First Secretary when he suggested that a slow and steady course, with little deviation, should be the guiding principle of the Congress. And indeed, there was some dissatisfaction and a sense of anticlimax that marked a Congress most notable for its lack of either transparency or popular engagement (Cameron 2016, reporting from a usually sympathetic observer). But slow and steady also proved to serve as a reminder of the power of the traditional Cuban vision of its core organizational principles, as well as its commitment to a Cuban Marxist approach to law, governance, and economics. Raúl Castro also noted the dilemma of the future of socialist macroeconomic planning, balancing between direction by the state, open markets, and managed economic activity.

> El reconocimiento del mercado en el funcionamiento de la economía socialista no implica que el Partido, el Gobierno y las organizaciones de masas dejen de cumplir su papel en la sociedad de enfrentar cualquier situación que dañe a la población, ni mucho menos decir: "es una cuestión del Gobierno, yo no me puedo meter." (Castro 2016, 9).[1]

Those remarks were just ambiguous enough to be appealing to Cuba's Chinese allies, even as it might have been off-putting to those who before the Seventh PCC Congress expected a more vigorous movement toward reintegration with the global economy and its legal structures. In the Chinese press, this was interpreted as a broad commitment to gradual movement toward what the Chinese might understand as a version of a Chinese-style socialist market economy. They quoted an official commentator to that effect:

> Rafael Hernandez, Cuban political analyst and head of the Temas magazine, said the task is among the hardest challenges facing Cuba in the last 20 years. "We are not rushing towards a free market economy, nor is our government taking us there. This is a gradual process of transformation, economic diversification and development of a nationalist private sector," Hernandez told Xinhua." (Xinhua 2016).

It is with this in mind that one should consider one of the principal documents that was produced by the Seventh PCC Congress, the "Conceptualisation of the Cuban socio-economic socialist development model" (*Conceptualización del modelo económico y social Cubano de desarrollo socialista*), which is intended to complement the Guidelines (*Lineamientos*) of the Sixth PCC Congress, and provide the theoretical foundation for its further implementation. Adopted in principle, the *Conceptualización* serves to answer the question: What sort of theoretical model will guide the development of socialism in Cuba. The Guidelines carried forward a tension between an emphasis on the state as the foundation and controlling force of economic activity, or a move toward regulated markets as a basis for economic development, without deciding between them. In contrast to the development of Asian socialist theory, grounded in the notion of socialist markets, distinct from capitalist market constructs (Backer 2016a), the *Conceptualización* appears to reject the primacy of markets, unable to distinguish markets from capitalism (as it understands that notion) and sets at its center the ideal of economic activity, including market activity, managed by and under the direction of the state as the highest expression of socialist economics—and politics.

To fully understand the Cuban position on reintegration, then, one must understand the principles and implementation strategies written into the *Conceptualización*. The *Conceptualización* (PCC 2016) is divided into four chapters; the first touching on sustaining principles and objectives (¶¶ 45–115), the second on the ownership of the means of production (¶¶ 116–202), the third on the core importance of economic central planning (¶¶ 203–264), and the last on social politics (¶¶ 265–311). These are preceded by an introduction (¶¶ 1–44) and completed with a brief set of "final considerations" (¶¶ 312–330). Their respective importance to the project of Cuban reintegration follows. The analysis is most useful for understanding those bright lines beyond which it is unlikely that the Cubans will be willing to compromise except in exceptional circumstances. Taken as a whole, however, the *Conceptualización* suggests a deep antipathy to the application of Western liberal models of civil and political rights, as well as a deep rejection of the notions of markets and market-based regulatory governance regimes for the ordering of their legal and economic orders.

The Introduction sets out the grand vision of the Cuban economic-social model. Its theoretical basis and characteristics: "Expone las bases teóricas y características esenciales del Modelo Económico y Social Cuba no de Desarrollo Socialista" (PCC 2016; *Conceptualización* ¶ 2).[2] The object is to create a superior society within Cuba ("con el objetivo de avanzar hacia una sociedad superior" (PCC 2016, ¶ 9). The characteristics of this society will be based on principles of socialism, prosperity, and sustainability ("en función de avanzar hacia una sociedad socialista, próspera y sostenible," PCC 2016, ¶ 10). The *Conceptualización* then turns to the specification of the foundational premises for the construction of Cuban socialism in this stage in its development, its structures, and its strategic goals. These are, in turn, embedded in history and context. First, Cuban society is in the midst of a process of constructing a true socialist society as a superior alternative to capitalist development, which alternative will contribute to the development of humanity ("La sociedad cubana se encuentra en el proceso histórico de construcción del socialismo, como alternativa viable para superar el capitalismo y, con ello, contribuir modestamente a la supervivencia de la Humanidad," PCC 2016, ¶ 8). Second, this long march toward a socialist society must adjust itself to new conditions, even on a temporary basis, in order to survive and prosper ("y se ajusta a las nuevas condiciones internas y el contexto internacional contemporáneo," PCC 2016, ¶ 12).

The essential basis for Cuba's political and economic (and legal) model is in turn embedded in what it gathers together as the concept of Revolution (2000) of Fidel Castro. That concept is grounded in a long entanglement with and development of strategies of opposition to the United States, leading to the reform and opening up of the *Lineamientos* (¶¶ 14–35). From these Revolutionary concepts were forged seven basic principles for advancing socialist development that is prosperous and sustainable ("para un desarrollo socialista próspero y sostenible," PCC 2016, ¶¶ 36–43). These include (1) unity and independence of the Cuban people; (2) popular support of the *leadership role of the PCC*; (3) the universality of social welfare services; (4) the strengthening of Cuban values; (5) active engagement of a socialist civil society; (6) productive capacity to engage in global commerce in specified sectors; and (7) augmented international prestige and standing among the community of nations. It is on the basis of these seven Revolutionary principles that one can discern the framework and constraints on Cuban engagement with global economic vectors or the rule structures through which they are organized and managed.

Chapter One then considers in more detail the principles that sustain the Cuban economic and legal-political model. The key objective of the chapter are to develop the core objective of the principles—to build a comprehensive (an "all around") socialist society ("impulsar y consolidar la construcción de una sociedad socialista próspera y sostenible," PCC 2016, ¶ 49). Sustainability, in turn, is understood as a function of development; development is understood as a function of the *Lineamientos* (PCC 2016, ¶¶ 50–51). Sustainable development targets both material and social productive forces to produce a rich and model state (PCC, 2016, ¶¶ 52–53).

The *Conceptualización* then turns to a more detailed consideration of socialist principles that sustain the model (PCC 2016, Chapter 1.1 "Principios de nuestro socialismo que sustentan el Modelo" (¶¶ 54–73 (Sustaining Principles))). These principles represent a synthesis of the continuation of the essential basis of Cuban socialism (¶¶ 57–73). These include nine core principles:

- *Socialist human rights and moral values* (¶ 58) ("Todo ello, en contraposición al egoísmo, el individualismo y el consumismo enajenante y depredador."); nondiscrimination (¶ 68); right to work, health, education, etc. (¶ 69), to ensure social welfare (¶¶ 70–71)
- *Leadership of the PCC* as the Leninist vanguard party (¶ 59)
- *The State as the guarantor and source of sovereign authority* (¶ 60)
- *Socialist democracy* is exercised through the legislature under the leadership of the PCC (¶ 61)
- *State as the source of popular rights* and obligations (¶ 62).
- *State control of the fundamental means of production* (¶ 63), legitimating/democratizing (¶¶ 64–65)
- Highest objective: *Preserving the state and Revolution* (¶¶ 66; 72)
- *Central planning* is the principal means of socialist development (¶ 67)

- *Control of individuals as a means of social production*; individuals' obligation to protect state property and work hard (¶ 73)

It is worth noting that though many of the core principles can be compatible to global reintegration, not all of them lend themselves to globalization of governance. This is particularly true in the context of human and labor rights. Both play prominently in the development of the *Conceptualización* that follows.

Having specified the principles, the *Conceptualización* then turns to the objects to which these principles are to be applied; that is, to the specific transformations necessary to the creation of a model socialist society that is prosperous and sustainable (PCC 2016, Chapter 1.2. "Transformaciones principales del Modelo" (¶¶ 74–115)). These transformations are sensitive to time and context (recall PCC 2016, ¶ 12) as necessary to move the socialist project forward ("Se refieren a las transformaciones que caracterizan los nuevos fundamentos del Modelo a partir de las condiciones internas y externas actuales," PCC 2016, ¶ 75). These touch primarily on three distinct categories of transformation; first the consolidation of state ownership of the means of production; second, the need to accommodate foreign notions of ownership of production and the complementary role of private enterprise in Cuba; and third, the enhancement of the state's role in the direct responsibility for economic planning and direction.

With respect to the need to consolidate the core role of social property (the means of production owned or managed by the state) (PCC, 2016, Chapter 1.2.1 "Consolidación del papel primordial de la propiedad social sobre los medios fundamentales de producción"). The necessary conditions for transformation revolve around the fundamental necessity of the creation of a *revolutionary working class* (Ibid., ¶ 80); the modernization of state-owned enterprises (SOEs) (organization, technology, innovation) (PCC, 2016, ¶¶ 81–2); the full application of a system of *socialist distribution to workers* (wage markets) (PCC, 2016, ¶ 83); rejecting the idea of wage labor markets); the enforcement of SOE self-financing for development and improvement (PCC, 2016, ¶¶ 84–85); the closer integration of SOE and state ministry planning and direction (PCC, 2016, ¶ 86); and lastly, the unification of the national currency (PCC, 2016, ¶ 87).

With respect to the recognition and diversification of forms of property and their ownership, especially around contact and interactions with foreigners, the *Conceptualización* offered an enhanced form of socialist foreign investment (PCC, 2016, ¶¶ 89–96). These would be wrapped around the conceptual framework of the current rules for foreign direct investment—carefully managed and mediated by the state (Republic of Cuba 2014). In addition, transformation required recognition of the complementary (rather than the primary) role of private property in the development of a Cuban socialist society. This complementary role of private property could be tolerated if confined to specifically designated means of production bent to the needs of perfecting the centrally planned economy (PCC, 2016, ¶¶ 91–96; "forma parte de los elementos que condicionan la necesidad objetiva del reconocimiento del mercado, en el que interactúen bajo la planificación como vía principal de dirección de la economía" (PCC, 2016, ¶ 94)). This approach is fundamentally incompatible with the approach of the United States since the administration of President Obama in the normalization process, which has always focused on shrinking the public sector in favor of a strong and robust private sector. And, indeed, it is well to remember that in the West, notions of property are at the center of economic and political organization (Gordley 2006, 7–31). However, a strong private sector is not incompatible as such with the objects of reintegration. But it poses a different problem, that of the conformity by the state and its instrumentalities with the requirements of all economic actors operating domestically and abroad.

With respect to the further development of state control over the economy, the *Conceptualización* offers a full-throated affirmation of classic European Marxist notions (Perez Lopez 1995, 11–20) of the inseparability of politics form economics, of the inseparability of politics from law, and of the convergence of public and private law within the state under the leadership of the vanguard Communist Party (Ibid., ¶¶ 97–115). The state was responsible for development of social and economic order (Ibid., ¶ 99). Central planning of the economy must control both the state sector and private markets (Ibid., ¶¶ 101–104). Import substitution and export growth as set as basic trade policy (Ibid., ¶ 105). Lastly, judicial norms to be developed in aid of this system con orden y disciplina (echoing Raúl Castro's widely distributed speech to the Cuban National Assembly [3](Castro 2013) ("También demanda el establecimiento de un clima permanente de ORDEN, DISCIPLINA Y EXIGENCIA en la sociedad cubana, premisa imprescindible para consolidar el avance de la actualización del modelo económico y no admitir retrocesos contraproducentes.")).

Chapter Two then takes up in more detail the issue of the ownership of the means of production in Cuba. It is divided into two parts. The first part (PCC, 2016; *Conceptualización* ¶¶ 119–191) considers the forms of state ownership of the means of production, as well as those forms for the organization of private property. It provides principles for the organization and operation of state enterprises, characterized either as noncommercial enterprises or commercial enterprises (PCC, 2016, ¶¶ 121–157). It then considers labor cooperatives (PCC, 2016, ¶¶ 157–168), a key method for the organization of private activity in Cuba (Piñeiro Harnecker 2011). Joint ventures (PCC, 2016; *Conceptualización* ¶¶ 158–167) and mass organizations (PCC, 2016, ¶¶ 187–191) are also considered. Lastly, the role and character of the organization of private property is specified (PCC, 2016, ¶¶ 168–186). This is property that cannot be accumulated or used for wealth creation beyond regulated maximums (PCC, 2016, § 176). The complementary role of private enterprise is emphasized, as well as its fundamental character as a means of contributing to socialist development under the management of the state (PCC, 2016). Their principal role is to contribute to employment and the efficiency of the socialist economy (PCC, 2016, ¶ 186). The second part (PCC, 2016, ¶¶ 192–202) focuses on the forms of engaging in economic activity permitted to the state. It is in this second part that one sees the emergence of Cuban conceptions of the rule of law. The system for the organization of entities for the purpose of engaging in economic activities are to be established through rules controlled by the state (PCC, 2016, ¶ 202).

Chapter Three then considers the role of central planning in the political economy of Cuba. This part of the *Conceptualización* is remarkable for the way it develops a sense of the role of the state in engaging with markets (PCC, 2016; *Conceptualización* ¶¶ 203–264). That engagement consists of two parts: internally, central planning supplants market-driven regulation; externally, the Cuban state serves the only participant in global markets. But that it is remarkable does not mean that it has appeared suddenly. The principles in Chapter Three have long been a cornerstone of Cuban governance, and it has played a central role in the construction of Cuban efforts to construct regional trading blocs, principally ALBA (Backer and Molina 2009). Yet here, more than anywhere, one encounters a challenge for reintegration. What appears possible is the reintegration of the Cuban state as a public and private enterprise within global trade. What is not possible is to penetrate within the territory of Cuba and bring the structures sensibilities and legal frameworks *within Cuba*. Private enterprise, the private sector, in a sense, within Cuba is understood as another element of the state sector, the operation of which is much more fully delegated. *It is the resulting impermeability of the Cuban economy that poses the greatest challenge to the full reintegration of Cuba, at least as understood in Western terms and according to Western sensibilities.*

State central planning is understood as made up of four components. The first is socialist planning (PCC, 2016; *Conceptualización* ¶ 209; "El desarrollo socialista se erige en función del ser humano considerando las dimensiones política, económico-financiera, social, demográfica, territorial, científico-tecnológica, formativo-cultural, de protección y conservación de los recursos y el medioambiente, entre otras." PCC, 2016, ¶ 220). The second is regulation through law (PCC, 2016, ¶ 207). It is here, perhaps, that one encounters rule of law in action in its most pristine Cuban form. What is meant is the use of law as the means of market regulation (PCC, 2016, ¶ 245 et seq.). That regulation covers: (1) the regulation of market access and inducement (through law) of rational consumption; (2) the identification of areas suitable for market functioning (market ghettos); (3) the establishment of standards and the regulation of (internal) competition; (4) consumer protection; and (5) the restriction of monopoly conditions contrary to societal interests. The third touches on the management of the state (PCC, 2016, ¶ 208). These cover resource management and regional economic integration in the shadow of Cuba's current policies and allegiances. The fourth, and perhaps most important element, are those touching on control. These are also the most problematic for reintegration—at least to the extent that they are not deployed for emerging sensibilities around accountability (Backer 2019). For Cuban theory, accountability is an important element of control—but accountability to the state, to the vanguard party, and to the basic line of both. Monitoring, surveillance, and regulatory structures are to be developed further to detect offenses and enforce planning. ("El sistema nacional de estadísticas da respuesta a las necesidades del nuevo escenario en que interactúan diferentes formas de propiedad y gestión, utilizándose de manera combinada métodos directos e indirectos de captación de información, como registros administrativos y contables, censos, encuestas y otros métodos de estimación." (PCC, 2016, ¶ 264)).

Chapter Four (PCC, 2016, ¶¶ 265–311) then turns to what might be the most problematic aspect of Cuban socialism, at least in terms of its compatibility with emerging global consensus around human rights and labor.

Chapter Four focuses on what may be the most important element in the construction of a socialist economy and political system in Cuba—socialist culture and the construction of the revolutionary worker. It ties together economic and social development ("El ideal de prosperidad de los ciudadanos se sustenta en perspectivas alcanzables de materialización de proyectos racionales de vida, individuales y colectivos, en correspondencia con los valores de nuestra sociedad, sustentados principalmente en los ingresos provenientes del trabajo, y los derechos constitucionales." PCC, 2016, ¶ 268). The chapter is divided into two parts. The first considers economic and social rights of the Cuban worker (PCC, 2016, ¶¶ 273–298). It sets out fairly standard welfare state principles. But it also looks to education and culture as critical tools for the socialization of the masses. Both are understood, then, as political in character, as well as central to socialist economic development in specific application. Regulations and governance systems are targeted in this respect both to a cultivation of a taste for beauty (PCC, 2016, ¶ 284), and for rules for maximizing the management of free time (PCC, 2016, ¶ 286).

The second part of Chapter Four considers the political consequences (and regulatory aspects) of labor as a means of production. If labor, like capital, is understood as a means of production, then, like capital, labor must be centrally planned and managed. (PCC, 2016, ¶¶ 299–311). Wealth distribution and social justice are tied together (PCC, 2016, ¶ 300). Basic principles must be developed for the national regulation of consumer information to ensure responsible and sustainable consumption (PCC, 2016, ¶ 311). These are based on ethical principles tied to fraud prevention and the avoidance of offense to any social sector and must as well as the symbols and messages of colonialism and imperialism (Ibid.). Wage and wealth differentials may be permitted within the parameters of social justice goals (PCC, 2016, ¶¶ 300–302). These principles apply to accumulations derived from private property as well (PCC, 2016, ¶¶ 306–307). Lastly, product markets must be managed to permit access to basic necessities (¶¶ 308–310).

The *Conceptualización*'s "Final Considerations" evidence the extent to which its provisions were drafted in the shadow of pressure to reintegrate into the global economy. And indeed, were there any doubts about the scope of the rejection of that pressure to reintegrate, and the rejection of the conventional terms under which such reintegration would be expected to occur, these are eliminated in the *Conceptualización*. Cuba will reintegrate, but on its own terms. At the heart of those terms is a firm determination to create a strong barrier at the borders of the national territory. Beyond Cuba, the state acknowledges and will engage with global economic structures and their governance on the best terms it can manage. That engagement will be undertaken by the state and for the purpose of advancing the state's internal objectives. But within the state there will be no effort to reintegrate. The state will stand between the nation and globalization. Those are the terms under which reintegration may occur. To that end, the model offered through the *Conceptualización* is bent to the preservation and development of Cuban socialism ("una necesidad para lograr la irreversibilidad y el desarrollo de la construcción del socialismo en Cuba." PCC, 2016, ¶ 312). But while the model imposes strict duties on the state, it also develops substantial responsibilities imposed on individuals—discipline, exigency, and a willingness to be socialized in accordance with the principles developed for socialist culture by the vanguard party ("Es preciso asegurar más explicación al pueblo, más disciplina y exigencia y un mayor y más cercano seguimiento al proceso de cambios. Hay que tener, como ya hemos dicho, los oídos y los pies bien puestos sobre la tierra." PCC, 2016, ¶ 319). The object is not reintegration of objectiveless progress, but rather the perfecting of the Revolution applied to changing global conditions (PCC, 2016, ¶ 322; "para consolidar los logros de la Revolución e impulsar la construcción de nuestro socialismo próspero y sostenible." PCC, 2016id, ¶ 329). These are undertaken especially in the shadow of the United States (not to be trusted) and perhaps facilitated by regional integration solicitous of Cuba's march along its socialist path (PCC, 2016, ¶¶ 325–327).

Perversely, that interest is generated in large part by its anachronisms. Ironically, the advent of big data, of the algorithms that now increasingly automate markets, may itself make it possible to move the mechanism of the markets out of the private sphere and back into the state. But that touches on the markets and not on states, and the *Conceptualización* fails precisely because it inverts cause and effect. The state can manage markets—can substitute itself for markets—only by becoming the market maker itself. And data management in transactions may make that possible (Automated Trader 2015). And that is possible only because markets themselves are becoming free of individual volition, except in those areas that the Cuban state has left to the individual—the detritus of economic activity with the lowest value added and the most marginal expressions of power. In this form, in the form that big data, that technology, makes possible, that this poses the most interesting challenge not just to Chinese socialist market theory but also to the core of Western neoliberal market ideology.

These characteristics were well displayed in the construction (and now the operation) of the *Plan nacional de desarrollo económico y social hasta 2030* (National Plan for Economic and Social Development Through 2030 (PNDES)) (PCC, 2016; PNDES). PNDES elaborates six "intimately interwoven and systematically designed" core strategic themes around which economic planning will be undertaken (PCC, 2016; PNDES ¶ 44). These are identified at ¶ 45 as (1) efficient and socialist government and social integration (Ibid., ¶¶ 49–77); (2) transformation and internationalization of production (Ibid., ¶¶ 78–101); (3) infrastructure development (Ibid., ¶¶ 102–129); (4) developing human potential through science, technology, and innovation (Ibid., ¶¶ 130–157); (5) development of natural resources and environmental concerns (Ibid., ¶¶ 158–184); and (6) human development, equality, and justice (Ibid., ¶¶ 185–220). These are meant to serve as the qualitative categories through which development will be structured (Ibid., ¶ 46). Around these six strategic themes, PNDES establishes 22 general objectives and 106 specific objectives (¶ 47) that constitute the bulk of the rest of the Plan. All of these are tied to the *Lineamientos* (Ibid., ¶ 46) and the efforts at modernization and preservation that has marked the policies of the Cuban state since the elevation of Raúl Castro as First Secretary of the PCC. This structure of a rules-based central planning suggests the way that Cuban authorities approach issues of law as a means of structuring decision-making. But it also suggests that economic planning as a rules-based system is inherently riven with very large areas of overlapping discretion to be exercised by officials. These, too, suggest a large area of challenge for aligning Cuban practice to global expectations. Where Cuban officials see careful consideration of decisions to build a market-alternative form of viable economic policy, others may see high transaction costs and the serendipity of decision-making that varies from official to official. And international organizations may see in systems substantially dependent on the exercise of administrative discretion a potential for corruption—or at least for the inability of the system to act consistently. As a consequence, demand for Cuban goods and services and the benefits of inbound investment tend to diminish measured against these additional costs. But measured against the objectives of the *Conceptualización*, that may not matter to Cuban officials, who use a different scale to measure success.

A European Alternative?

But where does this leave reintegration? Certainly, the euphoria—and expectations—that followed the initial gestures toward U.S.-Cuba normalization inflated expectations in ways that could only lead to disappointment. Cuba and the United States, each in their own way, have signaled their lack of interest in a reintegration of Cuba. Both, in their own way, continue to adhere to their baselines positions about engagement. For the United States, that means an emphasis on substantial political reform before full normalization can be possible (Trump 2017). For the Cubans it means almost the opposite—a stronger embrace both of the basic premises of a Marxist-Leninist Party state structure and a deeper commitment to a central planning model of economic policy that rejects a substantial role of markets. That position, in turn, suggests that at least *within Cuba*, there is little likelihood of deep changes to the domestic legal order along the lines that reflect global consensus. On the other hand, it does suggest that *between Cuba and its outside business partners* reintegration is possible, but that the changes to law, policy, and economics would apply only between the Cuban state (as owner of all Cuban productive forces) and outsiders. Whatever the value of the private sector, that was to remain tightly controlled through the imposition of complex systems of approvals and restrictions. Thus, Cuba appears to mean to place its state organs between global economics, politics, and law, on the one hand, and its internal legal and economic order, on the other.

Yet the emerging state of affairs in early 2018 does not entirely suggest a failure of the possibilities of deeper reintegration. Even as the United States retreated from direct economic connections with Cuba, the European Union sought to step into the space left by the American action. That strategic initiative, the Political Dialogue and Cooperation Agreement (PDCA) (Council of the European Union, 2016) took final form accelerated in the wake of the prior U.S. administration's policy of opening up. "The agreement has been under negotiation since April 2014 and was signed by EU foreign affairs chief Federica Mogherini in December 2016." (European Parliament 2017). In parallel, the agreement was submitted to the EU member states' national parliaments and the Cuban National Assembly for ratification. The European Parliament gave its consent on July 5, 2017, extolling the PDCA's provisions for the promotion of dialogue and economic cooperation's, as well as its possibilities for joint action and bilateral trade that contributes to the living conditions and social rights of Cuban citizens (Ibid.). The European Parliament also endorsed an accompanying resolution calling on Cuba to respect human rights (Bouchenaki and Kosova 2017). Most parts of the agreement started to be provisionally applied as of November 1, 2017.

The Political Dialogue and Cooperation Agreement entered into provisional application on November 1, 2017. This agreement—the first of its kind between the European Union and Cuba—constitutes the new legal framework for EU-Cuba relations. It foresees an enhanced political dialogue, improved bilateral cooperation and the development of joint action in multilateral fora. PDCA is the successor policy to the European Union's Common Position, which was repealed December 12, 2016. Indeed, "[t]he EU's willingness to make progress with Cuba has been interpreted by many as an attempt to respond to US President Donald Trump's frosty approach to the island nation." (Bouchenaki and Kosova 2017). The repeal of the Common Position and its replacement with PDCA represented a positive gain for the Cubans, especially when measured against the state of their relations with the United States. The Common Position had mirrored the U.S. position of requiring unilateral changes in Cuba's human rights and political openness, as measured by the European Union in ways that mirrored the U.S. position (Council on Hemispheric Affairs 2010). Cuba maintained that this constituted an intolerable interference in its internal affairs (Ibid.). After years of work by Spain on Cuba's behalf, and despite the opposition of other member states, there was a move toward encouraging dialogue with Cuba that became a reality when it appeared that the U.S. position was changing as well after 2008 (Bouchenaki and Kosova 2017).

While PDCA represents a change in the character of EU-Cuba relations, it was not undertaken in a vacuum. Even during the period of the Common position, the European Union maintained some connection to Cuba, mostly through aid projects, including a development cooperation instrument that had allocated to Cuba about €55 for the period 2014–2020. These funds were directed toward national priorities that had been identified in the *Lineamientos*: sustainable agriculture, sustainable use of natural resources, and sustainable economic and social modernization, plus funds for projects supporting vulnerable groups and cultural projects through grants to local organizations (European Commission, n.d.). Cuba also participated in a number of European regional efforts in Latin America through which it received funds (European Commission, n.d.). Most interesting is the possibility that in return for stronger ties the European Union might have waived the application of its strong business and human rights measures to EU-Cuba bilateral relations. The European Union appears to be willing to pay for its influence—from supporting the realization of Ciba's sector driven 2030 Economic Plan, to the European Union's help in avoiding or weakening the effects of the Cuban embargo. And, indeed, the willingness of the European Union to align its multilateral and bilateral arrangements to the economic development plans of its partner provides both an opportunity and challenge for the European Union if its role is to be understood in part as an agent of Cuba's reintegration into the global economy sensitive to emerging global norms on human rights, property, and markets.

The PDCA binds the European Union other than potentially the United Kingdom and or Ireland (Council of the European Union 2016; PDCA, CU/EU/en 9). The General Principles (Art. 1) reaffirm general commitments to a set of ambiguous concepts: multilateralism, respect for international law and the principles of the UN Charter; the principles of equality, reciprocity, and mutual respect; and to the promotion of sustainable development. (Ibid., Art. 1 ¶¶ 1–2, 4). Of course these are likely understood in almost diametrically different ways by the European Union and Cuba, but it provides sufficient cover for moving forward along pragmatic lines without losing face. That fig leaf is made clear by the agreement that implementation of PDCA would be undertaken "in accordance with their respective constitutional principles, legal frameworks, legislation, norms and regulations, as well as the applicable international instruments to which they are parties." (Ibid., Art. 1 ¶ 3). Complicating these initial principles are declarations of "respect for and the promotion of democratic principles, respect for all human rights and fundamental freedoms laid down in the Universal Declaration of Human Rights and in the core international human-rights instruments and their optional protocols which are applicable to the Parties, and respect for the rule of law." (Ibid., Art. 1 ¶ 5). But this is limited both by the provisions of ¶¶ 1–2 as well as by the provisions of ¶ 6 in which both sides "recognize that all peoples have the right to freely determine their political system and to freely pursue their economic, social and cultural development." (Ibid., Art. 1, ¶ 6). Taken together, these Principles balance nicely the political needs of the European Union and Cuba in a way that recognizes both but permits each to ignore the contradictions of their respective positions applied to the condition of the other.

Article 2 specifies the objectives of the PDCA. These are both straightforward and general. It is meant to help Cuba update its economy and society

(Art. 2 ¶ (b)) through dialogue and cooperation (Ibid., ¶¶ (a), (g)), promote mutual trade (Ibid., ¶ (e)), and the achievement of the 2030 Agenda for Sustainable Development (Ibid,. ¶ (d)). Most interesting is the objective of enhancing regional trade in the Caribbean and Latin America (Ibid., ¶ (f)).

To those ends, Part II of PDCA speaks to the contours of political dialogue. These touch on the usual: promoting exchanges, enabling broad exchanges of views, centering exchanges on the UN system, and promoting strategic partnerships between the European Union and CELAC (Ibid., Art. 3). The latter is particularly useful to Cuba, which has had long-term ambitions to lead at least the Caribbean regional trade and political framework (Backer and Molina 2009). But it is particularly useful as a means of avoiding OAS constraints on the manner of its global integration (see above Part II). All of this cooperation is to be undertaken at the state to state level—no people-to-people focus here (Ibid., Art. 4). That approach serves as the heart of an open-ended and vague provision respecting human rights. Article 5 provides in its entirety:

> Within the framework of the overall political dialogue, the Parties agree to establish a human rights dialogue, with a view to enhancing practical cooperation between the Parties at both multilateral and bilateral level. The agenda for each dialogue session shall be agreed by the parties, reflect their respective interests and take care to address in a balanced fashion civil and political rights and economic, social and cultural rights.

The key is in the last sentence. The Cubans will emphasize economic, social, and cultural rights, while the Europeans will push civil and political rights. To some extent this serves U.S. interest as well—to the extent that the European Union can be used as a proxy for pushing for political reform acceptable to the Americans. The Cubans, anticipating this, will likely negotiate hard.

In addition, the PDCA covers illicit trade in small arms and light weapons and other conventional weapons (Art. 6); disarmament and nonproliferation of weapons of mass destruction (Ibid., Art. 7); antiterrorism measures (Art. 8); international criminality (Art. 9); and unilateral coercive measures (Ibid., Art. 10). Additional areas of cooperation include combating trafficking in persons and migrant smuggling (Ibid., Art. 11); trade in illicit drugs (Ibid., Art. 12); and combating race discrimination, xenophobia, and related intolerance (Ibid., Art. 13). With respect to the latter, the focus is on exchanging best practices. Lastly, Article 14 focuses on sustainable development, mostly through the exchange of views.

Article 10, of course, is the most interesting to the extent that the specter of the U.S. embargo hangs over it. But it does appear to produce a common position seeking to work toward the weakening of the U.S. embargo, which is compatible with the position of both Cuba and the European Union. More problematic is the potential effect of Article 10 on the ability of the European Union to export its increasingly effective extraterritorial regime for the promotion of human rights. It is not clear from PDCA whether this provision is meant to prohibit the application of new measures—the U.K. Modern Slavery Act (2015) and the French Supply Chain Due Diligence Law (2017) in relations between the EU and Cuba, where ever they might manifest. The issue is particularly acute as European inbound investment meets an increasingly self-referencing Cuban conception of human rights applicable within its own economic activities (Backer 2015). The European Union will resist that reading by emphasizing the language "that are contrary to international law and commonly accepted rules of international trade." (Council of the European Union 2016; PDCA, Art. 10 ¶ 1). The Cubans, on the other hand, would emphasize the language: "which are used as a means of political and economic pressure against States and affect the sovereignty of other States." (Ibid.). How this will be decided remains to be seen—but for the moment it is clear that both sides believe they have protected their respective principles and thus created a contradiction that will manifest itself the first time a human rights–related charge is brought against enterprises operating in or through Cuba or its SOEs. One might expect to see this resolved potentially through the OCED Guidelines for Multinational Enterprise NCP mechanisms (OECD 2011, "Procedural Guidance National Contact Points").

Part III gets to the root of things: the provisions on cooperation and sector-policy dialogue. These touch on the core areas of development set out in PNDES (PCC, 2016; PNDES) discussed in Section III. In particular, Part III, Title VI then deals with sector-specific economic development that ties EU-Cuba cooperation to the focal points of PNDES. These touch on agriculture (Council of the European Union 2016; PDCA, Art. 50); tourism (Ibid., Art. 51); science, technology, and innovation (Ibid., Art. 52); technology transfer (Ibid., Art. 53); energy production (Ibid., Art. 54); and transport (Ibid., Art. 55).

However, Title I on cooperation sectors (Ibid., Art. 20) follows an EU pattern: "(a) sustainable development, (b) human rights and good governance, (c) environmental sustainability, (d) disaster prevention, (e)gender perspective, (f) persons in a situation of vulnerability, (g) building national capacities, and (h) knowledge management." The objectives (Ibid., Art. 15) emphasize focus on Cuban economic development goals within the sustainable development framework. The principles (Ibid., Art. 16) focus on cooperation through which each side makes the best deal it can (echoing, ironically enough, the recasting of trade policy by the Trump administration (e.g., Backer 2016c)). Sector policy dialogue (Art. 17) is centered on information sharing, the harmonization of standards, and capacity building through best practices sharing. Implementation of dialogue (Art. 18, Cooperation modalities and procedures) is meant to be enhanced by EU money (Art. 18 ¶ 1(a) ("technical and financial assistance")), and by coordination that "furthers and complements Cuba's development strategies and policies." (Art. 18 ¶ 1(b)). Also interesting is the focus on the European Union's help in securing financing for Cuban economic ambitions (Art. 18 ¶ 1(g) ("innovative cooperation and financing modalities and instruments in order to improve the effectiveness of cooperation")). Cuba for its part agrees not to use cooperation as a means of enhancing its revenues and not impede travel by officials (Art. 18 ¶ 5). Article 19 then identifies relevant actors covered by the cooperation arrangements. In addition to the usual international public actors, Article 19 ¶ (e) also identifies "civil society, including scientific, technical, cultural, artistic, sports, friendship and solidarity associations, social organisations, trade unions and cooperatives." Again, the provision is vague enough to give Cuba the authority to ban civil society groups that it deems politically threatening, while the European Union might take the position that all such organizations come within the umbrella of this provision. Expect some friction here. Some clarity, however, is attempted in Article 36:

> The Parties recognise the potential contribution of civil society, including academia, think tanks and media, to the fulfilment of the objectives of this Agreement. They agree to promote actions in support of greater civil-society participation in the formulation and implementation of relevant development and sectoral cooperation activities, including through capacity-building.

In light of the *Conceptualización* and its premises, one might well expect that the Cubans would read this provision narrowly. For example, they might suggest that the support for civil society extends only to academics, think tanks, and credentialed media; alternatively, they might suggest that civil society consists only of those mass organizations recognized by the state, as contemplated under the *Conceptualización*. There would be precedent as other states (e.g., China) move toward that position respecting civil society. Yet it is likely that the European Union will tend to read the provision far more broadly, and in the shadow of the Common Position. One would thus expect some friction as well in the context of the anti-fraud and corruption provisions of Article 21.

Part III, Title II deals specifically with the European Union's great concerns: democracy, human rights, and good governance. These provisions give the European Union some leeway in tying economic benefits to political reform, but the potential hidden in those provisions may require substantial work for their realization—at least as the European Union might see things. Article 22 touches on human rights. Its first paragraph nicely evidences the mishmash resulting from an attempt to push together two very different views of human rights:

> Mindful that the protection and promotion of human rights and fundamental freedoms is the first responsibility of governments, bearing in mind the significance of national and regional particularities and of various historical, cultural and religious backgrounds and acknowledging that it is their duty to protect all human rights and fundamental freedoms regardless of their political, economic and cultural systems, the Parties agree to cooperate in the area of democracy and human rights.

One might well note here the tensions in the provisions, the balancing of distinct approaches that will be difficult to untangle and that provides neither side with an advantage. The likely result will be little beyond the usual rhetoric and claims to victory by both sides as their respective enterprise seek to make money. Article 23 (good governance) and Article 25 (modernization of public administration) provides the Cuban with necessary capacity building that aligns with the focus of the Cuban *Lineamientos* on the development of governance in furtherance of their economic model.

It is not clear in what direction Article 24 (rule of law) will develop. It is likely that this will be used to ensure a measure of protection of investors from the European Union operating in Cuba through agreements negotiate under the umbrella of PDCA, something to which Article 26 (prevention and resolution of conflicts) is also devoted. Indeed, given the way that the *Conceptualización* approaches rule of law—as a cage of regulation that might constrain the exercise of administrative discretion in central planning and in the administrative operation of the state—it is likely that this provision will produce long-term disagreement. The European Union will likely use this to push for the constitutionalization of the rule of law in Western conventional terms. The Cubans may well respond by moving more openly toward a Chinese conception of the constitutionalization of politics within the vanguard party (Jiang 2018).

Part III, Title II then focuses on issues of justice, citizen security, and migration. These include issues around the protection of personal data (Council of the European Union 2016; PDCA, Art. 27), an issue quite dear to the European Union and less so to the Cubans. It also touches on trade in illicit drugs (Art. 28); money laundering (Ibid., Art. 29); organized crime (Ibid., Art. 30); anticorruption measures (Art. 31); illicit trade in small arms (Ibid., Art. 32); antiterrorism (Ibid., Art. 33); migration (Ibid., Art. 34); and consular protection (Ibid., Art. 35). Part III, Title IV then touches on social development and social cohesion. This furthers basic Cuban policy elaborated in the *Conceptualización* directly. Article 37 essentially summarizes the Cuban position on the integration of socialist economic and social development from its Seventh PCC principles. Article 38 may be more problematic for Cuba, aligning cooperation around International Labor Organization (ILO) standards. Article 39 speaks to educational cooperation, Article 40 to public health, and Article 41, tersely, to consumer protection. There is a wide scope of agreement possible with respect to a number of related areas of cooperation: culture and heritage (Ibid., Art. 42); protection of vulnerable persons (Ibid., Art. 43); a focus on gender (Ibid., Art. 44); interaction of youth (Ibid., Art. 45); and local community development (Ibid., Art. 46, with respect to which Cuba has a long history especially with EU-based nongovernmental organizations).

Part III, Title V focuses on environment, disaster risk management, and climate change. These are areas in which cooperation is likely to produce a substantial amount of positive effects. The principal focus (Ibid., Art. 47 ¶ 4) includes conservation and sustainable development, protection of fresh and marine waters, and climate change issues generally. Disaster risk management (Ibid., Art. 48), of critical importance to Cuba, looks to "common commitment to improving prevention, mitigation, preparedness, response and recovery measures in order to increase the resilience of their societies and infrastructure, and to cooperate, where appropriate, at bilateral and multilateral political level to improve disaster-risk-management outcomes." Water sanitation (Ibid., Art. 49) has also been a concern of Cuban planning as its infrastructure, especially in the older portions of its major cities, has been deteriorating. This also aligns with Cuban central planning goals for 2030.

Beyond its focus on the sectoral development of the Cuban economy that aligns with the Cuban 2030 Economic and Social Plan, Part III, Title VI touches on modernization of the economic and social model. But this modernization is narrowly tailored to avoid the complications of political repercussions or back-door regime-change strategies. Article 56 ¶ 1 focuses on strengthening Cuban public administration and the development of Cuban cooperatives and enterprises. This is somewhat sensitive in light of recent efforts by the Cuban state to stop licensing cooperatives and to better control the private sector (Frank 2017 ("The backtracking on the private sector hints at unease among some in the ruling Cuban Communist Party that free market reforms may have gone too far, amid a broader debate about rising inequality on the island.")). Article 56 ¶ 3 makes the "helpful but not threatening" approach explicit:

> The Parties agree to promote and encourage cooperation between institutions, including sector-based institutions, that promote instruments to support SMEs, particularly those whose efforts are aimed at improving competitiveness, technological innovation, integration in value chains, access to credit and training as well as strengthening the institutional capacity and institutional framework. They also agree to promote contacts between companies from both Parties to support their insertion into international markets, investments and technology transfer.

Lastly, issues of good governance in taxation (Council of the European Union 2016; PDCA, Art. 58) and statistics and data production (Art. 57) are covered. The last is particularly important as regulation moves form command to big data management systems. It encourages "including the exchange of scientists; the development of improved and consistent methods of data collection, disaggregation, analysis and interpretation; and the organisation of seminars, working groups or programmes complementing statistical capacities."

Part IV then turns to trade and trade cooperation. Article 60's objectives include the usual. There are some more interesting points that might be made to better understand the consequences of the unequal element in the cooperation deal that the PDCA represents. Cuba has a need that the European Union does not—to be integrated into the world economy (Art. 60 ¶ (b)). That means not merely integration into economic globalization but also avoidance of the U.S. trade sanctions in place since the 1960s. That is a tall order, especially as the United States moves from global embargoes to precision-targeted blacklists. This is especially likely with expanded use of Global Magnitsky Human Rights Accountability Act (2016) sanctions, which allows the executive branch to impose visa bans and targeted sanctions on individuals worldwide who are determined to be responsible for committing human rights violations or acts of significant corruption (Human Rights Watch 2017; United States, 2017). The European Union has also adopted a similar approach, seeking targeted sanctions against individuals identified in the context of tax fraud and avoidance (Council of the European Union 2017). It will likely have effects directly on CARICOM members and potentially indirectly on Cuba. As important, Europe is seen as an important target zone for the exploitation of a key area of sectoral development in Cuba under its 2030 Plan—pharmaceuticals (e.g., Council of the European Union 2016; PDCA, Art. 60 ¶ (f)).

Part IV, Title I focuses on trade and the outlines of bilateral investment terms. It is meant to be developed to reduce trade barriers (fiscal and otherwise; ibid., Art. 61 ¶ 1), and to be grounded on "rule-based multilateral trading system under which the Parties are responsible for maintaining the primacy of rules and their effective, fair and balanced implementation" (Ibid., ¶ 2). The parties pledge to accord most favored nations treatment to each other with the usual exception in accordance with WTO agreements (Art. 62) as well as to each accord national treatment to the goods of the other (Ibid., Art. 63). There are affirmances of transparency of trade measures (Ibid., Art. 64) and of mutual commitment to the WTO Trade Facilitation Agreement (Ibid., Art. 65) and the WTO Agreement on Technical Barriers to Trade (Ibid., Art. 66), along with standards agreements (Art. 67), trade defense (Art. 68), and existing obligations under Article XX of GATT (Ibid., Art. 70), all subject to mutually agreed revision (Ibid., Art. 69).

Part IV, Title II then focuses on trade-related cooperation. These include customs (Ibid., Art. 71), and administrative measures around trade facilitation (Ibid., Art. 72). These later commitments will pose something of a challenge for both the rules rigid European Union and the sometimes heavy-handed administrative control cultures of Cuba. But it is the thought that counts, and many of these measures are written as inspirational goals rather than as implementable measures. Protection of intellectual property is the focus of Article 73, which itself can pose problems given the messiness on that score that was generated after the 1959 Revolution. Going forward, deals, on the other hand, may be easier. Capacity building is an important focus on measures regarding cooperation on technical barriers to trade (Ibid., Art. 74) and trade defense (Art. 78). Increasing trade in agricultural products is the core of the provisions around food safety and animals welfare (Ibid., Art. 75), with a similar objective for trade in traditional and artisanal goods—from both sides (Ibid., Art. 76), though in the absence of strong consumer markets in Cuba it is hard to see how this flows any way but out of Cuba and into the hands of wealthy European consumers. A sustainable development chapeau is also provided (Ibid., Art. 76). The European Union secured recognition of the importance (to it) of protection of rules of origin (Ibid., Art. 79), and both parties pledged greater and better coordinated mutual investment (Ibid., Art. 80).

All of these aspirations have to be institutionalized somehow, and Part V serves to memorialize these new institutional structures. Given the heavily bureaucratized cultures of the European Union and of Cuba, it comes as no surprise that:

> A Joint Council is hereby established. It shall oversee the fulfilment of the objectives of this Agreement and supervise its implementation. It shall meet at ministerial level at regular intervals, not exceeding a period of two years, and extraordinarily whenever circumstances so require, if the Parties so agree. (Ibid., Art. 81 ¶ 1)

Beyond the policy and direction of the Joint Council, a working directorate, the Joint Committee is established to actually attempt implementation (Ibid., Art. 82). It meets once a year. It is unlikely to have much control of the day-to-day movement on the agreement, which suggests that the driving force will be elsewhere within the EU and Cuban bureaucracies. That "somewhere may be overseen by the various subcommittees that may be established under the Joint Committee" (Ibid., Art. 83), though these too meet infrequently albeit regularly.

Taken together, the PDCA appears to give both parties what they want most. For the Cubans that is a counterweight to both their friends (the Russians and Chinese) and their frenemies (the Americans). It provides a more solid basis for the fulfillment of key areas of the PNDES 2030 Economic Plan through entry into lucrative European markets—but only if the Cubans can deliver. And that may take a bit of financial help from either the Europeans (intimated in the PDCA) or from their friends. Even better, the PDCA might help Cuba avoid the effects of the U.S. embargo—especially those aspects targeting the economic drivers of the Cuban economy that have been targeted by the latest round of U.S. sanctions. For the Europeans, it appears to broaden their influence abroad. It also appears to provide a wedge in reform on two levels. The first is with respect to human rights–related reforms on the political level. The second, and much more achievable in part, is the opening to human rights and sustainability-based business conduct.

The fruits of this approach are only now beginning to form. In January 2018, the European Union's Federica Mogherini paid an official visit to Cuba for talks aimed at implementing the PDCA. The agenda focused on the need to structure the Joint Council established by the PDCA to oversee the fulfillment of the agreement (PDCA, Art. 81), and the Joint Committee (Art. 82) charged with the actual implementation of the PDCA (Art. 82). The European Union's press release announced the visit this way:

> The High Representative/Vice President Federica Mogherini will travel to Cuba on 3–4 January, reconfirming the strong EU-Cuban relationship. During her visit, she will meet with government representatives, with a view to an ambitious and swift joint implementation of the Political Dialogue and Cooperation Agreement (PDCA) between the EU and Cuba. Together with Cuban Foreign Minister Bruno Rodriguez Parrilla she will also prepare for the first EU-Cuba Joint Council meeting at ministerial level within the framework of the PDCA. (European Union External Action Service 2018)

But Cuba and the Europeans have been down this road before (Hare 2008). It is far too early to determine whether this time there will be greater success over the long term than in the past. Given the potential instability of the beginning of the transition era, it is likely that success will have to target very long-term targets. But it is not too early to begin to see the structures of that relationship unveiled. At the end of May 2018, it was reported that Cuba and the European Union held a first Joint Council meeting for the purpose of identifying issues for future resolution (Jessop 2018). As a long-term project, this may hold promise. But it is worth noting, that even as global actors view the promise of this EU approach, some in the Cuban nongovernmental sector worry. And the worry centers precisely on issues of democratic participation that is at the heart of U.S. policy and human rights at the heart of the EU political project abroad (Gomez Manzano 2018). It remains to be seen whether or to what extent the promise of the European Union's approach will be fulfilled.

Conclusion

How does one build a revolutionary working class that the state can exploit to perfect its control of the economy? That seems to be at the core of the Cuban approaches to the construction of their own internal legal-normative system for economics and politics. It is premised on the notion that labor and capital can be treated alike as regulable means of production. It assumes that labor as a productive force must be managed in the societal and cultural sphere like capital. And those assumptions may not be compatible with core notions at the vase of global economic governance.

Likewise, Cuba has sought to confront the question: How does one construct socialism without markets in a global context grounded in the value of markets? Their answer is to substitute direct control for objectives-based management through markets. At its core, the Cuban system would view economic activity as instrumental, which can be invested with moral values only through the direct control through leadership of Leninist vanguard. These notions may also be hard to harmonize with the core market-driven premises of economic globalization and transnational governance.

In the face of the need to reintegrate, Cuban theory is driven, in part at least, by reaction. That reaction is made up in part of a continuing fear of the United States and its intentions. But it is also driven by fear of losing control of the state in the face of the paramount power of global norms within states deeply embedded in global production. That latter fear is not unreasonable. For a state that prizes its autonomy and sovereignty, globalization and integration can be a hard concept to accept. Resistance is more comforting and more compatible with deeply held values. But that fear is also driven by what may in the end be unfortunate miscalculations about the compatibility of market-based governance and Marxist Leninist political and economic systems. Fear of engagement beyond the power of the vanguard to control or mediate may inhibit economic development to the point where the viability of the state becomes an issue—the Cubans have managed to avoid those straits well enough since 1989, but it is not clear that the possibility of avoidance can continue indefinitely. But for the moment (and the moment may last years), it is this state of affairs that confronts us all.

This chapter has sought to answer the question: What internal Cuban legal adjustments will be necessary for Cuba to enter into a fully normalized relationship with the United States and the rest of the world? That question itself suggested that the process of normalization had proceeded along lines to make efforts at conventional reintegration both feasible and plausible, that Cuba was willing to make those changes, and that there were no alternatives. Those assumptions, then, raise the three questions considered as a necessary predicate to approaching the question of Cuban reintegration. The first question centered on consideration of the adjustments Cuba might have to undertake if it is to embed itself within the structures of global trade and finance. To that end, this chapter analyzed the legal changes Cuba would need to undertake to join international financial institutions and global and regional trade organizations. The second question examined the extent to which Cuba is disposed to consider these possible reforms. Against the objective of socializing Cuban legal and economic practices with global norms, the chapter critically assessed the extent to which the current Cuban sociopolitical framework can produce these modifications and the consequences for such limitations, including with respect to the limits of political reform and the relevance of human rights norms in the construction of economic legal and governance structures. The third question then examined what may be possible now. The examination suggested the value of the European Union's strategic initiative, the Political Dialogue and Cooperation Agreement (PDCA) as a viable basis for Cuban reintegration in the global economy.

Taken together, what emerges now is a certainty about the strength of path dependence. Cuba will continue to adhere to its path for as long and to the extent it can; classical reintegration 1980s Eastern European style is out of the question; but then so is Chinese-style integration. The

Conceptualización made that clear in the absence of regime change in Cuba. The United States will continue to seek that regime change as a means of shortcutting the process of inducing Cuba to undertake global reintegration along classical lines. Whether that move toward regime change is done in a friendly and nonthreatening way as under the Obama administration, or more aggressively as undertaken by the Trump administration, is almost irrelevant from the perspective of the Cubans. The United States, like Cuba, remains fundamentally unchanged in outlook and committed to their own classical principles in defining their mutual relations. Lastly, it remains to Europe to play a mediating role. Europe is now attempting to do just that in the form of its PDCA. It represents a plausible effort to accept the tentative and state based re-engagement of Cuba while creating avenues to seek more deeply profound engagement within the state. The EU effort represents the most likely means of avoiding the possibility, as yet uncertain, of a tilt, not toward reintegration into the global economy as one has come to know it now, but rather as one that increasingly has Chinese characteristics.

Notes

1. "The recognition of the role of the market in the functioning of the socialist economy does not imply that the Party, the Government and the mass organizations stop fulfilling their role in society to confront any situation that harms the population, let alone say: "it is a Government issue, I can not get involved."
2. "It exposes the theoretical bases and essential characteristics of the Economic and Social Model Cuba not merely of Socialist Development"
3. "It also demands the establishment of a permanent climate of ORDER, DISCIPLINE AND EXIGENCY in Cuban society, an essential premise to consolidate the progress of actualization of the economic model and not accepting counterproductive setbacks."

12
Big Chills
How U.S. Choices Will Affect Cuba's Environmental Future

Robert R. M. Verchick and Karen C. Sokol[*]

In its penultimate year, the Barack Obama administration effected two reconciliations. The first was the re-establishment of diplomatic relations with Cuba in July 2015 (Felter, McBride, Renwick 2015). The second was the re-entry of the United States into a global consensus to fight climate change. This culminated in the adoption of the Paris Agreement in December 2015 (though it would not take force until almost a year later) (United Nations 2014). In this way, 2015 embodied a political spring thaw. U.S. and Cuban leaders were on speaking terms, U.S. travel and trade restrictions were melting, and Cuba seemed poised to further liberalize its economy and pay more attention to human rights (Felter, McBride, Renwick 2015). At the global level, climate change policy was finally settling into the right groove, with a chance of ramping up more fully in the near future.

Both developments were crucial to Cuba's environmental future. Full reconciliation with the United States—including an end to the embargo—would stabilize Cuba's economy and open a way for improved infrastructure, a more resilient power grid, and better protection of natural resources.[1] In addition, the Paris Agreement supported funding mechanisms to help Cuba and other poor countries cope with rising seas, stronger storms, and other climate hazards that even worldwide carbon reductions will not forestall.

But in the first year of the Donald Trump administration, President Obama's spring thaw now seems to be cycling back into another big chill. Nothing is certain. As a candidate, Trump once supported Cuban

* Robert R. M. Verchick, Loyola New Orleans, College of Law, verchick@loyno.edu; Karen C. Sokol, Loyola New Orleans, College of Law, kcsokol@loyno.edu.

The Cuba-U.S. Bilateral Relationship. Michael J. Kelly, Erika Moreno, and Richard C. Witmer, II.

rapprochement, but he has since hinted at a reversal if Cuba's economic and human rights reforms move too slowly (Felter, McBride, Renwick 2015). It is unlikely that today's majority-Republican Congress would have the appetite to revoke the trade embargo anyway. That said, the trade reforms President Obama put in place are very popular with the business community and, for that reason, would be risky for President Trump to undo (Whitefield 2017). What is more, President Raúl Castro's departure from office, and the transition to a new leader, may offer another chance to reset U.S.-Cuban relations.

The Trump administration's booming opposition to climate policy is less ambiguous. The administration is now trying to unwind nearly every climate-related program in the federal arsenal, including the Paris Agreement.[2] Still, some experts believe the Paris Agreement, because of its flexibility and broad international support, will motor forward even without the United States.[3]

What does this mean for Cuba's future? In a country where any enduring social or environmental good is ineluctably tied to climate, how will the government manage under such uncertainty? Are Cuba's environmental and climate policies resilient enough to suffer a cold spell in Washington or a petite *froidure* after Paris? Are there choices Cuba's leaders could be making now to hedge their bets? And against this backdrop, what would be best for the United States?

This chapter takes up these questions and hazards at least a few tentative answers.

The first part of this chapter discusses the environmental challenges that Cuba is facing and those that it will face as climate change accelerates, exacerbating the island's current environmental problems and creating new ones.[4] Next, the chapter provides an overview of Cuba's environmental and energy law and policy, which has increasingly incorporated the need to address climate change since the fall of the Soviet Union in 1991.[5] The following section sets out Cuba's top goals for addressing climate change and its impacts, as described in the government's recent report to the United Nations. Finally, the chapter assesses how U.S. decisions regarding its relations with Cuba and its involvement with the international effort to combat and respond to climate change will affect Cuba's ability to achieve its goals along with its own regulatory and policy tools as well as the resources that may be made available to poorer, vulnerable countries through the United Nations.

Cuba's Environmental Challenges, Backlit by Climate Change

Called the "Jewel of the Caribbean" (Dougherty 2015), there is no denying the island's natural beauty. The country boasts verdurous forests and some of the best-preserved reefs and shorelines in the region. But look further and you will find great vistas of urban dilapidation, leaking sewer systems, and vast carpets of contaminated marsh. Among Cuba's environmental problems, soil degradation—caused by poor farming techniques and intensified by drought—tops the list, affecting an estimated 60 percent of the land surface (see Rey Santos et al. 2008, 2.1.3). Water shortages are also on the rise, as result of overuse, pollution, saline intrusion, and drought. The loss of biodiversity and forest cover have also drawn national and international attention.[6]

Climate change makes problems like this even worse by increasing temperatures, raising sea levels, disrupting rain patterns, and contributing to "climate-related extremes."[7] According to the UN Intergovernmental Panel on Climate Change (IPCC), climate-change effects are now occurring "on all continents and across the oceans." (Field et al. 2014). The impact of climate change on the environment is contentious and notoriously hard to pin down. But in a 2012 report, the IPCC summarized the current scientific consensus (IPCC 2012). The panel's experts say it is "likely" that "the frequency of heavy precipitation or the proportion of total rainfall from heavy rainfalls will increase in many areas of the globe" (IPCC 2012, 13). Such downpours will affect landslides in some areas ("high confidence") and probably increase flooding in catchment areas ("medium confidence") (IPCC 2012). The IPCC finds it "likely" that tropical cyclone speeds will increase, posing particular threats to small island states (IPCC 2012, 13–15). It predicts with "medium confidence" that droughts will "intensify . . . in some seasons and areas, due to reduced precipitation and/or increased evapotranspiration" (IPCC 2012). Susceptible areas include, among others, Central America and southern Africa (IPCC 2012). Droughts can also produce secondary effects by withering crops that become fuel for wildfires and promoting soil runoff and landslides when the rain returns (IPCC 2012, 42).

These general conclusions are consistent with what is happening in Cuba right now. The country's average annual temperature has risen nearly a full degree Celsius.[8] Episodes of extreme weather, including hurricanes and searing dry periods, are mounting (Nachmany et al. 2015).[9] UN experts estimate a possible sea level rise of up to 1.5 meters over the next century, which means the island could lose more than 3 percent of its land by 2050 (Nachmany 2015, 4). Alarmed by the social and economic consequences of such projections,[10] Cuban leaders have made preparing for climate change impacts a priority of their environmental policies and the centerpiece around which all sustainability efforts should be arranged.[11]

Cuba's Environmental and Energy Law

Poor but always resourceful, Cuba in some ways appears a good candidate for a climate success story. It already has a strong, comprehensive environmental code, and it has long embraced international agreements aimed at both economic development and environmental protection. Since the 1959 Revolution, Cuba has wielded an outsized influence in the global political arena and nurtured a formidable cultural identity. The populace is also well educated, with high levels of scientific and technological resources for a country its size.

In December 2016, Cuba ratified the Paris Agreement under the UN Framework Convention on Climate Change (UNFCCC) (Granma 2016). The accord sought to bring all nations "into a common cause to undertake ambitious efforts to combat climate change and adapt to its effects, with enhanced support to assist developing countries to do so." (UNFCCC). The Paris Agreement is the long-awaited international commitment to specific obligations designed to give effect to the broad goals of the UNFCCC.[12] In its report to the United Nations on its progress and plans for meeting the goals of the UNFCCC (known as Intended Nationally Determined Contributions, or INDC), Cuba emphasized that it and other developing countries—particularly vulnerable island nations—are counting on promised financial and technological resources from developed countries in order to continue and increase their mitigation and adaptation efforts.[13]

In its report, Cuba highlights its long-standing recognition of the relationship between human welfare and environmental protections.[14] This relationship was brought into even sharper relief after the fall of the Soviet Union left the island without petroleum products to fuel its transportation, industrial, and agricultural sectors. Cubans' lives and well-being were suddenly almost entirely dependent on the island's natural resources.[15] In 1992—the year after the Soviet Union's dissolution—Cuba signed the UNFCCC and the Convention on Biological Diversity and began strengthening its environmental laws.[16]

The link between public welfare and environmental protection is rooted in the Cuban constitution. Article 27 of that document charges the government with "protect[ing] the environment and the natural resources in the country" and citizens with "contribut[ing] to the protection of the water and the atmosphere, and to the conservation of the soil, flora, fauna, and all the rich potential of nature" (Verchick 2016). An amendment to Article 27 added in 1997 introduces the concept of sustainable development (Cuba INDC): "[The State] recognizes th[e] close link [of the environment and natural resources] with the sustainable economic and social development for making human life more sensible, and for ensuring the survival, welfare, and security of present and future generations" (Verchick 2016).

Article 27 finds shape in Law No. 81, known as "the Law of the Environment."[17] In 1997, Cuba's legislature—the National Assembly—enacted Law 81 to update Cuba's environmental law framework in light of the need for greater protections and to promote sustainable development.[18] Law 81 is ambitious and sweeping: It requires the adoption of necessary acts and regulations, provides for the adoption of environmental standards, promotes broad public participation, and establishes mechanisms for environmental licensing, assessment, and enforcement (Verchick 2016). Law 81 creates one central agency—the Ministry of Science, Technology, and the Environment (CITMA)—charged with "proposing environmental policy and guiding its execution through the coordination and control of the nation's environmental management" (Verchick 2016, 217). More specifically, CITMA promulgates and enforces environmental regulations, coordinates environmental initiatives among other national agencies, and exercises oversight to ensure that all levels of government consider the nation's environmental goals before acting (Verchick 2016, 214–215).

In its INDC, Cuba states that its National Environmental Strategy is one of its principal tools for implementation of Law 81 (Cuba INDC). Like Law 81, the National Environmental Strategy is sweeping in scope. Unlike Law 81, however, the Strategy specifies the need to address climate change through both adaptation (preparing for and responding to climate change impacts that are inevitable) and mitigation (reducing greenhouse gas emissions) (Verchick 2016). The Strategy is particularly concerned with the need to adapt to climate change impacts (Verchick 2016, 215), which the island is already experiencing at an increasing rate (Verchick 2016).

Cuba is also concerned with modernizing its energy infrastructure and moving toward renewable sources of power generation. This would not only reduce Cuba's greenhouse gas emissions but also make energy production more efficient and reliable. Cuba's current infrastructure is both dirty and wasteful. Engineered from a patchwork of industrial relics bestowed first by the United States and then the Soviet Union, the system barely chugs along, powered almost entirely (96 percent) by cheap crude oil shipped from Venezuela (Ferris 2015). Cuban leaders desperately hope to change this. Today the nation appears to be following a credible path to one day light up the island with a more robust and reliable power grid fueled mostly by local sustainable energy (Nachmany et al. 2015). This path has been years in the making. In 1993, Cuba launched the National Energy Sources Development Programme, which brought electricity to scores of communities then off the grid. The effort, which relied heavily on solar installations, has helped ensure that up to 96 percent of residents now have access to electricity (Nachmany et al. 2015).[19] Cuba's "Energy Revolution" strategy took wing in 2005, aspiring to increase the share of renewable energy in gross energy generation from 4 percent to 24 percent by 2030 (Nachmany et al. 2015; Kolopic 2016). The government now strongly supports developments in solar power, wind generation, biogas, and hydroelectric power. In addition, Cuba's recently updated Law on Foreign Investment (Law No. 118) requires increased use of renewable energy.[20]

The government also promotes advances in energy efficiency. Resolution No. 136/09,[21] for instance, establishes efficiency standards for electrical appliances and equipment. It introduces a process for obtaining required energy labels and lists penalties for importing appliances that are not in compliance. The government also plans to install millions of LED lamps in homes and public spaces and to replace millions of less efficient kitchen appliances (Ferris 2015).

Cuba's Climate Change Goals

In its INDC, Cuba again declares climate change adaptation to be its "policy priority."[22] Given Cuba's situation, the statement is hardly surprising, but it takes on deeper political meaning when read alongside the history of global climate negotiations. The nations of the Global South have long resented the priorities and the moral proddings of the Global North. At bottom is the understandable complaint that increased standards of living in the North come at the expense of environmental destruction in the South. For more than a century, the North pumped carbon dioxide into the atmosphere beyond its "fair share." Today, the nations most threatened by famine and flood are in the South. The richer countries of the North—farther away from the direst impacts near the equator and more able cope with environmental hazards of all kinds—understandably emphasize the need for global greenhouse gas reduction. The poorer countries of the South—already burdened by the high temperatures and a lack of resources to respond—understandably emphasize the more local and immediate needs of climate adaptation. And because many of their climate-based threats derive in part from wealthy nations' overuse of the atmosphere's carrying capacity, poorer nations believe they are entitled to remedial aid.

Indeed, when the notion of INDCs was first discussed by FCCC parties, wealthier nations sought to limit national commitments to mitigation efforts only. Poorer countries, such as Cuba, pushed strongly for the inclusion of adaptation and for the transfer of financial and technological resources (South Centre 2015). The parties ultimately agreed to leave the content of the INDCs up to each country.[23] Although Cuba does address mitigation in its INDC, it makes clear that adaptation, along with financial and technical assistance, are its main concerns (Cuba INDC, 12).

Mitigation

In the portion of its INDC report on mitigation, Cuba highlights its progress in increasing the use of energy efficient bulbs and appliances, increasing forest cover, and developing renew able energy technologies (Cuba INDC, 15). Its principal mitigation goals are the development of new energy technologies, and, more specifically, building the infrastructure to generate electricity from them and connect them to the national grid (Cuba INDC, 17). More specifically, the government would like to build:

- 19 bioelectric plants connected to sugar mills with 755 MW from cane and forest biomass;
- 13 wind farms with 633 MW;
- 700 MW solar cells; and
- 74 small hydroelectric plants.[24]

Cuba estimates in the report that this infrastructure would allow the country to generate over 7,000 gigawatt hours each year from renewable energy sources, which would decrease its CO_2 emissions by over six million tons (Cuba INDC). This would make significant progress toward Cuba's goal of developing a strong, reliable energy system (Nachmany et al. 2015). Currently, its power system is in disrepair and fueled almost entirely (96 percent) by crude oil from Venezuela (Verchick 2016), which is decreasing as a result of Venezuela's precarious economic situation (Parraga and Ulmer 2016). In order to achieve this shift to renewables, Cuba strongly emphasizes that it will need assistance from industrialized nations through the UNFCC transfer mechanism and even specifies an amount: $4 billion.[25]

Adaptation

In its INDC, Cuba lists several climate adaptation goals:

1. Reducing the vulnerability of coastal settlements threatened by sea level rise land storm surge from hurricanes;[26]
2. Restoring the mangrove areas of the Cuban archipelago that have been most affected and stop the deterioration of the coral reefs if possible;[27]
3. Incorporating the dimension of (climate change) adaptation into the programs, plans, and projects linked to food production, water management, land use, forestry, fishing, tourism, and health;[28]
4. Establishing an environmental monitoring network that allows for the systematic evaluation of climate and environmental trends for decision-making;[29]
5. Reducing vulnerability in the health sector, based on a better knowledge and understanding of the relationship between climate variability, climate change, and human health, in two essential areas: infectious diseases and the System of Vigilance and Early Warning in the health sector;[30] and
6. Sustaining and developing research to protect, conserve, and rehabilitate the environment and adapting environmental policy to new economic and social projections. Prioritizing studies aimed at tackling climate change and the country's sustainable development

> generally. Emphasizing the conservation and rational use of natural resources such as the soil, the water, the beaches, the atmosphere, the forests, and biodiversity, as well as the promotion of environmental education.[31]

These are sizeable goals, yet they are clearly on target in light of the grave threats that climate change presents for Cuba. Whether Cuba can achieve them, however, depends on several factors and the interaction among them, including its domestic law and policy, the state of U.S.-Cuban relations, the state of U.S. involvement in global climate change policy, and a wild card: whether the global community is able to support an effective mechanism for helping poorer countries cope with the "loss and damage" associated with catastrophic risk. In the following assessment, we look at both mitigation and adaptation, but devote most of our analysis to Cuba's area of emphasis in its INDC report, adaptation.

Assessment

Cuba's Domestic Law and Policy

In theory, Cuba's national environmental framework and energy law are well suited to its climate change goals. Law No. 81 gives CITMA broad powers to shepherd environmental priorities through many aspects of government decision-making. The law provides mechanisms for comprehensive land-use planning, sustainable methods of development, the licensing of polluting facilities, environmental impact reviews that can demand substantive outcomes, and means of civil and criminal enforcement.[32] Cuba's "Energy Revolution" initiatives and efficiency standards are also promising, but depend on much greater funding than now seems available. Cuba also has a coastal zone management law (Decree Law No. 212) that can substantially limit shoreline development as far as 80 meters inland (depending on geographical features).[33] Finally, the government maintains a National System of Protected Areas (Decree Law No. 201), containing an impressive array of national parks, ecological reserves, wildlife refuges, and more.[34] The framework nature of Cuba's environmental law makes it amenable to the relatively easy incorporation of an overarching climate change adaptation strategy. Indeed, the government indicated in its last update of the National

Environmental Strategy in 2011, that Law No. 81 could be amended or retooled to further account for climate change impacts (Verchick 2016).

The government also created the National Program to Face Climate Change, administered by CITMA, which is largely devoted to adaptation measures (Nachmany et al. 2015). Since CITMA has broad authority to implement Law No. 81, it seems that a regulatory framework is already in place that is well suited to integrating adaptation considerations and measures throughout decision-making processes, including those that impact mangroves, coastal communities, and coral reefs, and other particularly vulnerable resources. In addition, Cuba has long been recognized for its remarkable hurricane response program,[35] and it has consolidated its educational initiatives on disaster adaptation over the years in its National Strategy on Adaptation (Nachmany et al. 2015). Its most recent update of that Strategy in 2010 identifies climate change as the first priority in moving forward (Nachmany et al. 2015).

Further, as Cuba notes in its INDC report, it has made significant investments in education since the 1959 Revolution, and, as a result, has a tremendous wealth of human capital (Cuba INDC).[36] Cuba also highlights that it has long drawn on the knowledge and expertise of its citizens to accumulate important data over a long period of time about climate, sea level, public health, and other areas that are relevant to developing climate change response strategies (Cuba INDC, 1). Its many scientists and medical and public health experts thus provide it with invaluable resources for creating effective climate change adaptation policy and developing systematic educational and research programs regarding climate change.

Still, serious challenges remain involving both implementation and resources. Consider coastal protection. Based on a comprehensive climate vulnerability study completed in 2013, the Cuban government has been able to identify the coastal properties most vulnerable to sea level rise and allocate resources accordingly (Ines Perez 2014). When, for instance, planners found that neighborhoods abutting Havana's Malecón esplanade were vulnerable to cold fronts, saltwater intrusion, and storm water overflow, officials were able to restrict development using authority originating in Law No. 81 (Cuba INDC). But what about structures already in place? In the years immediately following the fall of the Soviet Union, a resulting economic crisis in Cuba led to a dramatic sprawl of homes and other facilities on the coast that led to shoreline degradation. In 2000, authorities imposed a coastal protection law establishing 40-meter setbacks from high tide. But until 2011 these laws were seldom enforced. To protect the fragile coast, and the billions of dollars in tourism it supports, the government began a campaign in 2012 to bulldoze hundreds of buildings located too close to the beaches of Varadero. Flattened structures included nearly 287 state-owned buildings and 198 illegally built privately owned houses (Cuba INDC). Government efforts to relocate households to safer areas were slow and by many deemed insufficient.

In addition, the Cuban government is pursuing a broad campaign to restore natural coastal barriers by rebuilding dunes, protecting reefs, and reseeding mangrove forests (Cuba INDC). These efforts cannot prevent sea level rise, but they can help buy time. Cuba's environmental framework can ensure that the mangroves are protected and that agencies have access to the best scientific and technological information available. But money and labor is not unlimited, so, again, Cuba is eager to turn to the international community.

Cuba states in its INDC that, although it has allocated resources for adaptation in its annual budget, the country will need "much greater amounts in order to respond to the increasing impacts of climate change."[37] Undoubtedly, Cuba and other developing countries will need outside resources to undertake projects such as protection of coastal communities, restoration of mangroves, and stopping the deterioration of coastal reefs. Further, Cuba should continue to advocate for international cooperation through the mechanism of the transfer of financial and technological resources from developed to developing countries as called for by the UNFCCC, as it does repeatedly in its INDC report (Cuba INDC, 4).

In addition to the UNFCC transfer mechanism, Cuba's ability to pay for its climate change mitigation and adaptation efforts could be significantly affected by how its relationship with the United States plays out, as well as by what appears to be a likely withdrawal of the United States from its international climate change obligations.

U.S. Relations with Cuba

It seems obvious that normalized trade relations with the United States would help Cuba strengthen its economy and protect its environment. Deeper commercial ties would boost gross domestic product and shore up the country's debt. It would give the public and private sectors more resources to pursue renewable energy goals and climate resilience. As the Latin-American scholars Julia Sweig and Micahel Bustamante write, "the U.S. embargo remains a formidable obstacle to the island's long-term economic prosperity" (Sweig and Bustamante 2013). Freer trade with the United States, they suggest, would also give Cuban reform advocates "more leeway and increasing support on the island for greater economic and political liberalization" (Sweig and Bustamante 2013). Greater economic liberalization would grow the private development sector. Proper regulations, including strong zoning laws and building codes, would certainly make these changes sustainable. Because they would bear some financial risk of climate-related hazards, they would have incentives to develop resilient designs and locate buildings in safer areas.

Political liberalization is also key. Think of those bulldozed homes in Varadero, and all the families queued up for relocation assistance. In Cuba, tens of thousands of people live in ramshackle homes, many built illegally, on eroding coasts and interior flood plains. Assisting these communities will require not just technology and resources, but a carefully planned public process. Communities at risk will need access to information, decision-making tools, and meaningful opportunities to express their needs and help design their future. Without such process, people could end up in even worse shape than before, without social ties or accessible jobs. Grassroots opposition could scuttle any hope of transformation at scale.

Here we should add two points. First, economic and political liberalization—though clearly a desirable goal—poses its own challenges to climate adaptation. Stronger economic ties with the United States will mean more tourism and trade in Cuba. That will put more pressure on Cuban officials to open the island's scenic and fragile coasts to developments like hotels or port facilities. This will be an important test of Cuba's environmental protections. It's possible to see a pause in U.S. trade reforms as an opportunity for Cuba to catch its breath and prepare its regulatory and permitting apparatus for the U.S. onslaught whenever it comes. Liberalization on the political side, while also necessary, will unquestionably slow down efforts to control when and how people build—and when they move. This comes with the territory, to some extent. Again, Cuban leaders would do well stay on course with political liberalization, incorporating land-use decisions in its model.

Our second point is that although Cuba's economic liberalization seems to some extent inevitable, the trend toward political liberalization is more fragile. Human Rights Watch, for instance, reported in 2016 that Cuban authorities continued to "to repress dissent and discourage public criticism" (Human Rights Watch 2015). The Cuban Commission on Human Rights and National Reconciliation documented a total of 9,940 arbitrary detentions by the Cuban government last year (Deutsch Welle 2017). The key to progress on human rights issues is U.S. pressure, deployed best, we think, in the context to active economic engagement. Thus, if the United States retreats from President Obama's reform-based course, progress in this essential area could stall. This would be bad for Cubans in general, but it would put at risk the kinds of local planning and community engagement that are important to building climate resiliency at the ground level.

U.S. Retreat from Climate Change Action

In addition, Cuba will suffer indirectly when the United States retreats from its commitments under the Paris Agreement and the UNFCCC. We noted earlier President Trump's disdain for climate change action. His proposed budget for 2018, released in March 2017, shows what, as of this writing, may be in store.[38] For starters, the White House proposal "[e]liminates the Global Climate Change Initiative and fulfills the President's pledge to cease payments to the United Nations' (UN) climate change programs by eliminating U.S. funding related to the Green Climate Fund and its two precursor Climate Investment Funds" (Office of Management and Budget 2016). Operating within the U.S. Department of State, the Global Climate Change Initiative (GCCI) is the government's central hub for overseas climate change aid. The GCCI not only supports bilateral agreements of assistance, but has in recent years been in charge of meeting U.S. financial commitments to the UNFCCC and the IPCC (in its work assessing the latest climate research). The United States is the world's largest contributor to the UNFCCC and the IPCC, responsible for about 20 percent of the UNFCCC's $54 billion biannual budget (Matthiessen 2017). The GCCI also supports clean energy and climate-tracking initiatives in developing countries.[39] Cuba has not, to date, been involved in any of these programs. But if U.S.-Cuban relations continued to grow and Cuba maintained a course toward liberalization, it seems plausible that Cuba could join such initiatives in the future, providing they still exist.

President Trump's budget proposal would also end contributions to the United Nation's Green Climate Fund, which is intended to help poorer nations, including Cuba, prepare for catastrophic effects of climate change. While the Obama administration pledged $3 billion to the fund, only $1 billion has so far been paid (Matthiessen 2017). Finally, the budget proposal would "reduce by $650 million funding over the next three years to multilateral development banks, including the World Bank." (Office of Management and Budget 2016). These institutions play a major role in financing mitigation and adaptation projects in the Global South. Even though Cuba withdrew its membership from the World Bank in 1960, some observers speculate that the country may be interested in rejoining the bank—and that it may be interested in forming ties with other development banks as well (Morris 2017; Sosin 2015). If this were to happen, Cuba would tap into another source of funding for climate resilience projects. Continued U.S. support of development banks in this area has been crucial. Should this support be cut, the global community will be left scurrying to fill the gap.

The Special Case of the "Loss and Damages" Mechanism

In the midst of our discussion on mitigation, adaptation, and poor countries like Cuba, there is an elephant standing firm. It's called "loss and damages," and we will explain what that means. Recall that at the beginning of negotiations within the UNFCCC, wealthy nations voiced a priority for mitigation over adaptation, and that priority has remained. This is not to say adaptation was not recognized—we have seen that it is—but that such concerns often took a backseat. And early adaptation initiatives were short on details. Over decades, the UNFCCC struggled with how to facilitate and fund local adaptation projects in the South through myriad schemes. In 2011, the efforts were finally captured under a single umbrella known as the Cancun Adaptation Framework (Caripis 2014).

The Cancun Framework includes a coordinating body, a program to encourage national adaptation plans, and, most importantly for our purposes, something called the "Warsaw Mechanism for Loss and Damage." This process aims "to address loss and damage associated with impacts of climate change, including extreme events and slow onset events, in developing countries."[40] Parties in the Global South believe that "loss and damage" assistance should come *in addition to* assistance made available for more ordinary coping methods. For them "loss and damage" describes the kinds of extraordinary, more extreme climate impacts that cannot "be reduced by adaptation" (United Nations 2014).[41]

A related set of agreements make commitments on technology sharing, capacity building, and financing. So far, parties have committed US$100 billion per year until 2020 for mitigation and adaptation purposes. These funds are to be collected and disbursed by the UNFCCC's Green Climate Fund, from which, as we mentioned, President Trump is hoping to withdraw. In addition, the parties have recognized the need for "additional, predictable and adequate funding" for poorer countries that are in the climate-change crosshairs (UNFCCC 2011).

What does this mean? Though discussions on this point remain fluid, it appears that even assuming a heroic rush toward mitigation and adaptation, the global community understands that some poorer nations will be hammered hard by residual impacts. The "loss and damage" mechanism appears to be the beginning of a supplemental "Plan B." While it is too soon to say what a concrete plan would look like, an eventual package could draw from a range of tools from insurance, to emergency relief, to recovery assistance, to special compensation funds, to relocation assistance and even immigration privileges.[42] What we *do* know is that the size and cost of "Plan B" will be inversely related to the success of the original "Plan A" (that is, everything else the UNFCCC is doing). Put another way, the more harm we fail to avoid through mitigation and adaptation, the more harm we will have to pay for through the "loss and damage" mechanism.

Just as there are limits to what Plan A can realistically achieve, there are also limits for Plan B. Insurance programs, for instance, work best where risk is predictable and claims are spread out over time and extent of severity. When uncertainty expands and claims concentrate, insurance markets implode. Compensation funds work well when damage is easy to measure and verify, and where disbursements are large enough to put people back on their feet and discourage litigation, civil unrest, and other forms of backlash. They run into trouble where claims are too complex and large. Developing a successful "loss and damage" plan might be possible *as long as it is capable of carrying the load*. But if residual risk gets too big, the system will fail. For that reason it is important to examine the projected load of residual risk under chosen climate scenarios. The Paris Agreement calls for holding the rise in global average temperature to "well below 2°C above pre-industrial levels," while "pursuing efforts to limit the temperature increase to 1.5°C." (United Nations 2017). How much difference is in that half of degree? In terms of residual load—quite a lot.

According to a 2016 study published by European Geosciences Union, a third of an increase in global average temperature could result in some impacts that are disproportionately larger and concentrated in the tropics, where more poor countries are situated (Schleussner et al. 2016). With another half a degree increase in temperature, Central America, in particular, would see a twofold *decrease* in crop yields (Schleussner et al. 2016). Droughts, too, could worsen in dramatic ways (Schleussner et al. 2016). A half degree could mark the difference between having some living coral in the tropics near the end of the century and having none (Schleussner et al. 2016). For the "loss and damage" mechanism, the difference between an increase of 1.5ºC and 2ºC could mean the difference between success and failure. What this means for Cuba—or any island nation in a tropical "hotspot"—is that adhering to the 1.5º ceiling could be essential for any reasonable chance of normalcy. Beyond that, Cuba's adaptive efforts would buckle and the global community's mechanism to bail it out would collapse. Cuba's economy could fall into a tailspin. Its political institutions could break apart. Citizens might flee the island toward Florida shores. This is not a pretty scenario. Yet it is far from certain, or perhaps even likely. With an increase of 2º or more, it is certainly *plausible*.

The odds are not trivial. This is the situation the United States and other rich countries must ponder carefully. In the end, the chances that Cuba—or any other country similarly situated—will be able to prosper in the face of climate change will depend as much on its actions as it will on the actions of others around them. A U.S. failure to meet its emissions goals or a bar on overseas adaptation funding would be bad enough. But the real threat is that U.S. intransigence would encourage other rich or populous countries to drag their feet too. That is a future neither Cuba nor the United States could comfortably endure.

Conclusions

Cuba is understandably alarmed by the catastrophic risks that climate change presents to its land, people, and, indeed, continued existence.

Given the immensity and global nature of that threat, however, Cuba also recognizes that concerted international initiatives, including transfer mechanisms, are a necessary part of any response that has the chance of succeeding. The Global South has consistently urged the Global North to recognize the importance of placing adaptation on the same footing as mitigation, and of ensuring that the countries of the South have the resources to adapt and mitigate, and, now, compensation to recover from inevitable climate harms to which the South cannot adapt. Before the election of President Trump, the apparent renewed commitment of the United States to global climate change efforts and its easing of tensions with Cuba collectively bore significant promise for Cuba's ability to meaningfully address climate change within and outside its shores. We hope—for the sake of both countries and the rest of the world—that we do not all lose out on the potential power of this promising combination.

Notes

1. An end to the U.S. trade embargo against Cuba would add to the U.S. economy too. The U.S. International Trade Commission estimated in 2001 that the embargo cost U.S. exporters $1.2 billion annually in lost sales, a number that has likely grown significantly since then. U.S. Chamber of Commerce, Comments on the Economic Effects of U.S. Restrictions on Trade with and Travel to Cuba U.S. Chamber of Commerce for the U.S. International Trade Commission Investigation No. 332-552, "Overview of Cuban Imports of Goods and Services and Effects of U.S. Restrictions," June 2, 2015, available at https://www.uschamber.com/sites/default/files/u.s._chamber_submission_for_the_record_for_usitc_investigation_no._332-552.pdf.
2. *See, e.g.*, Coral Davenport & Alissa J. Rubin (2017, at A1), reporting that, at this signing ceremony, "Mr. Trump made clear that the United States had no intention of meeting the commitments that his predecessor had made to curb planet-warming carbon dioxide pollution, turning denials of climate change into national policy"; also EPA 2017, 16–22), detailing how President Trump's proposed budget "eliminates or cuts funding for most EPA climate programs, which account for much of the reductions in carbon and other greenhouse gas pollution that the U.S. government has worked to achieve to date." As for staying in the Paris Agreement, the Trump administration appears undecided (Davenport 2017).
3. *See* Hale (n.d.). Indeed, the United States, itself, might still meet its emissions targets under Paris thanks to actions being taken at the subnational level and in the private sector. *See also* Bloomberg (2017).
4. The first section draws from Robert R. M. Verchick (2016).
5. This section draws from Verchick, *supra* note 4, §§ 11:3–11:9.

6. *See* Ministry of Science, Technology and Environment, Proyecto Estrategia Ambiental Nacional (2011/15) [Environmental Strategy Project (2011/15)] §§ 2.1.2, 2.1.4 (2011) (hereinafter "Proyecto Estrategia Ambiental Nacional") (describing deforestation and loss of biodiversity). For a concise discussion of Cuba's environmental challenges, *see* Daniel J. Whittle, Kenyon C. Lindeman, & James T. B. Tripp (2003).
7. UNISDR (2009), http://www.preventionweb.net/files/9414_GARsummary.pdf, 6–7.
8. *See* República de Cuba, Contribución Nacionalmente Determindad Convención Marco de las Naciones Unidas Sobre el Cambio Climático ("Intended Nationally Determined Contributions") (2015) [hereinafter Cuba INDC].
9. *Id.* at 5.
10. *See, e.g.*, Cuba INDC, *supra* note 8, in which Cuba discusses the great danger to its security presented by climate change as a result of, inter alia, diminished water supply, food security, human health, and biodiversity.
11. *See infra* Parts II & III.
12. The United Nations Framework Convention on Climate Change (UNFCCC) sets up just that—a "framework" obligating state parties to eventually reduce carbon emissions and implement adaptation measures. (*See* UNFCCC, 1992, 31 I.L.M. 849.) *See also* United Nations (1997). "In short, the Kyoto Protocol is what 'operationalizes' the [UNFCCC]." It commits industrialized countries to stabilize greenhouse gas emissions based on the principles of the [UNFCCC]. *The Convention itself only encourages countries to do so.*") (emphasis added). Some of the developed-country UNFCCC parties did assume some more specific mitigation and adaption obligations five years later, when the Kyoto Protocol to the UNFCCC was adopted. Kyoto Protocol to the United Nations Framework Convention on Climate Change, Dec. 10, 1997, 37 I.L.M. 22 (entered into force Feb. 15, 2005). Those obligations, which were in any event largely considered to be severely inadequate, expired in 2012. *See* UNFCCC Website, *Background on the UNFCCC: The Initial Response to Climate Change*, at http://unfccc.int/
13. Cuba INDC, *supra* note 8, at 10–11.
14. Cuba INDC, *supra* note 8 at 1.
15. *See* Pamela Stricker (2007). "One could argue that (the dissolution of the Soviet bloc) inadvertently made Cuba independent for the first time in history." (Jonathan Benjamin-Alvarado ed., 2010).
16. *See* Cuba INDC, *supra* note 8, at 2; *see also* Stricker (2007, *supra* note 34, at 74) describing Cuban government officials' recognition that the environmental laws and implementation mechanisms in place at the time of the fall of the Soviet Union were inadequate for a number of reasons, including that "the law did no cover the loss of biological diversity, the depletion of the ozone layer, global warming, and the international movement of hazardous wastes."
17. Code Civil [C. Civ.] no. 81.
18. Stricker (2007, *supra* note 14, at 77) quoting then President of the National Assembly, Richard Alarcón, who explained "the need for this new, more comprehensive law" in a written statement: "the current conditions of economic and social development

demand a legal framework more in line with the current situation," "a legal instrument that will adequately reflect the requirements of environmental protection and the attainment of sustainable development."

19. *Id.*
20. Code Civil [C. Civ.] no. 118. A side note: in 2016, the U.S. Department of Commerce amended its Export Administration Regulations to promote exports of renewable energy technology from the United States to Cuba. (Cuba Licensing Policy Revision, 81 F.R. 4580 (Jan. 27, 2016) (to be codified at 15 C.F.R. pt. 746).
21. Resolución 136/2009, available at http://bit.ly/28MgJFB.
22. Cuba INDC, *supra* note 8, at 7 (authors' translation; original reads: "el Gobierno cubano reconoce como prioridad de su política la adaptación al cambio climático").
23. Cuba INDC, supra note 8 at 2. The South Centre's policy brief, which is available through a link on the UNFCCC website, explains the negotiations about the INDCs and provides developing countries with guidance on drafting them. At the beginning, the Centre notes:

    > In fact, it is important to note that in the INDCs that have been submitted thus far by developed countries such as the EU, US, Switzerland, and Norway, no one has indicated their contribution on finance and technology transfer, and have only focussed their communication on their mitigation contribution. This clearly signals the skewed way in which developed countries view the INDCs— which to them are only about mitigation commitments of all Parties.

    Id.
24. Cuba INDC, *supra* note 8, at 17 (authors' translation; original reads: "19 bioeléctricas anexas a los centrales azucareros con 755 MW a partir de la biomasa cañera y forestall"; "13 parques eólicos con 633 MW"; "700 MW Fotovoltaicos"; "y 74 pequeñas centrales hidroeléctricas").
25. Cuba INDC, *supra* note 8, at 17.
26. Cuba INDC, supra note 8 at 13 (authors' translation; original reads: "Disminuir la vulnerabilidad costera para los asentamientos amenazados por el aumento del nivel del mar y la sobreelevacción de este por los huracanes y el oleaje.").
27. Cuba INDC, supra note 8 at 13 (authors' translation; original reads: "Recuperar las áreas de manglares más afectadas del archipiélago cubano y detener en lo posible el deterioro de las crestas de arrecifes de coral.").
28. Cuba INDC, *supra* note 8, at 13 (authors' translation; original reads: "Incorporar la dimensión de la adaptación a los programas, planes y proyectos vinculados a la producción de alimentos, el manejo integral del agua, ordenamiento del territorio, forestal, pesca, el turismo y la salud.").
29. *Id.*at 13 (authors' translation; original reads: "Conformar una red de monitoreo ambiental, que permita la evaluación sistemática de las tendencias climáticas y medioambientales para la toma de decisiones.").
30. *Id.* at 13 (authors' translation; original reads: "Reducir la vulnerabilidad en el sector de la salud, a partir de un mejor conocimiento y entendimiento de las relaciones entre la variabilidad del clima, el cambio climático y la salud humana, en dos ejes

esenciales: las enfermedades infecciosas y el Sistema de Vigilancia y Alerta Temprana del sector.").

31. *Id.* at 13–14 (authors' translation; original reads: "Sostener y desarrollar investigaciones integrales para proteger, conservar y rehabilitar el medio ambiente y adecuar la política ambiental a las nuevas proyecciones del entorno económico y social. Priorizar estudios encaminados al enfrentamiento al cambio climático y, en general, a la sostenibilidad del desarrollo del país. Enfatizar la conservación y uso racional de recursos naturales como los suelos, el agua, las playas, la atmósfera, los bosques y la biodiversidad, así como el fomento de la educación ambiental.").
32. Code Civil [C.Civ] no. 81. For a more detailed description of Law No. 81, *see* Verchick (2016, *supra* note 4, § 11:7).
33. *See* Code Civil [C.Civ] no. 212; (Verchick 2016, *supra* note 4, § 11:12).
34. *See* Code Civil [C.Civ] no. 201; (Verchick 2016, *supra* note 9, § 11:14).
35. *See, e.g.*, Press Release, U.N. Office for Disaster Risk Reduction, (2015), noting that Cuba is "already a recognized leader in the field" of disaster risk reduction and community resilience to hazards such as hurricanes.
36. *See* Cuba INDC, *supra* note 8, at 1–2; *cf. also* Benjamin-Alvarado (2010, *supra* note 34, at 6) ("Since the 1970s, energy development schemes in Cuba have included dedicated attempts to link such development to the material well-being of Cuban society overall. Thus, energy policy has been infused with policy initiatives in higher education, science and technological advancement, and increasing domestic human capital resources.").
37. Cuba INDC, *supra* note 8, at 14 (authors' translation; original reads: "Cuba identifica expresamente, en el Plan Anual de la Economía, recursos destinados a la adaptación. Estas cifras hacia futuro tendrán el nivel que permitan las posibilidades financieras del país. Para responder a los crecientes impactos del cambio climático se requerirán montos muy superiores.").
38. Keep in mind that completing the federal budget is a circuitous process that starts with the president's proposal and bears many rounds of review in Congress. The final results could be different from what we describe.
39. The clean energy program is administered through the Clean Energy Ministerial, the Climate and Clean Air Coalition. The climate-tracking program is part of an initiative called Enhancing Capacity for Low-Emission Development Strategies.
40. Draft Decision, Warsaw international mechanism for loss and damage associated with climate change impacts, Decision-/CP.19 para 9.
41. *Report of the Conference of the Parties on Its Nineteenth Session, Held in Warsaw from 11 to 23 November 2013—Addendum—Part Two: Action Taken by the Conference of the Parties at Its Nineteenth Session*, UN Doc FCCC/CP/2013/10/Add.1 (31 January 2014) Decision 2/CP.19. For further commentary, *see* K. Dow K & F. Berkhout (2014).
42. For speculation of what the mechanism could or should look like, *see* Verchick, (2017), Burns (2016), and Burkett (2015).

13
Conclusion

*Michael J. Kelly, Erika Moreno, and Richard C. Witmer, II**

This volume has examined in significant depth the opportunities and challenges that shape the bilateral relationship between Cuba and the United States. In each of the three sections—politics, economics, and law—the contributors provide important insight into where progress is likely given existing and emerging opportunities in the bilateral relationship, and where existing challenges are likely to inhibit change. The political chapters highlight the path that led to increased engagement and a warming of relations between Cuba and the United States with LeoGrande's chapter 2 providing important insight into how Presidents Raúl Castro and Barack Obama arrived at their historic agreement. Chapter 3 provides context into the debate over succession versus transition and how succession scenarios are much more likely than a transition to a liberal democracy. The challenge this presents is clear, as U.S. law as currently written precludes full normalization of relations with a government in Cuba that is not democratically elected. Yet as Johnson and Lin note in chapter 4, the Chinese have a vested interest in Cuba retaining its centralized governmental structure while also advocating for a warming of relations with the United States. China stands as a model, along with Vietnam, for U.S. relations with countries that have an open economic system and a nondemocratic government.

A greater understanding of the economic relationship between Cuba and the United States is spelled out in the four chapters in the second section of the book. Here the major changes in the Cuban agricultural sector are covered by González-Corso and Nova-González in chapter 5, including a reduction in centralized control, which highlights the opportunities that have developed for farmers in the recent past and are likely to continue on

* Michael J. Kelly, Creighton University School of Law, michaelkelly@creighton.edu; Erika Moreno, Creighton University, erikamoreno@creighton.edu; Richard C. Witmer, II, Creighton University, witmer@creighton.edu.

The Cuba-U.S. Bilateral Relationship. Michael J. Kelly, Erika Moreno, and Richard C. Witmer, II.

the island. Similarly, opportunities exist for U.S. farmers looking for an expanded market in Cuba. Henken's chapter 6 expands on the theme of economic change in Cuba by highlighting the new ethos of entrepreneurship in a single market in Havana. Here again, recent changes have created new opportunities for the citizens of Cuba while providing goods that are in demand while engaging in a socially responsible, non-zero-sum, economic transactions. So, while the potential economic openings on the island have tapped into the ingenuity and entrepreneurial spirit on the island, new models of economic transactions have sprung up even if at a small scale.

The opportunities that market demand and supply provide for the Cuban-U.S. relationship is no more apparent than in the final two economy chapters. Here the growing demand for tourism services among U.S. and other non-Cuban citizens has been met with both opportunities to meet this expanding market and with challenges for providing needed services. Walsh in chapter 7 provides the context for investment in Cuba's tourism industry as well as identifying what seems to work and what is not necessary for market entry. Finally, Betancourt wraps up this section by identifying the variation in immigration, tourism, and trade that has occurred over the last decade or so in chapter 8. While challenges clearly remain for the flow of goods, services, and individuals between Cuba and the United States, this untapped market promises great potential to be a driving force in the warming of relations between the two countries.

Finally, section three provides additional context for the legal relationship between Cuba and the United States. Central to these chapters are the challenges that currently impede a warming of Cuban-U.S. relations. Yet these chapters, in identifying the challenges, also provide a valuable insight into how the two countries may be able to address existing impediments. In the United States, the Helms-Burton Act outlines a number of conditions that must be addressed before two sides can fully formalize relations. Benjamin-Alvarado addresses, in chapter 9, how the law continues to haunt efforts between the two countries and is likely to cast a shadow over efforts in the near future as support for repealing Helms-Burton seems unlikely to emerge any time soon. Kelly, Moreno, and Witmer address one of the key impediments to improved relations as noted in Helms-Burton, in chapter 10. Here, the authors provide a road map for resolving property rights claims that have existed for nearly sixty years. Their approach, which they describe as a means to benefit both countries, provides for quickly settling most outstanding claims.

Understanding the complexity of the legal landscape as it applies to the Cuban economy is at the heart of Catá Backer's chapter 11. Given the fragile state of the island's economy, the challenges are many, however, this does note preclude meaningful legal changes in Cuba, and with them, economic growth and opportunity. In posing and then answering three questions about these economic changes, Catá Backer provides valuable insight into the possible economic future of Cuba and its relationship with the United States and the rest of the world. Backer's insightful and thorough analysis of Cuba's economic and social priorities, as laid out in the Communist Party's most recent *Lineameintos* published in 2011, provide opportunities and some notable limitations to the islands' ability to re-engage the global economy. Meanwhile, opportunities presented to the Cuban government in the form of a European alternative, as manifested in the Political Dialogue and Cooperation Agreement (PDCA), may offer some hope for Cuban efforts to engage the global economy.

While the legal structure that facilitates economic development in Cuba is central to Backer's analysis of Cuban and international legal developments, chapter 12 forces us to contend with the environmental externalities that arise from economic and social development. In chapter 12, Verchick and Sokol address Cuba's vulnerability to environmental degradation, driven by global climate change and lack of domestic environmental regulation. Chapter 12 presents possibilities to bring Cuba in line with international agreements, including the Paris Accords. Yet, the United States' resistance to addressing climate issues since 2016 has the potential to place the island in a more vulnerable position, which the authors note could have effects that reverberate throughout Cuba's economy, society, and politics. For an island nation like Cuba, choices made there and by its neighbor just ninety miles away will continue to have important consequences in the years ahead.

While the three sections of this book offer a convenient mode of thinking about the policy areas that will be central to a *rapprochement* between Cuba and the United States, there is sufficient crossover between the three that all of them must often be considered simultaneously, as the existing and emerging opportunities and challenges push the relationship forward. For example, reading through the chapters that address the political relationship between the two countries, it becomes clear that government officials in Cuba and the United States are constrained by both the existing political *and* legal landscape. In the United States, the Helms-Burton Act, as outlined by Benjamin-Alvarado in chapter 9, was passed to limit the options that political leaders would have to alter the relationship with Cuba without meeting specific standards outlined in U.S. law. By codifying the need to address issues of property rights, as well as Cuba's transition to a liberal democracy, political and legal realities provide some of the most stubborn challenges that the two countries continue to face. Yet the solution to these two issues is also addressed in this volume. Prior to the efforts of Cuban President Raúl Castro and U.S. President Barack Obama to reduce the animosity between the two countries, the administration of U.S. President George W. Bush sought legal and policy options for addressing the property rights issue through the U.S. Agency for International Development (USAID). The result of this call for a workable policy is outlined by three of the study's original authors in chapter 10. Here, key recommendations for addressing the challenge of property rights includes allowing current inhabitants to continue to remain in their homes by offering financial compensation for those with smaller claims rather than recovery of property lost nearly sixty years ago. For larger claims, working to coordinate business opportunities between Cuban and U.S. companies is supported as a win-win strategy. This approach would not require a change in the Cuban regime, nor would it disrupt current uses of property in Cuba. The suggested model would have both sides move forward on resolving this long-lasting issue, allow for the continued development of a tourism industry in Cuba to generate much-needed hard currency, and remove one legal roadblock that continues to hamper bilateral relations. While the proposed property resolution model would not address outstanding political issues, like the transition to democracy in Cuba as noted in chapter 3, it would represent a highly credible signal to the Cuban government that a full normalization of bilateral relations is achievable in the near future. What is more, this particular solution suggests that diplomatic efforts at the state-to-state level (or track one diplomacy) are front and center for both governments. Both of these features, as we noted in chapter 1 (this volume), would represent a wholesale reversal of the Cold War status quo between these two neighbors.

The transition to democracy, while generally viewed as a precondition for the United States to normalize relations with Cuba, is not wholly consistent with the scope of current U.S. foreign policy. Nowhere is this more evident than in Johnson and Lin's chapter 4, which highlights the desire of China to see a warming of relations between Cuba and the United States. The irony is that China is the United States' largest trading partner despite its authoritarian government. Moving forward, the Chinese economic and political model, with an open economic system and centralized state control of the government, may serve as an archetype for Cuba. While this would fall short of stated U.S. policy requiring the transition to democracy, the succession of the Castro regime by leaders supportive of the revolution not named Castro who are also supportive of greater engagement with the United States, may find it possible to move toward a warming of bilateral relations. If the succession were to also result in the further opening of the Cuban economy to allow U.S. investment while addressing property rights and human rights issues, political pressure in the United States to further engage the new regime would likely follow. In this example, it is possible that legal, political, and economic influences could converge in the near future and impact the direction of Cuban-U.S. relations. While the likelihood of the United States abandoning its interests in seeing a regime change on the island are slim (as noted by Benjamin-Alvarado in chapter 9), relegating the language and policies of "regime change" on the island would represent significant policy change along the state-to-state track of diplomacy. But, as we note, it is far more likely if political pressure, facilitated by nonstate officials (track two diplomacy), business (track three diplomacy), and citizen interactions (track four diplomacy) are brought to bear on leaders in both states.

In section two of this volume we see additional examples of how economic developments over the last decade have the potential to shape the future of the bilateral relationship. This is true given internal changes in both Cuba and the United States, as well as between the two countries. As González-Corzo and Nova-González note, in chapter 5, the decentralization and opening of the agricultural sector in Cuba has been an important step in efforts to expand the production of food and other agricultural products on the island. While these reforms have expanded domestic production, the United States remains an important supplier of foodstuff for the island, accounting for nearly 40 percent of imports. The Cuban market represents an important opportunity to expand U.S. exports in an increasingly competitive global marketplace. In an environment where the demand is apparent, and the supply is available and looking for a market, further expansion of the agricultural relationship between the two countries may apply force on the two governments to expand their interaction. Increased demand in the United States to travel to the island, and the concomitant need to provide for more visitors in Cuba, may pressure both sides to expand their formal interaction. Again, economic demands in both Cuba and the United States may facilitate the reconsideration of the two country's political engagement and legal limitations, in light of economic opportunities. The effectiveness of an economic argument may be more likely during the Donald Trump years, as he has spoken often of the need to consider economic factors, even in nondemocratic regimes with a questionable human rights record.

In this volume's introduction we also touched on other thematic elements that help shape our understanding of Cuban-U.S. relations. This includes the level of interaction, whether at the governmental or individual level, and the signaling between the two governments that may facilitate continued thawing of the relationship. First, for much of the post-Cuban revolution era that began in the late 1950s, interaction between the two countries has existed mainly at the governmental, or elite level. Here, influences from the Cold War, claims and counterclaims of meddling in each others' governmental affairs, efforts on both sides to cast the other as an enemy and worthy adversary, and economic maneuvers, especially on the part of the U.S. government to punish its smaller neighbor, have resulted in generations of mistrust and limited political engagement. Even so, as LeoGrande outlines, there have been openings and opportunities that most recently resulted in a dialogue and re-establishment of limited relations between Cuba and the United States. This culminated with the administrations of U.S. President Barack Obama and Cuban President Raúl Castro, who negotiated with the assistance of the Catholic Church, to re-establish diplomatic ties between the two nations. The agreement between the two presidents also contained a number of credible signals of warming relations, including a prisoner exchange, a loosening of travel and trade restrictions by President Obama, and a commitment on the part of President Castro to engage nongovernmental organizations on issues of human rights. Yet, despite the efforts of Cuban President Castro and U.S. President Obama to formally establish a lasting and ongoing political dialogue that would lead to the normalization of relations, Obama's successor, President Donald Trump, took the relationship a step backward with a rhetorical swipe at the increased interaction between Cuba and the United States. Trump's announcement came with limited policy changes, including a reduction in legal opportunities to visit the island, a reduction in U.S. embassy staff in Cuba, and additional restrictions on U.S. business relations on the island. A result of President Trump's reversion to Cold War–era rhetoric and a pre-Obama policy focus has been to stall the progress that seemed inevitable just a few years prior. Whether formal opposition to warmer relation on the part of the United

States toward Cuba remains will likely depend on the next administration to occupy the White House.

The Trump policy interlude may be short-lived in any case given the observations of Ambassador Jeffrey DeLaurentis. As he points out in his foreword to this book, the many direct connections and similarities between the people of Cuba and the United States are likely to help shape future relations between the two countries. For generations, individuals on each end of the Florida Strait have linked Cuba and the United States. This includes families separated by the Cuban revolution, U.S. property owners who have a connection to expropriated land, homes, and business interests on the island, and immigrants and refugees fleeing economic downturns and political pressures in Cuba. More recently, following the easing of travel restrictions in the United States, the growing tourism and educational travel industries have expanded, as Betancourt notes in chapter 8, resulting in an influx of visitors and their hard currency. Travel from the United States has especially grown following the relaxation of travel requirements for U.S. tourist during the Obama administration. For businesses interested in this growing market, as Walsh in chapter 7 notes, the opportunities in Cuba can be made easier by following the example of successful companies that have managed to navigate the political, economic, and legal environment on the island. While there has been a small retrenchment with the Trump administration, it is unlikely that tourism from the United States will fall precipitously without further action on the part of the U.S. government. An increase in educational travel, cruise ship visits, and other planned travel appears more likely.

With the opening of travel, in both directions, between Cuba and the United States, we believe we are beginning to see where pressure on both countries will emanate from in the future. The kinds of outcomes result from the toppling of barriers that have kept people apart are profound. Change is possible, and we believe likely, as the political, economic, and legal policies identified in this book are likely to continue to develop in response to increased interaction between the two countries. From a political perspective, Obama's successful efforts at opening up additional avenues of interaction between the citizens of Cuba and the United States are expected to manifest themselves in a desire for more cooperation at the governmental level in the long term. However, as discussed in chapter 3, the future of Cuba's political leadership is unlikely to make a quick move toward a liberal democracy. This is unlikely to deter the pressure exerted on political leaders in the United States by businesses, agriculture, and other exporters, and citizens, to engage the Cuban people and government. As noted previously, politicians in the United States work with nondemocratic regimes around the world. Pressure to engage at the governmental level may also come from a realization on the part of the United States that external actors like China are poised to step in and build relationships, especially economic connections, with the Cuban regime. The multilevel game of diplomacy that the two states have played for decades could converge as economic, legal, and social demands facilitate a change of policy direction.

For *rapprochement* to occur, political pressure from the bottom up will need to build to address two related issues in the United States. The first, repeal of Helms-Burton, will be necessary for the resumption of normal diplomatic relations. The second, settlement of property rights claims by U.S. citizens, will be necessary before economic relations can be restored and foreign investment in Cuba allowed. As more and more U.S. citizens visit Cuba, and Cuban citizens visit the United States, person-to-person diplomacy has the potential to weaken long-entrenched views on the necessity to retain an adversarial relationship and the need for Helms-Burton and rigid enforcement of property claims. Similarly, as a new generation of political and opinion leaders who have visited the island replace those in the United States most opposed to reconciliation with Cuba, an additional thawing of relations is likely. Cuban-American political leaders in Florida, and especially south Florida, will likely be pivotal in this movement. Here, travel by U.S. citizens to Cuba to visit family, as well as generational replacement, are likely to be key contributing factors.

Finally, and perhaps most importantly, changes in Cuban-U.S. relations are likely to be influenced by the economic demands in both countries. For Cuba, U.S. tourists and U.S. businesses represent a potential source of much-needed hard currency. For U.S. businesses and tourism-related enterprises, Cuba represents an opportunity to invest and profit from an increase in travelers to the island, which is coupled by a lack of adequate infrastructure and supply to meet that demand. These business opportunities in Cuba may represent yet another source of pressure on political leaders in the United States as companies seek investment opportunities and a return on their investment in Cuba. The recent effort to strike an agreement between Major League Baseball and the Cuban government on allowing the movement of players to the United States highlights the ongoing efforts to forge additional business ties between the two countries.

Moving forward, we anticipate the window of opportunity for an increase in cooperation between Cuba and the United States will continue to open even as a rhetorical flourish would suggest otherwise. In the United States, the demands of individual citizens, businesses, and farm interests, should they find a common voice, are likely to lead the call to improve relations and take advantage of the opportunities that lie just ninety miles away. In Cuba, pressure on the government to provide for its citizens during a time of economic change and increased interaction with citizens from the United States may provide the impetus needed for leaders to alter their approach to their neighbors to the north. This will likely mean the relaxation of some economic oversight while retaining close, centralized control of governmental functions.

In the end, the key ingredient is the importance of political will to envision and act on the potential opportunities presented to both countries while paying keen attention to the potential roadblocks that have long challenged the bilateral relationship between the United States and Cuba. For the moment, both governments can benefit from the presence of a template to structure a new set of outcomes and possibilities. While the two governments cautiously watch each other for potential signals, whether costly or cheap, continued movement across the two states, by citizens, educators, members of the business community, and the like continue unabated. The question is not really whether the two states will turn the page on the Cold War era; rather, the question is: When will pivotal actors in both states catch up to the other players that have made their peace with the past to forge ahead to the future?

Afterword
Influencing Havana: Is It Possible?

Gary H. Maybarduk

The chapters in this volume present a comprehensive understanding of U.S.-Cuban relations and their influencing factors. Fierce and uncompromising debate has long been a characteristic of U.S.-Cuban policy. By now, however, it should be clear the inability to influence significant reform by either of the polar opposites of the debate—those who support isolation and sanctions on Cuba and the Obama concept of an opening without concessions from Cuba—should cause all parties to step back from strong advocacy to a period of greater analysis and reflection. That reflection should start with causes of Cuban resistance: the barriers to change.

The most commonly mentioned barrier to change in Cuba is simply that those in power do not wish to relinquish it. The goal of the regime is to keep its movement and party alive and in power. Members of the regime believe, probably correctly, that keeping power requires the continued economic dominance of the state, and the prevention of concentration of power by others, including in the economy. Any policy of reform that would challenge those requirements is unlikely.

Support for the status quo also comes from the army, the Party, and the lower level officials of both. All stand to lose status, power, and even their jobs if the Party loses power or a free market economy should rise. There is considerable commentary that bureaucratic opposition has been a major problem in implementing even the minor reforms promised by the Sixth Party Congress of 2011 (Castro 2016).

All the above-mentioned parties share with the public another fear: How will they fare in a competitive economy? Under the current system, they have reasonable job security, do not have to work hard or perform at elevated levels of competence, and enjoy a modicum of a social safety net. For three generations citizens have been taught that the safety net would not exist in a capitalist system. The failures of the Cuban economic system, the

The Cuba-U.S. Bilateral Relationship. Michael J. Kelly, Erika Moreno, and Richard C. Witmer, II.

exposure of Cubans to their diaspora, and general globalization of information have given many Cubans a different view of their system compared to the possible alternatives. Nevertheless, in conversations, many middle-aged and older Cubans will often raise fears of their ability to adapt.

Winding its way through all the concerns of the various parties is the thorny vine of ideology. Presumably a critical concern to some and of much less concern to others, ideology provides legitimacy to the existing order, and it provides structure that constrains debate on reform. Larry Catá Backer, probably the foremost expert on Cuban ideology, very effectively describes the ideological problem in his chapter and elsewhere by creatively comparing the ideologies of the Cuban and Chinese Communist parties. Catá Backer argues that Cuban Marxism is wedded to the early years of the revolution and the abolishment of private enterprise and the establishment of state corporations. Now *perfeccionmiento* of state enterprises is the goal of the party and state. In contrast Asian Marxism has been willing to step back to create a society "so rich it can produce a communist social and economic order." (Backer 2016).

> This is reflected in their respective approaches to wealth differentiation. For Asian Markets Marxism, the rise of income and wealth differentiation must be tolerated as the nation develops its productive forces. ¶85 For Cuban Central Planning Marxism the state must use law to avoid the development of wealth differences. The determination that private enterprises may be limited to the extent they amass too much wealth is a central element of this approach (Backer 2016). ¶86

If Catá Backer is correct and if these ideological views extend to the upcoming generation of party leaders, then those views will be a barrier that might survive another decade or two.

However, Catá Backer's view of the importance of ideology is not universally shared. Arturo López-Levy has argued that the more significant difference between China and Cuba has been the power of the nomenklatura and lower level bureaucrats in the party, in the government, and in the state enterprises, all of whom benefit or believe they benefit from the current system. He argues that Deng Xiaoping's reforms in the late 1970s came after Chinese bureaucracy had been decimated or at least cowed by Mao's Cultural Revolution. Cuban bureaucracy has encountered no such disruption or purge.[1] In this context, Raul's efforts to "democratize the Party" ironically may have made change more difficult, since it would make change subject to the consent of those most likely to oppose it.

Finally, even if a critical mass of actors at all levels are ready to make major reforms the question becomes how to proceed. Cuban authorities have recognized that economic efficiency requires the elimination of the dual currency system (essentially a system of multiple exchange rates), and a policy of market prices. Yet to achieve those goals they would have to allow the bankruptcy of many state organizations, and the loss of employment and opportunities for corruption for the lucky and politically reliable people who run them.[2] Other needed policy changes such as entrepreneurship in the public and private sector, and the accumulation of wealth for investment are either not understood or viewed as a challenge to the system.

Prospects for the Future

Cuba is in a Thucydidean stasis, in back-and-forth movements between the roughly equal forces of reform and the status quo. There is a lot of observable movement, but very little ever changes, and when change does occur, it comes slowly. Given the internal tension around the equilibrium, outside influences should be able to shift the balance, but the Cuban system has antibodies that resist such influences, especially those specifically directed to induce change. Then, of course, the outside influences often push in opposite directions. Exogenous economic events have disrupted the stasis, but once they pass, the pendulum swings back. The question for American policy makers is therefore: What can they do to encourage political and economic reform in Cuba?

The answer seems to be, not much! There should be little shock at this conclusion. Although not often expressed in writing, the author senses many if not most observers of Cuba policy came to this conclusion some time ago.[3] At least all sides of the American debate should be willing to question their own assumptions and logic. It is time to rethink our expectations and strategies.

I begin by summarizing, with appropriate modifications, the two polar strategies that have dominated the American debate, and then discuss a blend of the two strategies that might be more likely to bring about positive results.

The Passive Approach

The first, which most closely reflects Obama's policy, is to accept that change is likely to come slowly in Cuba, unaffected by U.S. policy. Therefore, our goal should be to help the Cuban people economically through the lifting of the embargo and the encouragement of American investment in the island. The expectation would be that in the more distant future, after the departure of the current leadership, a new generation of Cuban leaders, less threatened by American policy, would come to see the advantages of economic and political reform.

The passive approach suffers from at least two objections. It does not comfortably fit with the traditionally strong U.S. emphasis on the need for democracy and human rights in the Americas and the theory behind it appears counterfactual at least so far. President Obama's opening to Cuba allowed for several useful government-to-government agreements, but there has been no improvement in human rights, and the new constitution further curtails freedom of expression. Far from expanding economic freedom in Cuba, the regime has limited it still further. Since at least the 1980s, the history of the Cuban government has been to curtail private economic activity when times are good and to loosen controls when times are tough. Taking pressure off the regime is just as likely to work against economic reform and do little to advance political freedoms.

The Activist Approach

The activist approach, which would most closely resemble the pre–Obama era, would keep active and public pressure on the Cuban government to update its economy, with greater free markets, and to provide greater political freedom. Its measures could include preserving the embargo, preventing American investment, discouraging Americans traveling to Cuba, and limiting remittances. Such a policy would be less concerned with current Cuban standards of living, but instead focused on creating a much higher standard of living in the future. Its advantage is that even if it fails, it would allow the United States to place emphasis on the importance of democracy.

The active approach, of course, was tried for fifty years without success. It can be argued, however, that its failure was the result of the compensating policies of, first, the Soviet Union and later Venezuela to provide massive assistance to the regime. Success would depend on the continuing loss of Venezuelan assistance and the absence of a new patron. Even then, Cuba is better prepared for that possibility than when it lost Soviet assistance in the early 1990s. There are other alternative scenarios for this policy, including President Trump's, but it is hard to give high probabilities of success to any of them.

There are numerous gradations of policy action between the two polar approaches. The author's own preference would be a variation of the constructive engagement policy the United States adopted toward Eastern Europe during the cold war, responding positively only when Cuba moves toward economic and political reform. It would accept that Cuba's internal policies are locked tight by intersecting forces that act together to resist change and are cemented by hostility to outside influences. So instead of confronting Cuba and challenging its sovereignty directly, this indirect approach would instead put the burden of ethical conduct on American firms. In a variation of the Sullivan principles used in South Africa, U.S. corporations wishing to invest or trade with Cuba would have to abide by U.S. labor laws, allow employee organizations to represent their employees, and as much as possible use inputs and services from the Cuban private sector.[4]

Will Anything Work?

It is not clear that anything will work, even this author's constructive engagement proposal. In its Thucydidean stasis, Cuba barely can respond to offers of foreign investment from other countries, although it has a clearly stated policy of wanting that investment. Cuba still has not resolved the issues brought forth in the Sixth Party Conference of 2011. It is not even clear that a Cuba with an updated, mostly market economy would accept political reform. Ultimately, after years of arguing that an economic reform would lead to political reform, the author has concluded that a political revolution, hopefully peaceful, must come before economic reform can take place. The best we can do is to offer the Cuban authorities a choice such as constructive engagement and then sit back, until the Cuban government or the Cuban people decide to make a change.

Notes

1. Conversation with author in the spring of 2017.
2. The closing of state enterprises would also be a challenge to ideology, since it violates the principle that the state must guide the pillars of the economy. This is where the desires to maintain power, preserve ideology, and protect bureaucratic privilege all interlock.
3. The author does not include in my observation those who have long argued that we should let the Cuban people decide on their own system of government and economy. It is one thing to argue that we must recognize our influence is limited and quite another to assume that the government of a one-party state, with serious limitations on free speech and no political freedom, represents the will of its people.
4. For a greater elaboration of this proposal, *see* Maybarduk, 2011, pp. 361–367.

References

Abbott, K. W. and D. Snidal. "Hard and Soft Law in International Governance." *International Organization* 54, no. 3 (2000): 421–456.

Abrams, E. "Pressure Points: Digs in Deeper on Cuba." Council on Foreign Relations, 2015. http//blogs.cfr.org/abrams/2015/12/14/Obama-digs-in-deeper-on-cuba.

AFP. "Peluquero Incursiona En Responsibilidad Social Empresarial En Cuba." *Revista Lideres*, June 16, 2015.

AIN. "Nuevos Acuerdos De Cooperación Biotecnológica Entre Cuba y China." *Granma*. Accessed December 20, 2015. http://www.granma.cu/cuba/2015-06-30/nuevos-acuerdos-de-cooperacion-biotecnologica-entre-cuba-y-china.

Airbnb. "About." 2015. https://www.airbnb.com/.

Alcalá, Victoria. "Arte Corte Papito's." LaHabana.com 2010.

Allio, Lorene. "Post Communist Privatization as a Test of Theories of Institutional Change." In *The Political Economy of Property Rights: Institutional Change and Credibility in Centrally Planned Economies*, edited by David Weimer. Cambridge, UK: Cambridge University Press, 1996.

Almond, Gabriel. "Communism and Political Culture Theory." *Comparative Politics* 15, no. 2 (1983).

Almond, Gabriel and Sidney Verba. *The Civic Culture: Political Attitudes and Democracy in Five Nations*. Princeton, NJ: Princeton University Press, 1963.

Alonso, J. F. "Marabú, Charcoal, Exports and Dollars." Miami, FL, Association for the Study of the Cuban Economy (ASCE), 2017.

Altinay, L., P. Chatoth, R. Harrington, and M. Ottenbacher. "Strategic Management Research in Hospitality and Tourism: Past, Present and Future." *International Journal of Contemporary Hospitality Management* 26, no. 5 (2014): 778–808.

Álvarez, Carlos Manuel. "Propiedad De Todos, Socialismo De Nadie." *El Estornudo*, February 20, 2018.

Álvarez, María Elena. "¿Desaparecen Las BET, Las BUTS y Las FAPI?" *Juventud Rebelde*, July 23, 2011.

American Law Institute and National Conference of Commissioners on Uniform State Laws. "*Uniform Commercial Code* (Philadelphia: ALI)." 2015. https://www.law.cornell.edu/ucc.

American Society of International Law. "Reform of U.S. Sanctions Relating to Agriculture and Medicine." *The American Journal of International Law* 95, no. 2 (2001): 413–414.

Appel, Hillary. "Justice and the Reformulation of Property Rights in the Czech Republic." *East European Politics and Societies* 9, no. 1 (1995): 22–40.

Armony, Ariel C. "A View from Afar: How Colombia Sees China." *The China Quarterly* 209 (2012): 178–197.

The Cuba-U.S. Bilateral Relationship. Michael J. Kelly, Erika Moreno, and Richard C. Witmer, II.

ASCE. "Panel Discussion, 'Experiencas De Cuentapropistas,' with Ted A. Henken, Niuris Higueras, Camilo Condis, Roberto Díaz Vázquez, and María Werlau." Miami, FL, Association for the Study of the Cuban Economy, July 26–28, 2018.

Associated Press. "Low-profile U.S. Diplomat Helped Negotiate with Cuba." *Washington Post*, December 30, 2014.

Associated Press. "Pope Francis Wrote a Book About Cuba 1998." *US News and World Report*, December 19, 2014.

Auge. *Resumen Ejecutivo: Nuevas Regulaciones Sobre El Trabajo Por Cuentapropia*. Vol. July 14. Havana, Cuba: 2018.

Azicri, Max. *Cuba Today and Tomorrow: Reinventing Socialism*. Gainesville, FL: University of Florida Press, 2001.

Azieri, M. "An Introduction to Cuban Socialist Law." *Review of Socialist Law* 6 (1980): 153–163.

Backer, L. C. *"Let's Make a Deal" as Economic Policy*. Jurist Forum. 2016c.

Backer, L. C. "Are Supply Chains Transnational Legal Orders? What We Can Learn from the Rana Plaza Factory Building Collapse." *Journal of International, Transnational, and Comparative Law* 1, no. 1 (2016b): 11–65.

Backer, L. C. "Central Planning Versus Markets Marxism: Their Differences and Consequences for the International Ordering of State, Law, Politics, and Economy." *Connecticut Journal of International Law* 32, no. 1 (2016a): 1–47.

Backer, L. C. "The Cooperative as a Proletarian Corporation: The Global Dimensions of Property Rights and the Organization of Economic Activity in Cuba." *Northwestern Journal of International Law and Business* 33, no. 3 (2013): 527–618.

Backer, L. C. *Cuba Sonic Weapons Affair*. Law at the End of the Day. 2018.

Backer, L. C. "The Cuban Communist Party at the Cusp of Change." In *Reforming Communism: Cuba in a Comparative Perspective*, edited by Scott Morgenstern and Jorge Pérez López. Pittsburgh, PA: University of Pittsburgh Press, 2018a.

Backer, L. C. "Cuban Corporate Governance at the Crossroads: Cuban Marxism, Private Economic Collectives, and Free Market Globalism." *Transnational Law & Contemporary Problems* 14, no. 2 (2004): 337.

Backer, L. C. "Embracing a 21st Century Planning Marxism Model: The Cuban Communist Party Confronts Crisis, Challenge and Change in Its 7th Congress." Miami, FL, Association for the Study of the Cuban Economy (ASCE), July 2016, 2016.

Backer, L. C. *The EU to the Rescue of the Cuban Economy? The Political Dialogue and Cooperation Agreement (PDCA)*. Law at the End of the Day (January 3, 2018). 2018b.

Backer, L. C. "Global Corporate Social Responsibility (GCSR) Standards with Cuban Characteristics: What Normalization Means for Transnational Enterprise Activity in Cuba." Miami, FL, Association for the Study of the Cuban Economy (ASCE), July 2015.

Backer, L. C. "Unpacking Accountability in Business and Human Rights: The Multinational Enterprise, the State, and the International Community." In *Accountability and International Business Organizations: Providing Justice for Corporate Violations of Human Rights, Labor, and Environmental Standards*, edited by Liesbeth Enneking et al. New York, NY: Routledge Press, 2019.

Backer, L. C. and A. Molina. "Cuba and the Construction of Alternative Global Trade Systems: ALBA and Free Trade in the Americas." *University of Pennsylvania Journal of International Law* 31, no. 3 (2009): 679.

Bailey, Michael A., Anton Strezhnev, and Erik Voeten. "Estimating Dynamic State Preferences from United Nations Voting Data." *Journal of Conflict Resolution* 61, no. 2 (2017): 430–456.

Baker, Peter. "U.S. to Restore Full Relations With Cuba, Erasing a Last Trace of Cold War Hostility." *New York Times*, December 17, 2014.

Ban, C. "Is There More Room to Negotiate with the IMF on Fiscal Policy?" Boston, MA, CEGI Working Paper, November 9, 2014.

Barnett, M. and M. Finnemore. *Rules for the World: International Organizations in Global Politics*. Ithaca, NY: Cornell University Press, 2004.

Barreiro Pousa, Luis Alberto. Personal Communication 2018.

BBC News. "Obama and Castro in Historic US-Cuba Meeting." 2015. http://www.bbc.com/news/world-latin-america-32263880.

Bell, Daniel A. *The China Model, Political Meritoracy and the Limites of Democracy*. Princeton, NJ: Princeton University Press, 2015.

Benjamin Alvarado, Jonathan. "The Prospects for U.S.-Cuba Cooperation on Energy Policy." In *Cuba's Energy Future: Strategic Approaches to Cooperation*, edited by Jonathan Benjamin Alvarado. Washington D.C.: Brookings Institution, 2010.

Beoto, Anabel. "Proyecto Comunitario Artecorte." *Amano Oficio y Deseño*, March 30, 2016.

Berend, I. T. "The Economic Response to Globalization, Recovery, and Growth, the Integration of Eastern and Western Europe." *Society and Economy* 36, no. 1 (2014): 5–20.

Betancourt, R. R. "Cuba's Reforms: A New Institutional Economics Perspective." In *Perspectives on Cuban Economic Reforms*, edited by J. Perez-Lopez and M. Travieso-Diaz. Tempe, AZ: Arizona State University Press, 1998.

Betancourt, R. R. "Should the US Lift the Cuban Embargo? Yes; It Already Has; and It Depends!" Miami, FL, Association for the Study of the Cuban Economy (ASCE), 2013.

Betancourt, R. R. "USA-Cuba Migration Policy: A Political Economy View." Miami, FL, Association for the Study of the Cuban Economy (ASCE), 2016.

Betancourt, Rafael. *Construyendo Socialismo Desde Abajo: La Contribución De La Economía Popular y Solidaria*. Havana, Cuba: Editorial Caminos, 2017.

Betancourt, Rafael. Personal Communication 2018.

Betancourt, Rafael. "La Responsabilidad Social Empresarial En Cuba." *Estudios Del Desarrollo Social: Cuba y América Latina* 4, no. 2 (2016): 34–43.

Betancourt, Rafael. *Social and Solidary Economy and the Transformation of the Cuban Economic Model*. Havana, Cuba: Catalejo, Revista Temas Blog, 2014.

Betancourt, Rafael. "Working Group on Social and Solidarity Economy for Local Development." Universidad Central "Marta Abreu" de Las Villas, Cuba.

Betancourt, Rafael and Julia Sagebien. "Para Un Crecimiento Inclusivo: Empresas no Estatales Responsables En Cuba." *Temas* 75 (2013): 58–65.

Beyond Conflict. "The Emerging Fields of Brain and Behavioral Science, Combined with 25 Years of Real-World Experience, Offer a Powerful New Approach to Conflict Resolution, Reconciliation and Positice Social Change in the U.S. and Abroad." 2015. http://www.beyondconflictint.org/.

Biglaiser, G. and Karl DeRouen. "Economic Reforms and Inflows of Foreign Direct Investment in Latin America." *Latin American Research Review* 41, no. 3 (2006): 51–75.

Birch, B. P. "Without Pause but without Haste: Economic and Political Change in Cuba (Masters Dissertation)." M.A., 2015.

Birchtree Global. *The Global 20th Century*. Bedford Hills, NY: Birchtree Global Publications, 2014.

Blázquez-Lidoy, Jorge, Javier Rodríguez, and Javier Santiso. *Angel or Devil? China's Trade Impact on Latin American Merging Markets*: OECD Development Centre Working Paper No. 252, 2006.

Blonigen, B. A. and J. Piger. "Determinants of Foreign Direct Investment." *The Canadian Journal of Economics* 47, no. 3 (2011).

Bloomberg, M. "Climate Progress, with or without Trump." *New York Times*, March 31, 2017.

Bloomberg, M. and C. Pope. *Climate of Hope: How Cities, Businesses, and Citizens can Save the Planet*. New York, NY: St. Martin's Press, 2017.

"Blue Bank International & Trust (Barbados) Ltd. v. the Bolivarian Republic of Venezuela (ICSID). Case no. AARB 12/20." https://www.italaw.com/sites/default/files/case-documents/italaw8769.pdf.

Boeglin, N. "ICSID and Latin America: Criticisms, Withdrawals and Regional Alternatives." Bilaterals.org. https://www.bilaterals.org/?icsid-and-latin-america-criticisms&lang=fr.

Booth, W. and J. McAuley. "Europeans Haven't Given Up Hope that Britain Will Change Its Mind on Brexit." *The Washington Post*, June 12, 2018.

Borchers, Patrick J., Michael Kelly, Erika Moreno, Arthur Pearlstein, Richard C. Witmer, and James Wunsch. *Report on the Resolution of Outstanding Property Claims between Cuba and the United States*. Omaha, NE: Creighton University Press, 2007.

Bouchenaki, I. S. and O. Kosova. "EU-Cuba Relations Enter New Era." Euroactiv, 2017. https://www.euractiv.com/section/global-europe/news/eu-cuba-relations-enter-new-era/.

Brand, Alexander, Susan McEwen-Fial, and Wolfgang Muno. "An 'Authoritarian Nexus'? China's Alleged Special Relationship with Autocratic States in Latin America." *European Review of Latin American and Caribbean Studies* 99 (2015): 7–28.

Brewer, T. L. "Government Policies, Market Imperfections, and FDI." *Journal of International Business Studies* 24, no. 1 (1993): 101.

Brida, J., O. Driha, A. Rodriguez, and R. Scuderi. "Dynamics of Internationalisation of the Hotel Industry: The Case of Spain." *International Journal of Contemporary Hospitality Management* 27, no. 5 (2015): 1024–1047.

Brouthers, K. D., L. E. Brouthers, and S. Werner. "Real Options, International Entry Mode Choice and Performance." *Journal of Management Studies* 45, no. 5 (2008): 936–960.

Bu Marcheco, J. V. B. "100 Questions and Answers about the Mariel Special Development Zone in English." *Cuba Business News*, October 16, 2013.

Buncombe, Andrew. "Where Is Rolando Sarraff Trujillo?" *Independent*, 2015.

Burbach, R. "A Cuban Spring?" *NACLA Report on the Americas* 46, no. 1 (2013: 10–12.

Burkett, M. "Rehabilitation: A Proposal for a Climate Compensation Mechanism for Small Island States." *Santa Clara Journal of International Law* 8 (2015).

Burns, W. "Loss and Damage and the 21st Conference of the Parties to the United Nations Framework Convention on Climate Change." *Journal of International and Comparative Law* 22 (2016).

Cameron, M. "Cuban Communist Party to Launch Post-Congress Debate Amid Divergent Visions." *Green Left*, May 8, 2016.

Cancio Isla, W. "EEUU: En Suspenso Entrega De 20,000 Visas Anuales Para Cubanos." *Marti Noticias*, July 3, 2018.

Caporaso, James and David Levine. *Theories of Political Economy*. New York, NY: Cambridge University Press, 1992.

Caribbean Tourism Report—Q1 2018. London, UK: Business Monitor International, 2018.

Caripis, L. "The International Regime for the Adaption to Climate Change Internal Working Paper." Working Paper, Centre for Climate Resilience Research, Santiago, Chile (2014).

Carmody, Pádraig R. and Francis Y. Owusu. "Competing Hegemons? Chinese versus American Geo-Economic Strategies in Africa." *Political Geography* 26 (2007): 504–524.

Carty, V. "Capitalist Measures within a Socialist Model: A Commodity Chains Analysis of the Emerging Cuban Tourism Industry." *Canadian Journal of Latin American & Caribbean Studies* 34, no. 67 (2009): 163–195.

Castro, R. "El Desarrollo De La Economía Nacional, Junto a La Lucha Por La Paz y La Firmeza Ideológica, Constituyen Las Principales Misiones Del Partido; Informe Central Al 7mo. Congreso Del Partido Comunista De Cuba, Presentado Por El Primer Secretario Del Comité Central, General De Ejército Raúl Castro Ruz." *Granma*, April 16, 2016.

Castro, R. "The Development of the National Economy, Along with the Struggle for Peace, and Our Ideological Resolve, Constitute the Party's Principal Missions, 7th PCC Congress Central Report" *Cubadebate*, April 4, 2016.

Castro, R. "Intervención Del General De Ejército Raúl Castro Ruz, Primer Secretario Del Comité Central Del Partido Comunista De Cuba y Presidente De Los Consejos De Estado y De Ministros, En La Primera Sesión Ordinaria De La VIII Legislatura De La Asamblea Nacional Del Poder Popular, En El Palacio De Convenciones, El 7 De Julio De 2013." *Cubadebate*, July 7, 2013.

Castro, Raul. "Discurso Del General De Ejército Raúl Castro Ruz." *Juventud Rebelde*, December 18, 2010a.

Castro, Raul. "Speech to Cuba's National Assembly." *Gobierno De Cuba*, July 11, 2008.

Castro, Raul. "Speech to Cuba's National Assembly on August 1." *Gobierno De Cuba*, August 1, 2010b.

Castro, Raul. "Statement by the Cuban President." *Ministry of Foreign Relations press release*. December 17, 2014.

Castro, Raul. "Statement by the Cuban President." *Cuba Debate*, 2015. http://en.cubadebate.cu/news/2014/12/17/statement-by-cuban-president/.

Castro Morales, Yudy. "Qué Cambia Con Las Nuevas Normas?" *Granma*, 2018.

Caulfield, John. "Cuba's Next President Faces Choice between Economy and Communism." Accessed April 15, 2018. http://thehill.com/opinion/international/381294-cubas-next-president-faces-choice-between-economy-and-communism.

CBS News Miami. "Raul Castro Nominated for Cuba's Parliament." Accessed February 15, 2018. http://miami.cbslocal.com/2018/01/23/raul-castro-cuba-parliament/.

Centeno, R. I. "The Cuban Regime after a Decade of Raúl Castro in Power." *Mexican Law Review* 9, no. 2 (2017): 99–126.

Centro para la Promoción del Comercio Exterior y la Inversión Extranjera de Cuba (CEPEC). "How to Do Business with Cuba." 2015.

Cheibub, Jose Antonio. "Democracy and Property Rights: Is There a Link?" New York, NY, American Political Science Association, September 1–4, 1994, 1994.

Chenail, R. J. "Interviewing the Investigator: Strategies for Addressing Instrumentation and Researcher Bias Concerns in Qualitative Research." *The Qualitative Report* 16, no. 1 (2011): 255–262.

China View. "Sino-Cuban Relations." Accessed February 7, 2016. http://news.xinhuanet.com/english/2004-11/08/content_2191273.htm.

Chinadaily.com.cn. "U.S.-Cuba Relations Still Face Many Challenges." December 15, 2015. http://www.chinadaily.com.cn/opinion/2015-08/15/content_21606827.htm.

Chinafocus.com. "China Welcomes Move to Restore U.S.-Cuba Diplomatic Relations." Accessed February 10, 2016. http://www.chinausfocus.com/foreign-policy/china-welcomes-move-to-restore-u-s-cuba-diplomatic-relations/.

Chong, Alberto and Cesar Calderon. "Causality and Feedback between Institutional Measures and Economic Growth." *Economics and Politics* 12, no. 1 (2000): 69–81.

Chow, D. C. K. "Why China Established the Asia Infrastructure Investment Bank." *Vanderbilt Journal of Transnational Law* 49 (2016): 1255–1298.

CiberCuba. "Habaguanex S.A. Pasa De Eusebio Leal a Manos De Las FAR." *Cibercuba*, 2016.

Colby-Oizumi, H. "Overview of Cuban Imports of Goods and Services and Effects of U.S. Restrictions." Miami, FL, Association for the Study of the Cuban Economy (ASCE), 2016.

Comisión Económica Para América Latina y el Caribe. *La Economía Cubana: Reformas Estructurales y Desempeño En Los Noventa.* México, D.F.: Fondo de la Cultura Económica, 2000.

Comisso, Ellen. "Property Rights, Liberalism, and the Transition from 'Actually Existing" Socialism.' *East European Politics and Societies* 5, no. 1 (1991): 162–188.

Community of Latin American and Caribbean States (CELAC). "Caracas Declaration." CELAC. December 3, 2011. http://www.pnuma.org/forodeministros/19-reunion%20intersesional/documentos/CARACAS%20DECLARATION.pdf.

Community of Latin American and Caribbean States (CELAC). "Welcome." CELAC. 2017. http://celacinternational.org/.

Condis, Camilo. Personal Communication 2018.

Consejo de Ministros. "Fundamentación De Los Proyectos De Normas Jurídicas Para El Perfeccionamiento Del Trabajo Por Cuenta Propia." Havana, Cuba.

Corrales, Javier. "The Gatekeeper State: Limited Economic Reforms and Regime Survival in Cuba, 1989–2002." *Latin American Research Review* 39, no. 2 (2004): 35–65.

Corrales, Javier. "The Gatekeeper State: Limited Economic Reforms and Regime Survival in Cuba, 1989–2002." *Latin American Research Review* 39, no. 2 (2004): 35–65.

Cortés, Raúl. "La Peluquería De 'Papito', Escuela, Museo y Espejo De La Lenta Reforma Cubana." *El Nuevo Herald*, September 15, 2012.

Costello, T. G. and A. O. Costello. "Globalization: Payoffs, Multinational Corporations and Public Policy Makers—A New Paradigm." *The Business Review* 20, no. 1 (2012): 26–32.

Council of the European Union. *The EU List of Non-Cooperative Jurisdictions for Tax Purposes; Council Conclusions (Adopted on 5/12/2017). 15429/17; FISC 345, ECOFIN 1088.* Brussells: European Union, 2017.

Council of the European Union. *Political Dialogue and Cooperation Agreement between the European Union and its Member States, of the One Part, and the Republic of Cuba, of the Other Part (PDCA). COLAC 76; CFSP/PESC 753.* Brussels: European Union, 2016.

Council on Hemispheric Affairs. "The European Union and Cuba: The Common Position." COHA. http://www.coha.org/the-european-union-and-cuba-the-common-position/.

Creswell, J. W. *Qualitative Inquiry and Research Design: Choosing among Five Traditions.* Thousand Oaks, CA: Sage Press, 1998.

Crowley, Michael. "We Have to Talk." Politico 2015.
Cruz, Consuelo and Ana Seleny. "Reform and Counterreform: The Path to the Market in Hungary and Cuba." *Comparative Politics* 34, no. 2 (2002): 47–65.
"Cuba Arbitrary Arrests Soared in 2016, Dissidents Say." *Deutsche Welle*, January 6, 2017.
Cuba Licensing Policy Revision, 81 F.R. 4580 (2016).
Cuba Posible. "Artecorte: Pensando Cuba." *Cuba Posible*, May 10, 2016.
Cuba Posible and Ovidio D'Angelo. "Alianzas Intersectoriales Solidarias Públicas-no Estatales: ¿una Vía Para El Desarrollo?" *Cuba Posible*, November 4, 2016.
Cuba Research Institute. *2016 FIU Cuba Poll: How Cuban Americans in Miami View U.S. Policies Toward Cuba*. Miami, FL: Florida International University, 2016.
Cuba/Gallup. Gallup Historical Trends. Accessed February 5, 2018.
"Cuba's Report on Resolution 72/4 of the United Nations General Assembly Entitled 'Necessity of Ending the Economic, Commercial and Financial Blockade Imposed by the United States of America Against Cuba.'" December 7, 2017. http://www.cubavsbloqueo.cu/en.
Cuban Communist Party. *Conceptualización Del Modelo Económico y Social Cubano De Desarrollo Socialista*. Havana, Cuba: Cuban Communist Party, 2016.
Cyert, R. and J. March. *The Behavioral Theory of the Firm*. Englewood Cliffs, NJ: Prentice-Hall Inc., 1963.
Dahl, Robert. *Polyarchy*. New Haven, CT: Yale University Press, 1971.
Daley, D. *Ratf**ked: The True Story Behind the Secret Plan to Steal America's Democracy*. New York, NY: W.W. Norton, 2016.
D'Angelo, Ovidio. "Apuntes Hacia Una Sociedad De Economía Social y Gestión Popular." *Inter Press Service*, April 16, 2016b.
D'Angelo, Ovidio. "Es La Autogestión Social Una Opción De Desarrollo Para Cuba?" *Observatorio Crítico*, January 1, 2012.
D'Angelo, Ovidio. "Vuelta Al Capitalismo o Más allá Del Socialismo Estatal?: Riesgos y Desafíos." *Cuba Posible*, May 18, 2016a.
Davenport, C. "*Top Trump Advisers Are Split on Paris Agreement on Climate Change*." *New York Times*, March 2, 2017.
Davenport, C. and A. J. Rubin. "Trump Signs Executive Order Unwinding Obama Climate Policies." *New York Times*, March 27, 2017.
De la Nuez, René. "La Clandestinidad" Cartoon Shared by Oniel Díaz Castellanos. Facebook, 2018.
Deering, C. and F. Maltzman. "The Politics of Executive Orders: Legislative Constraints on Presidential Power." *Political Research Quarterly* 52, no. 4 (1999): 767–783.
DeGeorge, G., D. Tweed, and C. Donville. "Why 'Complicated' Cuba May Not See a 'Gold Rush' from the Opening of U.S. Relations." *Bloomberg News*, December 26, 2014.
Delgado Legon, E. "Cuba's Ongoing 7th Party Congress." *Havana Times*, April 27, 2016.
Delgado, Y. "Cuban Coal Shipment Marks First Export to U.S. in 60 Years." *Pan Am Post*, January 6, 2017.
DeYoung, Karen. "White House Implements New Cuba Policy Restricting Travel and Trade." *Washington Post*, November 8, 2017.
Diamond, Larry. "The Global State of Democracy." *Current History* 99, no. 2 (2000): 641–702.

Diaz Castellanos, Oniel. *Nuevas Reglas Del Sector Privado: El no Sobre El sí*. Havana, Cuba: ONCuba, 2018b.

Diaz Castellanos, Oniel. "Se Entregó." Facebook, 2018.

Díaz Castellanos, Oniel. "Hubo Respuesta (Facebook Post)." Facebook, 2018.

Domínguez, Jorge I. *China's Relations with Latin America: Shared Gains, Asymmetric Hopes*: Inter-American Dialogue Working Paper, 2006.

Doornbos, M. "State Formation Processes under External Supervision: Reflections on 'Good Governance.'" In *Aid and Political Conditionality*, edited by Olav Stokke. London, UK: Frank Cass, 1995.

Dougherty, T. "The Cuba Factor in the Caribbean Equation." *Travel Weekly*, February 16, 2015.

Dow, K. and F. Berkhout. "Climate Change, Limits to Adaptation and the 'Loss and Damage' Debate." *E-International Relations*, January 31, 2014.

Duflo, E. "The Economist as Plumber. Richard T. Ely Lecture." *American Economic Review* 107, no. May (2017).

Eckstein, Susan. *Back from the Future: Cuba Under Castro*. London, UK: Routledge Press, 1980.

Eckstein, Susan. "Capitalist Constraints on Cuban Socialist Development." *Comparative Politics* 12, no. 3 (1980): 253–274.

The Economist. "Come and See My Villa; Foreign Investment in Cuba." *The Economist*, May 19, 2014.

The Economist. "Slim Pickings: Clueless on Cuba's New Economy." *The Economist*, September 30, 2017.

Economist Intelligence Unit. "Cuba." *The Economist*, 2015. http://country.eiu.com.

Economist Intelligence Unit. "Cuba Fact Sheet." *The Economist*, 2014. http://country.eiu.com.

El Toque. *Hacia Dónde Va El Cuentapropismo?* Vol. February. Havana, Cuba: 2018.

Election 2018. "Who Is Winning the Race for Congress?" FiveThirtyEight.com, 2018. https://projects.fivethirtyeight.com/congress-generic-ballot-polls/?ex_cid=rrpromo.

Ellis, R. Evan. *China on the Ground in Latin America: Challenges for the Chinese and Impacts for the Region*. New York, NY: Palgrave Macmillan, 2014.

Environmental Protection Network. "Analysis of Trump Administration Proposal for FY2018 Budget for the Environmental Protection Agency." National Association of Clean Air Agencies. Accessed March 22, 2017. http://www.4cleanair.org/sites/default/files/Documents/EPA_Budget_Analysis_EPN_3-22-2017.pdf.

Environmental Strategy Project (2011/15). Proyecto Estrategia Ambiental Nacional (2011): 2.1.2.

Escobar, Luz and Mario Pentón. *Los Militares Se Quedan Con Las Empresas Del Historiador*. 14ymedio. 2016.

Escobar, Reinaldo. *No Habrá Transición En Cuba . . . Ni Siquiera Al Comunismo*. 14ymedio. 2018.

Esencia Group. "The Carbonera Club." 2015. http://www.esenciagroup.com.

Estado de Sats. *Video: Castrismo vs. Cuentapropismo: El Patron Común De Las Nuevas Medidas Es Impedir Que Se Forme Una Clase Media En Cuba*. Diario De Cuba. Vol. July 19 2018.

Esty, D. C. "Good Governance at the Supranational Scale: Globalizing Administrative Law." *Yale Law Journal* 115 (2006): 1490–1562.

EULAC Focus. "EULAC Focus Brochure." EULAC 2016. http://eulac-focus.net/assets/dms/brochure_en_4pp.pdf.

European Commission. "Cuba." European Union 2018. https://ec.europa.eu/europeaid/countries/cuba_en.

European Parliament. "Press Release: MEPs Back First Ever EU-Cuba Deal" (2017).

European Union External Action Service. "Press Release: HR/VP Federica Mogherini on Official Visit in Cuba." 2018. https://eeas.europa.eu/headquarters/headQuarters-homepage_en/37943/HR/VP%20Federica%20Mogherini%20on%20official%20visit%20in%20Cuba.

Farley, Robert. "What Was Alan Gross Doing in Cuba?" FactCheck.org. 2015. https://www.factcheck.org/2014/12/what-was-alan-gross-doing-in-cuba/.

Feinberg, Richard. "Cuba's Foreign Investment Invitation: Insight into Internal Struggles." The Brookings Institute. http://www.brookings.edu 2014.

Feinberg, Richard. "Foreign Investment in the New Cuban Economy." *NACLA Report on the Americas* 46, no. 1 (2013): 13–18.

Feinberg, Richard. "The New Cuban Economy: What Roles for Foreign Investment?" The Brookings Institute, 2015. http://www.brookings.edu.

Feinberg, Richard. *Open for Business: Building the New Cuban Economy*. Washington D.C.: Brookings Institution Press, 2016.

Feinberg, Richard E. "Analysis: Cuba and the International Financial Institutions." *Cubatrade* (2017).

Feinberg, Richard E. *Reaching Out: Cuba's New Economy and the International Response*. Washington D.C.: Brookings Institution Press, 2011.

Feinberg, Richard E. *Reconciling U.S. Property Claims in Cuba: Transforming Trauma into Opportunity*. Washington D.C.: Brookings Institution, 2015.

Feinberg, Richard and Claudia Padrón Cueto. *Cuba Moves Backwards: New Regulations Likely to Impede Private Sector Growth*. Order from Chaos, Blog of the Brookings Institution. 2018.

Feinsilver, Julie M. "Cuba as a 'World Medical Power': The Politics of Symbolism." *Latin American Research Review* 24, no. 2 (1989): 1–34.

Felter, Claire, B. Lee, C. McBride, and D. Renwick. "U.S. Cuba Relations (Council on Foreign Relations Backgrounder)." Council on Foreign Relations. Accessed July 26, 2015. http://www.cfr.org/cuba/us-cuba-relations/p11113.

Ferchen, Matt. "China-Latin America Relations: Long-Term Boon or Short-Term Boom?" *The Chinese Journal of International Politics* 4, no. 1 (2011): 55–86.

Ferchen, Matt and Alicia Garcia Herrero. "Export Dependence: If China Stops, Then What?" *China Economic Quarterly* (September 2011): 33–37.

Fernandes, Sujatha. "Hairdressers of the World Unite! (You have Nothing to Lose but Your Locks . . . and a Community to Win)." *The Nation*, December 28, 2017.

Ferreira, Nery. "Is Cuba's Private Sector Heading in Reverse?" *Havana Times*, February 2, 2018.

Ferris, David. "Cuba Wants Clean Energy. Can the U.S. Deliver?" *Energy Wire*, June 25, 2015.

Field, C. B., V. R. Barros, D. J. Dokken, K. J. Mach, M. D. Mastrandrea, T. E. Bilir, M. Chatterjee et al., eds. *IPCC, 2014: Summary for Policymakers*. Climate Change 2014: Contribution of Working Group II to the Fifth Assessment Report of the Intergovernmental Panel on Climate Change 6: IPCC, 2014.

Fletcher, T. "La Revolucion Energetica: A Model for Reducing Cuba's Dependence on Venezuelan Oil." *The International Journal of Cuban Studies* 9, no. 1 (2017): 91–166.

Fligstein, Neil. "Markets as Politics: A Political-Cultural Approach to Market Institutions." *American Sociological Review* 61, no. 4 (1996): 656–673.

Foreign Claims Settlement Commission (FCSC). *Completed Programs Page for Cuba*. Washington D.C.: FCSC, 2018.

Forte, R. and R. Moura. "The Effects of Foreign Direct Investment on the Host Country's Economic Growth: Theory and Empirical Evidence." *Singapore Economic Review* 58, no. 3 (2013): 1.

Fraga, M. *Cuba-US Relations: Current State of Affairs*. LCBacker Blog. 2017.

Frank, M. "Cuba Tightens Regulations on Nascent Private Sector." *Reuters*, December 21, 2017.

Frank, M. "Cuba to Deregulate State Companies in 2013." *Reuters*, July 8, 2013.

Frank, M. and J. P. Rathbone. "Cuba's Communists Dig in as Castro's Reform Drive Hits the Sand." *Financial Times*, March 28, 2017.

Frank, Marc. "Cuba Binds Its Entrepreneurial Spirits with Red Tape." *Financial Times*, July 16, 2018.

Frank, M. "Cuba Tightens Regulations on Nascent Private Sector." *Reuters*, December 21, 2017.

Frank, M. "Cuba to Allow for Small Private Retail Barbers and Hair Salons." *Reuters*, April 13, 2010.

Freedom House. "Democracy Scores." October 2017. http://www.freedomhouse.org/template.cfm?page=1.

Freeman, C. "The Briton Who Languished in a Cuban Jail After Being Accused of Spying." *The Daily Telegraph*, July 6, 2013.

Freidman, Milton. *Capitalism and Freedom*. Chicago, IL: University of Chicago Press, 1962.

Gaceta Oficial. *No. 35 Extraordinaria—Sobre El Ejercicio Del Trabajo Por Cuenta Propia*. Havana, Cuba: Asamblea Nacional de Cuba, 2018.

Gaceta Oficial. *Resolución no. 22/2017. no. 31 Extraordinaria*. Havana, Cuba: Ministry of Labor and Social Security, 2017.

Gaceta Oficial de Cuba. *Acuerdo 6853*. La Habana, Cuba: Gaceta Oficial de Cuba, 2010.

Gaceta Oficial de Cuba. "For Sale in Cuba Extraordinary Official Gazette with New Regulations for Self-Employed." *Cuba Debate*, August 18, 2018.

Gaceta Oficial de Cuba. *No. 18 Extraordinaria*. La Habana, Cuba: Gaceta Oficial de Cuba, 2015.

Gaceta Oficial de Cuba. *Resolucion 136/2009*. Havana, Cuba: Ministerio de Justicia, 2009.

Gallagher, Kevin P., Juan Carlos Moreno-Brid, and Roberto Porzecanski. "The Dynamism of Mexican Exports: Lost in (Chinese) Translation?" *World Development* 36, no. 8 (2008): 1365–1380.

Gámez Torres, N. "Agricultural Exports to Cuba Would Help Compensate Those Whose Properties Were Seized." *The Miami Herald*, May 27, 2017.

Gámez Torres, N. "OAS Secretary General: 'We Cannot Allow the Cuban People to Continue to Be Oppressed." *The Miami Herald*, April 13, 2018.

Gámez Torres, Nora. "Cuba Frena El Sector Privado. ¿Quiénes Seran Los Afectados?" *El Nuevo Herald*, August 1, 2017b.

Gámez Torres, Nora. "Cuba Impone Más Controles e Impuestos Al Sector Privado y Censura a Los Artistas." *El Nuevo Herald*, July 10, 2018.

Gámez Torres, Nora. "El Partido Comunista De Cuba Determina: 'No Puede Haber Ricos'." *El Nuevo Herald*, July 14, 2017a.

Gao, C. "China Says Latin America 'Eager' to Join Belt and Road; China Invites Latin American and Caribbean States to Join the Belt and Road Initiative." *The Diplomat*, January 24, 2018.

García, Alejandra. "El Sindicato, Apoyo Para El Trabajador Cuentapropista." *Granma*, May 23, 2017.

García, Ivan. *Sin Eusebio Leal, Habaguanex Es Controlada Por Militares*. Desde La Habana. August 9 ed. 2016.

Gearan, Anne. "Hillary Clinton Agrees with Obama on Cuban Embargo." *The Washington Post*, December 17, 2014. https://www.washingtonpost.com/news/post-politics/wp/2014/12/17/hillary-clinton-agrees-with-obama-on-lifting-cuba-embargo/.

Giles, Chris. "World Economy Feels the Impact when China Takes a Knock." *The Financial Times*. Accessed January 8, 2017. https://www.ft.com/content/30441208-b548-11e5-b147-e5e5bba42e51.

Gladstone, Rick. "Majority of Americans Favor Ties with Cuba, Poll Finds." *The New York Times*, February 11, 2014. http://www.nytimes.com/2014/02/11/world/americas/majority-of-americans-favor-ties-with-cuba-poll-finds.html.

Glaser, B. and A. Strauss. *the Discovery of Grounded Theory: Strategies for Qualitative Research (2nd ed.)*. Piscataway, NJ: Aldine Transaction, 2007.

Gold, Hadas. "NY Times Editorial Page Hires Ernesto Londono." *Politico*, January 7, 2015. https://www.npr.org/2015/01/07/375628523/did-editorials-influence-obamas-decision-to-normalize-relations-with-cuba.

Goldberg, Jeffrey. "Fidel: 'Cuban Model Doesn't Even Work for Us Anymore'." *The Atlantic*, September 8, 2010.

Goldsmith, Arthur. "Democracy, Property Rights, and Economic Growth." *Journal of Development Studies* 32, no. 2 (1995): 157–174.

Gómez Armas, Sara. "El Parlamento Cubano Aprueba El Encaje De La Empresa Privada En El Socialismo." *El Nuevo Herald*, June 1, 2017.

Gomez Manzano, R. "La Democracia Que Ve Europa En Cuba: El Poder En La Isla Se Ejerce Desde Lo Alto. Y Durante Los Casi Seis Decenios De Régimen Castrista Ha Sido Unipersonal." *Cubanet*, January 24, 2018.

González, Ivet. "Sector Privado Se Pregunta Cuál Es Su Espacio En Cuba." *Inter Presse Service*, November 25, 2016.

González-Corzo, M. "Cuba's Agricultural Transformations: Moving Towards Market Socialism?" In *Handbook of Contemporary Cuba: Economy, Politics, Civil Society, and Globalization*, edited by M. Font and C. Riobó. Boulder, CO: Paradigm Publishers, 2013.

González-Corzo, M. *Update on Cuba's Non-Sugar Agricultural Sector. Cuba in Transition, 11, 123–132*. Washington D.C.: Association for the Study of the Cuban Economy, 2011.

González-Corzo, M. and A. Nova González. "U.S. Agricultural Exports to Cuba: Composition, Trends, and Prospects for the Future." *Choices* 28, no. 4 (2013): 1–6.

González-Corzo, Mario and Orlando Justo. "Cuba's Emerging Self-Employed Entrepreneurs: Recent Developments and Prospects for the Future." *Journal of Developmental Entrepreneurship* 19, no. 3 (2014).

Goodwin, M. J. and O. Heath. "The 2016 Referendum, Brexit and the Left Behind: An Aggregate-level Analysis of the Result." *Political Quarterly* 87, no. 3 (2016): 323–332.

Gordley, J. *Foundations of Private Law: Property, Tort, Contract, Unjust Enrichment*. Oxford, UK: Oxford University Press, 2006.

Górecka, D. and M. Szalucka. "Application of MCDA Methods and Stochastic Dominance Rules in the Entry Mode Selection Process in International Expansion." *Multiple Criteria Decision Making* 9 (2014): 5–13.

Granma. "Actualizar, corregir . . . fortalecer El Trabajo Por Cuenta Propia." *Granma*, July 9, 2018b.

Granma. "Anteproyecto De Constitución: Visión Hacia El Presente y El Futuro De La Patria." *Granma*, July 13, 2018a.

Granma. "Cuba Ratifies the Paris Agreement on Climate Change." *Granma*, December 12, 2016.

Granma. "Resolución Sobre Los Lineamientos De La Política Económica y Social Del Partido y La Revolución." *Granma*, April 19, 2011.

Granma International News. "The Cuban Five Discuss Their Release and Return to Cuba." *Granma*, January 20, 2015. http://en.granma.cu/cuba/2015-01-20/the-cuban-five-discuss-their-release-and-return-to-cuba.

Gross, Terry. *Did Editorials Influence Obama's Decision to Normalize Relations with Cuba?*, 2015. NPR. (Fresh Air).

Guerra, L. "Cuba Under Raúl Castro: Assessing the Reforms." *Cuban Studies* (2015): 219–221.

Guevara, Ernesto "Che". "Socialism and Man in Cuba." In *The Che Reader*, edited by Ernesto "Che" Guevara. Melbourne, Australia: Ocean Press, 2005.

Guidelines. *Cuba: Economic and Social Policy Guidelines for the Party and the Revolution*. Translated for *International Journal of Socialist Renewal*, edited by Marce Cameron. Havana, Cuba: 2010.

Guo, Cunhai. "Touching China's Rock to Cross Cuba's River? (Mo Zhongguo De Shitou Guo Guba De He?)." *Oriental Morning Daily* (July, 10, 2012): 12.

Gurrea Martínez, A. and N. Mesa Tejada. "Una Aproximación Al Régimen Jurídico De Las Empresas Cubanas: Regulación Actual y Perspectivas De Reforma (An Overview of the Law of Business Organizations in Cuba: Challenges and Proposal for a Future Reform)." Working Paper Series 8/2016, IIDF.

Gurrea Martínez, A. and N. Mesa Tejada. *Cuban Business Law: Current Situation and Future Challenges*. Oxford Business Law Blog. 2016.

Hagelberg, G. H. "If It Were Just the 'Marabú': Cuba's Agriculture 2009–2010." In *Cuba in Transition*, edited by ASCE. 20th ed., 32–45. Washington D.C.: Association for the Study of the Cuban Economy, 2010.

Haggard, Stephan. *Pathways from the Periphery: The Politics of Growth in Newly Industrializing Countries*. Ithaca, NY: Cornell University Press, 1990.

Haggard, Stephan and Robert Kaufman. *The Politics of Economic Adjustment*, edited by Stephan Haggard and Robert Kaufman. Princeton, NJ: Princeton University Press, 1992.

Hale, T. *The Paris Agreement Will Survive President Trump*. Oxford, UK: University of Oxford, N.D.

Hare, P. *The Odd Couple: The EU and Cuba 1996–2008*. Washington D.C.: Brookings Institution, 2008.

Harlan, E. "Behavioral Theory of the Firm: Historical Perspectives Influencing Current Applications." *Ethics & Critical Thinking Journal* 2 (2014): 78–96.

Harnisch, Sebastian, Sebastian Bersick, and Jörn-Carsten Gottwald. *China's International Roles: Challenging or Supporting International Order.* New York, NY: Routledge, 2016.

Harrison, G. *The World Bank and Africa: The Construction of Governance States.* New York, NY: Routledge, 2004.

Hawkins, Darren. "Democratization Theory and Nontransitions: Insights from Cuba." *Comparative Politics* 33, no. 4 (2001): 441–461.

Hayek, F. A. *The Road to Serfdom.* Chicago, IL: University of Chicago Press, 1994.

Hearn, Adrian H. "China, Global Governance, and the Future of Cuba." *Journal of Current Chinese Affairs* 41, no. 4 (2012): 155–179.

Hearn, Adrian H. *Cuba and China: Lessons and Opportunities for the United States*: The Cuban Research Institute, Commissioned Report, 2009.

Hearn, Adrian H. "Harnessing the Dragon: Overseas Chinese Entrepreneurs in Mexico and Cuba." *The China Quarterly* 209 (2012b): 11–133.

Heine, Jamie. "China's Claim in Latin America: So Far, a Partner, Not a Threat." Accessed March 8, 2009. http://www.coha.org/china's-claim-in-latin-america-so-far-a-partner-not-a-threat/.

Henken, Ted A. *El Éxito De Un Negocio Garantiza El Éxito Del Negocio Vecino.* 14ymedio. 2017a.

Henken, Ted A. "A Good Hair Day in Old Havana." *Cuban Counterpoints*, March 6, 2017b.

Henken, Ted A. "Condemned to Informality: Cuba's Experiments with Self-Employment during the Special Period (the Case of the Bed and Breakfasts)." *Cuban Studies* 33 (2002): 1–29.

Henken, Ted A. *Entrepreneurial Activity in Cuba's Private Sector.* Vol. February Engage Cuba Coalition and Cuba Emprende Foundation, 2017b.

Henken, Ted A. "Self-Employed but Not Alone: Artecorte and Social Entrepreneurship in the New Cuba." In *Cuba Facing Forward: Balancing Identity and Development in the Twenty-First Century,* edited by David White, Lucas Spiro, Victor Silva, and Anya Brickman Raredon, 273–292. Boston, MA: Affordable Housing Institute, 2018.

Henken, Ted A. and A. Ritter. *Abajo Con El Bloqueo En Contra De Los Emprendedores Cubanos, Tanto En La Habana Como En Washington.* 14ymedio. 2014.

Henken, Ted A. and A. Ritter. "Overcoming Cuba's Internal Embargo." *Current History* 114 (2002): 73–76.

Henken, Ted A. and Gabriel Vignoli. "Entrepreneurial Reform, Market Expansion, and Political Engagement: Risks and Opportunities for Cuba Today." In *A New Chapter in U.S.-Cuban Relations: Impacts on the Island and Beyond*, edited by Eric Hershberg and William LeoGrande. Washington D.C.: Palgrave Macmillan, 2016.

Henken, Ted A. and Gabriel Vignoli. "A Taste of Capitalism? Competing Notions of Cuban Entrepreneurship in Havana's *Paladares*." *Human Geography* 10, no. 3 (2017): 97–117.

Hernandez, Marcelo. *Raúl Castro Critica Las Irregularidades En El Sector Privade y Cooperativo.* 14ymedio. 2017.

Hernández Catá, E. *Cuba: Is It a Demographic Revolution or a Blip.* ASCE Blog. Miami, FL: Association for the Study of the Cuban Economy, 2016.

Hesse-Biber, S. N. and P. Leavy. *The Practice of Qualitative Research (2nd ed.).* Los Angeles, CA: Sage Press, 2011.

Hirschfeld Davis, J. "Alan P. Gross gains the Freedom from Cuba He Thought Would Never Come." *The New York Times*, December 17, 2014.

Hobolt, S. B. "The Brexit Vote: A Divided Nation, a Divided Continent." *Journal of European Public Policy* 23, no. 9 (2016): 1259–1277.

Hoffmann, Bert. "A Südpolitik Made in Washington?" Washington D.C., American University and the Social Science Research Council, April, 2015.

Holmes, M. G. "Seizing the Moment" (Master's Thesis). Available from ProQuest Dissertations and Theses Databases (UMI no. 1483567). M.A., 2010.

Homburg, C., M. Klarmann, M. Reimann, and O. Schilke. "What Drives Key Informant Accuracy?" *Journal of Marketing Research* 49, no. 4 (2012): 594–608.

Horowitz, Irving Louis. "Eleven Theses on Cuba After Castro." *Studies in Comparative International Development* 34, no. 4 (2000): 3.

Hughes, John. "Spring Delayed as Cuban Follows China Model." *Christian Science Monitor* (April 9, 2012): 1.

Human Rights Watch. "Events of 2015." 2017. https://www.hrw.org/world-report/2016/country-chapters/cuba.

Human Rights Watch. "The US Global Magnitsky Act: Questions and Answers. Human Rights Watch Website." 2017. https://www.hrw.org/news/2017/09/13/us-global-magnitsky-act.

Huntington, Samuel. *Political Order in Changing Societies*. New Haven, CT: Yale University Press, 1968.

Huntington, Samuel and J. Nelson. *No Easy Choice*. Cambridge, MA: Harvard University Press, 1976.

Hussein Haeri, H. and R. Dagli. "Cuba Libre—But with Investment Protection." *Global Arbitration Review*, November 12, 2015.

Hymer, S. *The International Operations of National Firms: A Study of Foreign Direct Investment*. Cambridge, MA: MIT Press, 1976.

IBIS World. "Global Tourism, Industry Outlook." 2015. http://clients1.ibisworld.com.

Iglesias, Maidolys and Gilberto Valladares. "'Artecorte' Una Experencia De Economía Social y Solidaria." In *Construyendo Socialismo Desde Abajo: La Contribución De La Economía Popular y Solidaria*, edited by Rafael Betancourt. Havana, Cuba: Editorial Caminos, 2017.

Infante, E. R. and H. J. Samra. *Back to the Future? Foreign Investment Protection in Cuba*. Latin American Law Blog. 2016.

Inter-American Development Bank. *Annual Report 2016: The Year in Review*. Washington D.C.: IADB, 2016.

Inter-American Development Bank. *The Emergence of China: Opportunities and Challenges for Latin America and the Caribbean*. Washington D.C.: IADB, 2004.

Inter Press Service. "Alianzas Necesarias Para Fortalecer Desarrollo Económico y Social Cubano." *Ips*, February 27, 2017.

IPCC. *Managing the Risks of Extreme and Disasters to Advance Climate Change Adaption*: IPCC, 2012.

Jackiewicz, Edward L. and Todd Bolster. "The Working World of the *Paladar*: The Production of Contradictory Space during Cuba's Period of Fragmentation." *The Professional Geographer* 55, no. 3 (2003): 372–382.

Jara, Francisco. "Peluquero Privado Abre Escuela En Cuba." *El Nuevo Herald*, June 16, 2015.

Jessop, D. "The View from Europe: Cuba the EU and a Post-Cotonou Agreement." *The Barbados Advocate*, May 27, 2018.

Jiang, S. "Philosophy and History: Interpreting the 'Xi Jinping Era' through Xi's Report to the Nineteenth National Congress of the CCP." *Open Times*, May 11, 2018.

Jiang, Shixue. "A Comparison of Socialism with Chinese Characteristic with Socialism with Cuban Characteristics (Zhongguo Tese Shehuizhuyi Yu Guba Tshe Shehuizhuyi Zhi Bijiao)." *Zhongguo Tese Shihuizhuyi Yanjiu* 2 (2010): 31–37.

Johnson, Gregg B. and Zhimin Lin. "The China Factor." San Juan, Puerto Rico, Annual Conference of the Southern Political Science Association, January 7–9, 2016.

Johnson, Gregg B. and Jesse T. Wasson. "China, Latin America, and the United States: The Political Economy of Energy Policy in the Americas." In *China's Energy Relations with the Developing World*, edited by Carrie Liu Currier and Manochehr Dorraj. New York, NY: Continuum International Publishing Group, 2011.

Jones, K. "Revolutionary Cuba and the GATT/WTO System." *Journal of World Trade* 51, no. 5 (2017): 1–26.

Jordan, E., B. Boley, W. Knollengergy, and C. Kline. "Predictors of Intention to Travel to Cuba Across Three-Time Horizons: An Application of the Theory of Planned Behavior." *Journal of Travel Research* 57, no. 7 (2017): 981–99.

Kalia, K. "Denunciation of ICSID: Does It Really Mean No ICSID Arbitration?" *University of Pennsylvania Journal of International Law* (April 2017).

Karl, Terry Lynn. "Dilemmas of Democratization in Latin America." *Comparative Politics* 23, no. 1 (1990): 1–21.

Katz, Mark N. "The Soviet-Cuban Connection." *International Security* 8, no. 1 (1983): 88–112.

Keefer, Phillip. *A Review of the Political Economy of Governance: From Property Rights to Voice*. Washington D.C.: World Bank Research Working Paper, 2004.

Keefer, Phillip and Stephen Knack. "Polarization, Politics, and Property Rights: Links Between Inequality and Growth." *Public Choice* 111, no. 2 (2000): 127–154.

Kiefer, Francine. "If Congress Objects to Obama's Move on Cuba, What Can It Do?" 2014. http://www.csmonitor.com/USA/Politics/DC-Decoder/2014/1217/If-Congress-objects-to-Obama-s-move-on-Cuba-what-can-it-do-video.

Kimber, Stephen. "The Cuban Five Were Fighting Terrorism. Why Did We Put Them in Jail?" *The Washington Post*, October 4, 2015. https://www.washingtonpost.com/opinions/the-cuban-five-were-fighting-terrorism-why-did-we-put-them-in-jail/2013/10/04/37c556a6-1fca-11e3-b7d1-7153ad47b549_story.html?utm_term=.5e6dfe0a890c.

Knack, Stephen and Phillip Keefer. "Institutions and Economic Performance: Cross-Country Tests Using Alternative Institutional Measures." *Economics and Politics* 7, no. 3 (1995): 207–228.

Kolopic, Sasha. "Solar Energy Outlook in Cuba." *Havana Times*, February 26, 2016.

Kornai, J. *From Socialism to Capitalism*. Budapest, Hungary: Central European University Press, 2008.

Kornbluh, Peter. "This US Contractor Has Spent Almost Five Years in a Cuban Jail. Why Won't the White House Act?" *The Nation*, May 2, 2014. https://www.thenation.com/article/us-contractor-has-spent-almost-five-years-cuban-jail-why-wont-white-house-act/.

Krauze, Enrique. "The New Cuba?" *The New York Review of Books*, March 19, 2015.

Krepp, S. "Cuba and the OAS: A Story of Dramatic Fallout and Reconciliation." Wilson Center Sources and Methods. December 18, 2017. https://www.wilsoncenter.org/blog-post/cuba-and-the-oas-story-dramatic-fallout-and-reconciliation.

Krogstad, J. M. *Surge in Cuban Immigration to U.S. Continued through 2016*. Washington D.C.: Pew Research Center (Fact Tank), 2017.

Kubny, Julia and Hinrich Voss. *The Impact of Chinese Outward Investment: Evidence from Cambodia and Vietnam*: German Development Institute Discussion Paper, 2010.

Labott, Elise. "Cuba Releases American Alan Gross, Paves Way for Historic Easing of American Sanctions." *CNN*, December 17, 2014. https://www.cnn.com/2014/12/17/politics/cuba-alan-gross-deal/.

Laitamaki, J., T. H. Lisandra, M. Tada, S. Liu, N. Setyady, N. Vatcharasoontorn, and F. Zheng. "Sustainable Tourism Development Frameworks and Best Practices: Implications for the Cuban Tourism Industry." *Managing Global Transitions* 14, no. 1 (2016): 7–29.

Laitamaki, J., M. Tada, L. Siying, N. Setyady, N. Vatcharasoontorn, Z. Feizhou, and L. T. Hechavarría. "Sustainable Tourism Development Frameworks and Best Practices: Implications for the Cuban Tourism Industry." *Managing Global Transitions: International Research Journal* 14, no. 1 (2016): 7–29.

Lake, D. "Presidential Address: International Legitimacy Lost? Rule and Resistance when America is First." *Perspectives on Politics* 16, no. 1 (2018): 12–17.

Lamrani, S. "Reforming the Cuban Economic Model: Causes and Prospects." *International Journal of Cuban Studies* 4, no. 1 (2012): 17–35.

Landler, Mark. "U.S. Swap for Bergdahl Shook Up Secret Talks with Cuba." *The New York Times*, December 31, 2014. https://www.nytimes.com/2014/12/31/us/how-cuba-talks-were-reshaped-by-the-release-of-bergdahl.html.

Landler, Mark and Michael R. Gordon. "Journey to Reconciliation Visited Worlds of Presidents, Popes and Spies." *The New York Times*, December 17, 2014.

Lehoczki, Bernadett. "Sino-Cuban Relations in the 21st Century." *International Journal of Cuban Studies* 4, no. 3/4 (2012): 291–306.

Lektzian, D. and G. Biglaiser. "The Effect of FDI on the Use and Success of US Sanctions." *Management and Peace Science* 31, no. 1 (2014): 70–93.

LeoGrande, William. "The Trouble with Cuba's New Economy." *Americas Quarterly*, October 11, 2017.

LeoGrande, William and Peter Kornbluh. *Back Channel to Cuba the Hidden History of Negotiations between Washington and Havana*. Chapel Hill, NC: University of North Carolina Press, 2015.

Levmore, Saul and William J. Stuntz. "Remedies and Incentives in Private and Public Law: A Comparative Essay." *Wisconsin Law Review* (1990): 483–499.

Levy, Pema. "Miami Nice: Are Florida's Power Brokers Mellowing on Cuba?" *Mother Jones*, August 12, 2015. https://www.motherjones.com/politics/2015/08/miami-nice-politicians-mellow-cuba/.

Li, Boya. "US and Cuba Formally Established Diplomatic Relations." http://world.huanqiu.com/hot/2015-07/6819747.html.

Li, S. Y., M. S. Wong, and S. K. Luk. "The Importance and Performance of Key Success Factors of International Joint Venture Hotels in China." *Chinese Economy* 39, no. 6 (2006): 83–94.

Lia, J. and A. Rugman. "Real Options and the Theory of FDI." *International Business Review* 16, no. 6 (2007): 687–712.

Lin, Ruxuan. "Cuban Ambassador: Sino-Cuban Relations Have Matured to a New Stage of Comprehensive Cooperation." Accessed November 29, 2015.

Lindbloom, C. *Politics and Markets*. New York, NY: Basic Books, 1971.

Linz, Juan and A. Stepan. *Problems of Democratic Transition and Consolidation: Southern Europe, South America, and Post-Communist Europe*. Baltimore, MD: Johns Hopkins University Press, 1996.

Linz, Juan and A. Stepan. "Toward Consolidated Democracies." In *Consolidating Third Wave Democracies*, edited by Larry Diamond, Marc F. Plattner, Yun-han Chu, and Hung-mao Tien. Baltimore, MD: Johns Hopkins University Press, 1997.

Lipset, S. M. *Political Man: The Social Basis of Politics*. Baltimore, MD: Johns Hopkins University Press, 1980.

Liptak, Kevin. "Alan Gross, Held in Cuba for Four Years, Ends Hunger Strike." *CNN*, April 8, 2014.

Liu, Yuqin. "Analysis of the Position of Cuba and the Cuban-American Policy in the Resumption of Diplomatic Negotiations." International Network. Accessed November 29, 2015. http://comment.cfisnet.com/2015/1007/1302688.html.

Londoño, Ernesto. "How a Cuban Spy and His Wife Came to Be Expectant Parents." *The New York Times*, December 12, 2014. https://www.nytimes.com/2014/12/23/opinion/how-a-cuban-spy-and-his-wife-came-to-be-expectant-parents.html.

López, Félix. "Paisaje Urbano y Desafíos Futuros." *Granma*, September 23, 2011.

Lopez-Gottardi, Cristina. "Make No Mistake, Raúl Castro Will Orchestrate Cuba's Election Results." The Hill. Accessed April 15, 2018. http://thehill.com/opinion/international/383183-make-no-mistake-raul-castro-will-orchestrate-cubas-election-results.

Lopez-Levy, Arturo. "A Post-Castro Era Looms for Cuba." Foreign Policy in Focus. Accessed February 10, 2016. http://fpif.org/a_post-castro_era_looms_for_cuba/.

Luis, R. Luis. *Recent Trends in Cuban Migration*. ASCE Blog. Miami FL: ASCE, 2017.

Luis, R. Luis. *Understanding Cuba's Capital Flows*. ASCE Blog. Miami FL: ASCE, 2016.

Luna, K. *Growing Number of Cuban Migrants in the US*. Washington D.C.: Center for Immigration Studies Report, 2016.

Main, A. *C'ELAC: Speaking for Latin America and the Caribbean*. Center for Economic and Policy Research Blog. CELAC, 2011.

Majeed, S., C. Lu, M. Majeed, and M. Shahid. "Health Resorts and Multi-Textured Perceptions of International Health Tourists." *Sustainability* 10, no. 4 (2018).

Marceau, G. and J. P. Trachtman. "A Map of the World Trade Organization Law of Domestic Regulation of Goods: The Technical Barriers to Trade Agreement, the Sanitary and Phytosanitary Measures Agreement, and the General Agreement on Tariffs and Trade." *Journal of World Trade* 48, no. 2 (2014): 351–432.

Marchi, G., M. Vignola, G. Facchinetti, and G. Mastroleo. "International Market Selection for Small Firms: A Fuzzy-Based Decision Process." *European Journal of Marketing* 48, no. 11 (2014): 2198.

Marsh, Sarah. "Cuban Draft Rules Propose Curtailing Fledgling Private Sector." *Reuters*, February 22, 2018a.

Marsh, Sarah. "Trump Task Force on Expanding Cuba Internet Meets for First Time." *Reuters*, February 8, 2018b.

Marshall, Monty and Ted Gurr. "Polity IV Project." October 2017. http://systemicpeace.org/polity/polity4.htm.

Martinez, L. M. "Enforceability of Industrial Property Licenses Agreements and Juridical Effects in Cuba." *Revista De Derecho* 44 (2015): 50–81.

Martínez Hernández, Leticia. "Trabajo Por Cuenta Propia, Mucho Más Que Una Alternativa." *Granma*, September 24, 2010.

Matthieson, K. "Trump Budget: U.S. to Stop Funding U.N. Climate Process." *Climate Home*, March 3, 2017.

Matysiak L. and A. Bausch. "Antecedents of MNE Performance: Blinded by the Obvious in 35 Years of Literature." *Multinational Business Review* 20, no. 2 (2012): 178–211.

Maybarduk, G. H. "U.S. Policy After the Sixth Party Congress: It Is Time to Try Constructive Engagement." Miami, FL, Association for the Study of the Cuban Economy, July 2011.

Mazzetti, Mark, Michael S. Schmidt, and Frances Robles. "Crucial Spy in Cuba Paid a Heavy Cold War Price." *The New York Times*, December 19, 2014. https://www.nytimes.com/2014/12/19/world/americas/cia-mole-now-out-of-prison-helped-us-identify-cuban-spies.html?emc=edit_th_20141219&nl=todaysheadlines&nlid=8280832&_r=1.

McMillan, D. "Capitalist Development in Cuba." 2015. http://davidmcmillangroup.typepad.com/consulting/cuba-hospitality/.

McMinimy, Mark. *U.S. Agricultural Trade with Cuba: Current Limitations and Future Prospects*. Washington D.C.: Congressional Research Service, 2015.

Melia. "Cuba Partners." 2015. http://www.meliacuba.com.

Melia. "Melia Hotels International: About." http://www.meliahotelsinternational.com.

Mesa-Lago, Carmelo. "*Cuba En La Era De Raúl Castro: Reformas Económico-Sociales y Sus Efectos*." In *Cuba After the Cold War*, edited by Carmelo Mesa-Lago, 133–196. Pittsburgh, PA: University of Pittsburgh Press, 1993.

Mesa-Lago, Carmelo. *Cuba En La Era De Raúl Castro: Reformas Económico-Sociales y Sus Efectos*. Madrid, Spain: Editorial Colibri, 2012.

Mesa-Lago Carmelo. "Institutional Changes of Cuba's Economic-Social Reforms: State and Market Roles, Progress, Hurdles, Comparisons, Monitoring and Effects." Brookings Institution Working Paper. Accessed November, 29, 2015. http://www.brookings.edu/research/papers/2014/08/cubas-economic-social-reforms-mesalago.

Mesa-Lago, Carmelo and Jorge Perez-Lopez. *Cuba Under Raúl Castro: Assessing the Reforms*. Boulder, CO: Lynne Rienner Publishers, 2013.

Mesa-Lago, Carmelo and Jorge Perez-Lopez. *Cuba's Aborted Reforms: Socioeconomic Effects, International Comparisons, and Transition Policies*. Gainesville, FL: University of Florida Press, 2005.

Mesa-Lago, Carmelo, Roberto Veiga González, Lenier González Mederos, Sofía Vera Rojas, and Aníbal Pérez-Liñán. *Voices of Change in Cuba from the Nonstate Sector*. Pittsburgh, PA: University of Pittsburgh Press, 2018.

Messina, W. *The 2008 Hurricane Season and Its Impact on Cuban Agricultural and Trade. Cuba in Transition*. Washington D.C.: Association for the Study of the Cuban Economy, 2018.

Miroff, Nick. "Heroic Homecoming for Cuban Agents Brings Speculation about Future in Politics." *The Washington Post*, January 18, 2015. https://www.washingtonpost.com/world/the_americas/heroes-welcome-for-cuban-agents-brings-speculation-about-future-in-politics/2015/01/18/390926fe-9a95-11e4-86a3-1b56f64925f6_story.html?utm_term=.96439f83a821.

Modern Slavery Act (2015). London, United Kingdom. Accessed August, 2018. https://www.gov.uk/government/collections/modern-slavery-bill.

Monreal, Pedro. *Nuevas Regulaciones Para El Trabajo Por Cuenta Propia En Cuba: Informalización Legal? El Estado Como Tal.* 2018.

Moore, Barrington. *Social Origins of Dictatorship and Democracy*. Boston, MA: Beacon Press, 1966.

Morales, E. *Se Desmorona Plan De Inversiones Del Puerto Del Mariel.* Miami, FL: Miami: The Havana Consulting Group and Tech, 2018a.

Morales, E. *Remittances to Cuba Diversify and Heat Up Payment Channels.* Miami, FL: The Havana Consulting Group and Tech, 2018b.

Morello, Carol and K. DeYoung. "Canada, Vatican Had Key Roles in Secret Diplomacy," *Washington Post*. December 18, 2014.

Morfessis, I. and D. Malachuk. "Economic Development in the Post Crisis Era." *Economic Development Journal* 10, no. 3 (2015): 19–27.

Morris, S. *Will Cuba Join the World Bank and Inter-American Development Bank?* Center for Global Development Blog. Washington D.C.: Center for Global Development, 2017.

Morris, S. "Will Cuba Join the World Bank and Inter-American Development Bank?" Center for Global Development. https://www.cgdev.org/blog/will-cuba-join-world-bank-and-inter-american-development-bank.

Mu, Chunshan. "Cuba and U.S. Sought to Establish Diplomatic Relations in Secret, China Might Have Known It 18 Months Ago." 2014. http://news.takungpao.com/world/exclusive/2014-12/2865525.html.

Mulet Concepción, Yailenis. "Self-Employment in Cuba: Between Informality and Entrepreneurship—The Case of Shoe Manufacturing." *Third World Quarterly* 37, no. 9 (2016): 1717–1729.

Muñoz Lima, Rosa. "Cuba: El Desafío De Trabajo Por Cuenta Propia." *Deutsche Welle*, July 31, 2018.

Mura, L., E. Grublova, I. Gecikova, and D. Kozelova. "An Analysis of Business Internationalization Models." *Studia Universitatis Babes-Bolyai* 56, no. 2 (2011): 16–28.

Murray, J. Y., M. Ju, and G. Y. Gao. "Foreign Market Entry Timing Revisited: Trade-Off between Market Share Performance and Firm Survival." *Journal of International Marketing* 20, no. 3 (2012): 50–64.

Murray, Mary and Sandra Lilley. "'A Human Thing': Senator Says No Politics in Cuban Sperm Deal." *NBC News*, December 18, 2014. https://www.nbcnews.com/storyline/u-s—cuba-relations/human-thing-senator-says-no-politics-cuban-sperm-deal-n273106.

Musso, F. and B. Francioni. "International Strategy for SMEs: Criteria for Foreign Markets and Entry Modes Selection." *Journal of Small Business and Enterprise Development* 21, no. 2 (2014): 301–312.

Nachmany, M. et.al. "Climate Change Legislation in Cuba." Working Paper, London School of Economics, London, UK (2016).

Nanda, Ved. "The 'Good Governance' Concept Revisited." *Annals of the American Academy of Political and Social Sciences* 603, no. 1 (2006): 269–283.

Nasr, R. "Airbnb: A US Firm Manages to Crack the Cuban Market." *CNBC*, May 5, 2015. http://www.cnbc.com.

"National Security Presidential Memorandum (NSPM-5) Strengthening the Policy of the United States." *Federal Register* 82, no. 202 (2017).

Nelson, Daniel. "Charisma, Control, and Coercion: The Dilemma of Communist Leadership." *Comparative Politics* 17, no. 1 (1984): 1–15.

Nessler, D. "Is Cuba the Next Land of Opportunity?" *Hotel Business* 24, no. 9 (2015): 32–34.

New York Times Editorial. "Cuba: A New Start." *The New York Times*, December 15, 2015. http://www.nytimes.com/interactive/2014/12/15/opinion/editorial-cuba-new-start.html.

New York Times Interactive. "Obama Visits Cuba." *The New York Times*, March 22, 2016. https://www.nytimes.com/interactive/projects/cp/international/obama-in-cuba/obama-spends-almost2-hours-with-cuban-dissidents.

news.takungpao.com. "The United States-Cuba 'Resumption of Diplomatic Ties' Could Cause Cuba to Abandon Military Cooperation with China." Accessed October 12, 2015. http://news.takungpao.com/world/exclusive/2015-05/3007200_wap.html.

Nieves Cárdenas, José Jasán. *Comentario Sobre Las Nuevas Regulaciones Para El Trabajo Por Cuenta Propia En Cuba*. El Estado Como Tal. 2018.

Noesselt, Nele. "China and Socialist Countries: Role Change and Role Continuity." In *China's International Roles: Challenging or Supporting the International Order*, edited by Sebastian Harnisch, Sebastian Bersick, and Jörn-Carsten Gottwald. New York, NY: Routledge, 2016.

NORC, Chicago. "A Rare Look Inside Cuban Society: A New Survey of Cuban Public Opinion." NORC (University of Chicago) 2017. http://www.norc.org/Research/Projects/Pages/survey-of-cuban-public-opinion.aspx.

North, Douglass C. *Institutions, Institutional Change, and Economic Performance*. New York, NY: Cambridge University Press, 1991.

Nova Gonzalez, A. "Agricultura." In *Miradas a La Economía Cubana*, edited by O. E. Pérez Villanueva, 43–71. La Habana, Cuba: Editorial Caminos, 2010.

Nova González, A. *La Agricultura En Cuba: Evolución y Trayectoria (1959–2005)*. La Habana, Cuba: Editorial de Ciencias Sociales, 2006.

Nova González, A. *Cuban Agriculture and the Current Economic Transformation Process*. Cuba Study Group, 2012.

Nova González, A. *El Modelo Agrícola y Los Lineamientos De La Política Económica y Social En Cuba*. La Habana, Cuba: Editorial Ciencias Sociales, 2013a.

Nova González, A. "Un Nuevo Modelo Cubano De Gestión Agrícola." *Temas* 77 (2013b): 84–91.

Nova González, A. "El Sector Agropecuario En Cuba." *Nueva Sociedad* 216, no. 1 (2008): 77–89.

Nova González, A. "Sector Agropecuario y Lineamientos." In *Handbook of Contemporary Cuba: Economy, Politics, Civil Society, and Globalization*, edited by M. Font and C. Riobó, 81–96. Boulder, CO: Paradigm Publishers, 2013.

Obama, President Barack. "Remarks to the People of Cuba." Gran Teatro De La Habana. Vol. March 22. Havana, Cuba: 2014.

Obama, President Barack. "Statement by the President on Cuba Policy Changes." The White House. Accessed August 9, 2018. https://obamawhitehouse.archives.gov/the-press-office/2014/12/17/statement-president-cuba-policy-changes.

Obama, President Barack. "Transcript of Press Conference of Barack Obama and Raúl Castro, Havana, Cuba 21 March 2016." *Time*, March 22, 2016b.

O'Donnell, Guillermo. *Modernization and Bureaucratic-Authoritarianism: Studies in South American Politics*. Berkeley, CA: University of California Press, 1973.

Oficina Nacional de Estadística e Información. *Anuario Estadístico De Cuba (Tables 3.21, 15.3 & 15.12)*. Havana, Cuba: Gobierno de Cuba, 2015.

Oficina Nacional de Estadísticas e Información (ONEI). *Anuario Estadístico De Cuba, 2014, 2013, 2015*. La Habana, Cuba: Oficina Nacional de Estadísticas e Información (ONEI), 2016.

Oficina National de Estadistíca e Informacíon. "Annual Tourist Visitors by Country." Gobierno de Cuba 2015.

Okafor, G. "Locational Determinants of US Outward FDI into Sub-Saharan Africa." *The Journal of Developing Areas* 49, no. 1 (2015): 187–205.

Olsen, Mancur. "Dictatorship, Democracy and Development." *American Political Science Review* 87, no. 3 (1993): 567–76.

Olsen, Mancur. *The Rise and Fall of Nations*. New Haven, CY: Yale University Press, 1982.

Oppenheimer, Andrés. "Los Consejos De China a Cuba." Accessed January 8, 2018. http://www.analisislatino.com/notas.asp?id=861.

Oppmann, Patrick and Josh Levs. "'I'm Free': American Alan Gross' Emotional Return from Cuban Prison." *CNN*, December 17, 2014. http://www.cnn.com/2014/12/17/world/americas/cuba-alan-gross/.

Oppmann, Patrick and Evan Perez. "Cuban spy's ultimate mystery: How he got his wife pregnant from a U.S. prison." *CNN*. January 4, 2015.

Orsi, P. Business Insider. Retrieved from http://www.businessinsider.com/tourists-want-to-visit-cuba-before-americans-ruin-it-2015-3.

Orsi, Peter. "Raul Castro to Step Down: Who Will Run Cuba Next?" *The Christian Science Monitor*. Accessed March 1, 2016. http://www.csmonitor.com/World/Latest-News-Wires/2013/0224/Raul-Castro-to-step-down-Who-will-run-Cuba-next.

Orsi, Peter. "Wife of Cuban Agent Freed from U.S. Expecting Baby," *Associated Press International*. December 23, 2014.

Padrón Cueto, Claudia. "Artecorte: Un Alianza Entre Lo Estatal y Privado." *El Toque*, October 26, 2017.

Parker, Ashley and Jonathan Martin. "Change in Policy, Like Shift in Demographics, Could Alter Florida's Political Map." *New York Times*, December 17, 2014.

Parraga, M. and A. Ulmer. "Venezuela's Energy Woes Spread to Its Closest Ally: Cuba." *Reuters*, July 8, 2016.

Partido Comunista Cubano. *Conceptualización Del Modelo Económico y Social Cubano De Desarrollo Socialista y Plan Nacional De Desarrollo Económico y Social Hasta 2030. (Conceptualization of the Cuban Economic and Social Model and the National Economic and Social Development Plan through 2030)*. Cuban Communist Party. http://www.thecpe.org/wp-content/uploads/2016/05/Conceptualizacion-del-modelo-economico-PCC-Cuba-2016.pdf.

Partido Comunista Cubano. *Lineamientos De La Política Económica y Social Del Partido y Law Revolución*. Havana, Cuba: Cuban Communist Party, 2011.

Patillo Sanchez, L. *Establishing the Rule of Law in Cuba*. Miami, FL: University of Miami Institute for Cuba and Cuban American Affairs, 2003.

Paunescu, C. M. "Challenges of Entering the Business Market: The Pre-Entry Knowledge and Experience." *Management & Marketing* 8, no. 1 (2013): 63–78.

Peláez, Orfilio. "Nuevo Proyecto De Mapeo Cerebral: Cuba, China, y Canadá Aunarán Esfuerzos Para Desarrollar Un Proyecto Conjunto De Mapeo Cerebral." *Granma*. Accessed May 1, 2017. http://www.granma.cu/ciencia/2017-02-28/nuevo-proyecto-de-mapeo-cerebral-28-02-2017-23-02-48.

Perelló, J. L. "Desarrollo Del Turismo En Cuba: Tendencias, Políticas e Impactos Futuros." Miami, FL, 2016.

Perez, I. "Cubans Find Preparing for Climate Change Hard, Expensive and Essential." *Climate Wire*, June 16, 2014.

Perez-Lopez, J. "Coveting Beijing, but Imitating Moscow: Cuba's Economic Reforms in a Comparative Perspective." *Cuba in Transition* 5, no. 11 (1995).

Perez-Stable, Marifeli. "Caught in a Contradiction: Cuban Socialism between Mobilization and Normalization." *Comparative Politics* 32, no. 1 (1999): 63–82.

Pérez-Stable, Marifeli. *The Cuban Revolution: Origins, Course, and Legacy*. New York, NY: Oxford University Press, 2011.

Peters, P. "Cuba's New Real Estate Market." Working Paper, Brookings Institution, Washington, D.C. 2014.

Peters, Phil. *Cuba's Entrepreneurs: Foundation of a New Private Sector*. Vol. July 2012.

Peters, Phil. "Jobs, Anyone?" *The Cuban Triangle*, January 11, 2010c.

Peters, Phil. "Pilot Project Time." *The Cuban Triangle*, March 10, 2010b.

Peters, Phil. "The State Lightens Its Burden." *The Cuban Triangle*, April 13, 2010a.

Pickrell, E. "Other Nations, Not US, Will Seize Early-Entry Advantages in Cuba." *Monitor Global Outlook*, December 24, 2014. http://www.monitorglobaloutlook.com.

Pineiro, H. "Cuba's New Socialism: Different Visions Shaping Current Changes." *Latin American Perspectives* 40, no. 3 (2013): 107–25.

Piñiero Harnecker, C. *Cooperativas y Socialism: Una Mirada Desde Cuba*. Havana, Cuba: Editorial Caminos, 2011.

Poniachik, Karen. "China's Buying Spree: Life Beyond Commodities." Latin Trade. Accessed November 14, 2017. http://latintrade.com/china's-buying-spree-life-beyond-commodities/.

Prensa Latina. "Resaltan Relaciones Entre Fuerzas Armadas De Cuba y China." Prensa Latina. Accessed December 20, 2015. http://www.granma.cu/mundo/2015-12-04/resaltan-relaciones-entre-fuerzas-armadas-de-cuba-y-china-04-12-2015-23-12-15.

Price, E. "Five Questions for Cuba." *International Financial Law Review* 2 (2016).

Prohaski, Gueorgui. *A Review of Bulgarian Privatisation. Organization for Economic Cooperation and Development*. Geneva: OECD, 1998.

Przeworski, A. and Fernando Limongi. "Political Regimes and Economic Growth." *Journal of Economic Perspectives* 3 (7, Summer 1993): 51–69.

Puig Meneses, Yaima. "Trabajo Por Cuenta Propia: Por La Ruta De La Actualización." *Granma*, August 1, 2017.

Rainsford, S. "Is Cuba Ready to Open Up to Foreign Investment?" *BBC News*, May 30, 2014. http://www.bbc.com.

Ravsberg, Fernando. "El Emprendedor Individual y La Obra Social." *Cartas Desde Cuba*, October 27, 2016.

Recio, Milena. "Trabajadores Por Cuenta Propia Proponen Diálogo." *Oncuba*, December 14, 2017.

Redacción Digital. "Gerardo Hernández and Adriana Pérez Welcome Daughter, Gema, to the World." *Granma*, 2015. http://en.granma.cu/cuba/2015-01-06/gerardo-hernandez-and-adriana-perez-welcome-daughter-gema-to-the-world.

Redacción Nacional. "Díaz-Canel Ratifica Magnífico Estado De Relaciones Cuba-China." *Granma*. Accessed December 19, 2015. http://www.granma.cu/mundo/2015-09-02/diaz-canel-ratifica-magnifico-estado-de-relaciones-cuba-china.

Redacción Nacional. "Recibe Miguel Díaz-Canel Bermúdez a Delegación Parlamentaria De China." *Granma*. Accessed December 19, 2015. http://www.granma.cu/mundo/2015-12-04/resaltan-relaciones-entre-fuerzas-armadas-de-cuba-y-china-04-12-2015-23-12-15.

Regular Press Conference of the Chinese Ministry of Foreign Affairs. July 2, 2015.

Reinland, Don. "China Halts Overseas Investment Schemes." *The Financial Times*. Accessed February 28, 2016. http://www.ft.com/intl/cms/s/0/c64b3fc6-dc2e-11e5-a72f-1e7744c66818.html#axzz42j2fNww9.

Republic of Cuba. *Intended National Determined Contributions*. Havana, Cuba: Gobierno de Cuba, 2015.

Republic of Cuba. "Ley 188." *Granma*, March 29, 2014.

Resisen, H. "Will the AIIB and the NDB Help Reform Multilateral Development Banking?" *Global Policy* 6, no. 3 (2015): 297–304.

Resolution AG/RES. 2438 (XXXIX-O/09) Oas (2009).

Rey Santos, Orlando, Teresa Cruz Sardiñas, Anyeli de la C. López Garcia, Daniel Whittle, and Candice Kanepa. *Manual De Legislación Ambiental Para La Gestión De La Zona Costera De Cuba [, Manual of Environmental Legislation for the Management of Cuba's Coastal Zone* (2008): 2.1.3.

Rhodes, B. "Resident Obama Is Going to Cuba. Here's Why:" *Medium*, February 16, 2016.

Richter, Paul and Tom Kington. "Pope Francis Bridged Gap between U.S. and Cuba during Secret Talks." *Los Angeles Times*, December 18, 2014.

Ritter, A. "Canada's Economic Relations with Cuba 1990 to 2010 and Beyond." *Canadian Foreign Policy* 16, no. 1 (2010): 119–VII.

Ritter, A. "Cuba's Economic Strategy and Alternative Futures." In *Cuba at a Crossroads: Politics and Economics After the Fourth Party Congress*, edited by J. Pérez-López, 67–93. Gainesville, FL: University of Florida Press, 1994.

Ritter, Archibald and Ted A. Henken. *Entrepreneurial Cuba: The Changing Policy Landscape*. Boulder, CO: First Forum Press, 2015.

Rivera, Mario Antonio. "Elements of Political Restructuring in a Post-Castro Transition." Miami, Florida, Prepared for the Fourth Annual Meeting of the Association for the Study of the Cuban Economy, August 11–13, 1994, 1994.

Rodrigo, Norges. "Medidas Del Gobierno Cubano Para 2018." *2017* (December 28).

Rodríguez, Andrea. "Emprendedores Cubanos En Punto Muerto Esperan Nuevas Reglas." *El Nuevo Herald*, February 2, 2018.

Rodríguez, Jorge Enrique. "La Frase 'espanta Demonios' Que Raúl Castro Nunca Pronunció." *Diario De Cuba*, October 30, 2016.

Rojas, Rafael. "Nueva Constitución En Cuba: Lo Que Permanece y Lo Que Cambia." *Letras Libres*, August 6, 2018.

Romero, Simon and William Neuman. "Cuba Thaw Lets Rest of Latin America Warm to Washington." *The New York Times*, December 19, 2015. https://www.nytimes.com/2014/12/19/world/americas/a-brave-move-by-obama-removes-a-wedge-in-relations-with-latin-america.html?_r=0.

Rosales, Beatriz. "Emprender En Cuba Hoy: Gilberto Valladares, El Hombre Detrás Del Callejón De Los Peluquero." *Pan American World*, May 9, 2016.

Rosen, Daniel H. "How China Is Eating Mexico's Lunch: The Maquiladora System's Comparative Advantage Is Being Challenged Head On." *The International Economy*, Spring 2003.

Ross, J. "Cuba: U.S. Agribusiness Export Prospects Under Three Scenarios." *Cuba in Transition* 14 (2004): 369–380.

Roth, A. "The Economist as Engineer: Game Theory, Experimentation, and Computation as Tools for Design Economics." *Econometrica*, 70, no. 4 (July 2002).

Rottinghaus, B. and J. Maier. "The Power of Decree: Presidential Use of Executive Proclamations, 1977–2005." *Political Research Quarterly* 60, no. 2 (2007): 338–343.

Sagebien, Julia and Rafael Betancourt. "Non-State Socially Responsible Enterprises: The Key to Inclusive Economic Growth in Cuba." In *No More Free Lunch: Reflections on the Cuban Economic Reform Process and Challenges for Transformation*, edited by Claus Brundenius and Ricardo Torres Pérez. Switzerland: Springer International Publishing, 2014.

Sagebien, Julia and Eric Leenson. "Cuban Remix." *Stanford Social Innovation Review* (Winter 2015): 59–60.

San Diego Union Tribune. "Cuba Cancels Musical Performance in Taiwan Possibly Under Pressure from China." *San Diego Union Tribune*. Accessed March 8, 2016. http://www.sandiegouniontribune.com/hoy-san-diego/sdhoy-cuba-cancels-musical-performance-in-taiwan-2016mar08-story.html.

Sánchez, Yoani. *Twitter Feed*. 2013. https://twitter.com/yoanisanchez/.

Santiso, C. "Good Governance and Aid Effectiveness: The World Bank and Conditionality." *Georgetown Public Policy Review* 7, no. 1 (2001): 1–22.

Saslow, Eli. "Obama's Chief Speechwriter, 27, Works on Inaugural Address while Making His Own Transition." *The Washington Post*, December 17, 2008. http://www.washingtonpost.com/wp-dyn/content/article/2008/12/17/AR2008121703903.html.

Say, Jean Baptiste. *A Treatise on Political Economy*. Grigg, Elliot & Co., 1847.

Scarpaci, Joseph, Ted A. Henken, and A. Ritter. "Two Decades of Re-Aligning Mundane Entrepreneurship in Cuba." *Revista Economia, Sociedad y Territorio* 16, no. 51 (May–August 2016).

Schleussner, C. F., T. K. Lissner, E. M. Fischer, J. Wohland, M. Perrette, A. Golly, J. Rogelj et al. "Differential Climate Impacts for Policy-Relevant Limits to Global Warming: The Case of 1.5 C and 2 C." *Earth System Dynamics* 327 (2016).

Schmitt, Eric and Charlie Savage. "Bowe Bergdahl, American Soldier, Freed by Taliban in Prisoner Trade." *The New York Times*, June 1, 2014. https://www.nytimes.com/2014/06/01/us/bowe-bergdahl-american-soldier-is-freed-by-taliban.html.

Schroeder, Peter. "Can Obama Lift Cuba Embargo Alone?" *The Hill*, December 17, 2014. https://thehill.com/policy/finance/227442-can-obama-lift-cuba-embargo-without-congress.

Schumpeter, Joseph A. *The Theory of Economic Development*. Oxford, UK: Oxford University Press, 1974.

Schwartz, Felicia. "Cuba Officially Removed from U.S.S State Sponsor of Terrorism List." *The Wall Street Journal*, May 29, 2015.

Sesin, C. "U.S.-Cuba Bilateral Commission to Meet for First Time since U.S. Withdrew Embassy Personnel." *NBC News*, June 13, 2018.

Sheldon, D. "Assessing U.S. Cuba Trade: Prospects and Challenges" (Doctoral Dissertation). Retrieved from ProQuest Dissertations and Theses Databases (UMI no. 3322146). Ph.D., 2008.

Simones, Alexander J. G. and Carlos A. Hidalgo. *The Economic Complexity Observatory: An Analytical Tool for Understanding the Dynamics of Economic Development*: Workshops at the 25th AAAI Conference on Artificial Intelligence, 2011.

Skidmore, Thomas E. and Peter Smith. *Modern Latin America*. Vol. 5. Oxford, UK: Oxford University Press, 2001.

Small, Andrew and Carolina Ferrer Rincon. "Fidel's Choice." *The New York Times*. Accessed January 2, 2016. http://www.nytimes.com/2008/11/27/opinion/27iht-edsmall.3.18204430.html.

Small Business Association Office of Advocacy. "Survival Rates and Firm Age." Small Business Administration 2015. https://www.sba.gov/.

Smith, M. "Want to Do Business in Cuba? Prepare to Partner with the General." *Bloomberg News*, September 30, 2015. http://www.Bloomberg.com.

Smith, R. C. and I. Walter. "Understanding a Cuban Transition." *Independent Review* 20, no. 4 (2016).

Solorza, M. "Reformas Economico Financieras En Cuba: Reinsercion Al Capitalism En Una Etapa De Crisis-Problemas Del Desarrollo." *Revista Latinoamericana De Economía* 47, no. 185 (2016): 137–162.

Sosin, E. "What if Cuba Returns to the IMF and the World Bank?" *Progresso Weekly*, August 4, 2015.

South Centre. *Climate Policy Brief*. Geneva: South Centre, 2015.

Spadoni, P. *Cuba's Socialist Economy Today: Navigating Challenges and Change*. Boulder, CO: Lynne Rienner Publishers, 2014.

Spadoni, P. and J. Sagebien. "Will They Still Love Us Tomorrow? Canada-Cuba Business Relations and the End of the US Embargo." *Thunderbird International Business Review* 55, no. 1 (2013): 77–93.

SRELDC. *Annual Report of the Socially Responsible Enterprise, Local Development in Cuba Consortium*: SRELDC, 2013.

Staff. "Pope Francis Wrote Cuban Book in 1998 'Dialogues between John Paul II and Fidel Castro.'" *Huffington Post*, December 20, 2014. http://www.beyondconflictint.org/.

Staff. "Which Economic Ties Are Most Critical for Cuba." *Latin American Advisor*, January 18, 2018. http://www.thedialogue.org.

Staff. "Will U.S.-Cuba Relations Thaw Further in 2016?" *Latin America Advisor*, January 5, 2016.

The State Council. "China, Cuba Pledge further Development of Military-to-Military Relations." Accessed May 25, 2017. http://english.gov.cn/state_council/state_councilors/2017/03/30/content_281475611740322.htm.

Stein, Jeff. "The American Spy Traded in the U.S.-Cuba Diplomatic Breakthrough." *Newsweek*, December 18, 2014. https://www.newsweek.com/american-spy-traded-us-cuba-diplomatic-breakthrough-293070.

Stricker, P. *Toward a Culture of Nature: Environmental Policy and Development in Cuba*. New York, NY: Lexington Books, 2007.

Strobel, Warren, M. Spetalnick, and D. Adams. "How Obama outmaneuvered hardliners and cut a Cuba deal." *Reuters*, March 23, 2015.

Strüver, Georg. "What Friends Are Made Of: Bilateral Linkages and Domestic Drivers of Foreign Policy Alignment with China." *Foreign Policy Analysis* 12, no. 2 (2016): 170–191.

Sullivan, M. *Cuba: U.S. Policy in the 115th Congress*. Washington D.C.: Congressional Research Service Report, 2017.

Sullivan, M. P. "Cuba: U.S. Policy and Issues for the 113th Congress." *Current Politics and Economics of South and Central America* 7, no. 1 (2014): 39–131.

Sun, Chenghao. *The Ease of US-Cuban Relations and Its Implications (Meigu Guanxi Huanhe Jiqi Yingxiang)*. Beijing, China: Guoji Yanjiu Cankao (Reference of International Studies), 2015.

Sun Sentinel Editorial Board. "Finally: A Chance to End Cuban Abuses." *Sun Sentinel*, January 8, 2016.

Supply Chain due Diligence Law. TEXTE ADOPTÉ n° 924 «Petite Loi» Quatorzième Législature Session Ordinaire De 2016–2017 Relative Au Devoir De Vigilance Des Sociétés Mères Et Des Entreprises Donneuses d'ordre. Assemblée Nationale Constitution (1958).

Support Cuban Civil Society. "Open Letter to President Obama: Support Civil Society in Cuba." American University, 2015. https://www.as-coa.org/articles/open-letter-president-obama-support-civil-society-cuba.

Sweig, Julia and M. Bustamante. "*Cuba After Communism: The Economic Reforms that Are Transforming the Island*." *Foreign Affairs*, July/August 2013.

Talluri, V. S. "The Determinants and Motivations of United States FDI in Canada and Mexico: A Comparative Study" (Doctoral Dissertation). Retrieved from ProQuest Dissertations and Theses Database (UMI no. 9828085). Ph.D., 1998.

Taylor, Ariel A. and Daniyal B. Zuberi. "The Cuban *Paladar*: Ideological Subversion Or Substantiation?" *The Social Science Journal* 52, no. 4 (2015): 503–515.

Telesur. "Cuba and China Agree to Strengthen Military Cooperation." Accessed May 25, 2017. http://www.telesurtv.net/english/news/Cuba-and-China-Agree-to-Strengthen-Military-Cooperation-20170331-0006.html.

Tiezzi, Shannon. "Trump-Xi Summit: Much Ado about Nothing? The Feel-Good Vibes from the Meeting Were Drowned Out Amid Questions Regarding the U.S. Strike on Syria." *The Diplomat*. Accessed June 4, 2017. https://thediplomat.com/2017/04/trump-xi-summit-much-ado-about-nothing/.

Torres, Ricardo. "Cuentapropismo y Cooperativismo: Otra Decepción." *Progreso Semanal*, February 19, 2018a.

Torres, Ricardo. "Impoverish the Cuban People, So That They May Be Freer." *Progreso Semanal*, November 22, 2017.

Torres, Ricardo. "Por Aquí Ya Pasamos. . . ." *Progreso Semanal*, August 2, 2018b.

The Tourism Society. "Memorandum of Association." http://www.tourismsociety.org.

Trapczynski, P. "Does Foreign Direct Investment Theory Explain Subsidiary Performance? A Critical Literature Review." *Poznan University of Economics Review* 13, no. 2 (2013): 47–64.

Travieso-Diaz, M. "Alternative Remedies in a Negotiated Settlement of the U.S. Nationals' Expropriation Claims Against Cuba." *University of Pennsylvania Journal of International Law* 17 (1996): 659–82.

Trotta, Daniel. "The Man Next in Line in for Cuba's Presidency Wants to Modernize the Country." *Business Insider*, November 30, 2016.

Trump, D. *National Security Presidential Memorandum NSPM-5 Entitled "Strengthening the Policy of the United States Toward Cuba."* Washington D.C.: Federal Register, 2017.

"Trump Reverses Certain Steps Toward Normalizing Relations with Cuba." *The American Journal of International Law* 111, no. 4 (2017): 1027–1035.

U.S. Census Bureau. *Trade in Goods with Cuba*. Washington D.C.: Foreign Trade Statistics, 2017.

U.S. Chamber of Commerce. "U.S. Chamber Welcomes Progress in U.S.-Cuba Relations." Press Release. Accessed March 1, 2016. https://www.uschamber.com/press-release/us-chamber-welcomes-progress-us-cuba-relations.

U.S. Chamber of Commerce. *U.S. Chamber's Donohue to Lead Delegation to Cuba.* Washington D.C.: U.S. Chamber of Commerce, 2014.

U.S. Congress. *Freedom for Americans to Travel to Cuba Act of 2017.* 115 Congress. 1st Session sess., S. 1287 (2017).

U.S. Department of Agriculture. *Global Agricultural Trade System (GATS) Online.* Washington D.C.: USDA, 2016.

U.S. Department of Homeland Security. *Yearbook of Immigration Statistics.* Washington D.C.: U.S. DHS, 2015.

U.S. Department of State. *Commission for Assistance to Free Cuba.* Washington D.C.: U.S. Department of State, 2004.

U.S. Department of State. *On the One-Year Anniversary of the President's Policy of Engagement with Cuba.* Anonymous 2015. (Transcript).

U.S. Department of State. *One-Year Anniversary of the President's Policy of Engagement with Cuba: Fact Sheet.* Washington D.C.: Bureau of Public Affairs, 2015.

U.S. Department of Treasury (U.S. DoT). "Cuban Liberty and Democratic Solidarity (Libertad) Act of 1996." 2017. http://www.treasury.gov/resource-center/sanctions/Documents/libertad.pdf.

U.S. Department of Treasury (U.S. DoT). "*Cuba Sanctions*." U.S. DoT 2016. https://www.treasury.gov/resource-center/sanctions.

U.S. Department of Treasury (U.S. DoT). "*Cuba Sanctions*." U.S. DoT 2018. https://www.treasury.gov/resource-center/sanctions.

U.S. Department of Treasury (U.S. DoT). "Office of Foreign Asset Controls." U.S. D.O.T. http://www.treasury.gov/resource-center/sanctions/Programs/Documents/cuba.txt.

U.S. Government Accountability Office. *U.S. Policy Changes Increased Engagement with Private Sector, but Agency Information Collection Is Limited.* Washington D.C.: Government Accountability Office, 2016.

U.S. Office of Management and Budget. *America First: A Blueprint to make America Great again.* Washington D.C.: U.S. Office of Management and Budget, 2016.

U.S.-Cuba Trade and Economic Council Inc. "Economic Eye on Cuba." December 2015. https://www.cubatrade.org/.

UNFCCC. "Background on the UNFCCC: The Initial Response to Climate Change." UNFCCC. http://unfccc.int/essential_background/items/6031.php.

UNFCCC. *The Kyoto Protocol.* New York, NY: United Nations, 1997.

UNFCCC. *Report of the Conference of the Parties on its Sixteenth Session, Held in Cancun from 29 November to 10 December 2010—Addendum—Part Two: Action Taken by the Conference of the Parties at its Sixteenth Session.* New York, NY: United Nations, 2011.

UNISDR. *Summary and Recommendations: 2009 Global Assessment Report on Disaster Risk Reduction, Risk and Poverty in a Changing Climate.* New York, NY: United Nations, 2009.

United Nations. "Convention on the Recognition and Enforcement of Foreign Arbitral Awards." (1958).

United Nations. "Framework Convention on Climate Change, the Paris Agreement." United Nations. Accessed April 1, 2017. http://unfccc.int/paris_agreement/items/9485.php.

United Nations. *Report of the Conference of the Parties on its Nineteenth Session, Held in Warsaw from 11 to 23 November 2013—Addendum—Part Two: Action Taken by the Conference of the Parties at its Nineteenth Session*. New York, NY: United Nations, 2014.

United Nations. Resolution 47/19, "Necessity of Ending the Economic, Commercial and Financial Embargo Imposed by the United States of American Against Cuba." New York, NY: U.N., 1992.

United Nations Convention on Contracts for the International Sale of Goods (Vienna, 1980) (CISG). Uncitral (1980).

United Nations Council on Trade and Development. "World Investment Report 2015: Reforming International Investment Governance: Methodological Note." United Nations, 2015. http://unctad.org/en/PublicationChapters/wir2015chMethodNote_en.pdf.

United Nations General Assembly. "As General Assembly Demands End to Cuba Blockade for Twenty-Third Consecutive Year, Country's Foreign Minister Cites Losses Exceeding $1 Trillion." Accessed October 12, 2015. http://www.un.org/press/en/2014/ga11574.doc.htm.

United Nations Office for Disaster Risk Reduction. *Press Release: Showcasing Cuba's Hurricane Sandy Recovery*. New York, NY: United Nations, 2015.

United Nations World Tourism Organization (UNWTO). "About." United Nations, 2015. http://www2.unwto.org.

United States. "FAQ: Global Magnitsky Sanctions." Department of the Treasury, 2017. https://www.treasury.gov/resource-center/sanctions/Programs/Documents/12212017_glomag_faqs.pdf.

Global Magnitsky Human Rights Accountability Act. Public Law 114-328, Subtitle F, 130 Stat 2000 (2016).

Valladares, Gilberto "Papito". *Personal Interview*. February 23, 2017.

Valladares, Gilberto "Papito" and Camilo Condis. "El Proyecto Artecorte: Un Proyecto Comunitario De Desarrollo Local En La Cuba Actual." Miami, FL, Presentation given at the 26th annual conference of the Association for the Study of the Cuban Economy, "Cuba: What's Next?", July 28–30, 2016.

Vallely, Paul. "Hail Mary in Havana: Pope Francis' Divine Diplomacy." *Newsweek Magazine*, January 2, 2014. https://www.newsweek.com/2015/01/02/hail-mary-havana-pope-franciss-divine-diplomacy-294413.html.

Vasilak, R. "Cuba." *World Golf Report*, 2015. http://worldgolfreport.blogspot.com/2015_01_01_archive.html.

The Vatican. "Communiqué of the Secretariat of State." Press Release. December 17, 2014.

Verchick, R. R. M. "Can 'Loss and Damage' Carry the Load?" *Philosophical Transactions of the Royal Society* (2017).

Verchick, R. R. M. "Environmental Law in Cuba." In *Cuba: A Legal Guide to Business*, edited by Rand Rolando Cot. Anillo: Thomson Reuters, 2016.

Vidal, Alejandro P. and E. Hernandez Catá. "The Performance of Cuba's Gross Domestic Product, 2015–2016: The Role of External Factors, Business Confidence and Domestic Policies." Washington D.C., Association for the Study of the Cuban Economy (ASCE), 2016.

Vidal, Alejandro and Everleny Omar Pérez Villanueva. "Entre Al Ajustefiscal y Los Cambios Estructurales: Se Extiende El Cuentapropismo En Cuba." *Espacio Laico* 112 (October 2010).

Vidal, Alejandro and Omar Everleny Pérez Villanueva. "Aperturaalcuentapropismo y La Microempresa, Una Pieza Clave Del Ajuste Estructural." In *Miradas a La Economía Cubana: El Proceso De Actualización*, edited by Alejandro Vidal and Omar Everleny Pérez Villanueva. Havana, Cuba: Editorial Caminos, 2012.

Villaverde, O. "A Macroeconomic Approach of FDI in Post-Castro Cuba" (Doctoral Dissertation). Retrieved from ProQuest Dissertations and Theses Database (UMI no. 9828085). Ph.D., 2010.

Vinik, D. "The Strange Story of the First Cuban Import in Half a Century: Could Trump's New Policy Put a Fragile Opening at Risk?" *Politico*, June 16, 2017.

Voice of America United States Information Agency. *Cuba Annual Report: 1989*. Brunswick, NJ: Transaction Publishers, 1989.

Warsaw International Mechanism for Loss and Damage Associated with Climate Change Impacts. 14ymedio. *Cuba Cierra 2016. Con Más De 535.000 Trabajadores Por Cuenta Propia*. Vol. 2017. Havana, Cuba: 14ymedio.com, 2017a.

Warsaw International Mechanism for Loss and Damage Associated with Climate Change Impacts. 14ymedio. *Cuba Cierra 2016. Más Del 80% De Los Cuentapropistas Cubanos Pertenecen a Sindicatos Oficialistas*. Havana, Cuba: 14ymedio.com, 2017b.

Watts, J. and S. Brodzinsky. "U.S.-Cuba Thaw, One Year Later: Historic Breakthroughs but When Will They Trickle Down?" *The Guardian*, December 18, 2015. http://www.theguardian.com/world/2015/dec/18/us-cuba-relations-one-year-later-progress-report.

Weissenstein, Michael and Andrea Rodríguez. "Cuba Lifting Freeze on New Private Businesses." *Associated Press/Washington Post*, July 10, 2018.

Whitefield, M. "Mariel Is Cuba's Big Industrial Gamble. Could U.S. Companies Be among Investors?" *The Miami Herald*, October 23, 2017.

Whitefield, Mimi. "Hair Is Layered with Art and a Havana Street Is Transformed." *Cuba Today*, May 10, 2018.

Whitefield, Mimi. "New Cuba Regulations for Private Enterprise on the Island Have a Long List of Don'ts." *Miami Herald*, August 2, 2018.

Whitefield, Mimi. "A Trump Attempt to Reverse Obama's Cuba Policies Could Be Complicated and Costly." *The Miami Herald*, November 10, 2016.

The White House. *Background Conference Call on Policy Changes in Cuba and the Release of Alan Gross*. Vol. December 17 Office of the Press Secretary, 2014.

The White House. *Fact Sheet on Cuba Policy*. Washington D.C.: Press Office, 2017.

The White House. *Remarks by President Obama at the First Plenary Session of the Summit of the Americas*. Washington D.C.: Office of the Press Secretary, 2014b.

The White House. "Statement by the President on Cuba Policy Changes." U.S. Office of the Press Secretary 2017. https://obamawhitehouse.archives.gov/the-press-office/2014/12/17/statement-president-cuba-policy-changes.

Whittle, D., K. C. Lindeman, and J. T. B. Tripp. "International Tourism and Protection of Cuba's Coastal and Marine Environments." *Tulane Environmental Law Journal* 1 (2003): 539–44.

Wilkinson, Tracy. "In Cuba, Likely Castro Successor Keeps a Low Profile." *Los Angeles Times*. Accessed March 1, 2016. http://www.latimes.com/world/mexico-americas/la-fg-cuba-succession-20150207-story.html.

Wilson, W. A. I., II. "Research: Think Tank—Cuba—Is It Time to Heed Cuba's Call for Investment?" Foreign Direct Investment, 2015. http://www.fdiintelligence.com/.

Wolff, A. "DDG Wolff: WTO Accession Has Served as a Key Engine for Economic Transformation; Address to the Astana Economic Forum in Kazakhstan on 18 May 2018." *WTO News*, 2018. https://www.wto.org/english/news_e/news18_e/ddgra_22may18_e.htm.

World Bank. "Corporate Governance: Best Practices." World Bank, 2005. Retrieved from http://www.worldbank.org.

World Bank. "Ease of Doing Business." World Bank, 2014. Retrieved from http://www.worldbank.org.

World Bank. "Ease of Doing Business." World Bank, 2016. Retrieved from http://www.worldbank.org.cuhsl.creighton.edu.

World Bank. *International Bank for Reconstruction and Development Articles of Agreement*. New York, NY: World Bank, 2012.

World Bank. *Migration and Remittances Fact Book*. Washington D.C.: World Bank, 2016.

World Bank. "*World Development Indicators*." World Bank. Accessed June 5, 2017. http://data.worldbank.org/data-catalog/world-development-indicators.

World Trade Organization. *Working Party on the Accession of Viet Nam—Accession of Viet Nam—Report of the Working Party on the Accession of Viet Nam (Doc. no. 06-5202; 27 Oct. 2006)*. New York, NY: WTO, 2006.

Wu, Baiy. *Opportunities Along with Transformation A Multi-Perspective Analysis of the China-Latin American Relations*. Beijing, China: Economy & Management Publishing Press, 2013.

Wu, Baiyi and Liu Weiguang. *Annual Report on Latin America and the Caribbean (2010–2011)*. Beijing, China: Social Sciences Academic Press, 2011.

Wu, Baiyi and Liu Weiguang. *Annual Report on Latin America and the Caribbean (2011–2012)*. Beijing, China: Social Sciences Academic Press, 2012.

Wu, Baiyi and Liu Weiguang. *Annual Report on Latin America and the Caribbean (2012–2013)*. Beijing, China: Social Sciences Academic Press, 2013.

Wu, Baiyi and Liu Weiguang. *Annual Report on Latin America and the Caribbean (2013–2014)*. Beijing, China: Social Sciences Academic Press, 2014.

Wu, Baiyi and Liu Weiguang. *Annual Report on Latin America and the Caribbean (2014–2015)*. Beijing, China: Social Sciences Academic Press, 2015.

Wu, Baiyi and Liu Weiguang. *Annual Report on Latin America and the Caribbean (2015–2016)*. Beijing, China: Social Sciences Academic Press, 2016.

Wu, Tim. *The Master Switch: The Rise and Fall of Information Empires*. New York, NY: Vintage, 2011.

Wylie, L. "The Special Case of Cuba." *International Journal* 67, no. 3 (2012): 661–684.

Xinhua News Agency. *Xinhua News Agency*, June 15, 2017. http://news.xinhuanet.com/world/2017-06/15/c_129632923.htm.

Xinhua News Agency. *Xinhua News Agency*, June 17, 2017. http://news.xinhuanet.com/world/2017-06/17/c_1121161877.htm.

Xinhua News Agency. *Xinhua News Agency*, June 20, 2017. http://news.xinhuanet.com/world/2017-06/20/c_1121175010.htm.

Xinhua News Agency. *Xinhua News Agency*, June 20, 2017. http://news.xinhuanet.com/world/2017-06/20/c_1121180165.htm.

Xinhua News Agency. "Spotlight: Cuba to Embark on New Reforms After Communist Party Congress." *Xinhua News Agency*, April 20. 2016. http://www.xinhuanet.com/english/2016-04/20/c_135297508.htm.

Xu, Shicheng. *The "Upgrade" of Cuban Model and the Rise of Left in Latin America (Guba Moshi De "Gengxin" Yu Lamei Zuopai De Jueqi)*. Beijing, China: Social Sciences Academic Press, 2013.

Xu, Shicheng. "Cuba, 'Change' Socialist Economic Model (Guba, 'Gengxin' Shihuizhuyi Jingji Moshi—Yingjie Dang De 'Liuda' Zhaokai)." *Contemporary World (China)* 12 (2010): 35–38.

Xu, Shicheng. "On Trump's 'New Deal' on Cuba (Pinglun Telongpu Dui Guba De 'Xinzheng)." 2017. http://zh.apdnews.com/news/678534.html?node=698.

Yang, Lan. "Viva Sino-China." *Global Times*, June 2, 2015.

Yang, Wenzhong and Chunling Don. "The American Election and the Normalization of US-Cuban Relations (Meiguo Xuanju Yu Meigu Guanxi Zhengchanghua)." *Contemporary International Relation (China)* 1 (2016): 42–55.

Yuan, Dongzheng and Liu Weiguang. *Annual Report on Latin America and the Caribbean (2016–2017)*. Beijing, China: Social Sciences Academic Press, 2016.

Zahniser, S., Cooke B., J. Cessna, N. Childs, D. Harvey, M. Haley, M. McConnell, and C. Arnade. *U.S.-Cuba Agricultural Trade: Past, Present, and Possible Future*. Washington, D.C.: United States Department of Agriculture Economic Research Service, 2015.

Zhang, Deguan. *Collections from the Second Exchange Forum of Sino-Latin America and the Caribbean Think Tanks (Dier Jie Zhongguo-Lamei He Jialebi Zhiku Luntan Wenji)*. Beijing, China: Shijie Zhishi Chubanshe, 2013.

Zhonghou, G. and S. Yan. "The Research on the Risk Management Mechanism of National Defense Economy." *Acta Technica Corviniensis—Bulletin of Engineering* 6, no. 3 (2013): 79–83.

Zhongpingshe. "Trump's Tightening of Cuban Policy Created Shadow over US-Latin American Relations (Telongpu Shoujing Meiguo Dui Guba Zhengche Gei Mei-La Guanxi Touxia Yinying)." http://hk.crntt.com/crn-webapp/search/allDetail.jsp?id=104717097&sw=%E7%9A%84%E7%A1%AE.

Zhou, Hong and Xiong Hou. *China's Foreign Aid: 60 Years in Retrospect*. Beijing, China: Social Science Academic Press, 2013.

Zou, Zhipeng. "Cuba Update: Do Not Take the China Road." *World Expo* 6 (2013).

Index

For the benefit of digital users, indexed terms that span two pages (e.g., 52–53) may, on occasion, appear on only one of those pages.

Note: Tables are indicated by *t* following the page number

The Cuba-U.S. Bilateral Relationship. Michael J. Kelly, Erika Moreno, and Richard C. Witmer, II.